THE GREAT AMERICAN PRIORITIES

Edited by

George L. Berg Jr.

UNIVERSITY
PRESS OF
AMERICA

Lanham • New York • London

First published in 1992 by
University Press of America®, Inc.
4720 Boston Way
Lanham, Maryland 20706

3 Henrietta Street
London WC2E 8LU England

Copyright © 1991 by George L. Berg Jr.

Library of Congress Cataloging-in-Publication Data

The Great American priorities / edited by George L. Berg, Jr.
p.   cm.
Includes index.
1. United States—Politics and government—1989–   2. United
States—Politics and government—1945–1989.   3. Speeches,
addresses, etc., American.   I. Berg, George L., 1926–   .
E839.5.G74   1992   973.928—dc20   92–25027 CIP

ISBN 0–8191–8840–9 (cloth : alk. paper)
ISBN 0–8191–8841–7 (pbk. : alk. paper)

 The paper used in this publication meets the minimum requirements of
American National Standard for Information Sciences—Permanence
of Paper for Printed Library Materials, ANSI Z39.48–1984.

Three Cheers for Marian, Anne Marie and Scott

What we know
is a drop.
What we don't know
is an ocean.
• Isaac Newton

Contents
. . . .

Chapter 2

Chapter 3

Chapter 4

Chapter 5

Chapter 6

Chapter 7

Chapter 8

Chapter 9

Chapter 10

Chapter 11

Chapter 12

Chapter 13

Chapter 17

Chapter 18

Chapter 19

Chapter 20

Chapter 21

Foreword
• • • • • • • • • • • •

It is said that when Benjamin Disraeli became Prime Minister, he was asked by a new member of Parliament whether he advised him to take part in a debate. "No," replied Disraeli, "I do not think your ought to do so, because it is much better that the House should wonder why you do not speak than why you do."

My long-time friend and former fellow administrative assistant in the House, George Berg, knows that there are many occasions when those of us in public life would be better off taking Disraeli's advice, if only on the principle that what you don't say can't come back and haunt you.

But there are times when it is incumbent upon a House member or anyone else in public service, or with an interest in some area of controversy, to speak out. "The Great American Priorities" therefore meets a public need by collecting in one place speeches on a variety of subjects, ranging from agriculture to refugees, and from youth to patriotism, made by Representatives, Senators, business leaders, union leaders, historians and other Americans.

This collection makes no attempt to cover all the major issues in which the United States is concerned. The editor's sole purpose is to acquaint business, government and military leaders who are entering the ranks of top management with some of the more important business, social and political trends that are expected to take place at the turn of the century.

This book's agenda recognized the need for a global perspective now that the world is changing rapidly. Because the United States is the world's largest trading nation, and millions of American jobs are export related, there are several speeches with regard to the United States' relations with a number of countries.

Since our nation's strength—and its future—depends on our educational system, there are several speeches selected that emphasize how education is the key to opportunity. The "Philosophy of Teaching" and vocational education, which are often under-emphasized with respect to job preparation, has also been included

Health care programs are a top priority in the United States—and one of the critical items on the agenda of the Congress. The American private sector has provided an efficient health care system, the best in the world. However, as some of the speeches illustrate, there are still some unmet needs.

The great allied victory that drove Iraq from occupied Kuwait has shown the world that the first obligation of our government is to safeguard the security of the nation and to defend its interests and values. In the context of a shrinking world, the speeches by

Vice President Dan Quayle and former President Richard Nixon recognize the need to maintain a clear technological superiority in weaponry while working toward a verifiable system for disarmament.

The speeches selected on energy stress how important it is to find new ways to use geothermal steam, wind power, hydrogen as well as nuclear power. Concern for the environment must continue to be a top priority. We must recognize economic reality and set reasonable priorities and reachable goals to guarantee a healthy, pleasant environment for America's future.

One of our nation's greatest values is opposition to discrimination against anyone because of race, sex, color or creed. It is fitting, therefore, that several speeches with regard to women, blacks, refugees and discrimination in general are included in "The Great American Priorities."

Since transportation is one of the keys to America's prosperity, there are several speeches on this subject. With the exception of agriculture, transportation is the largest employer in America and we must do everything possible to preserve and improve our nation's transportation system.

Former President Ronald Reagan's comments on agriculture highlight the highly efficient and productive American agricultural community. The former President emphasizes the dual goals of protecting farm income while adding new foreign markets for our farm commodities.

Finally, there are several significant speeches by distinguished Americans on the subject of the nation itself. The speech by Mr. De Vos, president of Amway, discusses the small business person, the entrepreneur, the builder, the man or woman willing to take a chance to do something differently—and better, cheaper and faster. The speech by Mr. Ross Perot, the Dallas industrialist, is equally of interest in defending basic American principles.

The aforementioned subjects are only a few of the priority issues that readers will find in this book. Other speeches include ones on crime, drugs, labor, natural resources, religion, veterans, sports, children and the new world order. These speeches have been selected by George from *The Congressional Record* in a desire to help others who might be called upon to speak up and speak out for our Great American Priorities.

I am honored to be included among those whose speeches are found in this book, and delighted that my former colleague has taken the time and the effort to read, select and offer to readers everywhere a collection of speeches that addresses issues that are of importance today and that will define tomorrow.

Hon. Robert H. Michel
U.S. Representative
18th Congressional District of Illinois and
Minority Leader of the House of Representatives

Acknowledgments

I am pleased that the University Press of America is publishing "The Great American Priorities," my first book. I am also grateful to my friend, Congressman Bob Michel, the Minority Leader of the U.S. House of Representatives, for providing the Foreword to my publication and for his generous comments with respect to my desire to help others who might be called upon to speak up and speak out for our Great American Priorities.

I would like to gratefully acknowledge the sound advice and encouragement I received from Dr. Don Senese, director of the National Center for Presidential Research; to Bob Flaherty and Eloise Stinger of the Brookings Institute for their helpful suggestions and in regard to the preparation and marketing of my book; to my colleague, Carole Staus, for her untiring efforts in preparing the camera-ready reproduction and the proofreading of my manuscript. I also must express my gratitude to A. G. Manson, not only for his friendship but also for his understanding and moral support with regard to this project.

I also owe a special thanks to all those fine people who were kind enough to provide an endorsement of my book which I believe will help give this publication whatever interest and success it may have.

Finally, I am indebted to my wife, Marian, for her perseverence in bearing up through all the research and clutter necessary in editing "The Great American Priorities."

Chapter 1

America
· · · · · · · · · · ·
Selling America

Excerpts from Speech
in the Congressional Record
by
Richard M. De Vos, President
Amway Corporation

Almost 20 years ago I gave a talk called "Selling America," and at that time I thought about the greatness of this land as I saw it, and recounted some of the examples of that greatness.

Today, I want to refresh your memory, because all of our memories are so short. We live in watertight compartments, we live parcels of life. We say we're going to accomplish this or that in 30 days or 90 days or a year. Sometimes our long-term goals are overshadowed by the day-to-day activities which seem so important. Similarly, we can lose sight of the positive aspects of our nation if we spend most of our time complaining about those specific problems which plague us for the moment.

Each time I am a guest on a talk show, I talk to people calling in from across the country and realize that out there is the world of the disillusioned, the discouraged, the disheartened. One man said to me, "I don't know the difference between capitalism and communism—in one you're a slave to a state and in the other you're a slave to the capitalist pigs—we're all slaves to somebody."

I bled for him. His view of history is distorted. He has lost sight of the accomplishments of generations of free Americans. I think he reflects the fear of success—a distrust of those in leadership roles, which, while justified in some societies, is exaggerated greatly in ours.

The other day I re-read the words of Isocrates, an Athenian orator. He made this statement in the year 430 B.C., but I found it apropos of circumstances today. He said, "One must now apologize for any success in business as if it were a violation of the moral law, so that today it is worse to prosper than to be a criminal." He made that observation in 430 B.C.—and you thought we were the only ones ever condemned for achievement!

Despite the statement by Isocrates, the anti-success mood does prevail. Arguments about rich versus poor echo throughout the world. Those arguments must not be dismissed categorically. The feeling of frustration that poor people experience is not understood by many who are achievers. We may not always be as sympathetic as we should be. There is a source of potential tension that we must address.

We hear talk about the advantaged and the disadvantaged—the blacks versus the whites—management versus labor—Democrats versus Republicans—blue collar worker versus white collar workers—conservatives versus liberals and so on. We talk about Muslims versus Jews in the Middle East, communism versus capitalism, socialism versus free enterprise.

We wave our arms in frustration at inflation which has gone as high as 20 percent in recent years, but when we look around we find much of the world lives with 50, 60 and even 100 percent inflation. We complain about fuel shortages, and we are concerned about recession and unemployment. None of this is new. Like the statements which troubled Isocrates, those problems and others like them have been part of life for thousands of years. We will survive our frustrations, and with determination we will eliminate many of the problems which now concern us. I believe the best is yet to come.

I speak of the promise of America and the free world. The Communist World denies people the opportunity for achievement and progress. In my view, the Communist World moves backward, not forward, while the free world moves ever forward.

Let us look at the record of the free world. Let us examine some of the fruits of the labor of free people, their accomplishments—our accomplishments.

I guess Amway cannot be considered a small business anymore, but it was only 20 years ago that we were one of the smallest. Today we employ more than 5,500 people worldwide, and there are more than 500,000 Amway distributors in 13 countries—and they are small business people.

The small business person, of course, is the entrepreneur, the builder, the guy willing to take a chance, to do something differently and better, cheaper or faster.

This country achieved its greatness because of small business men and women, and I am concerned that we maintain the climate which made it possible for me and for millions of others to start a business and to build it and provide quality products and services and jobs and opportunities for so many millions of Americans.

Small business is indeed a large part of the great American success story. It has created 98 percent of all the new jobs in the last 10 years. Small business is where the innovators are. Dollar for dollar small business provides more than 24 times the innovation of big business and government combined.

Let me tell you about people in some other segments of our society who are doing their best to keep this country number one.

Let's talk about education. I, along with many of you, have been heard to complain that our education system is not up to par, that it's not like it used to be, that the kids aren't learning the way we did, that test scores are down, that government is corrupting the education process, that teachers' organizations are too powerful and so on.

Last June, a million of our young people came out of the colleges and high schools of America and entered the job market—to begin to make their contribution to the productive capacity of our nation.

Look back a few years and recall the great things that have been happening in the field of medicine. Think about those people a few years ago who were blind with cataracts and now find men with skilled microsurgery who can correct their vision problems, where before there was no hope.

I have a doctor friend in Grand Rapids who spends most of his waking hours performing delicate heart surgery. It wasn't long ago that those with heart ailments were told to rest—to take it easy to prolong their lives a few months. The miracles of medicine have now made possible transplants, valve replacement, bypass operations and much more.

The pioneers in arthritis surgery have made it possible for those afflicted with the pain of arthritis to enjoy more comfortable, productive lives.

Marvels of our age are also occurring in fields such as transportation. We are now making automobiles in this country that deliver 30 or 40 miles per gallon. Another important aspect of the transportation story is the fact that we are still producing in the United States about 10 million cars a year. We have over a hundred million cars and trucks on our highways. Our auto industry has suffered badly in recent years but we are not out of the automobile game—not by a long shot.

If you want more reasons to be proud and happy to be living in America, let's talk about our food industry—agriculture. In the United States today we continue to produce an abundance of food and grain. We continue to share that abundance with much of the world, but we can share only because we still have farmers who get up with the chickens and go to bed late at night. They are the people who really demonstrate their caring. Unlike those who so often talk about it, the farmers are the producers. They have created a product they can share—rather than idle talk about the value of sharing, which feeds no one.

Most of us never think about where we get our food. For most, there is no question of whether there's going to be food or not—at restaurants, fast food establishments or grocery stores. There's no question about whether there's going to be milk in the dairy case at the food store.

While this is true in America, it is not the case in large parts of the world. In Russia today, 30 percent of the people still work on farms but they cannot produce enough food to feed that nation. By comparison, in America 2 percent work on farms. Yes, this is a great land despite our problems.

What about energy. People argue, as a man did with me recently, about the problems with nuclear power. I responded that the number of people killed in connection with nuclear power generation is zero while those who die or suffer from black lung disease from mining coal are many. Yet, thousands of people continue to demonstrate against a viable alternative energy source which, in my opinion, may prove to be one of the safest systems we've ever known.

Another marvel of our time is communication. In America we pioneered modern communications techniques—some out of necessity in World War II, others for our ventures in space. There is no long distance anymore. It's all relative. It takes about the same amount of time to dial across town, across the country and halfway round the world.

But with all the wonders of new technology for food, for energy, transportation, for communications and all the rest, let us not forget that our greatest asset in America is people. One group that is too often overlooked or taken for granted are those in public service. Our firemen, policemen and rescue squad paramedics are great and dedicated people. There are, of course, dedicated men and women in the military service who serve our country—often at low pay and under trying circumstances—without whom all our lives would be in peril.

There is no question that there is much to be done in America. We all must play a part in making this nation even better for those generations which succeed us. But that is no reason to berate the system, to give up on all that free people have accomplished in less than 400 years.

I am proud to be part of that system—this land—I am grateful for the opportunities I have enjoyed. I am prepared to defend all of it in any forum at any time.

Yes. I have taken another look at our country and I am committed to selling America for another 20 years—and more.

Reference: (C.R. 12/10/80, Pg. H-12317)

American Values and Strength
in a Changing World
Excerpts from Speech
in the Congressional Record
by
Max M. Kampleman, Recipient
Jamestown Foundation's Freedom Award

It is an honor to receive your award this evening. It has been less than four months since I left government service with its different, exciting and enriching challenges. As a traditional Democrat who has served in a Republican Administration, it is useful for me to stand back and evaluate our country's evolving role as a leader in a world that is changing so fast and so dramatically that we can barely see its details let alone its scope.

The pace of change in the world today is so rapid that any statement we make about tomorrow is likely to be obsolete even today. The pace of change between 1900 and today is beyond calculation, probably greater than has taken place in all of mankind's previous history combined. And newer, greater scientific and technological developments on the horizon will probably make all previous discoveries dwarf by comparison.

We are brought up to believe that necessity is the mother of invention. I suggest the corollary is also true: invention is the mother of necessity. Technology and communication have made the world smaller. There is no escaping the fact that the sound of a whisper or a whimper in one part of the world can immediately be heard in all parts of the world. And yet the world body politic is not keeping pace with those realities.

What we have instead been observing is an intense fractionalization, as large numbers of people have had their emotions inflamed by nationality and religious appeals. It is as if a part of us is saying: "Not so fast, stop the world. We want to get off. We are not ready. We are not prepared for this new world we are being dragged into. We will resist the pressures by holding on tight to the familiar, the traditional, and we will do so with a determined frenzy!"

But the inevitable tomorrow is appearing. Changes in science and technology are producing fundamental changes in our material lives, and in our social and political relationships as well. There are new dominant sounds and among those most clearly and loudly heard are the sounds of freedom and democracy. The striving for human dignity is universal because it is an integral part of our human character. We see it in Burma, Pakistan, Korea, the Philippines, South Africa, China, Chile, Paraguay, the Soviet Union, Poland—different cultures, different parts of the world. A larger part of the world's population is today living in relative freedom than ever before in the history of the world.

We are in a time when no society can isolate itself or its people from new ideas and new information anymore than one can escape the winds of whose currents affect us all. National boundaries can keep out vaccines, but those boundaries cannot keep out germs or ideas. One essential geo-political consequence of that new reality is that there can be no true security for any one country unless there is security for all. Unilateral security will not come from either withdrawing from the world or attempting national impregnability. Instead, we must learn to accept in each of our countries a mutual responsibility for the peoples in all other countries.

In this world of increasing interdependence, the lessons for the United States and the Soviet Union—the most important security relationship in the present era—are evident. We cannot escape from one another. We are bound together in an equation that makes the security of each of us dependent on that of the other. We must try to learn to live together.

We are told by Soviet leaders that through the process of internal transformation that is demanded by the new technologies, they comprehend that repressive societies in our day cannot achieve inner stability or true security, that it is in their best interests to permit a humanizing process to take place, and that their domestic requirements are their highest priority.

Without doubt, that leadership faces the urgent need for drastic internal changes if the Soviet Union is to be a significant part of the 21st Century we are about to enter. The Soviet economy is working poorly, although it does provide a fully functioning military machine. Massive military power has provided the Soviets with a presence that reaches all parts of the world, but this military superpower cannot hide the fact that its economic and social weaknesses are deep. The Soviet's awesome internal police force has provided continuity to its system of governance, but a Russia which during czarist days exported food cannot today feed its own people. Productivity is low.

With absenteeism, corruption and alcoholism, internal morale is bad. The new leaders of the Soviet Union are fully aware of its problems. They are also aware of our strengths, reflecting the vitality of our values and the healthy dynamism of our system.

We hope the time is at hand when Soviet authorities, looking at the energy of the West, comprehend the systemic weakness that corrodes their society. We hope Soviet leadership today realizes that its historic aim of achieving communism through violence has no place in this nuclear age. We hope Soviet authorities will join us in making the commitment that our survival as a civilization depends on the mutual realization that we must live under the rules of responsible international behavior. We hope, but as yet we, regrettably, cannot trust.

When I began negotiating with the Soviet Union in 1980, human rights was beginning to be injected as a major item on our country's international agenda. The Soviet Union insisted that discussion of the subject was an improper interference in their internal affairs. When President Reagan asked me in 1985 to return to government service as head of our nuclear arms reduction negotiating team, an extraordinary change soon became apparent. Under the leadership of the President, the United States enlarged upon what President Carter initiated, and incorporated the concept of human rights as a necessary and ever-present ingredient in the totality of our relations with the Soviet Union.

In his 1975 Nobel Prize speech that he was not permitted to present in person, Dr. Andrei Sakharov said, "I am convinced that international trust, mutual understanding, disarmament, and international security are inconceivable without any open society with freedom of information, freedom of conscience, the right to publish, and the right to travel and choose the country in which one wishes to live."

The United States interacts and negotiates with the Soviet Union in that context. We have faith in our principles as we intensify our efforts, through our negotiations, to find a basis for understanding, stability and peace with dignity. To negotiate is risky. It is in the words of Hubert Humphrey, something like crossing a river while walking on slippery rocks. The possibility of disaster is on every side, but it is the way to get across.

We have begun a historic process. It may be working. It is in all of our interests to try and make it work. The process, furthermore, is likely to be a difficult and murky one. The USSR is not apt easily or quickly to undergo what Jonathan Edwards called a "great awakening," or see a blinding light on the road to Damascus. Their heavy bureaucratic crust of tradition is thick and not easily cracked. During a recent trip to Moscow, I heard it said, "There have been many books written on the transition from capitalism to socialism, but not one on the transition from socialism to capitalism." The problems are real and at times appear overwhelming.

We are also struck by the depth of ethnic nationalism that has survived the Marxist and

Leninist revolutions in the Soviet Union. That nationalism at times appears to be tearing at the fiber of the Soviet empire. There is violence, demonstrations, curfews, and the recurring question: How tolerant can Moscow afford to be? Can glasnost survive this strain and onslaught? Can the Soviet Union, with more than 100 nationalities and widely disparate cultures living in 15 republics, contain these demands for local sovereignty?

Just as the strains must not blind us to the changes so should the changes not blind us to the difficulties that still remain. Yes, the changes are stunning—Soviet troops out of Afghanistan; Solidarity legally recognized in Poland and free elections on the horizon; the prospect of Cuban troop withdrawal from Angola; Vietnam's agreement to withdraw from Cambodia; Communist Party officials challenged and defeated in Soviet elections; the beginning of a two-party system in Hungary; interesting Soviet proposals to reduce conventional arms along lines proposed by the West.

The great challenge to our diplomacy is how to adjust to a rapidly changing Soviet Union in a rapidly changing world without endangering our security and our values. As we do so, we must at the same time be sensitive to the judgment of history and take heed, lest future generations condemn us for having missed a decisive opportunity for peace with dignity.

Our task is to achieve the firm sense of purpose, readiness, steadiness, and strength that is indispensable for effective and timely foreign affairs decision-making. Our political community must resist the temptation of partisan politics and institutional rivalry as we develop the consensus adequate to meet the challenge.

Two hundred years ago this week George Washington took the oath of office as the first President of the United States. Our country, today the oldest democracy in the world, came into being. Our forefathers said that "America is the last great hope of mankind." It still is. Our political values have helped us build the most dynamic and open society in recorded history, a source of inspiration to most of the world. It is a promise of a better tomorrow for the hundreds of millions of people who have never known the gifts of human freedom. The future lies with liberty, human dignity and democracy. To preserve and expand these values is our special responsibility. We should look upon it as an exciting opportunity.

Reference: (C.R. 6/21/89, Pg. E-2234)

Straight Talk From Ross Perot
Excerpts from Speech
in the Congressional Record
by
Ross Perot

Today I would like to speak on behalf of millions of American citizens who never get to speak at the National Press Club, or present their views to a national television audience.

I am deeply concerned that the most important people in our country are becoming disillusioned and cynical. The people I am concerned about represent the majority of our nation's voters. They elect our political leaders. After elections, the people I am concerned about go back to their jobs and families.

They are not organized into special interest groups. Their daily presence is not felt in Washington, the state capitals or even at city halls. More and more they feel they have no effective voice.

Who are these people? These are the people who work hard, play by the rules. Operate in the center of the field of ethical behavior—not on the sidelines. Obey the law, rear good children, they are patriots. Are active in schools and churches, they attend PTA meetings, teach Sunday School, lead the scout troops and coach the Little League teams.

They come from all races—all religions. They are the steel and concrete that hold our nation together. They are givers in a world of takers. They are the people de Tocqueville wrote about when he toured America to learn why we were such a great country. He concluded, "America is great because her people are good."

The people I am concerned about represent the heart of this country's tax base. They pay the bills for our mistakes. Today, they are spending hundreds of billions of their hard-earned dollars to make government work. And, to clean up problems created by others. They are the majority of the electorate. And, finally and most importantly, these are the people—whose husbands, wives, sons and daughters make up the military forces in the deserts of Saudi Arabia.

Why are these people so frustrated? They pay substantial taxes at the local, state and national level and yet they are receiving very poor service in return from their government. Their money is being poorly spent and they know it. Let's look at the facts:

Just ten years ago, our great country was the largest creditor nation in the world. Today, we are the largest debtor nation in the history of man.

Our country is the most violent, crime-ridden society in the industrialized world. We have 450,000 men and women in the battlefields in the Middle East because of the rape, pillage and plunder in Kuwait, and yet we are unwilling to put the same emphasis on the same problems—yes, we have rape, pillage and plunder in our cities, and this city, Washington D.C.—the murder capital of the United States.

Forty-seven percent of our people are afraid to walk in their own neighborhoods at night. Entire sections of our cities have been abandoned to crime. Millions of other people I am talking about have been wrongfully put in jail—they have had to put bars on their windows and doors. Our leaders are willing to commit billions to solve problems in the Middle East, but are content to hold press conferences about these same problems in our own country.

This country now ranks at the bottom of the industrialized world in academic achievement. We have the largest number of functionally illiterates in the industrialized world. Our system of justice has failed the people. Our prison system is a mess—it costs more to keep a person in prison for a year than to send him to Harvard for one year.

Our people live in a nation with 5 percent of the world's population and 50 percent of the world's cocaine use. And yet we are willing to go to war in the Middle East because of Iraq's potential to produce chemical weapons, while we do little to solve the problems of chemical warfare that is being conducted every day against our children— on the streets of this nation.

The people are frustrated that organized special interest groups have taken control of our political process. The book "Agents of Influence" tells the story. For example:

The Japanese spend $400 million a year lobbying—an amount equal to the cost of all elections for the House and Senate in 1988—to protect the $50 billion a year Japanese trade surplus—not a bad return.

Congressional staffers routinely leak information to curry favor to position themselves for six-figure-income lobbying jobs later.

Between 1973 and 1990, one-third of the principal trade officials in the U.S. Trade Commission left to become foreign agents.

A former President received a $2 million fee from the Japanese. The Presidency is not for sale—now or later.

This practice is corrupting the United States political and economic system. It corrupts our institutions. We have put U.S. integrity and national honor up for sale. The people are disgusted and they should be.

The first three words of the Constitution are "We the people." If we were drafting this great document today and if we were honest with ourselves, the first words would have to be:

"We the special interest," or "We the big PAC contributors," or "We the international lobbyists," or "We the image-makers, spin doctors and sound byte specialists," or perhaps it should be "We the summiteers."

The people are frustrated that the business leaders of our country have allowed the job base to deteriorate. As one hard-working citizen said after his company closed its doors, "I didn't quit my job—my job quit me." In 1960, 75 percent of the vehicles made in the world were made in Detroit. Today, that number is 25 percent. The two principal exports from New York Harbor are scrap steel and scrap paper.

We are becoming a third world country; shipping lumber, iron ore and other basic products across the world to be manufactured into finished products and returned to our country to be sold. The good jobs paying top salaries are in producing the finished products. They have gone overseas.

Our people are disillusioned that the White House and Congress cynically covered up the savings and loan crisis until after 1988 elections. It was obvious in 1986. The delay, driven by personal political ambitions, increased the size of the problem from $50 to $500 billion, and the burden for paying for this mess rests with the ordinary citizen.

Whatever happened to "Watch my lips—no new taxes"? The tax bubble, lowering the income tax rate for the wealthiest Americans made no sense. Congress made the White House drop this one. The 15 percent capital gains tax made no sense. Again,

Congress refused to let this one slip through. The deficit gets bigger each year, while our leaders campaign that they will control spending and get rid of waste in government.

The people are frustrated by the budget shell game that forecasted unrealistic economic growth rates and 4 percent interest rates at the recent budget summit. We won't grow that fast. Interest rates won't go that low.

Our President blames the recession on the war in the Middle East. The recession is the result of ten years of excess spending and mismanagement in our country. Using the Middle East as an excuse is being untruthful with the people.

I hope that my years of service to this country have earned me the right to constructively criticize events occurring at his time. Why are we in the Middle East?

In the "Charge of the Light Brigade," Tennyson wrote, "Theirs was not to reason why. Theirs was but to do or die." Our Commander-in-Chief cannot make up his mind why we are there. At one time it was the price of oil. At another time we were there for jobs. Still later, the reason was we are fighting for a new world order. Then our mission was to eliminate Hussein's nuclear and chemical capability and try him in a Nuremberg setting as a war criminal.

Initially, we were told we were fighting for the American way of life—nobody bought that one. Lately, it seems that it was a combination of all of the above.

The American people can't understand why their sons and daughters are preparing to fight for kings and emirs. Americans fight only for great causes.

It is illegal and it is wrong for any one person in our country to put 450,000 lives at risk. Our system of government is based on checks and balances. If the President can't even appoint his Cabinet and spend money without congressional approval, do you think there is any possibility that the framers of the Constitution intended for the President to have the unilateral right to put lives at risk. The words of the Constitution are simply and plain. Here they are: "The Congress shall have the right to declare war." The lesson of Vietnam is: First commit the nation, then commit the troops.

On many occasions over the past 20 years, I have promised the men and women of the Armed Forces; the widows, children and parents of the men killed in action; and the wounded who will never again lead normal lives that before this country goes to war again, I would use the resources at my disposal to see that we first commit the nation and then commit the troops—that is the lesson of Vietnam. I will keep that promise.

Reference: (C.R. 1/14/91, Pg. S-428)

Abortion
• • • • • • • • • • •

A Congressman's Thoughts
on the Pro-Life Movement
Excerpts from Speech
in the Congressional Record
by
Honorable Henry Hyde
U.S. House of Representatives

I am pleased to speak to you this evening on what I conceive to be, since Dred Scott, the greatest civil rights issue of our time. The issue of the Right to Life deals with the most defenseless, voiceless and vulnerable of all human beings: the unborn. The dimensions and the significance of the issue are very great. We permit, tolerate and stand by quietly while over a million abortions every year occur in this country.

That is a staggering amount of human life wasted, and 300,000 of these abortions are paid for by taxpayers' funds through Medicaid—or at least they were until the last few years when we have tried to inhibit this use of tax money.

In discussing abortion, you have to start with what an abortion is. There are all kinds of highways and byways that you can get diverted onto that are interesting and controversial, but start first with this question: what is an abortion?

By definition and by intention, it results in the killing of somebody. It doesn't really happen to a woman, it happens to an unborn child, and every abortion is over somebody's dead body. What is being aborted? Is it a bad tooth, is it a diseased appendix, is it indeed a disease? Is it something to be exculpated and thrown away like a used piece of Kleenex, or, indeed, is it a human life?

Well, you see, that's the one issue the pro-abortionists do not want to discuss, and do not discuss: the humanity of the unborn. The medical books bristle with accounts of when human life begins. Not patented human life, but human life with potential, and to put it simply, life begins at the beginning.

Think of the euphemisms that the abortion lexicon contains: terminate a pregnancy. Do you terminate crabgrass on our lawn, do you terminate a mosquito when it bites you in the back of the neck? No, you kill a mosquito, you kill the crabgrass. You don't call the unborn anything recognizable, fetus is a nice cold word, or embryo, product of conception, pregnancy material. These are terms that are used very often.

The euphemisms don't stop with the question of the baby's personhood. I love this one: Pro-choice. Some choice. There is no choice at all for the victim. The choice is how we shall kill the unborn child. Shall we kill it with a curette, piece by piece? Shall we use the suction machine? Shall we insert a saline solution, substituting it for some of the amniotic fluid and literally scalding the unborn child to death? Or a hysterectomy? If the pregnancy is well along, past 24 weeks, we just perform a caesarean and leave the little infant gasping without any support until it suffocates. Now that is the choice they are talking about. A lot of babies die by chance, but I don't know of any that ought to die by choice.

But a child has a moral right to live, and getting on firmer ground; a civil right to be treated as a human being before birth. Birth is a change of address, medically speaking. There is no qualitative difference ten minutes after, ten minutes before or ten days before: it is a change of address. The unborn child, the fetus, the embryo is not a part of the women's body, in a medical sense. The mother is providing shelter and nourishment, but the child is an independent entity, with its own heartbeat, its own brain waves, its own circulatory system, its own blood type. It is just medical nonsense to believe that the unborn child, the embryo, that is implanted in the womb and growing magically and miraculously every day is a part of the women's body in the same way that an organ is part of her body. But, unfortunately, this argument must be used to justify abortion.

Child abuse reaches its ultimate in abortion. We think a lot more of animals than we think of unborn children. The snail darter is protected by law as one of the endangered species. The dolphin and the white whale are likewise protected and yet, the unborn child hasn't got any protection at any time during the nine months of gestation, should the mother desire an abortion.

The Supreme Court in its decision said that during the first trimester, neither the state nor the father has any interest in protecting the fetus. It's a private matter between the woman and her doctor. The Court said that during the second trimester, the state has no interest in fetal health, but only in maternal health. The unborn child has no rights through the second trimester. Now up to the third trimester, the state may have an interest in preventing abortion, except where the life or the health of the mother could be involved. The World Health Organization defines health as the absence of distress. So if a woman who is nine months along is distressed with her pregnancy, then her health is affected unless she has an abortion.

The Supreme Court said clearly that we have not permitted abortion on demand, but clearly we have permitted abortion on demand. The law has withdrawn protection from an unborn child.

We are told by the American Civil Liberties Union (ACLU) that we are breaching the separation of church and state by imposing on secular society a particularly religious (Catholic) view of when life begins. Hence, we are violating the First Amendment. This is a most interesting point of view. The religious antecedents of this country are tremendous, and to try and strip moral values out of our history and our traditions is just an incredible denial of everything that has ever happened in this country. When a mother, who should be that natural protector of her unborn child, becomes its adversary, then it seems to me it's the business of law to step in and say, just a minute, there is a victim there who is entitled to due process before he or she gets executed.

My own view, after dealing with this issue for many years, is the pro-abortionists are guilty of a three-count indictment. The first is oversimplication. They take the complicated problems of the unwanted pregnancy—the human tragedies of handi-capped children, and poverty, living in a ghetto and all those heart-rendering prob-lems—and their answer is to get rid of people. They are anti-people. To me, recognizing the human problems of unwanted pregnancies, poverty and disease ought to lead to human solutions, not the inhuman solution, which is abortion.

The second count of my indictment against these people is that they are guilty of pessimism. They surrender so easily to pessimism, as if every ghetto kid, every handicapped child, is going to be a loser. Going to be unhappy. The most unhappy people are those who are sated and jaded and live empty, pointless lives. The suicide rate among handicapped people is next to zero. Give them a chance to vote on the issue of whether they should be destroyed or not.

The last of my three-count indictment is that those who are in favor of abortion suffer from a failure of imagination. Do they ever think of the secrets that are undiscovered, the diseases that are uncured, the frontiers that are uncrossed, the music and the poetry that are unwritten? Do they ever think that maybe they have destroyed somebody who might have solved some of the great problems—space, time, disease? It never occurs to them because, otherwise, they might lose their minds.

But you don't compromise on this issue of abortion. How do you compromise when the issue is a human life—not you life, somebody else's life? I think the question you have to ask yourself is what does a caring, humane society do for the people living at the edge: its terminally ill, its incorrigibly poor, its profoundly handicapped, the senile, the hydrocephalic, the mongoloid—the people who are just a crushing burden? Do we put them out and let them die, let them freeze to death, or must society use its resources and its compassion to help those people and to recognize that they are God's creatures, accountable to God and the objects of God's redemptive love? It seems to me that the measure of a society is what it does for people, and what it does about people. That has to be the question we ask when people are postulating the solution of abortion.

The words of Rev. Anthony Padivano always impress me, when he talks about life. He said that those tragedies that break our hearts again and again are not more numerous than the healing influences that mend them. More impressive than the brokenness of our heart is the fact that we have a heart, and it is tender enough to suffer. Even the scar tells us of more than the wound we have sustained. It tells us that we have prevailed. And all the agony in the world cannot erase the fact that a man is born; and life and thought, emotion and choice, love and reason go on inside him.

So I have, through fate or circumstance, found myself in the middle of this issue. It hasn't been pleasant in many, many instances, but it has made me feel that whatever else happens to me in Washington or anywhere else, maybe, somewhere, a few lives—one life—has been saved and spared.

Reference: (C.R. 6/4/80 Pg. H-4513)

The Right to Choose an Abortion

Excerpts from Speech
in the Congressional Record
by
Ms. Heidi Hart
Elk Mountain, Wyoming

"I cannot understand the new view that life begins at conception. If this is true, why is it not customary to hold religious rites after a miscarriage? Why only after birth? It is obviously a concept trumped up to add righteous clout to the arguments of anti-abortionists."

This is the view held by Katherine Hepburn and me. I feel abortion should remain legal in all aspects, and especially in those cases involving rape, possible death of the women and teenage pregnancies and incest.

Imagine this: A woman walking home is attacked and raped. Because of this violation of her body, she is impregnated. She has probably also been mentally harmed by this experience. Why should she be harmed more, possibly irrevocably, by having to carry this child given to her by a criminal who took her by force? Wouldn't it be better to save this woman's sanity than to save the child that is not wanted. If she did have this child, it could end up a criminal just like the father. Or worse, it could end up mentally sick because of the stress the mother had to go through during the pregnancy. This child could also end up going from foster home to foster home all through its adolescent life. Wouldn't it be better to save this child from this hell?

Until 100 years ago no one punished abortion in the early stages of pregnancy—not even the Catholics punished it. The Christian Church gave the fetus a soul, and after 18 centuries of debate, the church took the conveniently loose view that the fetus became animated by the rational soul and abortion became a crime after only 40 days for a boy and 80 days for a girl. One problem with this is that no method of sex determination was given.

English common law was fairly tolerant of abortion up until the mother feels the fetus move, which usually happens between the fourth and fifth months. In the United States for a long time, the common law inherited from England protected the right of abortion in the early stages of pregnancy.

In 1869, Pope Pius IX eliminated the distinction between the animated and non-animated fetus. Since then, the Catholic Church has called all abortions murder and punished it severely. A succession of laws followed in outlawing all abortions except one needed to save the mother.

There were three main reasons abortion became a crime. The first was logical: abortion was a dangerous operation because of poor conditions and crude methods. The second wasn't quite as good: as biologists began to better understand conception, women began to use better contraceptives. Many countries looked down on this as they needed a higher population to keep up the number of workers in factories and on farms.

The third reason is the most dangerous: it is the idea that sex for pleasure is bad, and that pregnancy is the punishment for pleasure.

In 1973, the Supreme Court took a step toward legalizing abortion. The Court now affirms that the "right of privacy founded in the 14th Amendment's concept of personal liberty is broad enough to encompass a woman's decision whether or not to terminate her pregnancy." The Court held that up to the first trimester of pregnancy, the decision to have an abortion may be made solely by the woman and her doctor. After the end of the first trimester, the state's power to regulate abortion is limited to the establishment of rules governing where and by whom an abortion may be performed. "It is only after the fetus has reached a point of viability that the state may go so far as proscribing abortion except when necessary to save the mother's life or health."

Now legislators are trying to overrule this Court decision. Anti-abortionists say that "abortion violates the sacredness of human life." The legislators are being pushed to gain what they, the anti-abortionists, want.

One aspect of illegal abortions I don't think many people are looking at is the increase of criminals. Those women who get abortions and those doctors who perform the abortions are murderers thus making for more criminals in our court and prison systems if these people are charged and convicted of their crimes

Another aspect is the increased number of "back-alley" abortions. These can be done by various people and I will tell you of three.

The first person is the "quack" doctor who can't do an operation right. He might do the operation right, or he could tear up the woman's insides, perhaps ruining her chances of having a wanted child later on or he might end up mutilating both mother and child.

The second person is the mother herself doing the abortion. This has been done by many teenage girls in high school. Some adult women have given themselves abortions. One such woman died because she bled to death after she cut open her stomach to take out the baby. I believe abortion should be kept legal to save the women instead of them killing themselves.

The third person could be the woman's boyfriend. He might do the abortion right, but how many women have skilled surgeons as boyfriends? He could also end up killing both the woman and the child, making for two possible counts of murder.

Maybe we should all sit back and rationally look at all aspects of abortion. There could be some compromise that both sides could reach. I, however, would still be for abortion in all aspects, no matter what. Abortion should be kept legal and a woman's right to control her body. Just think of all the women dying because of self-inflicted abortions or abortions done by unskilled people. Do you want this? I think abortion should stay legal and that people should leave the conditions alone so they can work on more important things.

Reference: (C.R. 2/9/82, Pg. E-310)

Agriculture
In Recognition of Agriculture Day
Excerpts from Speech
in the Congressional Record
by
President Ronald Reagan

Agriculture Day is the day we commemorate stock cupboards, healthy children, the spirit of enterprise, railroad cars and trucks heavy with food, free men and women living and working on their own land, government workers researching and developing scientific farming techniques, fields overflowing with grain and cotton and vegetables, orchards laden with fruits and nuts, pastures dotted with cattle and hogs.

But most importantly, we commemorate all the people who plant and harvest, transport, market and distribute America's food and fiber.

Today, we salute an endeavor that is vital to our well-being, yet one Americans have been so successful at that it's often taken for granted: agriculture. All of us should be grateful to God for making American abundance possible and grateful to the families and all the others involved in agriculture for taking over from there.

Farm output has jumped more than 89 percent since 1950, with agricultural productivity rising more than four times faster than industrial productivity per hour worked. One hour of labor on an American farm produces 15 times as much as it did 60 years ago. American production of food and fiber, always admirable, now holds the rest of the world in awe.

With less than three-tenths of one percent of the world's farmers and farm workers, our country produces 65 percent of the world's soybeans, 48 percent of the corn, 32 percent of the sorghum, 25 percent of the oranges, 31 percent of the poultry, 26 percent of the beef and the list goes on and on.

Inscribed on the front of the Department of Agriculture building in Washington, D.C., are the words of George Washington. He said, "With reference either to individual or national welfare, agriculture is of primary importance."

This was never more true than today. With stores and markets overflowing, our citizens each consume 1,408 pounds of food annually. Their relative health, creativity and high energy level can, to a large degree, be traced to a diet that is the envy of the world.

The health of our economy is also tied to agriculture. American agriculture, taken as a whole, is an industry so vast that it stretches the imagination, with assets exceeding $1 trillion, employing 23 million people—22 percent of the American work force.

And we aren't just feeding ourselves. Today, wheat harvested in the Great Plains is eaten as pasta in Italy. Our soybeans are part of the soy sauce used in the Orient. Our cottonseed is pressed into oil and shipped to Venezuela. Our grain is consumed in Russia, and African children are fed by the tillers of Nebraska soil.

In 1983, our agricultural export revenue was five times what it was in 1970, helping to offset the increased cost of energy imports over this period. Today, two of every five agricultural acres are devoted to export. And over one-fourth of all farm income comes from sales overseas. Our agricultural exports use rural elevators, grain terminals, railroads, canals, seaports, ships, trucks, barges and warehouses. It is a vast network, incredibly efficient in providing income for tens of millions of people and feeding many millions more.

In the United States we're proud of what our free people, with a profit motive and private property, have produced, and that is especially true in agriculture. Our agriculture system is a national treasure, and this Administration is unflinching in its commitment to maintain and strengthen agriculture's role in the American economy.

Yet, as proud as we are of American agriculture, all of us should be aware of and sensitive to the weight borne by the American farmer in recent years. A decade of overspending and overtaxing shot interest rates sky-high and unleashed devastating inflation on all of us. Nowhere was it felt more than down on the farm. They were the greatest victims of the cost-price squeeze.

Bringing down interest rates, inflation and reducing fuel costs will help, but increasing farm income is better. Not by increasing subsidies or federal controls, but instead by opening markets and introducing alternatives in order to overcome excessive surpluses.

We believe in free trade, but we've no longer going to play patsy for those who would use this as leverage against us. Free trade means access for those trading with us and it also means access for Americans to their markets. Our trade representative must do everything it takes to tear down trade barriers and end unfair practices.

In this regard, we have sent trade teams around the world—to Europe, to Africa, to Latin America, the Middle East and the Far East—all with the intent to seek new markets. And these efforts are paying off. We expect to ship more grain to the Middle East, to have sizable grain sales to India, and, of course, we have a deal with Egypt that represents one-sixth of the world's wheat flour trade.

Although our large surpluses remain a problem, we can be grateful that even in economic downturns America has an abundance of food. This situation afforded us an opportunity last year to initiate a program to help those hard hit by the recession by giving away surplus cheese and dairy products—valued at nearly $400 million—to 10 million needy people during the past 14 months.

Emotional and often politically motivated attacks notwithstanding, overall nutritional assistance provided to the unemployed and the needy of this country is at a higher level now than ever before. This assistance takes the form of food stamps, school lunches, child and nutrition activities and donated commodities.

Getting control of farming costs, opening markets and coming to grips with the surplus problem will reap long-lasting benefits for farmers.

There is a federal role in agriculture. Consistent with this we've increased money for agricultural research and expanded the federal crop insurance program. We've strengthened the Department of Agriculture's market-development program, implemented the blended credit program to finance U.S. agricultural exports, increased the level of agricultural export credit guarantees to the highest level in history—$4.8 billion.

We have also ended the Soviet grain embargo and have pledged never again to single out agriculture from the rest of the economy for use as an economic weapon.

Throughout history, farming has been recognized as irreplaceable to the vitality of any society. The nobility of those who grow food has not escaped notice. In ancient Rome Cicero said, "Of all occupations from which gain is secured, there is none better than agriculture, nothing more productive, nothing sweeter, nothing more worthy of a free man."

Well, here in the United States where new dimensions have been added to the word "liberty," the Jeffersonian vision of free men working their own land is still rooted in our consciousness. So in many ways, we look to agriculture not just for sustenance of the body, but also to prove to ourselves that our ideals are still alive.

No matter how industrialized we become, America's heart, her soul, her sense of justice and decency will remain strong as long as the American farmer continues to be an integral part of our national life.

As a young boy growing up in that small town on the plains in Illinois, I remember those farming families. They were proud, church-going people. They were independent and yet always ready to lend a hand to a neighbor. We can all be grateful that these folks and their ideals are still with us today.

Today, Agriculture Day, we express our appreciation to them for the bounty of food and fiber they provide and for the strength they give us.

Reference: (C.R. 4/5/83, Pg. S-4108)

Aging

Public Policy and The Future of Aging

Excerpts from Speech
in the Congressional Record
By
Hon. Morris K. Udall
U.S. House of Representatives

In a country that seems to be obsessed with youth and with staying young, the problems of the elderly have been given short shrift. The programs we developed in the last decade for the elderly are a good beginning, but they have often fallen far short of expectations, reflecting our half-hearted commitment to real help for these 25 million Americans.

The way we treat our older citizens in this country is like certain ancient tribal societies where a person who became too old for hunting or warfare was placed ceremonially on a raft and allowed to float down a river.

In modern society we repeat in many symbolic ways that ceremony. There must always be a justifying mythology when a dominant group systematically disadvantages a less powerful minority. In this case, we have developed two stereotypes of the aged to justify our neglect—serenity and senility.

On the one hand our images of old-age are idealized images of the beloved and tranquil grandparents, the wise elders, the serene and gracious white-haired matriarch dispensing wisdom from the kitchen or the patriarch from the front porch rocker. On the other hand, the opposite image disparages the aged. Old age is viewed as irreversible decay, decrepitude and loss of mental powers.

Most tragically of all, these stereotypes are self-perpetuating. Cut off from the society they built, their self-esteem undermined by prejudice and discrimination, too many of our elderly lapse into patterns of despair and decay simply because they are afforded no opportunity to remain active.

Yet we need not look far to find abundant evidence that old age need not mean physical and mental disability. The artistry of a Picasso, a Casals, a Rubenstein is not cut off at 65. The heroic leadership of Winston Churchill, the humanitarianism of Albert Schweitzer, the moral and legal brilliance of Holmes and Black and Hand—all reached their greatest heroics years and decades beyond the age of 60.

There can be no higher national priority than the full and creative cultivation of our human resources—resources that flourish with age and experience. We must heed the words of the philosopher Paul Weiss who said, "America will never be of age until it knows how to make full use of its people, no matter what their color, sex or years."

Yet the men and women who brought this country out of a shattering depression and a cataclysmic world war today are discarded by society. We have no national policy for enriching their lives. Worse, the patchwork of well-intentioned programs which, in piecemeal fashion address the problems of the aging, have been poorly planned, underfunded, understaffed and undercut by those charged with carrying them out.

The outlook for older Americans today is bleak. It is getting bleaker. And it cannot get better until all of us—professionals in the field, policy-makers in government, the young and the elderly themselves—look behind the stereotypes and understand what it means to the old in America.

It means economic hardship. One in four Americans over the age of 65 lives below the official poverty line. In this poverty, older Americans must devote 80 percent of their income to food, shelter, health care and transportation—areas where prices have frequently risen faster than the national inflation rate while Social Security "catch-up" increases lag a year or more behind.

Being old in America means taking the leftovers from a health care system that caters to the young. The 10 percent of our people over 65 account for 28 percent of the nation's total medical bill. Yet Medicare—for all the good it has done—pays less than 40 percent of the medical bills of its recipients.

We have lengthened the lifespan of our people by eliminating many of the diseases of youth but we mask our failure to address the health needs of the elderly by ascribing their illnesses to "old age," and by putting the elderly out of sight in nursing homes.

Being old in America means living in fear. Urban renewal programs too often have destroyed vital neighborhoods, and those most likely to suffer are the black, the brown—and the gray. And the aged are the easiest targets for the crime inevitably bred by such overcrowding and squalor. A study involving elderly residents from 54 low-rent housing developments showed a pervasive fear of crime: two-thirds restricted their daytime activities in some way, and 60 percent never left home at night.

These are some of the problems. There are many others—a transportation system that all but excludes those who do not drive; environmental pollution that breeds heart and respiratory disease; nutritional deficiencies; and a dozen more.

Faced with prejudice, with poverty, with disease, with fear, aging Americans have sought help from the government. They have received endless reassurance, countless pious expressions of concern. In many ways, the problems of the aging reflect wider social failures, and can only be cured by fundamental reforms in our social and economic institutions.

We must shatter the myth that a person's social productivity ends at the age of 65. I believe we have an obligation to give every member of our society the chance to perform useful work. This basic right of social participation must not be cut off by the turning of a calendar; neither private nor public employers should be allowed unilaterally to impose mandatory retirement upon workers still capable of performing their jobs.

To the great majority who will at some time choose retirement, we have another obligation—the duty to help them obtain economic security in their last years. It's very important to reassure Americans that in spite of all these right-wing scare stories we hear, the Social Security Trust Fund is not bankrupt, and it is not about to go bankrupt. But it is also important that we understand the implications of declining birth rates for Social Security, and that we plan now to reallocate our social resources to follow shifts in age patterns expected for the future.

To begin with, we must reduce unemployment to get more people contributing to the trust fund. In addition, we should gradually increase the contribution base to restore the degree of participation intended by the designers of the system and reduce the regressiveness of the payroll tax.

In conjunction with private pensions, full employment and a national income maintenance program, these steps can help achieve the vital goal of adequate retirement income.

Six million Americans need better housing, and they need it now. We are in desperate need of a total revamping of the hodgepodge of federal housing programs. The special needs of the elderly must be recognized in our public housing system through improved design standards, a commitment of resources to rehabilitate existing homes, and secure long-term financing to enable non-profit groups again to take part in providing new housing for the aged.

Our efforts to reduce crime must focus on protecting the most vulnerable victims. Community support systems have proven effective in reducing crime rates in some areas; they should be expanded. Planning for community development must assure easier access to stores and mass transit for the elderly to reduce their exposure to potential assailants.

There are some improvements we can make to alleviate the heavy medical bill burden now borne by the elderly. One of the most basic of health costs to the elderly is for prescription drugs. Many individuals pay $20-$30 a month in drug bills, and this cost should be paid by Medicare. But even the best of the proposed health recommendations persist in ignoring the distinct needs of the aging. The health care needs of the elderly are less intensive but more chronic and continuous than those of the general population. At the same time, their social needs are more intensive and more acute.

Since these emotional and social problems often bear upon the aged person's eating and physical habits, they may seriously affect his health and in turn his need for professional medical attention. Our priorities in establishing national health care should concentrate on preventive and curative services so that fewer will face the prospect of hospital or nursing home confinements. Older Americans fear, above all, institutionalization—and we should do everything possible to alleviate this fear.

The policy changes I have outlined are needed. They are sound, reasonable, achievable steps toward dignified, humane treatment of our elders. But even if they were all enacted into law today, they could not achieve much. The essential element of improvement is commitment—commitment to making America work for all our people—and this kind of commitment simply has not been demonstrated by those charged with serving this nation's aged.

Old age is the last and most devastating segregation in our country. But, just as the other cruel and demeaning forms of degradation are slowly and painfully being erased, older Americans are rightfully demanding their just share in the rewards of our society. They are raising their voices and beginning to be heard. I am impressed and heartened by the vigorous growth of organizations committed to working for change, committed to achieving a better life for this neglected class of our people.

The French philosopher Montaigne once said, "I speak truth, not so much as I would, but as much as I dare; and I dare more as I grow older." I believe we will elevate the problems of the aging to their rightful level in the order of domestic priorities. We will because it is right, and because 25 million old citizens of this nation are finally demanding it. They have begun to dare more.

Reference: (C.R. 10/3/75, Pg. E-5205)

Alternative Fuels

Need for Alternative Fuels
Excerpts from Speech
in the Congressional Record
by
State Sen. Herschel Rosenthal (California)

I am pleased to be here to share with my colleagues information on the status of alternative fuel development in California. For many years, the California Legislature has promoted the use of alternative fuels as a means to (1) reduce our dependence on petrolelum based fuels and (2) insulate our state from fuel price shocks and supply disruptions.

We in California are mindful of our vulnerability. California is the third largest consumer of gasoline in the world, following the United States as a whole and the USSR. My state uses an average of more than one billion gallons per month, and its transportation system is 99 percent dependent on petroleum-based fuels.

The 1989 Exxon Valdez oil spill caused only a brief disruption of Alaska crude to California—yet California prices at the gas pump skyrocketed across the state.

In the last few years, California has discovered that alternative fuels also provide a remarkable opportunity to overcome what seemed to be insurmountable air quality problems. Even with the nation's most aggressive program to combat air pollution, California's major urban areas, do not meet federal air quality standards.

I believe that alternative fuel diversity is the insurance policy we need to combat both hazardous air pollution and dangerous petroleum dependence. In California we have active clean fuel demonstration programs in three major areas: (1) methanol, (2) compressed natural gas and (3) electricity.

For near-term, widespread market acceptance, the California Energy Commission believes that methanol fuel offers the simplest, most cost-effective option to petroleum fuel because (1) it is a clean-burning, cost-competitive liquid alternative that can substitute for both gasoline and diesel; (2) it is the least disruptive alternative for consumers, automotive companies and the fuel distribution industry; and (3) it provides equal or superior overall vehicle performance.

The California Methanol Fuels Program started in about 1978 with field tests of relatively small volumes of alcohol fuels blended with gasoline. Both ethanol and methanol fuel technologies were demonstrated. Methanol became our preferred alternative.

Most ethanol production facilities are concentrated in the Midwest grain-producing states. Due to the current federal subsidy, equivalent to about 60 cents per gallon, ethanol has been and will likely continue to be economically competitive as a gasoline blending agent. But without the subsidy, ethanol faces a serious cost problem. In addition, California air quality agencies have expressed concern regarding the higher emissions that come from ethanol-based gasohol. Since the clean fuel vehicles in California can run on ethanol, we are continuing to evaluate ethanol fuels, but this option may turn out to be best in other parts of the country.

In the last two years, the California Energy Commission has begun demonstrating flexible fuel vehicles manufactured by Ford and General Motors that are capable of operating on methanol, ethanol, gasoline or any blend of these fuels. They are totally automatic in operation—no switches, no adjustments whatsoever from the driver's perspective. With flexible fuel cars, the fear of running out of fuel or having a restricted driving range is no longer a factor.

California is implementing a flexible fuel demonstration program with the goal of operating at least 5,000 vehicles in the state by 1993. Agreements have been signed with Ford and General Motors to deliver a portion of these vehicles, and we are seeking additional participation by Toyota and Nissan.

Vehicle demonstrations alone will not create a self-sustaining market for clean burning alternative fuels. We also need to build a supply and distribution system. A few years ago, I introduced legislation that would have required oil companies to install methanol compatible storage tanks in gas stations at the time old, leading storage tanks were removed to comply with toxic pollution requirements. At the urging of the oil industry, the Governor vetoed the bill. Thereafter, however, ARCO and Chevron volunteered to place methanol fueling facilities across the state, and Shell and Exxon have recently joined the program. Up to 50 methanol fueling facilities will soon be operational.

In 1987, the California Legislature established the Blue Ribbon California Advisory Board on Air Quality and Fuels, composed of 17 members representing the automotive and oil industries, state agencies, local air quality districts, the business community, environmental groups and the public at large. The advisory board was directed to make recommendations on the need for and benefit of using mandates and incentives to facilitate the introduction of a variety of clean fuels.

The board completed its efforts in 1989, and concluded that the use of methanol, ethanol, propane, compressed natural gas, hydrogen, electricity and reformulated gasoline would all result in improvements in air quality and improved energy security.

I would like to comment on the advent of reformulated gasoline, which I believe was first introduced by ARCO in Southern California. I don't think that the oil industry would have come up with this clearer gasoline had not California, in its clean fuels initiatives and the President and the Congress in their debate over the Clean Air Act amendments, threatened to replace gasoline with alternative fuels. Reformulated gasoline, in my judgment, is not the best clean fuel. But I welcome the oil industry competing in this area as long as it does not convince the Administration and the Congress to discriminate against other clean fuels such as methanol, natural gas and electricity.

In contrast to petroleum-based gasoline, natural gas is comparatively inexpensive and plentiful in North America. Because of its clean burning characteristics and attractive costs, natural gas is inceasingly being viewed in California as the fuel of choice for stationary power generation. We are now beginning to look at natural gas as a clean transportation fuel.

Because of the increased efforts to seek air quality improvements, the gas utilities in California have begun an aggressive effort to initiate compressed natural gas vehicle demonstrations. Due to the expense of purchasing gas compressed fueling systems and vehicle range limitations, compressed natural gas vehicles in California will likely initially be used in metropolitan areas for commercial van fleets with central fueling facilities.

Electric vehicles hold the promise of virtually eliminating mobile source emissions. Battery-powered electric vehicles are currently being demonstrated in commercial fleet applications in California. General Motors, Chrysler and Ford are supporting the production of electric vans. Also this year five California electric utilities in cooperation with the California Energy Commission will begin an on-road demonstration of 38 electric vehicles.

A preliminary assessment of California's electricity supply system suggests that the state could comfortably accommodate the off-peak charging requirements for a considerable number of electric vehicles. It is my hope that the recent announcement by General Motors of the introduction of the "impact"—a passenger-sized commuter electric vehicle—may represent a technological breakthrough in this area.

California has over 20 state agencies and commissions that share responsibility for energy and environmental functions. In the area of clean-burning fuels, programs are being undertaken by our state's Energy Commission, Public Utilities Commission, our Resources Board, Department of Transportation, Department of Food and Agriculture and Department of General Services.

One of the goals of our Joint Committee on Energy Regulation and the Environment is to provide the next governor with options for reorganizing energy regulatory activities to promote environmentally sound energy programs, includng a comprehensive clean fuels program.

I want to emphasize California's commitment to a national energy strategy which includes an effective and diverse clean fuels component. I believe that California has led the nation in demonstrating the viability of alternative fuels, particularly methanol. We hope our efforts to commercialize clean fuel technologies will provide helpful guidance to other states and the federal government as we all move forward in this critically important area.

Reference: (C.R. 6/13/90 Pg. E-1952)

Acid Rain
• • • • • • • • • • • •

Conference on Acid Raid
Excerpts from Speech
in the Congressional Record
by
Dr. Mark MacGuigan
Secretary of State for External Affairs of Canada

It is undoubtedly obvious to all of those here today that acid rain—and all the damage it is inflicting—is a serious problem for both our countries. I do not intend to review in detail today the issues surrounding the dangers and control of acid rain. These have been examined exhaustively and expertly by the many specialists who have preceded me here. Rather, I want to examine the political components of this phenomenon—phenomenon which for Canadians is a question demanding answers in the present, and for both our countries is an issue which goes to the heart of our relationship.

Our relationship is one which spans much of our history and it has—for the most part—served us well. But beyond that, Canadians and Americans share a moral responsibility. Our prosperity and influence have not been solely the product of hard work or economic wisdom. From the very dawning of North American history, it was evident throughout the world that Canadians and Americans were the inheritors of one of the world's richest land masses. It was the promise of these that brought to this continent the millions of people who sought to fashion it into strong and influential economic and political entities.

But I want to suggest to you today that there is another dimension to that inheritance, namely our responsibility toward each other to ensure—through the rule of law—that what was given to us is not left ravaged and extinct because we lacked the foresight or the will to protect it for future generations of North Americans.

There are those, of course, who do not necessarily share our ominous view about the tragic effects of acid rain. There are others who are pessimistic about the prospects for action to effectively control those emissions which have resulted in acid rain and the profound damage it is causing to much of our environment. There are others whose approach fails to take account of the true nature of all the costs and benefits involved. Let me briefly address a comment to each of these views.

To those who doubt the seriousness of acid rain, I extend an invitation to come to our country and see for themselves. They will find signs of depredations of several millon tons of sulphur dioxide and oxides of origin—which are transformed chemically in the atmosphere and fall in our country each year in the form of acid rain. Many of our lakes have reached levels of acidity which make it impossible to support fish and related forms of life. In Nova Scotia, no less then nine rivers no longer support the salmon population. Elsewhere, the leaching of calcium and magnesium from the soil is threatening our boreal forest—a resource that provides employment to 10 percent of our labor force in Canada.

Those who are pessimistic about the prospects for halting the high level of emissions have, perhaps, ignored our own experience in Canada. The best example is the huge smelting operation of the International Nickel Company at Sudbury, Ontario— the largest single producer of acid-causing emissions in our country. Had no controls been imposed, that smelter would today be producing some 7,200 tons of sulphur dioxide daily. However, for several years it has been operating at 50 percent control or below.

This is one major example, but there are others. Sulphur containment at a new copper smelter in Timmins, Ontario, will reach 97 percent. And Ontario's thermal power stations have been required to reduce total sulphur dioxide emissions by 43 percent during the 1980s, even though, like the United States, we are anticipating considerable growth in demand for electricity.

I cite these examples to illustrate what can be accomplished through the joint efforts of scientists, industry and government where there is a determination to make an impact on a situation which can only get worse if left unchecked.

To that third group—those who propound the view that economic and energy considerations make significant controls unfeasible—I would submit that significant emission reductions, if wisely applied, need not detract from economic and energy goals. Nor should the legitimate costs of production be passed off to another party— in this case another country. This is spurious in economic terms and irresponsible in the spirit of international legal considerations.

With respect to coal conversion there is considerable economic benefit to be derived from a switch to coal from imported oil. In effect, this benefit is sufficiently attractive that we can more than afford the cost of ensuring that resulting damage to the environment be minimized to the extent possible.

It can be argued, of course, that legislators will respond only to the expressed concerns of their constituents, and while there is a very high level of concern and sensitivity in Canada about acid rain, there is a relatively low level of concern in the United States. But this point of view overlooks some present day realities and ignores the nature of our historic relationship.

For one thing, media reports and conferences such as this clearly demonstrate accelerating interest in the United States. I understand this reflects a growing awareness of extensive environmental damage in such areas of the United States as New England, the North Central Region, part of the Rocky Mountain region and the Appalachian area. And so, while the acid rain phenomenon has not yet had as profound a recognition generally in the United States as it has had in Canada, alert Americans appear to be heeding the warning signs.

I believe also that legislators in the United States are unlikely to fly in the face of our historical methods of resolving problems common to our two countries. Canada and the United States developed a long tradition over the years of solving their environmental problems effectively, fairly and with careful attention to international law and responsibility.

The importance of acid rain in Canada-United States relations is also demonstrated by the attention it received during the recent visit of President Reagan to Ottawa. It was among the major bilateral issues discussed. I can assure you that Canada was pleased to receive the President's assurances that negotiations of an agreement to deal with the problem would proceed as planned.

We regard this as an important commitment by the United States government.

Our ultimate hope, of course, is the successful conclusion of a bilateral air quality agreement. In that connection, our two countries signed a Memorandum of Intent which enunciated three specific objectives.

The first is to commit our countries to begin negotiations on an air quality agreement.

Secondly, the Memorandum of Intent provided for the establishment of five joint Canada-United States working groups, charged with developing a common information base.

Thirdly, the Memorandum of Intent calls on both Canada and the United States to undertake interim measures of control to reduce transboundary air pollution, pending the conclusion of a bilateral agreement.

It has been said that acid rain constitutes a test of the rule of law in the relationship between Canada and the United States. The legal principles involved are clear. Both our governments support Principle 21 of the 1972 Stockholm Declaration, which provides that states have "the responsibility to ensure that activities within their jurisdiction or control do not cause damage to the environment of other states or of areas beyond the limits of national jurisdiction."

With regard to boundary waters, this principle has been embodied in our bilateral treaty obligations for more than 70 years. The Boundary Waters Treaty of 1909 prohibits the pollution of waters on either side of the boundary "to the injury of health or property on the other." This was the basic principle applied in the Great Lakes Water Quality Agreement of 1972, an agreement which must inevitably be of particular significance to both Americans in this region and to Canadians in the "Golden Horseshoe" on the Canadian side of Lake Ontario.

I am certain that all responsible Americans accept that the rule of law should guide their relations with other countries as well as their internal activities. I am also certain that responsible Americans recognize that our mutual obligations must be met by dealing with the causes of acid rain to prevent further damage rather than concentrating on remedies for damage after it has occurred.

For our part, we accept the fact that there will have to be a more focused concentration on the problem of acid rain in both countries, necessitating heightened awareness and sensitivity to the damage associated with it.

One such mechanism is conferences such as this, in which skilled and informed specialists, legislators and others can elucidate our difficulties and focus on avenues for problem resolution. It is an action that is in the finest tradition of our two countries and one that offers to Canadians the ray of hope we need to press on with our neighbors in overcoming one of the most serious environmental problems we share in this continent.

Reference: (C.R. 5/14/81, Pg. S-5110)

Arts and Humanities

Collaborations in Arts Education

Excerpts from Speech
in the Congressional Record
by
Frank Hodsoll, Chairman
National Endowment for the Arts

I am delighted to be here with so many distinguished figures in the Bay State's artistic, educational and philanthropic communities.

The Cultural Education Collaborative has made singular contributions to richer, fuller, more creative teaching and learning. I can't imagine a more fitting tribute to the Collaborative on the occasion of its tenth anniversary than the growing consensus that its partnership approach to cultural programming for public school students has become a model for action in other states and cities across the nation.

As Chairman of the National Endowment for the Arts, I can assure you that the Collaborative has a most appreciative collaborating partner in Washington. We are excited about the potential which the Institute for the Arts represents, and we look forward to a process of sharing and mutual consultation as your important work goes forward.

As most of you know, the Endowment has made arts education a major priority. We believe that arts education is critical, not only to the future vitality of the arts in America, but also to the "compleat" citizen. It is sad indeed that so many of our young people graduate from our high schools without being able intelligently to see and hear the arts.

Serious studies of arts audiences show educational attainment to be the key predictor of future arts participation. But when even college graduates have had little or no exposure to the arts, it is not surprising that the seminars we held about our various programs repeatedly cited the need for more and better arts education.

I like to point out to all who will listen that those of us advocating arts education now have a body of unimpeachable authority on our side. Three of the most significant reports published last year on the state of American education are in close agreement as to the basic place of the arts in effective education.

The College Board and the Carnegie Foundation for the Advancement of Teaching specifically include the arts among the subjects they recommend as essential for high school graduation.

We should take full advantage of the key finding of the National Commission on Excellence in Education, as set forth in "A Nation at Risk," that "the curriculum in the crucial eight grades leading to the high school years should be designed to provide a sound basis for study in those and later years in such areas as English language development and writing, computational and problem-solving skills, science, social studies, foreign language, and the arts."

While the Commission did not go so far as to include the arts among its recommended "Five New Basics" for high school students, it did declare that "a high level of shared education in these basics, together with work in the fine and performing arts and foreign languages, constitutes the mind and spirit of our culture."

We at the Endowment are convinced that American youth cannot adequately apprehend "the mind and spirit of our culture" without an understanding of the arts. We also know what a tremendous challenge we face, in attempting to convince state and local educational authorities that math and science—as important as they are—cannot by themselves open up "the mind and spirit of our culture." Our Survey on Public Participation in the Arts, for instance, shows that most Americans have never had any form of artistic instruction at all; 53 percent have had no instruction in music; 76 percent, no visual arts; 82 percent, no creative writing; 91 percent, no theater; and 93 percent, no ballet. For the vast number of young Americans, the arts remain the forgotten part of educational experience and growth.

We think that the College Board has made an especially valuable contribution by summarizing the levels of competence which college-bound students should achieve in the arts. The College Board recommends that all such students should possess:

- The ability to understand and appreciate the unique qualities of each of the arts;
- The ability to appreciate how people of various cultures have used the arts to express themselves;
- The ability to understand and appreciate different artistic styles and works from representative historical periods and cultures;
- Some knowledge of the social and intellectual influences affecting artistic forms; and
- The ability to use the skills, media, tools and process required to express oneself in one or more of the arts.

However one formulates the goals of arts education, it will be up to teachers, artists and their local collaborators to bring these goals to fruition. In assisting this process, the role of the Endowment must remain modest. We do not—and cannot—set arts education policy; nor can we become a source of funding for programs that must derive their principal support from state and local sources.

Within these limits, we have put forward several focal points for Endowment encouragement of arts education.

First, we are working with the National Assembly of State Arts Agencies in co-sponsoring a series of regional seminars; these seminars will concentrate on identifying the best ways to build effective arts education programs, and on the relationship between public advocacy and educational policy-making at the local level.

Second, the Endowment is cooperating with the Getty Trust in an effort to assemble the best possible project team to undertake the development of a pilot series of television arts programming for young people. In the long run, our interest is in taking advantage of the unique capacities of television to assist the acquisition of artistic literacy among young people.

Third, we are exploring ways in which the artistic education of teachers might be strengthened. In this area we may test the merits of an approach developed by the National Endowment for the Humanities, to enhance humanities teaching through discipline-intensive seminars for classroom teachers. But we will also want to study the Institute for the Arts' new Program of Artist/Education Interchange.

Fourth, the Endowment is interested in encouraging a greater involvement in arts education on the part of arts institutions. We are especially interested in following the development of the Institute for the Arts' Program of Art Partnerships, which build upon prior experience to develop long-term collaborations between schools, individual artists, cultural institutions and academic researchers.

Finally, we are committed to continuing and, wherever possible, to improving the Endowment's Program of Artists in Education. This program assists artists' residencies in schools and other community sites in all 50 states as well as the District of Columbia and five special jurisdictions. Since 1969, over 14.3 million students have benefitted from residencies which have involved approximately 30,700 artists, 454,700 teachers and administrators, and 57,800 school and community sites nationwide.

In summary, the Endowment fully subscribes to the assumptions of the Collaborative with respect to the value of partnerships between schools and cultural institutions. We agree that the involvement of cultural institutions in arts education helps students learn to look and listen with understanding; to expand their awareness of the world around them; to develop awareness about other cultures; to discover a sense of their own capabilities; to develop their intellectual faculties, including the capacity to comprehend non-verbal modes of knowledge; and to communicate effectively in the world of concepts and ideas—as well as to become literate artistically.

If I were to state a dream, it would be that no American would graduate from high school without a general literacy in the arts. Impossible? Perhaps. But it surely is a worthy dream. It is for us, the collaborators, to fashion practical means to approach the dream. I pledge the Endowment to help to this end.

Reference: (C.R. 5/14/84, Pg. S-5695)

Chapter 2

Biotechnology
From Green to Gene: Another Revolution?

Excerpts from Speech
in the Congressional Record
by
Hon. Christopher S. Bond
United States Senate

It is fitting that you have assembled at one of the most prestigious institutions in the world, the National Academy of Sciences. As members of the first graduating class of National Needs Fellows, you have exhibited an intellect of remarkable proportion.

The next century will reveal technological advances unmatched since the beginning of time. We must encourage this change, not fear it. Technology is something which evolves, it is not bestowed upon a population or country. Failure to recognize this will only impede our nation's progression from the Green Revolution to the Gene Revolution. As Winston Churchill once said, "Unless the intellect of a nation keeps abreast of all material improvements, the society in which that occurs is no longer progressing."

As professionals with educational backgrounds in agriculture, you must look beyond current surpluses and excessive production. What will the structure of agriculture be in 25 years? Fifty years? One hundred years? Recent projections state that there will be 9 billion people on earth in the year 2025. World demand for food production is expected to double in the next 30 years. Without a doubt, biotechnology will play a major role in whether the United States changes the path of modern history or simply hitchhikes its way through the 21st Century. The course which we chart will be determined by many: academia, the scientific community, government agencies, Congress, farmers, ranchers and, ultimately, consumers.

As many of you already know, technological evolution is not a given and there are those who will fight it every step of the way. One outspoken opponent has stated that "biotechnology stands to increase surpluses, soil loss, pollution, and to wipe out what's left of small farms; not to mention the bigger picture of the potential disaster inherent in releasing mutant life forms."

I'm more of an optimist than that. Human health benefits aside, biotechnology will lead to the development of new plant varieties with greater resistance to disease, improved adaptability to climatic factors, increased herbicide tolerance and enhanced plant growth and photosynthetic efficiency.

According to Dr. David Pimentel of Cornell University, significant benefits will result "when organisms such as bacteria, viruses, fungi, nematodes and insects are engineered to control insect pests, weeds and plant diseases. He indicates that the gains could be enormous given the fact that one-third of all U.S. crops—about $50 billion worth—are annually lost to pests. Additional savings, up to $500 million, could be generated by reduced pesticide costs.

In livestock, Bovine Somatotropin (BST) has increased dairy cattle milk yields by 10 percent to 25 percent per day within several days of use. Porcine Somatotropin (PST) may lead the way to adapting pork to meet today's demand for leaner meat products. Other possibilities include mouth disease, scours and shipping fever. Genetic engineering of chickens, swine and cattle may also become a reality.

Efforts to improve agricultural inputs and outputs must be supported by the entire production processing and distribution chains. The development of new crops will be of little use without the proper equipment for planting and harvesting. Agricultural marketing will undoubtedly become much more sophisticated by dealing with products specifically tailored to meet consumer demand.

Current issues illustrate the increasing role which food scientists will play in the future. Consumer confidence in our nation's food supply may have been jeopardized by recent examples of salmonella in eggs and sulfamethazine residues in pork. I would hope that Congress acts soon to pass legislation to supplement organoleptic inspection with microbiological and chemical sampling. Again, such a thing can be done, thanks to advances in genetic engineering.

With all the talk about the possibilities of biotechnology, it is very easy to overlook an essential component—education. Future advances in agriculture will not be made solely as a result of research funding, but because of a national commitment to producing highly skilled researchers and educators.

Some months ago some startling figures were brought to my attention. Undergraduate enrollments in United States Colleges of Agriculture have declined by nearly 50 percent during the past decade. In 1986, the U. S. Department of Agriculture projected a 10 percent annual shortfall of college graduates in food, agriculture and natural resource disciplines through 1990. A 17 percent shortfall is projected for agricultural scientists, engineers and related specialists.

In my opinion, this could not come at a worse time. We must enact steps to reverse this trend and enlighten others of the opportunities existing within the agricultural sciences. For starters, increased efforts must be undertaken to increase funding for the National Needs Fellowship Program. Congress seems willing to appropriate research funds without questioning the quality of researchers. I am of the opinion the two are not mutually exclusive. Quality researchers lead to quality research.

Congress will undoubtedly play a role which extends beyond simply appropriating funds. While the federal government establishes scientifically acceptable testing guidelines, Congress must also ensure they do not become unnecessary deterrents. Public safety will remain the utmost concern and must always be considered. We must also keep in mind that it takes years to regain the public's confidence once the assurance of safe products has been compromised. Congress must be in a position to ensure safety, thus an oversight role of the regulatory system will most likely continue.

Along these lines, one concern which continues to surface in Congress relates to the deliberate release of genetically engineered organisms into the environment. Although guidelines have been established by the National Institutes of Health, an increasing number of localities are passing ordinances implementing more stringent regulations. A way to minimize this trend is to ensure that the federal government, including Congress, does not lag behind the advances made by the scientific community.

An area which may require additional resources is the Office of Trademarks and Patents (OTP). Recent rulings have affirmed that patents can be awarded for genetically engineered seeds, plants, plant tissue cultures and animals.

However, it is my understanding that companies must wait about two and a half years before their application is reviewed. It then takes another two years on average before a final decision is rendered. As of the beginning of 1988, OTP's backlog of application appeals and amendments was 6,907.

It is evident that technology has progressed at a faster rate than our ability to evaluate it. While basic research holds the key to advanced technologies, applied research assumes the responsibility for providing the benefits to society.

If current legislation is any indication of the future, Congress will deal with a full spectrum of technology issues related to agriculture. Bills now pending range from prohibiting the patenting of animals altered through genetic engineering to the authorization of a plant modification research program.

Good will or good intentions are not a substitute for action. Neither the federal government, in general, nor Congress, in particular, should impede the evolution of technology. Let me again assert that progress results from sound research not a resounding fear of the future.

As George Bernard Shaw said, "All progress is initiated by challenging current conceptions."

We have at hand the opportunity to challenge the current conception—or misconception—that biotechnology stands to increase surpluses, soil loss, pollution and to lead to disastrous mutations.

Only by doing so can we achieve progress.

Reference: (C.R. 4/25/88, Pg. S-4636)

Banks
· · · · · · · · ·

Will the U.S. Banking Industry Remain Competitive in the Global Marketplace?

Excerpts from Speech
in the Congressional Record
by
Hans Angermueller

My thesis is quite simple and, if you are an American, quite disturbing. In a world order which is more and more becoming based on economic, and not military, might, the efficiency with which a nation's financial institutions can facilitate the flow of capital from the ultimate suppliers to the ultimate users of capital will be a major factor in determining that nation's economic well-being and its position in the global marketplace.

In my view, foreign financial institutions are today much better positioned than United States financial institutions to mobilize capital and help direct it to its most productive uses. Foreign financial institutions have the flexibility to respond to changes in the marketplace. United States financial firms do not.

Foreign financial institutions have the opportunity to diversify and to tap new sources of revenue. United States financial institutions do not.

Foreign financial institutions can therefore expect to be stronger and more competitive than U.S. institutions. Consequently, in today's global marketplace, U.S. institutions operate at a disadvantage not only in the international markets but in the United States as well.

This is bad news not only for U.S. financial institutions, but given the pivotal role that financial institutions play, there will be adverse consequences for the U.S. economy.

For almost half a century, the military confrontation between the U.S. and the Soviet Union has led to their respective roles as the world's superpowers. However, it is now becoming increasingly clear that the world leadership role of the U.S. can no longer be based on its rivalry with the Soviet Union. The U.S. must adjust its priorities in a world in which other nations aggressively pursue their own economic interests and are becoming less dependent on U.S. military strength. This means that the U.S. must position itself to remain competitive in the global marketplace which, in turn, means that U.S. financial institutions must be able to operate effectively in that marketplace.

However, that marketplace is undergoing fundamental and irrevocable changes. Today, as we are all aware, major advances in information technology, shifts in savings from depositories to mutual funds and pension funds and the use of options, futures, swaps, and other derivative instruments are revolutionizing the business of finance.

As a result, financial institutions can now disassemble any financial asset into its basic risk components and recombine those components, those basic components into a new instrument with completely different maturity, liquidity, interest rate, foreign exchange and credit characteristics. This enables the users and the suppliers of capital, including intermediaries themselves, to determine how much, and what kind of, risk they wish to bear.

Most OECD countries are in the process of taking, or have already taken, the steps necessary to permit financial institutions in their countries the opportunity to adopt to this changing financial marketplace. They are doing this by permitting their financial institutions to exercise a broad range of powers and thus to offer their customers whatever combination of products and services they may demand and which the institutions feel competent to provide.

These countries are developing a regulatory climate that is hospitable to a global financial service business. The premier example is the United Kingdom. But other countries are also streamlining their financial systems for defensive reasons—to prevent any further erosion of their position.

In preparation for 1992, countries within the European Community are rapidly dismantling the remaining barriers between banking, securities and insurance. In a blunt report on where European banking is headed, Sir Leon Brittain, vice-president of the Commission of the European Communities, recently told a Washington audience that the European Community "in one bound has moved from 12 fragmented and confusing structures of national banking regulation to a single market of a size and simplicity unmatched anywhere else in the world." He took pains to point out that the European Community is not taking these stops "merely to benefit banks. We are doing it to increase the competitiveness of European industry by giving it access to the cheapest, most efficient, and most innovative financial products in the world. So don't say you weren't warned."

With incentives like this, the Japanese minister of finance is speeding up the process of exploring options for the future of Japan's financial system.

In sum, public policy toward the financial sector in other parts of the developed world is changing rapidly and, from the point of view of their financial institutions and their customers, it seems to be changing for the better.

What, in contrast, has been happening with the United States in response to the basic changes in the world of finance? The short answer is, at best, basically nothing.

Without a major restructuring of our laws and regulations, I am afraid that U.S. financial institutions will be relegated to playing bit parts on the world financial services stage. Handicapped by a weak domestic franchise, U.S. financial institutions generally, and U.S. banks in particular, face a narrower range of options than do foreign institutions. United States banks may withdraw into the United States. Indeed, many U.S. banks have already cut back substantially on their operations overseas. Others may retain a global presence, but only in selected markets or for selected groups of customers. Still others may find it necessary to find a foreign partner or seek adoption by a foreign parent.

It is noteworthy that U.S. commercial bank write-offs in the last five years were $60 billion. This is more than twice as much as the write-offs during all of the 1950s, 1960s and the 1970s! One wonders whether the U.S. economy, in which 35 large bank holding companies hold about one-half of all U.S. banking assets, really needs all the 13,000 banks plus 3,000 thrifts that we have. Perhaps a smaller number of larger institutions operating in a national market with greater flexibility might be better for the public interest—even though perhaps not for the special interests.

Bad as this picture of U.S. banking may be, it could even get worse, for I see some disturbing parallels between the banking crisis of 1933 and the thrift crisis of 1990. Hopefully, it will not take another 50 years to understand why thousands of thrifts have failed and why it will cost the U.S. taxpayer more than $300 billion—some now say up to $500 billion— to resolve the problem. In my view, the real villain is the government itself.

The government allowed hundreds of thrift institutions to continue in operation long after they were insolvent. When these insolvent institutions had exhausted their own capital, they were permitted to continue to raise money from the public by soliciting above market rate insured deposits. With none of their own funds at stake, they had every incentive literally "to bet the bank."

Think for a moment how the thrift crisis could have been averted or brought under control if the federal authorities had simply refused to extend deposit insurance to cover any new deposits of thrifts whose capital levels were below minimum requirements.

In sum, the thrift crisis was a consequence of the collision of the narrow thrift charter in a competitive world with an abrupt shift in monetary policy. That collision was exacerbated by lax regulation and supervision and compounded by the inability of the FSLIC to close down insolvent institutions.

This then brings me to my last subject—what should the Congress do?

It seems to me that Congress must deal with two fundamental issues: deposit insurance reform and structural reform. Whether the issues are dealt with successively or concurrently, the fact is that both issues must be addressed and soon. Deposit insurance reform should be designed to protect the deposit insurance funds and to assure that the U.S. taxpayer is not once again exposed to risk. However, deposit insurance reform, by itself, will do nothing to assure that financial firms will remain competitive and able to generate earnings sufficient to maintain adequate capital. That ability to generate earnings that maintain and attract capital is ultimately the best protection for the deposit insurance funds and for the U.S. taxpayer.

Similarly, the problem with structural reform must be confronted and solved directly and independently. Here, too, there are a variety of proposals by trade associations as well as by regulators. All warrant consideration. Some have already been introduced in the Congress in legislative form.

Thus, after nearly two decades of debate, reams of congressional testimony, countless conferences and hundreds, if not thousands, of academic papers and studies, the ideas are all here. But where is the political will to implement them?

I began my remarks by pointing out that national rivalries will increasingly be played out on economic, as opposed to military, battlefields. Europe, in the person of Sir Leon Brittain, has warned us as to how it intends to conduct the economic battle insofar as financial services are concerned. Will the U.S. Congress rise to this economic challenge of the 1990s as it did to the military challenge of the 1950s?

Reference: (C.R. 5/3/90 Pg. E-1366)

Blacks
• • • • • • • • •
Honoring Martin Luther King Jr.
Excerpts from Speech
in the Congressional Record
by
Hon. Edward M. Kennedy
United States Senate

Two decades ago the dreamer we honor this morning asked his own congregation to remember him as a drum major for justice, a drum major for peace, a drum major for righteousness.

Today, the community of Boston, and especially this Church, are blessed because the Rev. Charles Stith is our drum major. Through his work, the dream of Dr. King on racial justice and full civil rights still lives. By his ministry, Rev. Stith is bringing all of us closer to the day when Dr. King's great dream comes true for our city, our commonwealth and our country.

At the historic march on Washington a quarter century ago, Martin Luther King stood before a quarter million people assembled at the memorial to our greatest Republican President. And on that famous day, Dr. King, heir of Abraham Lincoln, addressed the crowd in these words:

"We have come to our nation's capital to cash a check. When the architects of our republic wrote the magnificent words of the Constitution and the Declaration of Independence, they were signing a promissory note to which every American was to fall heir. This note was a promise that all men would be guaranteed the unalienable rights of life, liberty and the pursuit of happiness."

In the 200 years since then, we have surpassed their aspirations beyond human measure and created a nation of unparalleled power and influence. But measured against the promise of America, we have also fallen short in ways that continue to plague us and divide us.

It is a national tragedy and a national disgrace that after 200 years of progress, the goal of racial justice now seems to be receding, not advancing.

After 200 years, where is justice in health care, when a newborn baby who is black is twice as likely to die in the first year of life as a baby who is white?

After 200 years, where is justice in education, when the doors to our colleges and universities are being closed and locked against minorities, when student aid is being slashed, and when campuses are becoming battlegrounds of racism instead of peaceful avenues to understanding?

After 200 years, where is economic justice, when black Americans are condemned to the bottom of the pay scale, and government abandons its commitment to affirmative action in employment?

After 200 years, where is justice in democracy, when intransigent public officials who fear the power of the black vote speak with tongues of hypocrisy about ballot security, and conspire to prevent black citizens from casting their votes on Election Day?

The check of which Dr. King spoke—the check for liberty and equality—was drawn on a bank account whose funds have been withdrawn by a national administration that speaks platitudes about doing better but persists in doing worse.

The proud independence of the Civil Rights Commission has been dismantled and destroyed. Even the extension of the Voting Rights Act was jeopardized, in spite of the overwhelming evidence that minorities are still denied the constitutional right to vote for the candidates of their choice.

This abject retreat on civil rights at the highest level of government has exacted a high price. Minority citizens have become targets of convenience for the fears and frustrations of other Americans seeking their own education, their own employment, their own economic security.

That attitude has spawned incidents of racism that would have been unthinkable ten years ago. The life of a young black man is lost to the sudden violence of white teenagers in Howard Beach. A black student at the Citadel is threatened by white cadets dressed as Ku Klux Klansmen. A white man in Kansas City, Missouri, attempts to force a black family to move from the neighborhood by attacking their home five times with guns and explosives.

These are not just isolated cases of violence and bigotry. As Dr. King taught us, "Injustice anywhere is a threat to justice everywhere." Racism feeds on itself. Each time an individual's rights are violated, it becomes easier the next time for others to lose their rights as well. Bad as they are, the episodes of racism that mar the American landscape today are nurturing worse incidents tomorrow.

The landscape I see has not been entirely barren over the past six years. Each individual can make a difference—and some of us have tried. As my brother Robert Kennedy told the students at Capetown in South Africa a few years ago: "Each time a person stands up for an ideal, or acts to improve the lots of others, or strikes out against injustice, he sends forth a tiny ripple of hope, and crossing each other from a million different centers of energy and daring, those ripples build a current that can sweep down the mightiest walls of oppression and resistance."

I am proud to stand here to day as the sponsor of the Martin Luther King holiday bill, the sponsor of the voting rights bill and the sponsor of fair housing.

I am proud to speak for legal services, for the poor, for school integration and for the integrity of the federal courts. I am proud to be the sponsor of the District of Columbia statehood bill and the Equal Rights Amendment to the Constitution.

In ways such as these, on the issue of full human liberty for the minority of Americans who are not white and the majority who are women, I will never give up and I will never give in.

When the timid say they fear even to try anymore, we reply that we still have a shining, powerful dream. When we hear a new version of the old refrain that speaks of gradualism, we reply "What about Americanism?"

And when we are told to wait for tomorrow and tomorrow and tomorrow, for the next election or the next generation, we reply, in the words of Dr. King: "Now is the time." Now is the time to commit ourselves to the dream of Dr. King.

I ask you when is the time for the right of every person who is able and willing to work to have a decent job? Now is the time. When is the time for the right of every young person to a decent education? Now is the time.

When is the time for the right for every man, woman and child in America to decent housing and decent health care? Now is the time.

And finally, when is the time for the right of even the least among us to rise from the shadow of poverty into the sunshine of liberty? Now is the time.

We need national leadership that is more committed to rights such as these in our own land and to full human rights around the world. We must understand that our national interest demands progress and justice for every citizen in America.

We know that the path ahead will not be easy. Change and progress never are. But now is the time—and today is the day—to reaffirm the goals of Martin Luther King and make them our own. May his vision be our vision, his strength our strength, his struggle our struggle. In the words of Dr. King's great letter to his fellow clergymen:

"Let us all hope that the dark clouds of racial prejudice will soon pass away, that the deep fog of misunderstanding will be lifted from our fear-drenched communities, and that in some not-too-distant tomorrow, the radiant stars of love and brotherhood will shine over our great nation with all of their scintillating beauty."

That is our prayer on this 58th anniversary of his birth. And with God as our guide, may we have the wisdom and courage to carry on his work, so that at long last we shall be able to rise together and say with him, "Free at last, free at last, thank God Almighty, we are free at last."

Reference: (C.R. 2/24/87, Pg. E-574)

The Future of Black America
Excerpts from Speech
in the Congressional Record
by
Marian Wright Edelman, President
Children's Defense Fund

It was the best of times, it was the worst of times, it was the age of wisdom, it was the age of foolishness.

For many of you sitting in this room, it is the best of times. Black per capita income is at an all-time high and many of you have moved up the corporate ladder even if the ladders you are on frequently don't reach toward the pinnacle of corporate power. Black purchasing power, now at $200 billion, exceeds the gross national products of Australia and New Zealand combined. But it has not yet been translated into commensurate black economic influence and benefit.

Black elected officials are more numerous than ever (6,681 in 1987, a 350 percent increase since 1970). The amassing of committee and subcommittee chairmanships (eight full House committee chairs including the Select Committee, and 18 subcommittee chairs) by members of this Congressional Black Caucus is impressive by any standards, although the main political game in town is cutting the budget deficit.

Bill Cosby is America's favorite Daddy, and Michael Jackson and Whitney Houston dot the top ten charts. Black leadership has permeated a range of mainstream institutions. Bill Gray chairs the House Budget Committee; Frank Thomas heads the Ford Foundation; A. Barry Rand is in charge of marketing at Xerox; and Richard Knight is the city manager of Dallas.

I am proud of these and many similar accomplishments and applaud the black middle class for whom the times are good tonight. We've worked hard to get where we are. However, we have to work harder still to stay there and to move ahead.

But there is another black community that is not riding high tonight and that is going down and under. If you and I don't build a bridge back to them and throw out some strong lifelines to our children and youths and families whom poverty and unemployment and hopelessness are engulfing, they're going to drown, pulling many of us down with them, and undermine the black future that our forebears struggled and died for.

I am grateful, therefore, that the Congressional Black Caucus has focused attention this year on Educating the Black Child. Just as Martin Luther King Jr. and others accepted the challenge of their time, so the challenge of our time is educating all of our children in mind, in body and strengthen the black future.

It is the worst of times for black babies born within a mile of this hotel and in many inner cities around the country who have less of a chance of living to the first year of life than a baby born in Costa Rica.

It is the worst of times for black youth and young adults trying to form families without decent skills or jobs and without a strong value base. Young marriages have essentially stopped in the black community. Sixty percent of all black babies today are born to never married single mothers; 90 percent of those born to black teens are born to unmarried mothers. One out of two children in a female-headed household is poor. Two out of three children in black female-headed households are poor. If that household is headed by a mother younger than 25, three out of four are poor.

To combat the poverty which is engulfing half of the black babies born today— half of our future as a black community, we must all work to prevent too early sexual activity and pregnancy and encourage our boys and girls to wait until they have the education and economic stability to form lasting families. If the share of single births in the black community grows at the rate of the last decade, by the year 2000, only one black baby in five will be born to a married woman. And if you don't care about these babies unselfishly, you'd better care selfishly, for the future black voting and economic base upon which much of the leadership status rests resides in the health and education of the black child and the strength of the black family.

Not only are too many black babies and youths fighting poverty and sickness and homelessness and too little early childhood stimulation, they are also fighting AIDS and other sexually transmitted diseases; drugs, tobacco, and alcohol addiction; and crime which hopelessness and the absence of constructive alternatives and support systems in their lives leave them prey to.

A black baby is seven or eight times more likely to be an AIDS victim than a white baby and minority teens are the highest risk group for a range of sexually transmitted diseases. A black youth is five times more likely than a white youth to end up in an institution and is nearly as likely to be in prison as he is to be in college. Between 1979 and 1985, the number of black youths in juvenile detention facilities rose by 40 percent while the number of black youths entering college after high school fell by four percent.

Just as our nation is committing moral and economic suicide by permitting one in four of its preschool children to be poor, one in five to be at risk of being a teen parent, one in six to have no health insurance, and one in seven to face dropping out of school at a time when the pool of available young people to support an aging population is shrinking, so we are committing racial suicide by not sounding the alarms and protecting our own children from the poverty that ravages their dreams.

We must recapture and care about our lost children and help them gain the confidence, self-esteem, values, and real world opportunities—education, jobs and higher education which they need to be strong future guardians of the black community's heritage. How do we do this? There are nine steps we must take if we are to help our children.

The first step is to remember and teach them that black folks have never been able to take anything for granted in America and we had better not start now in these waning years of budget deficits and looming economic recession. Frederick Douglass once said: "Men may not get all they pay for in this world, but they must certainly pay for all they get." Tell our children they're not going to jive their way up the career ladder. They've got to work their way up—hard and continuously. Too many young people want a fast elevator straight to the top floor and resist walking up the stairs or stopping on the floors of achievement between the bottom and the top. We must tell them to take the initiative in creating their own opportunity. They can't wait around for other people to discover them or to do them a favor.

The second step is to teach them the importance of getting a good education. While not a guarantee of success, education is a precondition to survival in America today. And we need to ensure that they get a liberal education and learn how to think so that they can navigate an ever-changing job market.

The third step is to tell them that forming families is a serious business and requires a measure of thoughtful planning and economic stability. Education alone, although of enormous value in itself, cannot guarantee a young black adult the income needed to raise children in economic safety today. But two black adults, both working, have the safety net of the second income when unemployment strikes.

The fourth step is to set goals and work quietly and systematically toward them. You can get a lot done in this world if you don't mind doing the work and letting other people take the credit. You know what you do and the Lord knows what you do, and that's all that matters.

The fifth step is knowing the difference between substance and style. Too many of us think success is a Saks Fifth Avenue charge card, or a set of wheels or coming to this Black Caucus dinner. Now these are things to enjoy, but they are not life goals. Don't confuse style with meaning. Get your insides in order and your direction clear first and then worry about your clothes and your set of wheels.

The sixth step is valuing family life. We must build on the strong black tradition of family and teach our children to delay family formation until they are economically and emotionally stable and ready to raise the new generation of black children and leaders. We must join together as an entire community to establish an ethic of achievement and self-esteem in poor and middle class black children.

The seventh step is to vote and use our political and economic power. People who do not vote have no line of credit with people who are elected and pose no threat to those who act against our interests. Don't even pretend that you care about the black community, about poor children, about your nation, even about your own future, if you don't exercise your political leverage.

The eighth step is to remember your roots, your history, and the forebears' shoulders on which you stand. As a black community today there is no greater priority than assuring the rootedness of all our children—poor, middle class, and Ivy League. Young people who do not know where they come from and the struggle it took to get them where they are now will not know where they are going or what to do for anyone besides themselves if and when they finally arrive somewhere.

The first step is to keep dreaming and aiming high. At a time when so many in public and private life seem to be seeking the lowest common denominator of public and personal conduct, I hope you will dream and set new examples of service and courage.

Dr. Benjamin Mays, a former president of Morehouse College and role model for me, once said, "It must be borne in mind that the tragedy of life doesn't lie in not reaching your goal. The tragedy lies in not having a goal to reach. It is not a calamity to die with dreams unfulfilled, but it is a calamity not to dream. It is not a disaster to be unable to capture your ideal, but it is a disaster to have no ideal to capture. It is not a disgrace not to reach the stars, but it is a disgrace to have no star to reach for. Not failure, but low aim, is sin."

We must aim high for our children and teach them to aim high. They desperately need our help on a one-to-one basis. We must all work to redirect the nation's foolish priorities which favor bombs and missiles over babies and mothers upon whom our real national and community security rest.

Reference: (C.R. 10/7/87, Pg. E-3897)

Chapter 3

Captive Nations
•••••••••••••••••••••

President Salutes Captive Nations Week
Excerpts from Speech
in the Congressional Record
by
President George Bush

For the last 32 years, Presidents from Eisenhower to Reagan have commemorated the on-going struggle of captive nations. And traditionally, this one has been the ceremony to commemorate the ongoing struggle of these nations to bear witness to the suffering of millions—a ceremony to honor courage, a ceremony to tell everyone still in captivity that they are not forgotten.

These previous captive nations ceremonies have not been moments of joy, but rather of rededication and sadness that so many in our world live in the throats of tyranny.

The Revolution of 1989 was stunning—thrilling, clearly a historic time and at this ceremony last year, we told the world that we would keep faith with those who were oppressed, and we did. And then taking their lives into their own hands, the very people who are in our hearts crafted an unforgettable year of triumph. The triumph of brave hearts. The triumph of people declaring they would control their own destinies.

And last summer while we were in Eastern Europe, I sensed that excitement in the air that some of you here had been telling me about. In meetings with the people of Poland and Hungary, I pledged America's strong support for their historic struggle. And like most Americans, we watched in joy as the barbed wire on that Austrian-Hungarian border came down. And we were deeply moved as the changes swept across the continent bringing within each the vision of a Europe truly whole and free.

For four long decades, America and her allies have remained united and strong in our mission for peace and freedom. That strength has at long last borne some fruit. What an amazing year this has been, a year of glory in lands that had been defined by those black watchtowers and walls and the drab emptiness of lost dreams.

But we are gathered here today, not just to celebrate the joyous change of this past year, but to celebrate it in a very special way. With us today are some of the young people whose countries were a part of this Revolution of '89. And each is proud of his country.

And so to honor that shining faith in the future, I dedicate this day to this new generation of freedom and to future generations who will never have to bear the burden of tyranny. For some of this new generation this freedom means a whole new world in their own backyard. On that unforgettable morning when the East German borders fell, parents gathered up their kids and brought them to the Brandenburg Gate, the final symbol of tyranny in Berlin. And still in their pajamas, these children on this day of new freedom were passed up from friendly hand to friendly hand to have the thrill of sitting on top of the Wall, looking across at the endless horizon of their dreams. And now, a new generation is coming of age in freedom.

In the audience today is a group of young interns from Poland, Hungary and Czechoslovakia. Supported by funding from private American organizations, they are spending the summer working and learning in our great country. And they are here learning how a free society works and will return to build a free Poland, a free Hungary, a free Czechoslovakia.

But while we celebrate for those who are now free, we must also remember those who are not. And I continue to be moved by what I see and hear throughout the rest of the world, where unfinished revolutions continue one heroic story at a time. In the Americas, where a boy with nothing but a board and sail windsurfed to escape the politics of repression. In Asia, where iron tanks were met by the iron will of the courageous lone man. And today, I also want to remember especially the people of Latvia, Lithuania and Estonia, and renew our unflagging support for their long quest for national self-determination. The road ahead is going to be difficult. But we can now join them in looking forward with hope to the day when their long-cherished dreams will become reality.

Alongside this success story of nations we also hear quiet stories of individuals who, even in darkness, could see the vision of liberty. Those who have risked everything in countries not yet free. The countries we must still remember today, the desperate people we must never forget.

Boys like Quang Trinh, a young Vietnamese teenager. He almost died escaping from the shattered life of a country where he had seen his mother killed, his father jailed, his brothers' spirits broken. Quang fled the only life he had known for freedom. And he jumped into shark-infested waters for freedom. And he starved in delirium for freedom. And after he was finally rescued and told he could enter the United States, he wept all night long.

When did something touch our lives so completely that we cried for joy throughout the entire night? Quang calls America "freedom country." And how many of us have stopped to think of our homeland in those terms?

You know, on my desk in the Oval Office, I have two special mementos with me at all times. One is a small American Flag, given to me in an army hospital by a soldier wounded while fighting to free our friends in Panama. It represents America's commitment to freedom and to the proud people wherever they may be who see that freedom.

And the other souvenir is a piece of the Berlin Wall. One of the first chiseled from that horrifying affront to humanity. I keep it as a reminder of the miracle which courage, strength and unity can achieve. It's sitting right here.

And I also wanted to bring with me today this piece of barbed wire which I brought to last year's ceremony. Some of you may remember. It came from the Austria-Hungary border. And these two symbols of tyranny should never be forgotten.

Sitting in this peaceful Rose Garden today are several generations of these nations of miracles, including the new generation. But there are also countries that are still waiting to be free. So let us all work together so that next year this dream of freedom extends to all those countries where it is now denied. Let us pray together that the light of liberty will shine across our entire planet, and that the next Captive Nations Week will be the last.

Reference: (C.R. 7/26/90 , Pg. E-2507)

Civil Rights
• • • • • • • • • • • • • • • • •
Enforcement of Civil Rights Laws
Excerpts from Speech
in the Congressional Record
by
William French Smith
Former Attorney General of the United States

It is a very special privilege for me to address the federal resources luncheon of the National Urban League.

My remarks today will be earnest and serious. They concern your organization and mine—and our primary goal, equal justice under the law. This organization's membership is as important to the Department of Justice as the Department is important to the well-being of minority Americans. The Justice Department remains one of the most important federal resources in the struggle to ensure all Americans equal rights and equal opportunity.

The goals we seek are the same goals you seek. Although we may differ in some cases on the best means of furthering those goals, in the overwhelming majority of instances, our approaches are the same as, or very similar to, those you advocate. In the course of public debate, however, these basic areas of agreement have sometimes been ignored. Today, I want to set the record straight. And I must say, right up front, that things are not as they have been portrayed by some of our critics.

One of the most important responsibilities of the Department of Justice is the enforcement of our civil rights laws. Twenty-five years ago, the Civil Rights Act of 1957 created a Civil Rights Division within the Department of Justice. Each of the major civil rights acts since then has added to the Department's responsibilities. Since the nation first roused from its long neglect of blatant racial discrimination, the Department of Justice has been in the forefront of the struggle to achieve equal opportunity for all Americans. That leadership role continues.

In his address last year to the NAACP, the President stated that this administration will vigorously investigate and prosecute those who, by violence or intimidation, would attempt to deny Americans their constitutional rights. We have done so. Our level of activity in that regard has exceeded every other Administration. There are currently pending in the Civil Rights Division approximately 1,300 investigations of alleged criminal violations of the civil rights laws, and over $11.5 million is budgeted for FBI investigations of such violations.

The largely unheralded Community Relations Service of the Department of Justice has also been actively working to defuse tensions before they erupt into violent confrontations. In the past year the Service has, to cite a few examples, worked to ease tensions in Atlanta growing out of the tragic murders of black youths in that city, mediated disputes between new refugees from Southeast Asia and other citizens, and sought to stem the unacceptable growth of harassment and intimidation in some areas of the country. We will continue to do everything within our power—both through criminal prosecution and the work of the Community Relations Service—to guarantee that no American is subjected to threats or violence because of his race, religion or ethnic background.

One of the most basic individual rights is the right to vote. The Department of Justice has reviewed over 9,000 proposed voting changes to determine whether they discriminated against minorities in violation of the Voting Rights Act. As you know, the President recently signed the extension of the Voting Rights Act. Under the new law, Section 2 of the Act was amended to adopt a "totality of the circumstances" standard for determining unlawful voting discrimination. We have already begun a vigorous enforcement effort under the amended Section 2 of the Act.

Our efforts have been no less vigorous in guaranteeing all Americans the right to be considered for employment on the basis of individual ability, irrespective of group characteristics such as race, religion or sex.

In the field of public education we have been working to ensure that no individual is denied equal education opportunity because of race. Even beyond the question of student assignments, we have begun investigations in several cases to determine if the quality of education offered in some schools was intentionally and illegally inferior to that offered in other schools.

We have been active in other areas as well. We have begun 26 new investigations of state and local institutions under the Civil Rights of Institutionalized Persons Act—and one has already resulted in a state's plan to close an institution. By successfully prosecuting a suit in Arizona, we stopped leaders from discriminating against Native Americans.

We have also attacked discrimination in housing. We opened some 82 new pattern-and-practice discrimination investigations—some of which have already resulted in our filing suit. In one case, we appeared as an amicus before the Supreme Court and took the position, with which the Court agreed, that under proper circumstances "testers" have standing to bring housing discrimination suits.

We in the Justice Department are proud of our record. It stands as clear and objective evidence of our commitment to guarantee the civil rights of all individuals, and to keep the doors of opportunity open to all regardless of membership in any racial, religious or ethnic group.

In spite of this record of accomplishments, some have mischaracterized the civil rights efforts and objectives of the Department of Justice. They have chosen to brand a debate over some remedies as a difference over rights. Clearly, we have been in the process of evaluating the means by which government has sought to promote equality of opportunity during the last decade. And we are therefore seeking new ways to promote and ensure the right of equal justice under law.

To this end, in the employment discrimination area, we work to ensure that individuals are treated on the basis of merit and not as members of some favored group.

Some have criticized us because we no longer seek to impose hiring or promoting quotas—in other words, precisely because we will not seek to have individuals treated as members of some group and marked for different treatment because of their race or sex.

In our employment cases we seek full relief for those individuals who have been discriminated against. For example, when an individual has been a victim of illegal discrimination, we seek affirmative remedies such as back pay, retroactive seniority, reinstatement, and hiring and promotional priorities. We attempt to ensure that he or she is placed in the position he or she would have attained in the absence of the illegal discrimination.

Confusion is also evident concerning our efforts to ensure equal educational opportunity regardless of race. No child should be assigned to a particular school solely because of race, and no child should receive less of an educational opportunity because of race. That is the mandate of Brown vs. Board of Education, to which we are fully committed. That landmark decision vindicated the "personal interest" of pupils, "in admission to public schools—on a non-discriminatory basis."

Some, however, focus not on the "personal interest" but on racial balance within the schools. They advocate mandatory busing of students on the basis of race to "correct" any perceived imbalance. Experience has demonstrated, however, that such busing does not guarantee equal educational opportunity and often promotes segregation by encouraging many to leave the public schools.

Today, I have reviewed our record in the area of civil rights and suggested why that record does not satisfy some of our critics. They would have us embrace remedies designed to achieve equal group results rather than secure the right of individuals to equal opportunity. They contend that we have abandoned civil rights because we have renounced quotas and busing for racial balance. We believe that those remedies disserve the Constitutional and statutory guarantees of freedom to participate in our society as an individual regardless of race, religion, sex or ethnic background. The Department of Justice continues to lead the fight for that freedom, and for a more just America.

In 1882—100 years ago—the first "separate-but-equal" state law was passed. It has taken us the better part of the last century to eliminate the vestiges of the pernicious doctrine that separation enforced by law could ever mean equality. Today, in ensuring the civil rights of all Americans, we are concerned that the law not be used to separate society by treating persons differently according to their race. Surely, our future as a nation would be best served by government action that treats individuals alike—that forswears and combats efforts to treat them differently because of their race. We are working to make that future a reality. By working together on those issues about which we truly agree, surely success will be guaranteed.

If progress is to continue on civil rights and it must—we cannot be afraid to try new means of guaranteeing progress. The central question must always be whether we are moving in the right direction—not just what methods are we using. In the case of this Administration's efforts, I am certain that the end we pursue is the same goal you cherish—equal rights and equal opportunity. I am also certain that while we may differ on some of the remedies, there is total agreement on most of the steps necessary to vindicate the basic rights involved.

Though our approaches may be new in some ways, our goal is to get this society and all of its members through the gate of equal opportunity. I am certain that the policies we are pursuing will help to ensure that all Americans end up on the right side. That truly is our aim—and our hearts, like yours, are in the effort.

Reference: (C.R. 8/4/82, Pg. H-5190)

Commencement
West Point Class of 1987

Excerpts from Speech
in the Congressional Record
by
General John A. Wickham Jr.
Chief of Staff, U.S. Army

One of the inevitable aspects of life is that the young take up the responsibilities of those who have gone before. You members of the graduating class are about to don the Army green at the same time as I, after 37 years as an officer, prepare to lay aside my Army uniform and retire from active duty. You will understand if I say that my emotions run deep today. West Point represents an inspirational starting point for all of us in the long grey line.

On this special occasion, let me offer several congratulations.

First, to West Point and its superb staff and faculty, congratulations on behalf of the Army and the nation. You have worked well. Your graduates continue to make history, as they have for 185 years, in the defense of our nation, in all segments of our society and even in the exploration of space. You educate, train and inspire young men and women so that they are ready to take their places as leaders of excellence in the Regular Army. There is no institution in the world that better prepares its graduates for the profession of arms than West Point.

Second, congratulations to the families and friends of the graduating cadets. Your support and encouragement have kept these young people on the right path. You can be proud of their accomplishment, which in a way is yours, too. West Point presents demanding challenges—and that's how it always should be. Family and friends provide the lifeline that helps us to weather adversity, and also to enjoy in full measure the success that came our way. Thanks on behalf of the Army and West Point to families and friends who are represented here today.

Third, congratulations to the Class of 1987. Clearly, your class has accomplished much these past four years: you have earned academic degrees, learned much about leadership, and developed yourselves mentally, militarily, physically and ethically. As you well know, today marks the end of one phase in your life, but the beginning of another. You have chosen a high road that will be demanding, and you should never shy away from the tasks ahead. A wise man once said:

"We live in deeds, not years; in thoughts, not breaths—he most lives who thinks most, feels the noblest, and acts the best."

The challenges that you face will stretch your capacities, but the rewards for services to your country and your own personal development will be worth your commitment. There is no greater satisfaction than that derived from one's devotion to comrades and our fellow citizens. I'm sure that you will never have the occasion to regret the choices you have made.

Our nation's roots, and those of the Army, are intertwined with the Constitution of the United States, a document that the framers designed for all centuries. Our values and beliefs are forever defined in this work that constitutes the legal and moral justification for the Armed Forces of the United States.

You understand the Constitution and Bill of Rights because you have studied Constitutional law. You know, better than most perhaps, that only members of the Armed Forces are charged to provide for the common defense. Only upon our shoulders falls the ultimate responsibility to secure the blessings of liberty for our generation and to pass them on, intact, to generations upon generations of Americans who will surely follow.

In a few moments you will take the oath of commissioning. This oath is a sacred trust—one that should never be borne lightly or forgotten. You will pledge, without reservation or regard for personal sacrifice, to "support and defend the Constitution of the United States against all enemies, foreign and domestic, and to obey the order of officers appointed over you."

Your commission will instruct you that the Commander-in-Chief, representing all the people of this nation, reposes "special trust and confidence" in your "patriotism, valor, fidelity and abilities." These are simple words but they involve the essence of character.

Upon receiving a commission, every officer accepts a lasting obligation—no matter what the assignment—to cherish and protect the country and to sustain the dignity and integrity of its sovereign power.

You assume leadership in the Army during historic times. Our challenges in peacetime, perhaps, have never been greater. At home, we face increasingly con-strained fiscal resources as the Congress struggles to allocate funds for competing national priorities. Abroad, the Soviets continue to modernize their armed forces and to expand their influence aggressively; regional and low intensity conflicts are ongoing throughout the world; and terrorism is an international threat that undermines peace and security. As a society, we see all around us values eroded and quality of leadership wanting in virtually every walk of life.

The global responsibilities of the Army demand balance, flexibility and readi-ness—and the need for quality soldiers as well as leaders of exemplary character. Landpower is what changes history, keeps the peace and protects all that we hold dear. The U.S. Army is the bulwark of American landpower. The total Army—active, Reserve and civilian components—includes 28 divisions, which, with our special operations forces, are prepared to operate across a complex, dangerous spectrum of conflict.

The Army is in the midst of an unprecedented modernization program—a program we must complete with the help of Congress and the American public. We have made great progress in recent years. We have better people, better equipment, better training and better support than ever before. Although we are a small Army given

the size of our assigned missions, we are a good Army—probably the best in the world.

First, about 40 percent of the Army is forward deployed. Thus the Army demonstrates our determination to honor defense commitments and to fight any aggressor that threatens our interests and those of our allies if deterrence fails;

Second, as the backbone of American strategic reserve, six active and 10 reserve divisions are available to handle contingency or reinforcement missions, especially our NATO commitment;

Third, five light infantry divisions and our airborne air assault and motorized rifle divisions, plus our special forces and rangers, can quickly deploy anywhere in the world to contain and defuse emerging crisis; and

Finally, the Army provides security assistance, performs peace-keeping operations and can fight terrorism. Thus, our 28 divisions and supporting forces perform absolutely essential roles in the execution of our national military strategy. Moreover, if we as a people are serious about reducing the risk of nuclear warfare, we must be committed to strengthening the conventional capabilities of our Army.

As you enter today's Army, you will find great opportunities awaiting you. As our inspired recruiting phrases say, "The Army is a great place to start" because you will be given the chance "to be all you can be." I urge you to get off to a fast start—make the most of this golden opportunity because service and life itself are shorter than we think.

Your soldiers are the best I have seen during my military career. They will expect you to be role models of the best—perhaps not perfect in every respect, but very good indeed. You must, therefore, be standard bearers of excellence throughout your life. This is what your family, your friends, the Army and the long grey line expect of you.

The difference between a good army and a great one is simply the quality of leadership. I have tried as Chief of Staff to nurture a climate of command in the Army with leadership that cares, teaches, mentors and allows our soldiers and families the "freedom to grow," so they can mature and capitalize on their God-given talents. You must help them to put those talents to full use. Your challenge will be to provide ethical, caring leadership that sparks the Army's greatest strength—its people and their spirit.

History tells us liberty is never free and every generation must make a down payment of service and perhaps sacrifice for its sake. If we enjoy peace today, it is because of our military strength and because of those who served before us. If we want peace for our children and our children's children, we as a people must remain ever vigilant, militarily and economically strong, and led in every walk of life by people of character so that their values can be emulated and ensured.

And so young officers of our Army, go out from this great Academy with its commitment to duty, honor, country, join the long grey line and really make a difference during your lifetime.

As St. Matthew said, "Let your good works glorify your Maker." Make history on your watch. Make all of us who cheer you and pray for you, proud. God bless you all.

Reference (C.R. 6/2/87, Pg. 219)

U.S. Air Force Academy, Class of 1981
Excerpts from Speech
in the Congressional Record
by
Secretary of Defense Caspar Weinberger

Twenty-six years ago, in a commencement address at another service academy on the banks of the Hudson River, President Eisenhower reminded the graduates of two missions they would be called upon to serve in their military careers. The first, of course, is to prepare to fight wars in defense of our society and our way of life. The second is less obvious, but just as much a part of our nation's tradition. "You are members," he said, "of a vast team, the American nation. Its historic objectives have always been human dignity, human peace, human prosperity. These, as a public servant, you must help attain."

These words of one of America's pre-eminent soldier-statesmen apply as well today, to this class, at the Academy as they did on that occasion over a quarter of a century ago. The concept of the military as an integral part, and indeed the servant, of its parent society, is an ancient and hallowed democratic ideal. The military draws its strength, its values and its reason for being from the society it is sworn to defend. Pericles, in his funeral oration, chose to honor fallen heros by paying particular tribute to the virtues of the society they died defending.

Historically, our economy has gone through cycles in which the basic positive and mutually reinforcing relations between the military and the rest of society have been interrupted by periods of tension, suspicion and even hostility. We are just now emerging from one of these darker periods, and all Americans, I am sure, will be relieved to have it behind us.

In terms of both President Eisenhower's two missions, these early years of the 80s are an exciting and an important time for you who are entering your careers as commissioned officers. Your mission as defenders of America will assume great importance as the decade unfolds, as the expansion of Soviet power continues, and as the further extension of the power looms as a greater threat in several areas of the world. It will become more critical as instability—economic, political, religious and social— plagues the regions of vital interest to us and to our allies and friends. Tense, uncertain, unpredictable, these times may yet call upon you to defend and not merely to deter.

Yet at the same time your mission as public servants is of equal importance. It behooves all of us—in and out of uniform—who care about the military to remember the heritage of past service and the continuing need today, for it is through this second mission that the military can most effectively confirm its identity as an organic part of our total society.

Addressing the graduating class at the University of San Diego earlier this week, I urged them to devote a good part of their future careers to participation in some form of public service. Our self-governing democracy cannot work unless most of us do devote some of our time to helping make it work by participating in various forms of public service.

You who have chosen it as your profession and your career are already aware of this. It is my belief, which I have held since long ago, that we must all contribute, if not our full time and devotion as you do, at least a substantial part of our endeavors to ensuring that this government of ours realizes the enormous potential that a government literally of the people and by the people can have.

For generations, the Armed Forces have been the nation's great provider of basic education, high school equivalency and entry level training. For millions of American youth, we have been the national high school, junior college and even graduate school.

Medical history is dotted with landmarks of military origin. Major Walter Reed's isolation of the mosquito, coupled with environmental and protective techniques developed and implemented by the Army Corps of Engineers, not only made possible the construction of the Panama Canal, but freed future generations from the fear of suffering and death from yellow fever. Today, in distant corners of the world, military medical research institutes are breaking paths in the treatment and prevention of malaria and other deadly diseases.

Similarly, we have made great progress in opening up opportunities for women and minorities in the Armed Forces. Last year, with the graduation of the first woman from our military academies, we took a symbolic and practical step forward. We will take more in the future.

President Reagan is committed to enhancing our ability to carry out both missions—to rebuilding America's military strength by providing greater equity in the standard of living of our military and their families and, by means of his leadership, securing a renewed pride in our military and a far greater appreciation by all American of the outstanding, dangerous and necessary job they do.

Last fall, the voice of the American people clearly demanded that our nation should be second to none in military power. Acting through their elected representatives in Congress, the people are backing this mandate with the resources necessary to bring it to fruition.

With the responsibility of this mandate and the considerable resources we are being granted—especially while our economy is still in the earliest stages of recovery—goes an even more demanding obligation for all of us in the Department of Defense to demonstrate that we deserve this public trust by doing our determined best to be faithful to it. We, more than any of the other 200 million Americans, hold in our hands and in our daily work, the potential to fortify or to erode the public consensus in favor of a stronger defense. If we are perceived as wasteful, or unreceptive to new ideas of strategy or tactics, or if we do anything to lose the people's confidence, we might destroy the fragile national consensus so recently formed for stronger defenses, and the new national resolve to fight if necessary for our future.

By your splendid and successful performance through the Academy, physical and military rigors of four years at the Air Force Academy, you have proven you have the resources to become outstanding officers and professionals.

There is a particularly moving feature to graduation ceremonies at all our great service academies. What our President calls the "torch of leadership," is being handed to you in this commencement ceremony today. You now have the right and the ability to accept that torch. Bear it proudly while you have it, and prepare others who will follow to receive it and do likewise.

That is one of the special obligations and privileges that will come to you as a graduate of this great institution.

I have no doubt whatsoever that you will so bear this torch that it will bring the very greatest credit upon each of you, your service, the Armed Forces and your country.
Reference (C.R. 6/12/81, Pg. E-2943)

Marine College and Staff College Graduation, June 1990
Excerpts from Speech
in the Congressional Record
by
Hon. Ike Skelton of Missouri

We gather today to celebrate the achievement of hard work well done. Those officers who have spent the past ten months at this command and staff college know well the exciting changes that have taken place at this institution of higher learning over the past few years.

Let me extend my sincere congratulations to all of you on today's achievements. Savor today's accomplishment, but now is not the time to rest, much work remains to be done.

The changes taking place at this command and staff college must continue if our hope to make this institution a world class center of military learning is to be fulfilled. Those in positions of authority—both here and at Headquarters Marine Corps—need to use this precious period of peace. They need to make the schools here at Quantico so good that you leave here knowing that you are par excellence, that senior strategists in the world would look to you for the most educated commentary on warfare, and that your battlefield decisions would be such that parents would want their sons under your command in time of conflict.

As you know, the Department of Defense is in its sixth straight year of real cuts in the defense budget. In the mid-1980s the pressures on defense spending came on two fronts—the internal one of budget deficits and the external one of trade deficits. Now, in the 1990s, the defense budget will come under even greater pressure as a result of the stunning events that took place in Eastern Europe in the last half of 1989.

The world in 1990 is a far different place than the world that existed just a year ago. The ideals of freedom, democracy and human rights, for which this country has sacrificed much blood and treasure over the past 50 years have been affirmed throughout the world—in Eastern Europe, Nicaragua, South Africa and even the Soviet Union.

But the world of 1990 is still a perilous one. Taking the long view of history, we should realize this is nothing new. We still live in the nuclear age, and the hazards of it are still with us, if less keenly felt. Even after the nuclear arsenals of the United States and the Soviet Union have been reduced through negotiations, each side will still possess thousands of nuclear weapons. This nation will still have to deal with a Soviet Union that will remain a great power.

Elsewhere, the United States will have to cope with the consequences of increasing military power in countries throughout the world. Nuclear and chemical weapons proliferation, in conjunction with the spread of ballistic missile and other technologies, affords the potential for countries such as Syria, Libya, Iraq, Iran and others to figure on the world stage. In the Far East, for example, Stalinism still holds sway in North Korea, China and Vietnam. I believe Korea must rank as the most probable country in the world where American forces could become engaged in large-scale combat.

So while we can relax a bit because of the improvement in American-Soviet relations, these other challenges will confront us for the foreseeable future. Before we disarm too far, I believe it would be better to assess the threats we face before we arbitrarily slash our defenses. In 1935 Winston Churchill warned his countrymen that "wars come very suddenly." It would be a warning well worth keeping in mind in 1990.

In many ways the present period is comparable to the months immediately after World War II. There was much joy then because the war had been won. The cry throughout the country was "bring the boys home"—and we did. Little did we realize the strategic threat that Stalin's Russia would assume in just a few short months and war in Korea in five short years.

Today, as in 1945, the call has gone out again to cut the defense budget. Once again, however, the future is unclear. Yet defense leaders have to make decisions today to design military forces that will defend the worldwide interests of the United States in the post cold war era. Unfortunately, many of those decisions are driven by budgetary pressures rather than strategic considerations. At the same time, trying to put together a military strategy is very difficult, if not impossible, when there is no consensus about a new national security strategy.

We in the United States succeeded at the higher level of strategic thinking prior to World War II because our command and staff and war college during the 1920s and 1930s produced officers of exceptional character and strategic vision. As a nation, we emerged victorious from World War II in no small measure because of the moral and intellectual strengths found at the highest levels of the American Officer Corps.

Unfortunately, after the war we became complacent. Strategic thinking atrophied after 1945. In the nuclear age many believed that the ideas and thoughts associated with classical military history and strategy had been rendered obsolete.

Doing what one knows, rather than what should be done, is a problem which many military commanders have faced throughout history. It's a problem not unfamiliar to the American military in the recent past. I would contend that in Vietnam the American military did what it knew—fighting the conventional war which it had fought in World War II and Korea—rather than knowing what to do—fight the revolutionary war in which it became engaged. It took ten years to put together a strategy to win the Vietnam War. By that time it was too late. The patience of the American people had come to an end.

The bitter experience in Vietnam, which resulted from a loss of strategic vision, sent American military men back to the study of war and military history. Many of you here today are the beneficiaries of that renewed interest in the study of the war. I hope you have learned that a military career includes a life-long commitment to self-development. It is a process of education, of study, of reading and of thinking that should continue for the rest of your professional military life.

Yes, tactical proficiency is very important, but so too is strategic vision. It can only come after years of careful reading, study, reflection and experience. You need to be aware of the natural yardstick of 4,000 years of recorded history. Thucydides, Plutarch, Sun Tzu, Clausewitz, Napoleon, Mahan and MacKinder have much to offer tomorrow's generals and admirals. Today's officer corps must be made aware of this inheritance. If you have been made aware of this inheritance over the past ten months, you will have fulfilled the sacred trust your superiors, and indeed your nation, have placed in your hands today.

Winston Churchill put this idea in these words: "Professional attainment, based upon prolonged study at colleges, rank by rank, and age by age, those are the title reeds of commanders of the future armies, and the secret of future victories."

I must confess to you the concern I have about the security of our country as I look to the future. My fear is that in some ways we may return to the difficult days for our military that we went through in the 1930s and more recently after Vietnam. In an address to the Military Schools and Colleges Association in 1923, Major George C. Marshall noted: "The regular cycle in the doing and undoing of measures for the national defense is that we start in the making of adequate provisions and then turn abruptly in the opposite direction and abolish what has just been done."

I do not believe our nation will make the drastic cuts it made in its security in the 1930s, but these next few years for those in the military will be difficult ones nevertheless. Many of my colleagues would not hesitate in cutting the Army numbers to 300,000. Some would be quite happy to do away with the Marine Corps by consolidating it with the Army.

The temptation to become discouraged for those serving in uniform will grow. Please do not give in to it. In moments of doubt, recall the words of Franklin Roosevelt: "The only limit to our realization of tomorrow will be our doubts of today. Let us move forward with strong and active faith." We do not know what tomorrow holds. There is no crystal ball in which to look to foretell the future. Only a kaleidoscope with its uncertain patterns gives us a clue to what lays in store for uniformed Americans. Whether you will march again to the Halls of Montezuma or sail to the shores of Tripoli we do not know. But you should be guided by the words of Robert E. Lee, "Do your duty in all things. You cannot do more. You should never wish to do less."

Reference: (C.R. 6/26/90 Pg. E-2134)

Washington College Commencement, 1983
Excerpts from Speech
in the Congressional Record
by
Walter Cronkite

In your lifetime, certainly in the lifetime of your parents, this world has almost simultaneously plunged into five eras, any one of which alone would qualify as an entire age of man—the Atomic Age, the Computer Age, the Space Age, the Petroleum-Chemical Age, the Telecommunications Age. Together they comprise a technological revolution perhaps greater in its impact than the industrial revolution of the last century. And there is evidence that we are living through it just as blind to its social, economic and political impact as did our grandfathers through the industrial revolution.

The very invention and development of these devices of the technological revolution give proof of man's intellectual capabilities. Can we really believe that he is incapable of applying equal brain power to solving the great problems?

There is going to be social and political and economic evolution, coming with such explosive suddenness as to have the character of revolution. The revolutionary forces already are at work today, and they have man's dreams on their side. It is up to us—to you—to get into the leadership of that revolution.

To do that we've first got to put our own house in order. There is a growing feeling that government doesn't work very well anymore; that it is ill-equipped to handle many of the more critical problems the nation will face in coming years.

Ways must be found for government to cope with the vast technological changes taking place today, anticipate new problems and to safeguard the health and interests of the people.

You will need to look at Congress and its procedures. For, if the government is to be updated, brought up to speed, some way must be found to make the legislative branch more efficient, more responsible and more knowledgeable.

The Presidency also needs careful examination—especially the way we pick our presidents. You should ask yourselves whether the talents and qualities that get a man elected have anything to do with those needed to run the country—whether the current process selects the best man for the job.

The relationship between the branches of government also needs review. You will hardly be able to afford the kind of paralysis that so often seems to afflict government today, just when the need for effective action is most urgent.

You also should re-examine the relationship between government and industry to see if there is not a more efficient and productive way of ordering the nation's economy. However you do it, you are going to have to get the country's economy moving again and competing effectively in the international marketplace.

You are going to have to develop a system for managing this nation's resources, while there still are resources worth managing.

You will have to devise a means of coping with the growing problems of immigration to this country from other nations whose borders are spilling over with excess people. That could provide one of the great policy challenges of your generation.

And you will have to look beyond our borders. Our house cannot be in order unless affairs abroad are as well. The approach of many developing countries to those global problems has been anything but enlightened. Typically, they argue that pollution controls hold back their development; efforts to contain nuclear proliferation are conspiracies to maintain a military status quo; suggestions that poor countries spend more on food and less on expensive military hardware draw similar responses; and population control is seen as a form of racism.

In the strengthened conditions this planet faces, it seems unlikely that freedom can endure easily for very long among an affluent ten percent or less of the world's population. We are going to need converts to the cause of freedom if it is to endure. Freedom must be a growth industry. And converts will not come from nations bulging with people so hungry they cannot think or work efficiently. And they will not come from countries with illiteracy rates of 70 and 80 percent.

It is high time the United States returned to full and active participation in the affairs of the world—a participation consonant with its wealth and power, and the interests it has at stake. We need to re-establish our credentials for leadership among the developing nations—and we can only do that by taking the lead in a serious effort, rationally and fairly, to recognize the global economy. We need the Third World. We need its people as allies, we need its raw materials, and we need its cooperation in tackling those global problems which threaten rich and poor alike.

That does not mean that we should be apologetic about our own success, or timid in our leadership, or suicidal in our generosity. Our first duty, to ourselves and to humanity's future, will be to preserve those beachheads of liberty which we and our friends already hold. To that end, we must strive to make America as self-sufficient and self-reliant as is humanly possible. We must reduce our dependence on foreign oil and other resources, in so far as that is possible.

But we must also make our peace with the fact that full independence no longer is possible in this world, with the fact that we will grow increasingly dependent on other peoples, other places—and they on us.

And that is the idea which I think must order this country's—your—agenda for the 80s and beyond. Our own values and traditions urge upon us a special mission in this world to help and to lead. Our interests demand it.

In the course of the 20th Century, America has grown up, or we hope it has. We have turned in some spectacular performances economically, militarily, in science and technology. We have added enormously to man's store of knowledge. We have begun the exploration of space, which may prove the great agenda for the 21st Century.

We also have learned the lesson, paid the price, particularly in Vietnam, for arrogance and the careless exercise of power, and we have learned, as well, the futility of cringing from its responsibilities. We have sinned and we have come of age. We have learned that we are neither omnipotent nor omniscient. Now we must apply those lessons.

In sum, our task will be to make America work again, to overhaul the system, discarding defective and outmoded parts and restoring those that still serve.

You should not be too quick to throw out the familiar, the traditional—for familiarity and tradition are values in themselves. But neither should you flinch from radical thought, hard questions and fundamental change—if they are necessary to pass on intact the heritage passed to you, the heritage of human freedom.

The historian Carl Bridenbaugh has written of your revolutionary counterparts of 200 years ago. He said, "Their equality and status questioned, the now united gentry became radicals, gentlemen revolutionists. They revolted to preserve what they had."

And that is what you will be doing, if you are faithful to the demands history will make upon you. You will be rebuilding, even redesigning, America to preserve what it always has been and must remain—a nation of free men, an example to all men, in Lincoln's phrase, "the last best hope of earth."

You have survived one of the more formidable intellectual obstacle courses in the world. You have made it all the way through the American educational system without apparent brain damage, and you have even managed to get an education. You are graduates today of an imminent institution which has turned out its share of the nation's moral, intellectual and political leadership.

The challenges ahead of you are immense, but the greater the challenge the sweeter the taste of victory. It is not a time for the fainthearted. Marshall your courage and convictions. Pick up your cudgels and man the barricades—seize with joyous enthusiasm the opportunity to carry on the fight that inspired your revolutionary forefathers on this continent—the dream of a world of liberty and justice for all.

Good luck, Godspeed—for the good of us all.

Reference: (C.R. 6/7/83, Pg. E-2742)

Competition
· · · · · · · · · · · · · · · ·

Europe 1992: We Are Not Ready
Excerpts from Speech
in the Congressional Record
by
Dr. James B. Holderman, President
University of South Carolina

It is a special pleasure to be able to address this distinguished audience, and to share this panel with such expert speakers.

As this forum addresses the science and technology challenges of 1992, I feel a special obligation as a representative of both the National Science Board and higher education generally.

I can think of no challenges greater than the fact that we are not educating people who can handle what 1992, and so many other events, have thrust upon us.

In confronting this fact, I want to stress three things:

First, the broader nature and implications of the extraordinary changes occurring around the world.

Second, how our universities and our entire education system have failed to adapt.

And third, how we can change that for the better. Events of just the last year make the need to change obvious.

One year ago, the reunification of Germany seemed an impossibility. Now, it is inevitable.

One year ago, in good conscience, South Africa and freedom could not be spoken in the same sentence.

Now, freedom in South Africa is on all our lips.

And who would have imagined a year ago, even a month ago, that Violeta Chamorro could be elected president in Nicaragua.

In effect, it is a world that has undergone paradigm shifts in loyalties. In the Soviet Union, loyalty to obsolete political ideals moves in favor of loyalty to progress.

In Eastern Europe, loyalty—albeit imposed—to personality cults is transformed by loyalty to individual freedom.

In Western Europe, loyalty to parochialism and loyalty to unity work together. Such transformations in loyalty underlie the social and political upheavals around the world, when we already face a world offering challenges enough.

A world beset by AIDS, poverty, and family dilemmas such as divorce, abortion and abuse.

A world in which ice storms strike Tokyo. London is besieged by hurricane-force winds, and in which rain forests disappear by the equivalent of almost a football field per second.

It is a world in which some of the gloomiest predictions say global warming could one day leave all but the torch of the Statue of Liberty under water.

Who else but our universities, with their tremendous resources of people and capital, can address these matters?

In the midst of all this comes Project 1992.

Elsewhere, the integration of individual freedom and politics has set the pace. But in Western Europe, it is an economic integration, and it is just as significant and courageous.

Yet, while the world has shifted toward integration, our universities remain trapped in ideas which no longer serve. We have not adapted.

As a result, we are unable to provide the help that Europe, and other nations, require, which leads to my next concern.

The American education system, the main source of talent to resolve today's greatest dilemmas, is crippled:

It is crippled when 50 percent of high school students in urban areas drop out, and when our high school students are lost in math, physics, chemistry and biology compared to other industrial nations.

It is crippled when the public school compensation system protects teachers not for their contributions as educators, but for their ability to survive and for their seniority.

And it is crippled when universities continue to reward the specialist disproportionately, while the world integrates.

Elementary schools are separate from secondary schools, secondary schools are separate from universities, and university departments separate themselves from one another.

Of course, in basic science, our universities still lead the world. American basic science is why in some fields, more foreign students get advanced degrees in the United States than our own students—an incredible irony.

Unfortunately, such specialized success has blinded us to other possibilities. How many times has someone else come along and turned our know-how into their technological advances?

At this conference, integration means primarily economic integration on one continent, mainly with white men in charge. But in another context, the meaning of integration makes America's glib talk of helping the Economic Community ring hollow.

How can we help provide an educated corps of young people from all races when 63 percent of black students drop out of college? How can we help when we have not prepared for an America, where by 2001, only 15 percent of the new labor force will be white males?

How can we help in an America that is producing a generation whose most notable quantity just might be its ignorance?

But what can and must we do, ourselves, now? What can we do when change is not only in the air, it is remaking the earth and the relationship between all its inhabitants?

Commitments to react have been made time and time again in recent years, but with little follow-through. Yet, ours is a rare gathering—a complex mosaic of leaders from two great continents, candidly discussing our mutual concerns.

That one continent, nearly half-a-century ago, helped the other recover from the ravages of a terrible war tells us that we can overcome grave challenges. With that in mind, we can work to insure that domestic crisis don't impede America from again becoming a true scientific and technological compatriot. The domestic chaos does not have to destroy our mutual hope.

First we know inspired young people have overcome such chaos before. Religion, athletics, poetry, finance, industry, even the chance to save this planet, can be such an inspiration again.

We must alert young people that such inspiration is very real, and very important.

Consider the European Community's own example. Jean Monnet, the Frenchman known as the father of the common market, who showed us all the potential of economic integration.

Or consider this academy, which has inspired so many universities to become first-class research institutions.

Or people from Berlin to Capetown, from Nelson Mandela to Vaclav Havel, turning the world on its ear. We must help our young people draw inspiration and courage from such examples. This is the first path to a solution.

Second, we must make education in grades K through 12 exciting again. We must find feeder mechanisms by which the resources of our universities can modernize and recast our educational system.

Third, and finally, and most importantly, our universities must change their role in society, and they must begin to do so immediately. Building from their strength in basic research, universities must develop professionals, and scientists and teachers who can recreate secondary and elementary education. Our universities must integrate across disciplines, across levels of education, across all sectors of our culture.

The new world we have entered requires that kind of integrated training. Our young people, our love for them, and our loyalty—not to yesterday but to our future and to their future—demands that we do all these things beginning now.

Everywhere, the alarms have gone off loud and clear. They are ringing in Europe and the Soviet Union, in Latin America and South Africa.

They are ringing in our skies and in our oceans, in our schools and in our factories, and in our streets and in our homes, and they are ringing louder with each passing day. They are the alarms which tell us to get up and to act.

We must enable our education system to meet the needs of your companies and of your industries. We are not ready.

We must enable the United States to work with the European Community where it is needed. We are not ready.

We must enable our teachers, our researchers and our children to appreciate the integrated world we have entered. We are not ready.

To get ready, to make these things happen, we must change the university's role in society, and we must begin now. Making all this possible is our challenge, and it is our hope, and I look forward to making it a reality with you.

Reference: (C.R.5/8/90 , Pg. S-5849)

Conservation
••••••••••••••••••
Izaak Walton League Speech
on Conservation Issues
Excerpts from Speech
in the Congressional Record
by
Secretary of Interior James Watt

One of the major reasons you belong to the Izaak Walton League is that you like to hunt and fish and enjoy the outdoors in our leisure. Perhaps because it satisfies instincts within us all which hark back to times when our ancestors had to hunt and fish for survival. Perhaps it is just an excuse to get out of the hassle of everyday living and to be close to nature.

You are able to hunt and fish and hike in the outdoors for pleasure, for recreation or re-creation. You can do so because you have adequate incomes to provide you with the time and the means to pursue these enjoyable, healthful and constructive pastimes.

Hunters and fishermen were the original conservationists—environmentalists long before that word became fashionable. Organizations such as the Izaak Walton League were established by people who realized that if we are to continue to use the land, we have to do so in ways that will assure that the land and its wildlife renew themselves. This philosophy was followed almost a century ago by one of your members, J. N. Darling, who launched the Federal Duck Stamp Program. This is one of the ways we have to give nature a helping hand to assure that these resources are cared for properly.

This certainly sums up my philosophy of stewardship—use the land and water resources as though we love them, harming them as little as possible so that the land and water will continue to help us meet our economic needs, help us to enjoy life more fully, help us to survive on Earth.

The natural resources of America are here for us to use for our needs—our economic needs, our recreational needs. Wise use will not diminish these values; but will enhance them. We are not destroyers but builders. We do not wantonly harvest the riches of the land. We do not decide resources questions without regard for our future or for the future of generations yet unborn.

Where this Administration differs from our critics is in our belief in the full equation.

We believe that use is a part of the equation, that you who hunt and fish can contribute to conservation, not undermine it.

We believe in management of natural resources and that hunters and fishermen are part of sound management.

We believe in our right of access to the public lands; your right to responsibly use and enjoy these lands. We trust you, and we believe that you and organizations like yours have been remarkably successful in instilling the environmental ethic in America.

When I became Secretary of Interior 13 months ago, we were not using our natural resources wisely. There was too much air and water pollution, the national parks had been allowed to deteriorate, our wildlife ranges and refuges had been neglected, and our multiple-use lands had not been managed properly for the taxpayers and consumers of this generation and those yet to come. America was on a starvation diet even though our pantry of natural resources was overflowing. We were rapidly losing the economic vitality needed to sustain the environmental ethic which I believe in, which all of us here believe in.

We can be a nation of environmentalists only if our citizens have jobs and incomes to support wise conservation. If you suffer economically to the point where you can no longer hunt, fish, hike—or even travel to the forests and streams—then our burning desire to conserve is going to dim quickly, and understandably so.

So I was determined to make changes at the Department of Interior that would restore balance, so that we could begin making better use of natural resources in order to maintain the economic strength that is fundamental to sound environmental stewardship.

Let me give you a quick summary of some of the changes we have made during these past 13 months.

We launched a program to repair and restore our National Park System which was neglected to a shameful degree.

We have improved programs for the exploration and production of oil and gas, both on land and under the sea, for coal leasing, for oil shale development, for tar sands, and for geothermal resources. In every case, we have been careful to maintain environmental protections.

These improvements are important because the federal government controls some 730 million acres—about one-third of America—and well over one billion acres of outer continental shelf. Estimates are that 85 percent of the crude oil yet to be discovered in America is likely to come from the 540 million acres of public lands open to multiple-use, as will 40 percent of natural gas, 35 percent of the coal, 80 percent of the oil shale, nearly all of the tar sands, and substantial portions of uranium and geothermal energy.

In addition to the 540 million acres of multiple-use public lands, the Interior Department has responsibility for managing 72 million acres dedicated to national parks, 84 million acres set aside as wildlife refuges and ranges (an area twice the size of the six New England states). The Secretary also has responsibility for various aspects of the 80 million acres of the federal lands set aside as wilderness.

Recently, I proposed to Congress a new approach for settling the muddled and overly-emotional debate about our wilderness system. Our proposal is an effort at a compromise between two extreme positions—those who want wilderness closed now and forever and those who want another 20 years of exploration. As a compromise there is the risk that it will please no one, but it should.

We propose a compromise: close wilderness now and specify a date, January 1, 2000, and leave Congress the choice of what to do thereafter. The date, we believe, would make it harder to reopen wilderness between now and the 21st Century.

The compromise we have proposed is similar to the one hammered out and adopted in 1980 in the Alaska Lands Act covering 56 of the 80 million acres in the Wilderness System. We thought it might be fair to apply the basic formula to the 24 million acres in the "lower 48."

This proposal provides an essential safety valve to protect our national security. In the event of urgent national need, the President could issue an order for the entry into a specific few acres of wilderness areas for the production of specifically needed energy or minerals. Congress, of course, could countermand that order and is given time to do so.

This proposal would tone down the rhetoric and give time for emotions to cool so that we can better manage and protect these wilderness areas for the rest of the century. It gives this nation time to clarify how we are to continue stewardship of these important areas in the 21st Century.

A study conducted for the U.S. Fish and Wildlife Service demonstrates that many Americans still do not know much about animals or wildlife conservation issues. Residents of large cities showed little knowledge of wildlife and conservation issues. People in large cities who knew the least about wildlife were the most opposed to hunting.

Unfortunately, there are those who play to the emotions of people who know little about wildlife. This makes it difficult for your organizations and for me to do our work. We have to do a better job of educating our people about wildlife and about conservation in general so that there is an understanding that managed use of resources —whether use be hunting, fishing, grazing, mining or drilling—is an essential part of the equation of stewardship.

As the Secretary of Interior, I must ask every time we are faced with a resource management decision: How will this affect the environment? How will this help create jobs? How will this impact on national security?

In response to these questions, I have brought a year of change to the Department of Interior. These changes are crucial so that we can restore America's greatness, so that we can protect our liberties, so that we can maintain our economy and our environment for ourselves and for untold generations to come.

Reference: (C.R. 3/10/82 Pg. S-1952

Crime
· · · · · · · ·

Double-digit Crime Inflation

Excerpts from Speech
in the Congressional Record
by
Warren E. Burger
Chief Justice of the United States

Today I will focus on a single subject, although one of large content. Crime and the fear of crime have permeated the fabric of American life, damaging the poor and minorities even more than the affluent. A recent poll indicates 46 percent of women and 48 percent of Negroes are "significantly frightened" by pervasive crime in America.

When I speak of "Crime and Punishment," I embrace the entire spectrum, beginning with an individual's first contact with police authority through the stages of arrest, investigation, adjudication and corrective punishment. At every stage, the system cries out for change, at each step in this process a primary goal, for both the individual and society, is protection and security.

Today, thatproud Americans boast that we are the most civilized, most prosperous, most peace-loving people leaves a bitter taste. We have prospered. True we are, and have been, peace-loving in our relations with other nations. Like it or not, today we are approaching the status of an important society whose capability of maintaining elementary security in the streets, in schools, and for the homes of our people is in doubt.

I have pondered long before deciding to concentrate on this sensitive subject and I begin by reminding ourselves that under the enlightened constitution and bill of rights, we have established a system of criminal justice that provides more protection, more safeguards, more guarantees for those accused of crime than any other nation in all history. This protection was instituted, and it has expanded steadily for nearly two centuries, because of our fear of the power of kings and states developed by an elite class to protect the status quo—their status above all else—and it was done at the expense of the great masses of ordinary people.

I ask you to ponder this question: Is a society redeemed if it provides massive safeguards for accused persons, including pretrial freedom for most crimes, defense lawyers at public expense, trials, appeals, re-trials and more appeals—almost without end—and yet fails to provide elementary protection for its decent, law-abiding citizens?

For at least ten years many of our national leaders and those of other countries, have spoken of international terrorism, but our rate of casual day-by-day terrorism in almost any large city far exceeds the casualties of all the reported "international terrorists" in any given year.

What people want is that crime and criminals be brought under control so that we can be safe on the streets and in our homes and for our children to be safe in schools and at play.

We talk of having criminals make restitution or haveing the state compensate the victims of crime. The first is unrealistic, the second is unlikely. Neither meets the central problem. Nothing will bring about swift changes in the terror that stalks our streets and endangers our homes, but I will make a few suggestions. I share the belief that poverty and unemployment are reflected in crime rates—chiefly crimes against property. But if poverty were the principal cause of crime as was the easy explanation given for so many years, crime would have been almost non-existent in affluent Sweden and very high in Spain and Portugal. But the hard facts simply did not and do not support the easy claims that poverty is the controlling factor; it is just one factor. The crime rate today far exceeds our crime rate during the Great Depression.

We must not be misled by cliches and slogans that if we but abolish poverty crime will also disappear. A far greater factor is the deterrent effect of swift and certain consequences: swift arrest, prompt trial, certain penalty, and—at some point—finality of judgment.

To speak of crime in America and not mention the drugs and drug-related crime would be an oversight of large dimension. The destruction of lives by drugs is more frightening than all the homicides we suffer. The victims are not just the young who become addicts. Their families and, in turn, their victims and all of society suffer over a lifetime. I am not wise enough to venture a solution. Until we effectively seal our many thousands of miles of borders—which would require five or ten times the present border guard personnel—and vastly enlarge the internal drug enforcement staffs, there is little else we can do. Our Fourth and Fifth Amendments give the same broad protection to drug pushers as they give to you and me, and judges are oath bound to apply those commands.

Deterrence is the primary core of any response to the reign of terror in American cities. Deterrence means speedy action by society, but that process runs up against the reality that many large cities have either reduced their police forces or failed to keep them in balance with double-digit crime inflation.

A first step to achieve deterrence is to have larger forces of better trained officers.

A second step is to re-examine statutes on pre-trial release at every level. This requires that there be a sufficient number of investigations, prosecutors and defenders—and judges—to bring defendants to trial swiftly.

Let me stop and simply repeat that governments were instituted and exist chiefly to protect people. If government fails in this basic duty they are not excused or redeemed by showing that they have established the most perfect systems to protect the claims of defendants in crime and proceedings. A government that fails to protect both the rights of accused persons and also all other people has failed in its mission.

Many enlightened countries succeed in holding criminal trials within four to eight weeks after arrest. First offenders are generally placed on probation, free to return to a gainful occupation under close supervision. I hardly need remind this audience that our criminal process often goes two, three or even four or more years before the accused runs out of all options. Even after sentence and confinement, the warfare continues with endless streams of petitions for writs, suits against parole boards, wards and judges.

The dismal failure of our system to stem the flood of crime repeaters is reflected in part in the massive number of those who go in and out of prisons. In a nation that has been thought the world leader in so many areas of human activity, our system of justice—not simply the prisons—produces the world's highest rate of "recall" for those who are processed through it. How long can we tolerate this rate of recall and devastation it produces?

What I suggest now is to "survey the wreckage" and begin a damage control program. It will be long, it will be painful, it will be costly, but less costly than the billions of dollars and thousands of blighted lives now hostage to crime. It is as much a part of our national defense as the Pentagon budget.

Should you look at the records you will find that the 300,000 persons now confined in penal institutions are heavily weighted with offenders under age 30. A majority of them cannot meet minimum standards of reading, writing and arithmetic. Plainly, this goes back to our school systems. A sample of this was reflected in a study of pupils in a large city, where one-half of those completing the third grade could not meet minimum standards. This should not surprise us, for today we find some high school graduates who cannot read or write well enough to hold simple jobs.

Here are a few steps which ought to be considered immediately:

A. We must accept the reality that to confine offenders behind walls without trying to change them is an expensive folly with short-term benefits—a "winning of battles while losing the war."

B. Re-examine treatment of first non-violent offenders—intensive supervision and counseling and swift revocation if probation terms are violated.

C. A broad-scale physical rehabilitation of all prisons (perhaps on a federally funded matching grant basis) to provide a decent setting for educational and vocational programs.

D. Make all vocational and educational programs mandatory with credit against the sentence for educational progress—literally a program to "learn the way out of prison," so that no prisoner leaves without at least being able to read, write and do basic arithmetic.

E. Generous family visitation in decent surroundings to maintain family ties, with rigid security to exclude drugs or weapons.

F. Counseling services after release, paralleling the "after-care" services in Sweden, Holland, Denmark. All this should be aimed at developing respect for self, respect for others, accountability for conduct, appreciation of the value of work, of thrift, of family.

G. Encourage religious groups to give counsel on ethical behavior and occupational adjustment

This will be costly in the short run, and the short run will not be brief. This illness our society suffers has been generations in developing, but we should begin at once to divert the next generation from the dismal paths of the past and try to make homes and schools and streets safe for all.

Reference: (C.R. 3/17/81, Pg. E-1115)

Promoting Public Safety in the 90s
Excerpts from Speech
in the Congressional Record
by
Commissioner Catherine M. Abate
New York City Department of Probation

Never before has this nation and this city been challenged on so many fronts. We are waging one war across our waters, the results of which will have a profound effect on the city for years to come. With the same determination, resolve and resources, we must fight our war against crime, drug abuse and violence at home. It is time for us to say, "Mr. President, you speak of freedom and human rights abroad, then let us speak of the same freedom of each and every citizen to live in their homes and walk through their neighborhoods free from fear and violence." 1991 must mark the time when we in government, joined with communities throughout this city, act with clarity, vigor and conviction. Together we must meet the challenge to restore and maintain public safety.

According to the National Institute of Justice, last year there were more than 1 million Americans aged 18 years and over in prison and jail in the United States, and more than 2.5 million on parole and probation. The grand total under the criminal justice system exceeded 4 million. That number is nearly two percent of the nation's adult population.

In New York State alone, the number of prison beds has doubled in the 1980s. Unfortunately, those who were incarcerated soon were replaced by too many others on the street who were willing to follow in their footsteps. Too many released from prison returned to their communities no better prepared to live a law-abiding life. Today more persons are incarcerated in New York State than ever before, yet crime has not diminished, arrests for violent crimes are ever increasing.

We must ask ourselves, how can we meet the challenge of crime's insidious and relentless assault upon the quality of life in our city. We know that not all the solutions are before us. But we have an opportunity to learn from our experience in the 80s to define an action plan for the 90s. One lesson we have learned is that the focus of the criminal justice system—whether that be corrections, the courts or probation—must involve more than punishment and control. We must be in the business of preventing crime and shaping behavior. Prevention, treatment and law enforcement must become the co-equal cornerstones of a justice system that can begin to effectively stem the tide of victimization.

With escalating prison costs, jail-overcrowding and increasing violence, the role that probation plays in the criminal justice system becomes even more critical. On any given day in New York City, over 60,000 people are under our supervision. That is almost three times the number incarcerated at Rikers Island.

Over 50 percent of our probationers come from the city's poorest neighborhoods. The average probationer is a minority male, between the ages of 16 and 25, placed on probation for a drug-related felony offense. He is abusing either drugs and/or alcohol. A high school dropout and unemployed, he is functionally illiterate with few, if any, job skills.

The mission of the Department of Probation is to promote public safety by providing community-oriented criminal justice sanctions and by assisting the offender to remain in his community as a law-abiding and productive citizen.

To that end, we have developed a resource delivery concept to enable the probation officer to provide the appropriate services to more fully meet the needs of our probationers. This model will include medical and mental health care, drug treatment, vocational training, job preparation, direct employment referrals, literacy and life skills development.

We are also establishing a Day Treatment Center for those probationers who, despite our best efforts, are on the road to violating the terms of their probation sentence. The Center will provide probationers with an intensive program of rehabilitative and remedial services for up to 12 hours a day, five days week, for a period of 90 to 120 days. Operating within the Center will be a Board of Education Alternative School, a Department of Employment Tap Center, and a Department of Mental Health psychiatric social work clinic.

To address the severe drug crisis facing the city, we have developed a specialized unit of probation officers to supervise "high risk" cocaine abusers. This case management strategy includes reduced caseloads, more frequent reporting requirements and home visits as well as routine drug testing. As a result of a city/state initiative, the Department will be able, for the first time, to contract for 1,100 drug treatment slots dedicated to probationers.

Responsible government must be responsive to the communities we serve. This shift in philosophy is reflected in the new direction of the Probation Department. If we effectively monitor and supervise offenders, our streets and our neighborhoods will become safer.

Because probationers pose the longest threat to their own communities, our efforts to establish neighborhood offices have been given high priority. Community probation will improve our ability to monitor offenders and link them to appropriate services in their own neighborhoods. Our Field Service Unit, a specially trained unit of armed probation officers, will continue to work with the Police Department to execute warrants against probationers wanted for new crimes or for violating the terms and conditions of their probation sentences, and to intervene in potentially volatile crisis situations.

One way of repaying their debt to society is through community service.

Community service acts as a constructive punishment reminding offenders that their actions have consequences and tying them in a positive way into the very neighborhoods that they victimized.

This effort will allow the Department to expand the community service programs well beyond the current 100,000 hours of service. It will mean cleaner parks, food and other services provided to the homeless, cleared vacant lots, graffiti free subways and rehabilitated apartments for the elderly. Community service teaches the probationer respect for his/her community and enables civic leaders to see offenders as potential assets. It will improve the quality of life in the neighborhoods and provide the offender with a positive work experience.

Communities throughout the city face the consequences of crime on a daily basis. Crime affects each and every household. The impact on its victims is severe and lasting. To address the needs of victims, we have created a Victims Advisory Panel made up of the leading advocates and service providers in this city. The panel is assisting the Department in developing improved victim impact statements. Better impact statements will lead to wider use of restitution to victims. We are automating our restitution program to provide more effective collection and disbursement of these funds. Victim advocates are training our staff to identify child, elder and spouse abuse when making family visits.

I hope I have dispelled the notion that probation coddles criminals and is soft on crime. Probation is punitive. It is punishment and it is tough. To many offenders, "doing time" is far less intrusive than being supervised on probation for up to five years. They know if they fail—do not undergo drug treatment—remain unemployed—do not go back to school or pay back their victims—they will be faced with longer terms of imprisonment.

Probation makes sense. Our leaders speak about investing in our future—in our children. I do not believe children are born to hate. They learn too well—growing up— the ways of violence, denial and apathy. We must do all we can to stop the vicious cycle once a child enters the criminal justice system. We must see that they graduate from school and go on to higher levels of learning and growth.

Probation cannot succeed without your support. Together we must assist probationers to become productive citizens by addressing their needs for an education, a decent job and a stabilized family life. By teaching them to resolve conflicts without violence, to reduce their dependency on alcohol and drugs, to manage family responsibilities and to find resources they need to improve their lives, we hope to restore the probationer to the community.

Adequately staffed, properly equipped and intelligently managed, probation is the most safety-conscious and cost-effective criminal justice sanction we have. Its unique blend of punishment, prevention and treatment will significantly contribute to a safer New York.

Reference: (C.R. 3/20/91, Pg. S -3816)

Chapter 4

Democratic Party
●●●●●●●●●●●●●●●●●●●●●●●●
Democratic National Strategy Council

Excerpts from Speech
in the Congressional Record
by
Governor Mario Cuomo of New York

I have been invited here today to give my views on what the Democratic Party should be saying in preparation for the election of 1984.

There is a syndrome that is particularly prevalent in campaign seasons: the tendency to push everything to absurd extremes; to use empty rhetoric, to deal in parody and hyperbole, on the assumption that voters will not understand or tolerate subtlety even if the truth lends itself to nothing else.

I think 1980 was a good example of that. The American people, tired, confused by inflation and tormented by a mad ayatollah, were desperate for simple answers and vulnerable to simplistic ones.

At the moment of their weakness they were confronted by the extraordinary charisma of a certified American hero—notwithstanding his certification was written on celluloid. He was, and is, a gifted communicator.

He chose to tell the people what a majority of the people wanted to hear, and gave them explanations that were as clear and simple as they were wrong.

He told them that if we had the biggest tax cut in history, rich people would take the money and invest it in Phoenix, and the South Bronx, thereby reigniting the engine of the economy for everybody's benefit. He said this would happen so surely and swiftly that he could also increase our military spending more drastically than at any point in our peacetime history, and still balance the budget in three years.

He even said that by having the government order a morality which ministers, rabbis, nuns and well-intentioned parents had failed to teach, he could rid us of sinners. A weary, confused, perplexed nation was offered a sweet-tasting capsule-sized placebo by an attractive hero, and swallowed it whole. We all know the record.

Instead of rewarding incentive, over 50,000 companies were put out of business.

Instead of giving our people new opportunities, the plan denied millions of them the simplest of human dignities, the chance to earn their own bread.

Instead of balancing the budget, it left us with the largest deficit known to American government.

Instead of fairness it caused a massive redistribution of the nation's wealth— unevenly and unfairly moving it from social necessities to armaments; from the poor and the middle class to the rich; from vulnerable old cities made weak by carrying the burden of the immigrants to affluent portions of the nation.

Group after group joined the disadvantaged; undernourished children; senior citizens worried over their futures; inner city youth suffocated by an evil drug culture that is allowed to flourish by the failure of the federal government to do anything meaningful to stop it; steel workers and auto workers; the people in wheelchairs, in hospitals, in community centers; people who can't speak the language, who are out of work, who need help.

In 50 years we Democrats have not had a clearer challenge to our assertion that our way is closer to the truth.

In 50 years we have not had a better opportunity to justify our existence as a party. It seems to me, that unless there is a real difference in what we believe, a real capacity to improve the conditions of people's lives, putting a Democrat in the White House will be only an exercise in political vanity.

But I believe there are differences, fundamental and crucial ones, if we are not afraid to state them. These fundamentals make up the soul of our party.

They are the same beliefs that have distinguished us since the awful, grim winter of 50 years ago when Franklin D. Roosevelt raised himself up from his wheelchair to lift this nation from its knees.

They are operating principles that produce specific policy judgements that touch peoples lives. What are those principles?

Our opponent said in 1980 that government was the problem, and to the extent that you withdraw government from everyday events, you improve the condition of our society.

We believe that, of course, we should have only the government we need, but we insist on all the government we need.

We believe that survival of the fittest may be a good working description of the process of evolution, but that a government of humans should elevate itself to a higher order, one which tries to fill the gaps left by chance or by a wisdom we don't understand.

We believe that to demand less of our government or of ourselves is to evade our proper responsibility. We believe in government's capacity to promote human dignity, to create an economy that supports rather than undermines families and communities, to nurture a respect for life and teach compassion by showing compassion.

We proclaim, as loudly as we can, the utter insanity of nuclear proliferation and the need for a mutual nuclear freeze—if only to reaffirm the simple truth that peace is better than war because life is better than death.

We believe that unions are a great institution that has provided justice and decency for millions of working people. We fight for privacy for people, for freedom from unnecessary restraint, for free choice.

We have always been strong enough to use words like "conciliation" and "compassion." And smart enough to find ways to make our highest aspirations, and our most beautiful dreams, an everyday reality.

Our insistence on a government that is positive, that seeks to improve the conditions of people's lives and that understands it must be reasonable—all this suggests a whole series of steps that need to be taken.

We are not against increases in defense expenditures, but we do oppose increases based solely on an attempt to make them higher than an opponent's percentage.

It was wrong—and is wrong—to impose so much of the pain on the least able, on the debilitated cities and states of this nation that, like my own, have carried, disproportionately—but proudly and gladly—the burdens of generations of immigrants.

Of course, protectionism that amounts to isolationism is wrong. In the end, we must welcome competition and be able to use it to goad us into increasing our own productivity and finding new uses for our potential strength. But that is not to say that we must allow other countries to close their markets to us by making it impossible to compete. Or that we should abandon the right to motivate them to be fair by an occasional act of response, or even retaliation.

Some of our older industries, like our steel industry, have fallen behind international competitors. But that is no reason to abandon these industries entirely, leaving thousands of middle-aged steel workers and their families without a job and without hope.

We don't believe in nationalizing our industries. But in this world of fierce competition, where other governments have learned how to support economic growth through partnerships of the public and private sectors, through subsidies, through national investments in research and development as well as capital formation, it is right—and wise—for us to do the same.

We urge the adoption of a federal capital budgeting program that will provide us with a coherent plan for balanced investment in the backbone of roads, rails, ports and bridges that supports our national economy.

And because we are Democrats, we need to recognize the importance of human resources as a foundation of our economic future. The most important investment of all is the investment in our people. Education, occupational training, on-the-job experience must all be given special emphasis.

The recognition that at the heart of the matter we are bound inextricably to one another, that the layoff of a steel worker in Buffalo is our problem, the pain and struggle of a handicapped mother in Houston, our struggle; the fight of a retired school teacher in Chicago to live in dignity, our fight.

The acknowledgement that to prosper we must be the family of America, the family of the United States of America. Feeling one another's pain, sharing one another's blessings, equitably, fairly, without respect to geography or race or political affiliation.

I believe that amid all the division and divisiveness that holds us apart, that has been with us so long now, it may seem insurmountable—we can rediscover the purpose and belief that brought this nation into existence, sustained it, made it as good as it was great.

And underlying everything else, I have the unshakable conviction that for all of our present travail—and we know it well—the deficits, the hordes of homeless, unemployed and victimized, the loss of spirit and belief, this country is still good enough to do what must be done, and more.

An entire nation has profited from 50 years of the progressive Democratic principles I've spoken of today. They have helped lift a generation up to the middle class—and higher. Given us the chance to work, to go to college, raise a family, own a house.

A whole nation—Democrats and Republicans alike—is better off today because of government's refusal to believe that only the rich, the already strong, the well born, the fittest should survive.

Yes, Democrats and Republicans, but only the Democrats appear to remember.

It would be a desecration of history and a sin against our party's soul—if we too should forget what we were, what we are and what we are supposed to believe.
Reference: (C.R. 5/16/83, Pg. S 6709)

A Democratic Foreign Policy Agenda
Excerpts from Speech
in the Congressional Record
by
Honorable Claiborne Pell
United States Senate

It gives me great pleasure to appear before you again to discuss American foreign policy. Will Rogers once said, "I belong to no organized political party—I am a Democrat," and no one could fail to find some truth in that characterization. But I am pleased to report that Senate Democrats have approached the 100th Congress with a particular sense of purpose and urgency.

I begin with nuclear arms control, for no issue is as important to the future of mankind as the careful management of United States-Soviet relations and the prevention of a superpower war. Clearly, the superpower relationship has, in the last six years, fallen into disrepair. Most importantly, in the area where substance is everything—namely, the negotiation of nuclear arms limitation—administration proposals have been designed more for public consumption than for paving the way to serious agreement.

The administration's reflexive hostility toward arms control becomes clear if we consider its actions in three respects—toward nuclear testing, toward Star Wars, and toward the SALT II Treaty.

Nuclear testing is one of the engines of the arms race, and I remain committed to the effort to switch it off. In this regard, the Foreign Relations Committee is currently engaged in the process of completing unfinished business—the ratification of two nuclear testing treaties signed in the 1970s during the Administrations of Presidents Nixon and Ford. These agreements, the Threshold Test Ban and the Peaceful Nuclear Explosions treaties, place important limitations on nuclear testing. And if we can achieve their formal ratification, they can provide a basis for moving ahead to impose steadily decreasing limits on testing until it is extinguished altogether.

Turning to Star Wars, we find in the President's so-called Strategic Defense Initiative still another sign of the Administration's inability to grasp the fundamental reality of the nuclear age—that weapons alone cannot safeguard our national security. Real security—long-lasting security, stable security—requires that we enter into cooperative arrangements with the Soviet Union that restrain the military competition. Among these agreements, none is more important than the Anti-ballistic Missile Treaty of 1972, which emerged from a clear understanding that technological gadgetry could not guarantee either Soviet or American security in an age when the superpower arsenals hold the destructive power of more than one million—I repeat, one million—Hiroshimas.

Given the Administration's actions on nuclear testing and Star Wars, perhaps we should not be surprised at the decision taken last November to violate, unilaterally, the SALT II ceiling—negotiated by the Ford and Carter Administrations—on nuclear missiles and bombers. The Administration's move has liberated the Soviets from the most important constraints of the SALT Treaty; and, ironically, the Soviets are better poised to take advantage of this removal of limits than we are. I believe strongly that the United States should immediately take the necessary steps to return to compliance with the treaty lest the entire offensive arms control regime unravels.

The Administration's approach to nuclear testing, STAR Wars, and SALT II reflects, I believe, the fundamental shortcomings of its policies—an unwillingness to accept that in the nuclear age our survival depends on the actions of our adversaries.

The weakness of the Administration's approach lies in its belief that cooperation is itself a form of weakness. Under the guise of "realism," it has pursued a policy of unilateralism; and this policy has short-changed American security. A policy truly rooted in realism would recognize that arms control agreements complement our defense and strengthen our security.

Let me turn to Central America, where American policy has been a source of sharp division between Democrats and the present Administration.

In some cases, this tension has yielded positive results. Specifically, the Congressional emphasis on human rights has obliged the Administration to focus on the domestic policies of the regimes we support. Four countries of Central America—Guatemala, Honduras, El Salvador and Costa Rica—now have democratically elected governments operating with varying degrees of autonomy from their military establishments. In each case, our economic assistance has begun to address the root causes of regional instability—namely poverty, ignorance and oppression.

For Congress, the real policy background on Central America will center on the issue of continued assistance to the Nicaraguan Contras. President Reagan has sought to make the Nicaraguan issue a moral one. He has described the Contras as "freedom fighters" and likened their leadership to our own revolutionary heros—George Washington, Thomas Jefferson and Benjamin Franklin.

Democrats, too, should see Nicaragua as a moral issue. But in my view, the Contras are "our terrorists," and they include,—in all too many cases—thugs, drug runners, and murderers. Terrorists urge war on innocent people, they carry out acts of violence in order to change the policy of a government, and for that reason the President has declared war on terrorism. But how should we describe the conduct of the Contras when they attack unarmed villagers or plant mines to blow up buses, often killing innocent women and children.

During the last two years, the Congress sought to distance the United States from such activities by cutting off military assistance to the Contras. But the White House sidestepped this law by promoting—and then orchestrating—private efforts of Contra support.

Efforts to end-run the Congress by contracting out American foreign policy cannot be ignored or tolerated. The policies of the United States government must be formed and implemented as the Constitution prescribes; and we cannot allow policies that lack the approval or support of the American people to be sustained by private entrepreneurs and gun-runners who pretend to speak for this nation.

Such private efforts were rendered less important when the Congress bowed to administration pressure last August and voted to resume official military aid to the Contras. But as we push not to cut off Contra aid once and for all, we must ensure that our efforts are not defeated by hired hands not accountable to the American people.

This brings me to the Iran fiasco, which, I believe, epitomizes the incoherence endemic to this Administration's conduct of our international affairs. Let me cite two glaring inconsistencies.

First with regard to terrorism, the Administration has talked a hard line and even, in raids on Libya, matched words with action. But while the President was talking tough to Qaddafi, his emissaries were secretly arranging the sale of weapons to a regime that took American diplomats hostage and which actively supported Lebanese radicals who murdered 241 American servicemen, assigned to peacekeeping duties, while they slept in their quarters in Beirut.

Second, in the Iran-Iraq war, the Administration has talked neutrality while in fact tilting—and with some good reason—toward Iraq. This policy makes clear sense if you believe, as I do, that Iran's conquest of Iraq would be a disaster for United States security interests in the vital Persian Gulf region. Yet, meanwhile, the President's men were secretly providing the wherewithal to Khomeini's Iran to do the one thing that would most harm our interests—that is, to win the war.

As we move now to set American foreign policy on a more even keel, I believe that we should be guided—in our approach to arms control, central America, and the Middle East—by this maxim: that the most effective foreign policy is one which not only serves American interests but which also reflects American values, and which the American people understand and support.

Such a policy should, I believe, contain the following elements:

First, a respect for the norms of international law. The law of nations, as it has evolved, owes much to the moral leadership of the United States. We can hardly demand that other nations adhere to those standards if we ourselves do not.

Second, a consistent human rights policy. American freedom is what distinguishes us as a society from much of the world and constitutes the principal reason the United States is so widely admired. To be effective, however, the United States must have a single standard for oppressive regimes on the left and on the right.

Third, we must restore the American commitment to the purpose and goals of the United Nations. Today, the United Nations remains an underutilized resource of vast potential. In a dangerous, contentious, and uncertain world, American interests—moral, political, economic—can be bolstered by a stronger set of international institutions and norms.

Fourth, if the United States is to speak with a single voice around the world, there must be a clear understanding that the State Department has primary responsibility for the execution of American foreign policy. The recent Iran-Contra affair has demonstrated the danger of an ad hoc foreign policy, and a strong State Department is essential if we are to avoid such fiascos in the future.

Fifth, the United States should spearhead new forms of international cooperation. Hunger, disease, and pollution know no boundaries. The international community shares the same oceans and the same ozone. Rather than spurning international opinions, the United States should be seeking to pull the international community together to tackle the mutual problems of our global environment and our global welfare.

As Chernobyl vividly demonstrated, nuclear radiation is not simply one country's "domestic" problem.

Ralph Waldo Emerson once said that "nothing can bring you peace but the triumph of principles." If the new Democratic Congress adheres to the principles to which I have referred—I believe we can build a coherent foreign policy that will be a tribute to American values and ideals, that will serve our interests, and that will earn the respect of an admiring world.

Reference: (C.R. 1/19/87, Pg. S-2318)

Disabled
· · · · · · · · · · · ·

Jobs, Jobs and More Jobs—for the Disabled

Excerpts from Speech
in the Congressional Record
by
Hon. Robert Dole

It's an interesting coincidence that tonight's seminar, which focuses on employing disabled Americans, should take place during the week of Labor Day—two days after President Reagan outlined the economic policies of his Administration as "Jobs, Jobs and More Jobs."

Well, we all agree with that, and we look to the President and the Congress to make certain that the millions of new jobs we believe his economic program will create in the next few years will go to people regardless of whether they walk to work or ride in a wheelchair—whether or not they can hear the sounds of an office around them— whether they stand tall in physical posture or personal spirit.

This is the year of the disabled person. It is not the year of the handicapped. The distinction is important. For a disabled person is handicapped only as long as he or she is prevented from achieving a goal, earning a living, realizing a dream. Throughout my life, I have known persons who might have been physically disabled, but who attained great things of the mind or the spirit. I have known in my own life the call to self-discovery that comes with a physical disability—and I learned many years ago that sympathy is no substitute for a chance to develop one's skills.

There are 35 million other Americans who have learned or will learn that same lesson. They represent a vast and largely untapped human resource. They ask nothing but a chance to share their talents. And they demonstrate every day of their lives the meaning of what Tennyson meant when he wrote, "To strive, to seek, to find, and not to yield."

The last decade has seen a lot of striving, seeking and finding. The only yielding done was by the barriers—architectural, economic or psychological—that have traditionally blocked the way to personal independence and employment of the disabled. Physical mobility was increased. Now the same thing must happen with economic mobility.

I hardly need remind anyone in this room that we live in a time of fiscal austerity. The federal budget is under siege to some hard economic realities. The federal government itself is trying to restore the historic concept of federalism before that foundation of American self-rule is smothered beneath Washington's deficits, Washington's rules, Washington's regulations and Washington's smug conviction that it knows best.

The demands on our dollars have never been greater. But that does not mean any diminution in the needs of the disabled. What is just a time of heavy spending remains just in a time of belt-tightening. Fortunately, I can report that programs for the disabled had, by and large, escaped the budgetary ax. I think the Administration is sensitive to the needs of disabled Americans. I see no desire—and no possibility—for a retreat of the commitment of recent years.

But I do see a greater reliance upon the private sector as a partner in meeting the economic needs of the disabled. To be blunt, business will be invited to pick up some of the slack that government alone can no longer handle.

And I've seen encouraging evidence that the private sector is anxious to meet that responsibility. Not long ago I had the chance to speak with a Menninger Foundation Council sponsoring the Projects With Industry (PWI) program. PWI is the best evidence I know to support the theory that a small investment in the disabled can lead to a substantial payoff, both financial and social. Ninety PWI programs across the country put 5,500 people to work. Taxes on their $50 million wages alone will more than double the entire public expenditure on the program. PWI works because it stresses the capabilities—not the disabilities—of the individuals it employs. It works because it advocates competition as well as compassion. It instills independence, it disclaims impairments. It gives people a reason to hope, as well as a paycheck.

In the course of its work, PWI has educated a lot of businessmen as well. Employers have discovered that it takes less accommodation than they thought to hire handicapped workers. They have removed architectural barriers. They have launched PWI training programs. They have hired and they have promoted qualified disabled job applicants.

This is a country whose people have always believed in work. Give a man a job, and you give him a stake in society. You give him a reason to share in the great central dream of this republic, which was founded, after all, as a vast, on-going experiment in social mobility. Give a man a job and you give him reason to hope for better days ahead— for himself, for his family, for generations yet unborn. Give a man a job and it doesn't make any difference the color of his skin, the place of his birth, the nature of his faith.

PWI extends that belief and that tradition to the largest minority group of all—the disabled. By itself, it is only a beginning. But it can and ought to serve as an example to both government and business of what can be done when determined individuals set about to find innovative ways of employing disabled workers. Tax incentives to employers can help further such programs. We have managed to amend the Social Security Act to provide fresh incentives for the disabled to return to work. And we continue the fight for adequate funding for a whole range of educational, rehabilitation and employment efforts.

Budgets in Washington may face trimming. But our commitment to economic justice for the disabled can never be cut back. This nation has no intention of muffling the disabled in a cloak of fiscal austerity. Rather, I think we are already searching for better ways to tap their human resources. In that search, private businesses and concerned individuals must be willing to assume partnership status with government at all levels. Economic common sense suggests it. Conscience demands it.

We have broken down some barriers. Now we must raise up the disabled to their rightful place in society. We must measure our progress in economic as well as medical terms—and hasten the day when "Jobs, Jobs and More Jobs" applies to every American regardless of physical or emotional handicaps.

We've come a long way already. We have a long way to go. But it's good to know that the road ahead will be traveled in the company of people like yourselves.

Reference: (C.R. 9/10/81, Pg. S -9427)

Discrimination
· · · · · · · · · · · · · · · · · · · ·

The Elimination of All Forms
of Racial Discrimination

Excerpts from Speech
in the Congressional Record
by
Ambassador Patricia M. Byrne
U.S. Representative to the United Nations

The United States is a multiracial nation built by people of every country, race and religion in the world. The principal reason tens of millions of persons have come to this country is the old one of the search for freedom: political, religious and economic freedom. We pride ourselves on having built a country based on an ideal: that a person not be judged by his religion, politics, ethnic origin or race; that everyone has rights that must be protected so that he can participate in the nation's social, economic and political life.

Living up to this ideal is not easy; on many occasions we have failed to do so. Unlike some political systems, we do not claim perfection; we hide nothing; we admit our failings. You can hear and see us debating solicitations to our problems in our publications, television programs, election campaigns and legislatures. One problem with which we have grappled has been that of racism. We have made great progress; our struggle against racial intolerance has been characterized by some of the worst and some of the most inspiring chapters in our history. That struggle is not over; it is one which will be won.

Our history, our ideals, the nature of our people leave us no option but to oppose ideologies and systems based upon the rule of a self-appointed elite claiming a "revealed truth" justifying oppression. In case anyone would doubt it, let me state that the United States firmly believes that apartheid cannot be justified. Apartheid must end. The international community has the responsibility to work for the eliminating of apartheid. All ideas, attitudes and economic and political systems that condone slavery, segregation, discrimination or any other form of subjugation of the individual denigrate victim and perpetrator. Apartheid denigrates all the people of South Africa.

As we have stated on previous occasions, our opposition to that inhumane system which has brought so much death and misery pushes us to seek ways to dismantle apartheid without increasing the suffering of the people of South Africa. We must consider carefully the consequences of our actions less they increase the suffering of the people in whose behalf we act. Calls for violence will bring violence. They serve only to undermine the determined struggle by the majority in South Africa, who—let us not forget—even more skillfully use their economic clout in the cause of a better life.

Despite a hardening of South Africa attitudes since our imposition of sanctions, the United States will not disengage from efforts to promote peaceful change in South Africa. The realities there are grim—increased repression, censorship, violence and fear.

But there are also elements of hope. Our policies seek to build on those elements of hope. We aim to provide assistance to the victims of apartheid and to prepare them for increased economic and political responsibilities in the future. Our assistance has focused on increasing educational opportunities for the black majority, training in leadership skills and strengthening community organizations, labor unions, legal resources centers and black-owned enterprises.

These efforts will continue. We support practical steps to bring a peaceful end to apartheid. Secretary of State Schultz spoke before the Business Council on International Understanding and discussed our hope for South Africa's future. We would like to see in South Africa:

• A new constitutional order establishing equal political, economic and social rights for all South Africans without regard to race, language, national origin or religion;

• A democratic electoral system with multiparty participation and universal franchise for all adult South Africans;

• Effective constitutional guarantees of basic human rights for all South Africans as provided for in the Universal Declaration of Human Rights and the canons of democracies everywhere;

• The rule of law, safeguarded by an independent judiciary with the power to enforce the rights to be guaranteed by the constitution to all South Africans;

• A constitutional allocation of powers between the national government and its constituent regional and local jurisdictions in keeping with South Africa's traditions; and

• An economic system that guarantees economic freedom for every South African; allocates government, social and economic services fairly; and enables at South Africans to realize the fruits of their labor, acquire and own property, and attain a decent standard of living for themselves and their families.

In the words of Secretary Schultz, "These are ideas that we believe would help South Africans chart their own path to a democratic and prosperous future. We Americans do not claim a monopoly on democratic concepts for another country, but we have every reason to make clear our hopes and visions. I challenge South Africa to rise to the test of building a future which takes these ideas into account."

Another important factor Secretary Schulz discussed was the powerful force of religion in South Africa. The Secretary noted that South Africans are a devoutly religious people. Churches, some of them integrated, represent "institutional channels for dialogue and reconciliation across racial barriers." The Dutch Reform Church, the largest Africkaner Church, claimed, until last year, that apartheid was not only allowed but actually required by the teachings of the Bible. Last year, after months of internal debate, the Church announced that its previous teachings were wrong: apartheid is not justified by the Bible and is not in accordance with Christian principles. According to Secretary Schulz, "This simple but powerful truth hit like a thunderbolt among

Afrikaners. Suddenly the spurious moral basis for apartheid had been stripped away, revealing it for the unjust and unsanctified system that it is."

In conclusion, we think that the only effective manner to fight apartheid in South Africa is through peaceful change. Violence brings only suffering, and violence will mean only defeat for the democratic foes of apartheid, it will leave only a devastated landscape and economy incapable of giving life to the dreams so many of us have for South Africa. My country stands ready to assist, as it has done for over 200 years, all those who seek to promote democracy and justice.

Reference: (C.R. 1/14/87, Pg. H-8675)

Drunk Driving

Alcohol Enforcement and Education Project

Excerpts from Speech
in the Congressional Record
by
Bruce B. Madsen, Managing Director
Traffic Improvement Association of Oakland County

I would like to begin my presentation of the Oakland County Alcohol Project by quoting a few paragraphs from an *Oakland Press* editorial.

"Our world is filled to overflowing with 'programs' that do not work. Some are public, some private, some a little of both, but they share one distinguishing characteristic. Their grand aims are seldom achieved. So brace yourself. We have a program here in Oakland County that seems to be working. No doubt about it."

The editorial then goes on to describe our current drunk driving project; the fact that it is a four-year, $1.2 million project administered jointly by the Traffic Improvement Association (TIA) of Oakland County and the Oakland County Sheriff's Department. I am pleased to report that the project is an outstanding success—exceeding our most optimistic expectations.

The following is a summary of the basic findings of two years of operation.

DUIL (Driving Under Influence of Liquor) arrests on a countywide basis were increased by 30 percent.

DUIL arrests within the Oakland County's Sheriff's Department increased by 130 percent.

The special alcohol enforcement (AE) team—which includes six to seven officers who work four nights a week—issued over 1,700 DUIL citations.

There were over 11,000 DUIL arrests made throughout the county during this two-year period.

Alcohol related traffic accidents were reduced by 21 percent. This meant that there were 2,500 fewer accidents as compared to the preceding base years, about half of which would have been in the fatal or seriously injured categories.

During the two years immediately preceding our program, alcohol was a factor in 55 percent of fatal accidents. That has been reduced to approximately 48 percent.

Approximately $550,000 was spent on this project during the two-year period. During this period, there was an estimated $14 million reduction in the costs of alcohol-related accidents.

Before summarizing the activities of the Oakland County project, let me pass along some demographics so that you might better understand the environment within which this project operates.

Oakland County borders the city of Detroit to the north. It is nearly as large as Rhode Island—approximately 900 square miles.

Our population is approximately one million, making it larger in this respect than 13 of our states.

We have 63 local units of government.

We have 15 courts with traffic authority.

We have 42 police departments.

The annual average number of traffic fatalities for the past three years stands at 155. Personal injuries average about 18,000 per year. It's a big county with big problems. Certainly one of the largest in human and economic losses caused by the drunk driver. In the five years preceding our project, alcohol-related accidents took 450 lives, injured over 20,000 people and cost about $168 million.

To combat this problem, we launched our program with great media fanfare. The project incorporates two major thrusts. Emphasis is placed on selective enforcement and on public information and education (PI& E). Here's how the enforcement operations work:

Through our sophisticated traffic data system, we identified the days of the week and times of the day when the greatest number of alcohol-related accidents occur. We also pinpointed the locations where these accidents were occurring with the greatest frequency.

We established 10 specific locations, each about 15 miles in length, which became the target areas for special AE teams. They work Wednesday nights through Saturday nights from 11 p.m. to 4 a.m. Although these hours represent only 12 percent of the total time in a week, 65 to 70 percent of all alcohol-related accidents occurred during these hours.

The AE teams are comprised of six sheriff's deputies, two Michigan State Police officers and two to three officers from the local communities within which they operate.

Each of the officers who works on the AE teams attended a one-week course in drunk-driving detection, apprehension, arrest and adjudication conducted at Michigan State University. At this moment, we are providing this training to an additional 100 officers in three locations within the county.

As we all recognize, one cannot expect improvement in enforcement if only one link in the total enforcement chain is strengthened. Considering this, our total project has included a series of seminars, demonstrations and conferences specifically directed to the needs of prosecutors and judges. Reports indicate that our judges are taking a tougher stand on this offense.

Now to the second part of our total project. We have included an intensive public information and education program which has addressed two major objectives: (1) to create a greater public awareness of the magnitude and cost of the drinking driver problem, and (2) to develop a perception of a high probability of arrest for this offense in Oakland County. This perception of high risk is the single greatest deterrent to the drinking driver offense—more so than even severe penalties.

Our total PI&E activities include a special saturation mass media campaign conducted during the months of November, December and January. This campaign has received an exceptional level of support by local media and has included news releases, feature stories, drinking driver profiles, editorials, full-page display ads, billboards and television and radio spots—all provided as a public service. The campaign theme is: "Drunk drivers, the party's over."

During the remaining nine months of the year, special attention is directed to speakers' bureau activities, special training for high school driver educators in alcohol and the drinking driver problems, involvement of professional and service organizations and feature articles for magazines, newsletters and trade journals.

As the statistics which I have reported indicate, the Oakland County Alcohol Enforcement project is working very well and, quite surprisingly, we are seeing continuing improvement in all areas of the total project—from enforcement to the reduction in traffic losses. There are now many believers who agree that his program is the most important public undertaking in Oakland County.

In the several drunk driving conferences in which I've participated or attended, a significant portion of the deliberation has focused on problems, needs and counter-measures at the state level or on a statewide basis. In shaping policy recommendations, I would strongly urge that major focus and emphasis be placed upon ways and means of meeting this problem at the local level.

I believe this to be particularly so with respect to drunk driving countermeasures for certainly enforcement, prosecution and adjudication is notably autonomous and local in nature. In this sense dealing with the drunk driving problem is conspicuously different than many other functional areas of traffic safety—such as establishing traffic engineering design standards which must be initiated at the federal and state levels.

Certainly local authorities need good state legislation as a basis for operations. In that respect, we know that our Oakland County project will benefit substantially from the recently enacted Michigan law providing for the use of preliminary breath testers.

But these valuable additions to our legal framework will have precious little impact on the drunk driving problem in areas where no management systems exist for upgrading the level of official performance or creating the necessary climate of public awareness, concern and support.

And, in particular, I would urge that emphasis also be placed on means for providing the financial support to local programs. While local revenues raised through drunk driving fines may be used for enforcement, certainly consideration should be given to providing funding for soundly based programs such as we have had the pleasure of introducing in Oakland County.

Reference: (C.R. 6/21/83, Pg. E-3071)

Drugs
• • • • • • •

The Campaign Against Drugs:
The International Dimension

Excerpts from Speech
in the Congressional Record
by
Honorable George P. Shultz
U.S. Secretary of State

I speak today about a problem that directly or indirectly affects the well-being of all Americans. That problem is narcotics. And I would like to discuss, in particular, the large international dimension of the problem and what we are doing to confront it.

All of you know what narcotics are doing to our cities and our society. In Miami, in New York, in Chicago, Detroit, Los Angeles, in Washington—indeed in almost every American city—we see the drug problem in our streets and learn about it daily in our media. We see it preying on our nation's youth. We see it eroding families and communities. We see the crime it brings—the murders, the robberies, and the organized crime rings that have made it such a lucrative business. We see it destroying lives indiscriminately—rich and poor, black and white, young and old. We can measure the cost of drug abuse in many ways—in lost productivity, in escalating health and social costs, and, most profoundly, in the senseless waste of life.

We see the drug problem in its enormity and sometimes we wonder how it can possibly be addressed. I will not stand before you and say that there are simple solutions. Drug abuse is one of the lingering symptoms of a deeper social and cultural phenomenon: the weakening of the traditional values of family and community and religious faith that we have suffered for some time in Western society.

Our founding fathers created a system of government that could protect the rights and freedoms of the individual. But they deeply believed that something more was needed to protect the spiritual health of the nation. And the founders also believed that upholding the public and private morality was not primarily the role of government, but of our educational, religious and social institutions, our families and communities.

So when we look at the nation's drug problems, we must bear in mind that government does not have all the answers. In our own public life we must restore the faith in family, church, and community that has kept democracies strong for over two centuries.

I believe such a restoration is occurring. Today, there is a spreading consensus across America that drug abuse is not fashionable, it is immoral. We have rejected the fatalistic view that drug abuse as a national phenomenon is here to stay. Parents, communities, organizations, education and religious institutions are heeding the President's call "to join the battle against drug abuse."

Government, of course, must do its part, with energy and determination. The Administration has set forth a comprehensive Federal Strategy for the Prevention of Drug Abuse and Drug Trafficking. This federal strategy has five central components that attack the problem at every link of the chain that extends from the grower to the user of narcotics. We have devised extensive programs for:

First, prevention, which includes educating our youth about the dangers of drugs.

Second, detoxification and treatment for drug abusers.

Third, research aimed at understanding the causes and consequences of drug abuse.

Fourth, drug law enforcement to destroy drug networks and interdict drug supplies before they reach consumers.

Fifth, international cooperation to control the production and shipment of narcotics.

This five-point strategy adds up to an aggressive approach to this drug problem and we are pursuing each path with great vigor.

It is clear, however, that we cannot meet the challenge of abuse here at home without also attacking the worldwide network of narcotics production and trafficking.

Each year drug traffickers smuggle into this country as much as 70 metric tons of cocaine, and as much as 15,000 metric tons of marijuana. These drugs come from all over the world: from Columbia, Peru, Bolivia, Mexico, Belize, Jamaica, Pakistan, Afghanistan, Iran, Thailand and Burma. Once the crops are produced in these countries they are often shipped elsewhere for processing, and then in their refined narcotic form are shipped again to local suppliers in Western Europe, the United States and throughout the industrialized world.

Our concern about this growing narcotics network is twofold. We've already noted the severe impact on our own people. But it also represents a threat to American interests of a different sort. The fact is, it is an example of a larger and relatively new kind of foreign policy problem that confronts the civilized world today. It is part of a trend toward international lawlessness that has been increasing ominously over the past two decades.

The civilized world faces, therefore, not just separate and isolated incidents of violence and banditry, but a systemic, global problem of growing proportion. And this growing problem poses a unique—and deliberate—challenge to the world order that Americans and all civilized people seek: a world order based on justice and the rule of law.

To meet the challenge of international narcotics trafficking requires, above all, international cooperation between those nations that share our concern about the growing threat to our society.

American officials at the highest levels, have continually emphasized to foreign leaders the importance we attach to their cooperation on the drug issue. We have placed our greatest emphasis on reaching bilateral agreements on crop control, eradication, and interdiction with nations where narcotics are produced, shipped and consumed. We have also worked hard in the United Nations to support international efforts to stem the flow of drugs and reduce production.

Many nations have taken significant steps. In Columbia, an aerial herbicide eradication program has destroyed more than 4,200 acres of marijuana. This initial effort alone could keep nearly $3 billion worth of marijuana off our streets. In Peru, despite the threat of terrorism, authorities have eradicated nearly 5,000 acres of coca bushes, used to produce cocaine. We are working with other South American governments to prevent the spread of drug production into new source areas.

In Asia, the government of Pakistan continues to extend its ban on cultivation of opium poppy into additional areas of the Northwest Frontier Province, and it has reported sharply increased seizures of heroin. The Thai government has increased its commitment to controlling opium cultivation in villages that receive development assistance. The Burmese government is exploring with us more systematic methods of eradication.

We know the difficulties involved in reducing crop production. In many producer countries, narcotics production is or has become an important fact of everyday life. There are parts of the world where opium and coca are used as part of centuries old traditions, and, of course, many nations have growing addiction problems of their own, which encourage narcotics production.

Our international narcotics policies are aimed at overcoming these obstacles. We have encouraged multilateral assistance through the United Nations Fund for Drug Abuse Control and other international organizations. The Department of State has worked with the U.S. Drug Enforcement Administration, the Customs Service and the Coast Guard to provide training to foreign governments in narcotics control, enforcement and interdiction.

But the toughest challenge we faced until recently was simply convincing other nations that narcotics trafficking is an international problem that requires international efforts. For a long time, foreign governments considered narcotics an exclusively American problem. Today, that is changing.

Other nations have come painfully to realize that narcotics is their problem, too, and that only through international cooperation can the world community hope to combat the international narcotic network.

For years, the world had good reason to suspect that narcotic smugglers were being aided by some governments; that they were getting money and protection, that they were being provided safe havens and support in shipping drugs to the United States and elsewhere. One of the most prominent suspects was Communist Cuba.

Over the years, the case against Cuba mounted until, finally, in 1982, four high-level Cuban officials were indicted by a Miami grand jury for helping a major Columbian narcotics trafficker. That case provided startling evidence of Cuban complicity in Latin American narcotics trafficking. Furthermore, the complicity of the Communist governments in the drug trade is cause for great concern among the nations of the free world.

The hurdles we face in confronting this problem are many, but we have made significant strides in recent years. Our international narcotics policy has rested on four basic principles:

First, countries where narcotics are produced or through which drugs are shipped must accept their responsibilities under international treaties to reduce crops and drug smuggling.

Second, the international community must assist those nations that lack the resources to take the necessary steps.

Third, worldwide emphasis must be on crop control and eradication—we have seen that interdiction alone is not the answer.

And fourth, in producer nations that need our help, our narcotics related economic assistance must be linked to agreement on reducing crop levels.

Our goals must be to control narcotics production in all geographic areas simultaneously. We cannot focus on only a few areas at a time. When we helped reduce heroin production in Turkey, for example, increased production in Mexico filled the gap. A truly international effort aimed at all producer nations is essential. And we are moving down that path.

Much has been done, and we are only beginning the fight. Obviously, we still have a long way to go. We know that the international narcotics network is larger, more efficient, and more sophisticated than ever before. The narcotics market is an ever-shifting phenomenon that adapts to each new method we devise to confront it. Drug smugglers have managed to find new ways of smuggling to elude our stepped-up efforts. Finally, we have seen that some Communist nations continue to use the drug trade for their own purposes and, therefore, have an interest in its perpetuation. The international drug problem presents an increasing challenge to our intelligence community to provide good estimates of narcotics production and trace the links between drugs, terrorism and Communist insurgencies.

But we are making progress. We have a policy in place that addresses all aspects of the international problem—the cultivation, production and distribution of drugs, the flow of profits, the impacts upon other countries as well as our own. And we have developed broad-based international support for controlling the narcotics trade.

But these substantial successes can be severely damaged by perceptions overseas about what is happening in the United States. To a greater degree than many people realize, our success in international narcotics control is dependent on the success of our assault on drug abuse at home. It will be hard to convince other nations to put an end to drug cultivation if they believe we are not living up to our responsibility to get a grip on the drug problem here. We cannot preach what we do not practice.

This is why what we do here and throughout our own country is so important to our overall efforts. The officials in every community across this nation must understand that effective foreign policies of narcotics control are clearly linked to an effective domestic program against drug abuse.

We are making significant progress. Success will take time. But we are building a foundation for the future, a future not only of reduced drug abuse in our country, but of a world where there is no room and no tolerance for outlaws.

It is an effort that calls for broad national support from all Americans.

Reference: (C.R. 9/19/84, Pg. E-3930)

Chapter 5

Economics
∙ ∙ ∙ ∙ ∙ ∙ ∙ ∙ ∙ ∙ ∙ ∙ ∙ ∙

Continued Economic Growth

Excerpts from Speech
in the Congressional Record
by
Hon. Robert W. Kasten Jr.
United States Senate

It's good to be among friends—among men and women who understand that a sound, job-creating economy ought to be the number one priority on America's political agenda.

If you believe the so-called "conventional wisdom" in this town, you'd think that jobs don't really matter, that economic growth isn't really important. You'd actually come to believe that the well-being of the American economy, and the integrity of our national spirit, depended on one key factor: the elimination at all costs of the federal budget deficit.

Now, I'm not about to tell you that the budget deficit doesn't matter, or that we can safely ignore it without eventual peril to our productive economy. But what I will tell you is that our budget is on the road to balance as long as we don't decide to raise taxes.

One of the easiest ways we can avoid bringing this budget into balance in the next few years is by choking off our revenues at the source. And the way to do that, of course, is by saying, "Damn the torpedoes, let's raise taxes—and nevermind the consequences."

The basic mistake of the tax increase proponents has been their assumption that tax increases somehow come free of charge. Many of them believe that a taxpayer dollar languishing in someone's pocket has no higher calling than to help reduce Washington's deficit.

But the plain truth is that each extra dollar that is diverted away from the productive economy and toward the public sector comes at a terrible cost—a cost we can measure in lost growth, lost jobs, lost productivity and lost opportunities for many Americans who really need them.

The economy can be compared to a large machine that produces goods and services. How it treats us—and especially the most economically needy among us—

depends entirely on how we treat it. The basic question we should be asking ourselves: What kind of a nation are we?

Do we prize the most creative and innovative people, the investors and the savers, the ones who create our nation's stock of wealth? Or are we afraid of what happens when men and women are free to create and produce to the limits of their potential?

To the extent that we Americans have succeeded in creating a good life for our people, and in establishing a just and happy social order—we have succeeded because we have had a truly free economy, free to produce, free to create, and free to open up ladders of opportunity to ever-expanding circles of citizens.

We really ought to stop concentrating so much on issues like the budget deficit, and start listening to the voices of the real economy—the voice of the entrepreneur trying to start a new business; the voice of the small business woman looking for a decent interest rate; the voice of a young parent trying to save for a child's education; the voice of the factory worker struggling to compete in a high-tech economy.

The chief danger, I think, in being deficit obsessed is that many widely hailed "solutions" to the deficit focus our attention on the demand side of the economy just when we ought to be concentrating on the supply side. Keynesian policy proposals— like high taxes and high interest rates—are hindrances to the real-life voices of the supply-side economy. In tending toward recession, they threaten the very roots of our national well-being.

Comments by federal officials to the effect that interest rates cannot come down until Congress brings down the deficit are equally unhelpful as long as the conventional wisdom refuses to admit that tax revenues are growing. Any plea for deficit reduction is automatically transformed by the financial markets into a tax increase ultimatum.

Congress ought to be paying a lot more attention to the things we can do to promote productivity growth. Enhancing the nation's productivity—the output per man hour— is the major challenge that we face in the 1990s. It's the key to higher living standards, international competitiveness, job opportunities—and even deficit reduction.

The most important way that Congress can boost our nation's productivity is by reducing the tax rate on capital gains. I have introduced a bill in the Senate called the Entrepreneurship and Productivity Growth Act, which offers a new approach to capital gains reform.

First, it reduces the tax rate on capital gains.

Second, it targets the new incentive to equity investment. The capital gains differential would only apply to investment in equities, direct investment in stock and purchases of stock sold by other investors.

Third, the bill indexes capital gains for inflation.

This bill seeks to restore the focus of economic policy back to the supply side. Lower capital gains rates are the spark of business innovation, technological advancement, job creation and GNP growth. What we do to promote the realization of lower capital gains rates is a useful indicator of the kind of society we are. How important is it to us to promote investment in our productive potential, in our economic future?

We can't honestly declare ourselves to be committed to economic growth if we remain unwilling to promote savings and investment in this way. Our chief trading partners realize how helpful it is to keep capital gains taxes low—most of them have a zero percent capital gains rate.

If we bring our effective rate down to 14 percent, we'll be increasing the availability of start-up capital, for the high-risk, growth-oriented small businesses that account for so much of our economy's job creation. We would restore the interest of our financial markets in long-term equity investment, and, correspondingly, take it away from short-term gains—like those available through investment in junk bonds and commodity options.

Our economy has great resources. Cutting the capital gains rate will free those resources up by increasing mobility—and therefore the efficiency of capital. When capital starts to flow from existing companies to new companies and growing businesses, we'll be able to measure the result in job creation and increased productivity.

President Bush won his election on the issue of taxes. He said we should bring down the capital gains rate to 15 percent. The bill I have introduced will prove a good legislative vehicle to accomplish this goal. Congress ought to be in the business of promoting high-risk, growth-oriented investments, not tax shelters and collectibles trading. That's why I've restricted the capital gains differential in my bill to investment in equities—equities that promote productivity and GNP growth.

And this rising GNP growth means higher tax revenues for the federal government. Even the Congressional Budget Office (CBO) admits—and this is a quote—that "lower tax rates on gains could increase savings and capital formation, and channel more resources into venture capital." What CBO failed to recognize, though, is that this increased capital formation, and especially new investment in venture capital, means that the entire tax base will grow even faster—and boost overall revenues.

I want to convince the Bush Administration to make this new approach to capital gains a major priority. Let's remember the optimism and dedication to the future that have marked us for centuries as Americans—and work together to promote this and other new departures for a growing economy.

Reference: C.R. 2/7/89, Pg. S-1210)

Education
America's Educational Future
Excerpts from Speech
in the Congressional Record
by
Wayne E. Hedien, Chairman, CEO
Allstate Insurance Company

A long time ago Sears' legendary chairman, General Robert Wood, said, "Business must account for its stewardship, not only the balance sheet, but also in matters of social responsibility." We've tried to put that principle into practice in a number of ways.

Since 1951, for instance, the Allstate Foundation has been making significant contributions to worthwhile causes across the country.

As a corporation, we've also crusaded for safety on the highways and in the home. We worked to increase the availability of affordable housing in urban neighborhoods.

We've helped promote health and fitness for all age groups in our society.

And above all, we've tried to lend a hand to our neighbors—wherever and however we can.

We even have an organization in Allstate called "Helping Hands," which supports the involvement of Allstate people in a wide variety of charitable projects. I'm proud to say that three out of every four Allstate employees are active in these volunteer programs across the country—from community gardens to Special Olympics to seniors' day celebrations.

So the idea of sharing our talents and resources with others is pretty well ingrained at Allstate. In fact, the commitment to society and community has been formally identified as one of our four basic principles that guide the decision-making process in our company.

For most leading corporations today, business as usual includes a dedication to corporate citizenship of the highest order. In some ways that represents a change from the prevailing attitudes of a century—or even a generation—ago.

But it's definitely a change for the better. And it's based on some very sound reasons. In the first place, community involvement makes good business sense. Better-fed, better-housed, better-educated employees make better workers, and better communities make it easier to hire and retain them.

We've also learned that corporate social responsibility is good for our image. And a good image is absolutely essential in today's media-conscious environment.

What about the issue we are addressing today. Why are corporations especially concerned with the future of American schools? And what can we do to ensure the success of our joint efforts? Let me briefly take a crack at answering those two questions.

As we begin the 90s, business people like me find themselves staring at a double-barreled dilemma.

On the one hand, we're facing a severe labor shortage by the end of the decade. Our population is increasing at a rate slower than in any era since the Great Depression. It's also getting older.

As a result, by the year 2000 the work force will be growing at less than 1 percent per year—while economists expect the GNP to be growing at something like 3 percent annually. But that's only part of the problem, because while we will have fewer workers to draw on, we will also be making more demands on them.

We may think that computers and cable TV already bombard us with too many facts. But as the information age unfolds, tomorrow's workers will have to know more than ever—about all kinds of things.

But in a world where change is the rule, rather than the exception, what we really need are people who know how to use the information at their fingertips. That means we need people who can make connections—explore options. We need innovation and entrepreneurship. So when business looks at the year 2000, we see a world where fewer workers will have to exercise more creativity and initiative than ever before.

Employees and corporations will have to learn how to work harder and, above all, smarter!

Which brings me to my second reason why business has become so involved with education—because corporations and the schools face many of the same issues and have many of the same goals.

By the year 2000, more than 85 percent of all new employees entering the work force will be minorities or women—while one out of every three American students will be members of minority groups.

For both our institutions, the real challenge will be to create environments that are truly "heterogeneous"—where people are neither advantaged nor disadvantaged because of their background—and where different people are encouraged to make the best possible use of their different talents.

We're moving closer and closer to a world marketplace. Europe 1992—the emerging economies of the Eastern Bloc and Pacific Rim—all the signs point to greater economic interdependence in the future.

Meanwhile, we're also moving closer to world culture. Fashions, music—the media—they look and sound familiar, whether you're in Tokyo, Turin or Toledo.

Now, globalization creates opportunities as well as challenges. But when more than half of all adult Americans can't find England or France on a map—and when the average American business school graduate knows about as much math as the average eighth grader in Japan, we're clearly not ready to become full-fledged citizens of the world.

Which brings me to my second topic. What can we do to ensure the success of our emerging business/education partnership?

To paraphrase "Pogo," when it comes to joint efforts by executives and educators—maybe the real enemy is us. Because even though we both have an enormous stake in the success of our schools, we still approach education reform from different directions—and envision solutions largely from our own perspective.

That's something we don't often say out loud. But it's an observation that's reinforced by the results of surveys done over the past year in conjunction with this forum.

The first, you may remember, questioned business leaders around the country.

The second survey was conducted this year by our Allstate Research Center. It was co-sponsored by the American Association of School Administrators.

We asked many of the same questions as in the first study. This time, though, we surveyed members of the education establishment. Comparing responses to the two surveys revealed some interesting differences of opinion and perspectives.

Educators, for instance, were more than twice as likely to place part of the blame on budget cuts, while executives cited inadequately trained teachers, low academic standards and lack of emphasis on basic skills. Both educators and executives believe getting parents more involved, making teachers more accountable and doing a better job of motivating students were key objectives.

Now based on these differing responses, I'm not saying who's right—or whose perspective make more sense. In most cases, the answer probably lies somewhere in the middle.

But one thing is clear. What we have is a real failure to communicate. And it's costing us. Look for example, at the survey's final question. We asked: "Overall, considering what you know about current involvement, how much difference do you think U.S. companies' efforts have made in the quality of education provided by our public education system?"

More than half said they hadn't made a difference at all. But, if business isn't having a major impact on education, it also reflects the fact that executives and educators still often see the world in different ways.

So what can we do about it? It seems to me we have two choices. We can draw a line in the dirt and say, "You stay on your side, and we'll stay on ours." That's been our traditional approach. That plan, however, hasn't really resolved some of the fundamental problems confronting American education.

In other words, we need to rub out the line between us—draw a big circle instead—and invite everyone in.

The best way to do all that is to tackle the issue where it matters most and where we can do the most good—at the local level.

Talk to those involved and you'll find that parents and teachers, executives and administrators, government officials and civic leaders don't have to sit down very long before they find that the other guys have something to offer, too. From there, it's possible to create a common agenda and a shared strategy; and from that vision springs success.

So that's our first recommendation—the revolution begins with one school, one district, one town at a time, and everyone plays a part.

Let me leave you with one final thought. This is our third such forum on education, and it's our biggest turnout yet, which suggests that more and more executives and educators understand the importance of such efforts. We realize we must act together, and soon, because we're not just talking about improving our productivity or raising SAT scores.

We're talking about improving our society and raising our expectations for generations to come.

When Dick Haayen opened the first Allstate forum on education, he talked about "the wealth of nations." He said Adam Smith's concept of people as a country's most valuable asset has been best illustrated by the history of the free enterprise system.

But history is full of little ironies. Today, we find millions of workers in Eastern Europe demonstrating and even dying for that ideal.

While back here at home, America goes on squandering its human resources by allowing our schools and our students to settle for less than the best. As Charles de Gaulle, another European leader of an earlier generation, said: "People get the history they deserve."

Let's agree to do what's necessary today—so that a generation from now, history can say we gave the children of America the education they deserved.

Reference: (C.R. 6/27/90, Pg. E-2172)

Education — The Ultimate Weapon
Excerpts from Speech
in the Congressional Record
by
Stephen Joel Trachtenberg, President
University of Hartford

I was a junior in college, waiting for my history professor to arrive to begin his lecture on October 4, 1957. When he rushed in, uncharacteristically late, he took the podium and asked us, "Well, gentlemen, how does it feel to be the citizens of a second-class power." That was the way I learned that the Soviet Union had just put Sputnik into space.

Without prior notice, the Russians had suddenly made it clear that the United States had neglected its educational and scientific affairs for altogether too long. A nation which, until 1917, had been ruled by a czar and which had to borrow armaments, food and other material from us in order to struggle through World War II had abruptly stepped out in front.

We Americans rallied, joined forces, and threw ourselves into the competition with enthusiasm and a commitment of both spirit and resources. Before long our astronauts were orbiting the moon and then proudly planting the Stars and Stripes on its soil.

It seems extraordinary that some of our fellow Americans have forgotten, or have elected to ignore, the lessons of Sputnik. In an appropriate effort to eliminate excesses found in the national budget, the current Administration has proposed a variety of fiscal initiatives to bring our expenditures into alignment with our income. Reasonable people can only wish that effort well.

I saw a bumper sticker the other day which read: "If you think education is expensive, try ignorance." The truth of that slogan is underscored by the vast infusion of cash that it now takes to maintain the products of ignorance: our welfare systems, our prison systems, and our reformatories. We are squandering our nation's "people potential." I am told it cost more to keep a man in prison for a year that it would cost to pay his tuition and room and board fees for an equal amount of time at Harvard.

In what we boldly hail as the richest nation in the world, we have an embarrassing low verbal and numerical literacy rate. A few years ago, the Department of Education released a study reporting that one out of every five Americans is functionally illiterate, a term used to mean that a person is unable to read advertisements, add up bills, or write grocery lists.

There may be disagreement concerning the causes and solutions to our problems, but to all who believe that education is crucial to the survival and future of American democracy, the signal is "Mayday."

When one looks at the struggling school systems of our large cities, or at our rural schools, or those in the suburbs, one is confronted with disagreeable news about conditions that deny our children excellence, competence and equality in education such as violence and drug abuse, lack of school safety, inadequate academic resources and support services, and overcrowded and unprofessional working conditions.

For the last 15 years, college board scores and other standardized examinations, as well as college admission officers and professors, have been telling us that young Americans read, write and figure less well than do their parents. Public perceptions of a high school education have been so downgraded that the term "high school graduate" is now as meaningful as "sound as a dollar."

At a time when the budget of the Pentagon is being increased and federal aid to education is being reduced, there's a growing belief that defense spending takes away from the education and training of America's young and inhibits the research and development on which future innovations are based. It sets a short-term agenda at the expense of unleashing problems which are contrary to long-term defense needs and which will come home to haunt us in the future.

The next decade will be critical. The most efficient energy source in an advanced, industrialized economy may be the midnight oil. Properly used, it fuels people to whom we look for skills, imagination, ideas, insights and productivity.

As a result of a diminished birth rate, the traditional college-age population will shrink by one-fourth between now and 1990. In Connecticut, we project a 43 percent decline in the number of high school seniors during that time. In the coming ten years, the military may have to recruit one out of every three male high school graduates if it expects to maintain its projected manpower needs.

The armed services will require a larger percentage of the available young people at precisely the same time that colleges and universities will have to deal with the implications of a shrinking population, concurring with escalating institutional operating costs.

Words like "retrenchment" and "no growth" are now on the lips of principals and school superintendents, deans and college presidents as frequently as "learning skills," "achievements" and "curriculum."

Elementary school administrators have had to lay off teachers, close schools, and diminish instructional programs. We now see a similar pattern developing at the high school level. Those of us in higher education look at our colleagues in the precollegiate sector, and we know that in the near future their present situation will become ours.

The National Association of Independent Colleges and Universities reports that more than 120 independent colleges have closed in the United States since 1970, and almost 50 other American post-secondary institutions have been obliged to merge.

University admissions were once a low-key enterprise in which as much time was devoted to telling some students why they were not acceptable as telling others why they were. Today, one finds admission officers being replaced with recruitment officers. Some bring a hard-sell approach to their activities which parallels the stereotype of the door-to-door appliance salesman of a bygone era.

The education community has much to learn from the profit-making sector of our society. However, the commercial model has no place on the not-for-profit college campus, if it means compromising the education of the young people for whom it is responsible.

Education at every level, from kindergarten to post-doctorate, is an investment in our future. A failure to invest in education today will have serious repercussions for the quality of education and, ultimately, for the quality of our life in the future.

Increasingly, political and other leaders share a concern that our schools be accountable, that social promotion be eliminated and minimum competency be established. In state after state we see the introduction of examinations seeking to measure school achievement. This initiative is encouraged by those in business, the professions and government. But accountability without support is a sham. We can only ask our schools to be as good as we are prepared to pay for.

I am a university president at an independent, modestly endowed university. I am obviously concerned with the future of higher education. But as an American, I think that we must first see to it that our primary and secondary schools give us citizens who understand democracy and are capable of defending it with their hearts and their minds, as civilians and as soldiers.

Vocational programs which help to prepare machinists and other skilled artisans, craftsmen and tradesmen may be as vital to the well-being of this land as our university-level programs which help to prepare engineers, physicists, philosophers and poets.

This audience is in the unique position of being able to communicate with credibility across the boundaries of the educational and military compounds. For example, it is one thing for someone in my role to point out that America's engineering schools are struggling with a shortage of faculty and obsolete facilities and equipment. It's another thing for you to speak up about that issue.

I believe that if something is not done in the near future, our engineering shortage will grow fluorescent and have an inimical effect on the defense industry and on national security.

There is much to be learned from farmers, who understand that some portion of a crop must be put aside for seed. The seeds are then used in the following season to generate a new crop. If we eat the seed corn today, there will be no crop tomorrow.

Without education we will not be able to defend ourselves and indeed there may not be much to defend. While joining forces under a single administrative agency may not be the answer, joining forces to achieve a common goal makes eminent good sense.

Education can respond to social needs, but it cannot do so alone. We must encourage a consensus in which it is agreed that education is the ultimate weapon. It will help to protect us from our enemies abroad, and it will help us in the war against poverty, racism, hunger and sickness as well.

One possible idea that may be worth exploring would be the indexing of the federal contribution to America's schools to the defense budget. Precise formulas, ratios, the floors and caps, I would leave to another occasion. But here may be something to be learned from the scriptural lessons about tithing, or from the agricultural example which I mentioned above, by which farmers protect a portion of each crop as seed for the next.

We hear talk of the reindustrialization and the revitalization of America. Their time has come. Our schools are the place to start. They can be fixed. We can fix them with your help.

Reference: (C.R. 5/21/81, Pg. H-2395)

Better Students Build a Better World

Excerpts from Speech
in the Congressional Record
by
Honorable Jennings Randolph
United States Senate

Nearly 60 years ago, the American philosopher Josiah Royce said that we have become more informed, more knowing, and more clever—but we have not become more profound or more reverent.

These words continue applicable to American society. Despite our knowledge, we often seem to lack wisdom. We possess sophistication, but life for many people lacks meaning and purpose.

Today, we feel a sense of purpose. Many students will overcome substantial obstacles to earn a degree. You work and study and will face future obligations. Bringing quality to your lives does not take a vacation. There are three challenges that are essential as you labor and plan for careers with constructive purpose and substance.

People are important. We are in a busy and complex world with increased emphasis on technology. We are prone to place people in restricted categories. We speak of "engineers," "professors," "bus drivers," "liberals," "conservatives," the middle class," and the "silent majority."

We must recognize human values—to probe what other people are thinking and what motivates them. We must know people—individuals who laugh, who cry, who love, who have unique talents and genuine aspirations, who grow old and lonely, and who have fears and doubts.

Possibly, in our technological society, we lose the charitable quality that enables us to be understanding of others—not merely tolerant but truly understanding.

We live in a world where our inventions have brought us closer together physically and have enabled us to communicate instantaneously. Yet, these same advances are driving us further and further from each other. Conveniences make families and individuals self-reliant and people live side by side and share few greetings. Our level of technology is so great, our pace so fast, that we work next to each other and have no common language. I ask: Will our inventions become so overwhelming that we depend more on them than on each other?

Many of you will pursue specialized fields. Do not become so engrossed with the details of your work and so reliant on technology that you forget that an individual is liberated from labor to enhance his or her dignity. Machines do not necessarily improve quality of lives. In pursuing your goals, keep your sensitivity high, direct your energies toward people. If you practice medicine, remember that doctors heal people. If you enter politics, keep in mind that government serves people. If you are an educator, remember that teachers teach people. If you work on a space shuttle, do not forget that shuttles transport people.

In the future you will realize successes and failures—good times and bad. I urge that you continue to believe that people are important. Do not just talk to your neighbors and co-workers. Counsel with them. Be concerned for people.

Maintain firmly your convictions. Act boldly on the ideals you know to be of value. We have convinced ourselves that we can be responsible citizens without taking sides, without expressing convictions on fundamental issues—we fail to vote.

We must understand that education does not inevitably humanize. We know that a truly great college not only extends student knowledge but also deepens convictions and values.

These qualities must be nurtured and cherished. This does not mean that you try to impose standards on others. Nor does it mean that you must be decisive, because we can have differences without being divisive. It does mean that you will be challenged to constantly give attention to your convictions and values—assess them—make them a part of your daily living and association with other people.

The quality of your future over the next 50 years and the history you will make will depend to an unprecedented degree on how well you develop and practice the art of communication—not only how well you learn to communicate with your next door neighbor, but how well you communicate with your neighbors across oceans—so far away and yet almost the same as being in your own backyards.

Nearly everything you will accomplish in this interdependent world will be done through the use of words—written, spoken and broadcast. Through language you will choose, make decisions, and help formulate policy in this country, domestic and foreign. You will communicate in many ways—but language will be the most effective tool. Learn all means of communicating available to you—and realize that the ballot box is a powerful form of communicating your views.

Good communication and only good communication will keep this world safe and secure—economically, educationally, politically and militarily.

Your college seeks to give you a humanistic education. This means a reverence for natural and human life; a respect for excellence; an understanding of others; a striving for achievement without arrogance; an empathy toward opposing views; a commitment to fairness and social justice; a dedication to integrity; and openness to change and an inquiring intellect. I have referred to many lofty ideals. Some of you may feel they are not very practical. I submit they are most practical and I am convinced they are within our grasp.

In 1946, John Masefield addressed the graduates of the University of Sheffield, England. He spoke a beautiful tribute to colleges worldwide. He said:

"There are few earthly things more beautiful than a college. It is a place where those who hate ignorance may strive to know and where those who perceive truth may strive to make others see. Wherever a college stands, it stands and shines. Wherever a college exists, the free minds of men and women, urged on to full and fair inquiry, may still bring wisdom into human affairs."

Reference:(C.R. 9/7/84, Pg.. 10816)

Philosophy of Teaching
Excerpts from Speech
in the Congressional Record
by
Rita Kay Beard, National Teacher of the Year
Hillcrest High School, Dalzell, South Carolina

John F. Kennedy delivered a prophetic statement: "We must educate people today for a future in which the choices to be faced cannot be anticipated by the wisest among us." We must educate students today in such a way that will enable them to function in tomorrow's world. We must provide for the development of knowledge and skills that will permit students, regardless of professional or vocational goals in life, to participate intelligently in society.

One of education's prime responsibilities is to bring relevancy into the learning program. We must strive to provide challenges and successes for each individual student entrusted to us. We realize the American society is an ever-changing society and we must keep abreast of these changes. Therefore, we must constantly evaluate developments in our disciplines and must systematically read literature relative to our own field.

"You can lead a horse to water, but you can't make him drink," says the old adage. In education, motivation is the desire to learn. As teachers, we should see that each individual student goes about his learning process possessing the highest possible degree of motivation.

The student's motivation is directly related to the teacher's success in making learning meaningful and interesting. Enthusiasm generates interest. Students become interested when the teacher exhibits enthusiasm for the subject. Enthusiasm is contagious—it spreads directly from the teacher, to the student, to the subject matter. Extreme care should be given in the planning for all classroom and class-related activities to take advantage of every opportunity to motivate each student to achieve.

Teachers should be positive role models for their students by advising student activities and attending school-related programs. The purpose of the school is to guide growth in knowledge, skills, habits, and attitudes which will enable students to live more effectively in the present as well as in the future. Extracurricular activities make a significant contribution to student growth. An adviser becomes part of student life.

By participating in these activities the teacher is given the opportunity to talk with students and parents in an informal atmosphere.

In dealing with students in the classroom, the teacher must deal with attitudes— attitudes about self, others and goals. He must set realistic goals of what he wants to do for his students. He also helps students set goals for themselves. He should take time at the beginning of each course to get to know the students—relate to them and their individual needs. Meeting each student's needs is the greatest challenge in teaching. The teacher must take notice of individual needs to help each student become the very best he or she is capable of becoming.

Teaching is a calling, not a job. To give it our best demands a positive attitude toward students, parents, administrators, the community, and our positions. No paycheck will equal the "extra" pay that comes when graduates call, write or drop by to say thanks for something we did to smooth their paths. Granted they may be few and far between, but one student saved from failure makes it all worthwhile.

Teachers should instill in their students the belief that they can succeed if they learn the basic course principles, if they believe in the worth, and if they are willing to work hard and take risks.

Education issues and trends of today include: teacher accountability, improving basic skills and standardized test scores, student and community apathy, cooperative learning, and choice in education. One of the most crucial issues, however, is the public's perception of education.

In an episode of a school-related television series, the principal made an interesting comment. He said that when he went to school, teachers worried about students chewing gum, talking in class, and failing to do their homework. Today, teachers deal with narcotics, weapons, violence and teenage pregnancies. These problems vividly indicate some of the changes which have occurred in schools in the past few years.

All the ills and problems of society have reached the schools. The expectation is that somehow schools should be able to solve them and at the same time educate the children; but who is to blame?

We live in a world of misplaced values. We need to remember that values are instilled in the home, by the parents. Parents need to become more involved in their children's education. Their involvement will determine how their child does in school. They need to be at home more for their child, set rules, and set a limit to the number of hours their child can work per week. They need to get involved with their child's education by attending school meetings, programs and activities. Too many of our young people get little encouragement from their parents to excel in school.

The minimum-wage job is killing education. Students are working too many hours and not spending enough time doing their homework. They arrange their schoolwork around their work schedule. They don't have time to do their homework or they don't have the discipline to make themselves do it. Our world is getting too advanced for our young people not to get an education.

As teachers we need to constantly strive to be an example by our own values and give strong values to our students. We need to help the students see the possibilities for themselves. We need to be a positive influence and a friend to them. We must encourage parents to participate in school activities. We must build quality relationships with our students. We must love them, nurture them, support them, be proud of them, and teach them all we can. As teachers we need to sell ourselves to the public by making the public aware of the consequences of a good educational system and one that comes from one under stress.

Teaching style plays a major role in determining the student's level of motivation. It affects classroom discipline and the level of communication between students and teachers.

My classroom activities are designed to build on individual student interests, strengths, needs and desires. Students are encouraged to assist in selecting projects and other class activities. Being involved provides more effective motivation.

Highly motivated students use time more effectively—an important factor in maintaining high motivation is the use of a wide variety of teaching methods from day to day and within each class period. Methods that work for me include: student/teacher demonstrations, role playing, problem solving simulations, gaming strategies of all kinds, overheads and other audiovisual materials, small group and individualized work, brainstorming, questioning techniques, panel discussions, resource speakers and micro-computers.

I make sure that my curriculum challenges all the students in the class regardless of their ability. I want all of my students to succeed.

I would recommend that my most capable students enter the teaching profession.

Teaching has been a very rewarding career for me for the last ten years even though it has not been easy being a teacher. Teaching is much harder and more time consuming than I expected. Teaching takes a lot of hard work, patience, strength, perseverance, and overcoming of frustration. If we are to attract our brightest students and equip them for a teaching career to ensure that tomorrow's youth is well taught, we must serve as a role model for our future teachers.

Be competent. There is no substitute for competence. An effective teacher never stops learning. It is important to keep current in one's subject area by attending conferences, joining professional organizations, and taking classes. Your intellectual skills with students will be remembered by more students and far longer than anything else you can do or say. Respect and trust each student as an individual. Care about each student and show a genuine interest in the student as a person worthy of your time and attention.

A teacher has to have the capabilities of becoming exemplary. He must take a long look at himself, recognize his weaknesses and set out to improve them.

An exemplary teacher will show willingness to accept leadership roles in the department and schools. He will work with the teachers in his department and school to provide the best curriculum of courses and programs to assure that students are getting the best education. He keeps professional ethics at a high priority, never undermining the school or the school system. He recognizes and complements his peers.

Teachers should feel that they are responsible for a trust. Our teaching will affect the future of each student who enters our classroom in some way. This result of teaching is a tremendous trust that is being placed on the shoulders of our profession.

In the process of improving education, not one single group should be held accountable, but rather all who are concerned with the education system must become involved and be at least partially accountable. This includes students, teachers, administrators, parents and the local community. We are each accountable to society and to ourselves.

A more competent and productive work force is needed to keep our nation competitive with other countries. The ability to work together using new technologies will ensure our country's success in the global economy.

America needs an educational system that does the job of preparing students to meet the demands of the job market. To cultivate such a system, we must specify the literacy and technological literacy skills that will be needed for competent performance in the workplace.

High school graduates are being called upon to have computer skills as they leave school, whether they go on to college or directly into the job market. Businesses are searching for talented and skilled computer literate workers to lead them into the 21st Century and the information age. What these two facts suggest is that computer education should be one of the highest priorities for schools now and in the future.

The impact of computers on society and education will largely be dependent on the effectiveness of our battle for men's minds. It is the teachers who play the key role in motivating and leading students. A rededicated commitment to encouraging students to maximize their talents will pay high dividends. Minimum competency, academic excellence, and intellectual development must be the central roles in education. Teachers' effectiveness will be enhanced by computers to give more time for individual attention, support, challenge and leadership. The result is a more productive, competitive America with the opportunity for more meaningful jobs and lives.

Reference: (C.R. 11/9/89, Pg. E-3744)

Three Key Words for Vocational Education: Rigor, Relevance — and Profit

Excerpts from Speech
in the Congressional Record
by
William B. Reed, President
Southern Co. Services, Inc.

Ladies and gentlemen, less than two months ago the United States Congress passed what was called a "jobs" bill. Whatever the effects of that legislation—I dare to make this prediction: You gathered here at this conference—and your colleagues back home who work in support of vocational education—will achieve more to get people into jobs than any law ever passed by any Congress.

You will achieve more—first because you bring to the task your own personal dedication. You have committed yourselves to deal with a need that exists, not here at the nation's political center, but in the nation's true center—which is back home, where America lives and works.

Secondly, you will achieve more because you have the wisdom to seek a partnership between vocational education and business. I'm confident you'll find most business people eager to enter into this partnership. Believe me, we know that we have a vital stake in vocational education.

Of course, many of you on the advisory councils are business people, too. But your main endeavor—through the advisory councils—is to build bridges between business and the field of vocational education. To the extent that you want to maintain those bridges and keep them open, you may feel some constraints—some reluctance to speak to your state educational and political establishments with a blunt and direct business viewpoint. I can speak without those constraints—hoping to give you a message from business that you can carry across the bridge.

I must preface my message with an observation of the obvious. This economy—this society—indeed, this world—is going through a painful process of change. Unless you've been marooned on a desert island, your ears must ring with the jargon of change—the terminology of high tech, the information age, knowledge industries, and the growing service sector.

All of this has had a tremendous influence on what we of the business world look for when an applicant walks into one of our employment offices. No longer is it enough for a worker to come in and offer us a pair of hands. Today, we're hiring minds as well and that's the problem—and the opportunity—for vocational education.

I've said that we in the Southern electric system are getting some good data processing people, some good technicians, some good drafting people. True. But the level of quality we're seeing is grossly inconsistent. It has reached the point where our employment managers can identify not only specific schools—but specific teachers—whose students come to us ready for the world of work. On the other hand, there's a large percentage of applicants—large enough to rate the word "tragic"—who come to us unqualified to assume any useful role in the workplace.

Let me relate one specific instance. One of our companies was accepting applications for a number of entry-level job openings. About 360 applicants lined up at the plant site, desperately hoping to land one of those jobs. Of the 360 applicants, the employment manager estimated that he would be fortunate to find 20 who could qualify for the work.

Where did the others fall short? If past experience is any guide, they will lack the basic skills of comprehension and computation—or, in layman's language—simple reading and writing and elementary arithmetic.

Nothing so advanced as algebra, mind you. We're talking abuot more than 50 percent of the applicants who came to us being unable to handle level two in numerical computation. That's addition, subtraction, multiplication, long division, simple fractions, and decimals.

Some say that teaching these fundamental skills is not the mission of programs in vocational education—that vocational education must concern itself only with training in specific workplace skills.

My answer to this—and I ask you to relay it back to your state education departments—is that we in business are not concerned about whose turf is involved. Reading, writing, addition and subtraction are essential workplace skills. No vocational education program which neglects these skills can hope to establish a fruitful partnership with business.

Let me offer some suggestions that may help our partners in the educational and political establishments to strengthen their state vocational programs. Let me offer you a message to carry across the bridge—a message based on three key words. These words are—rigor—relevance—and profit.

It appears that rigor has not been a popular word in American public school classrooms for many years. Believe me I'm including all courses and all levels of education in this charge. Students have been quick to perceive that a mere 65 percent—a grade of D is "passing," and that everybody passes and everybody graduates or gets a certificate eventually. Unfortunately, for these students, they step out the school door into a world where 65 percent is not good enough—and where everybody does not get by. I can assure you that our customers would be very unhappy if their electric service was reliable only 65 percent of the time. And you'd all be terrified if we ran our nuclear reactors with the attitude that 65 percent was good enough!

We in business and industry are not perfect. But we keep trying for perfection. It's a matter of attitude. Zero defects may be an unattainable goal—but it's a worthy goal.

Ladies and gentlemen, there's more to vocational training than learning to work a drill press, a weaving machine, or even a computer. Attitude counts. And I suggest that greater rigor in the schools will help build the right attitudes.

The second key word in my message from business to those in the field of vocational education is relevance. Again I refer to the almost revolutionary transition that business and industry are now going through.

This change isn't limited to the high-tech laboratories and computer rooms. Recently, a sawmill in my home state began operations—and it differs as much from the sawmills of 20 years ago as an astronaut differs from Paul Bunyan. This sawmill uses lasers, electronic sensors, computer analyzers and microprocessor controllers. The sawmill does not need a staff of engineers to operate that kind of installation. They do need people who are trained in today's technology—and who will be retrainable in tomorrow's technology.

We in business recognize the problems that education systems face when they try to develop programs that match today's technology. We understand that budget limitations makes it difficult to get state-of-the-art equipment and qualified instructors. I believe many business people stand ready to help—through equipment donation plans, through instructor exchange programs and through workplace training programs. But the educational establishment and the political powers will have to make some matching commitments before this can be called a real partnership.

I won't embarrass you by asking for a show of hands of how many of your states offer 10 to 20 programs in cosmetology for every one in instrumentation technology. How many have far more programs and instructors in upholstery or auto body work than in industrial electronics?

I don't mean to cast any stigma on the trades I've named but there's a rather severe limit to the number of cosmetologists that the world of tomorrow will need—while there is almost no practical limit to the number of electronic technicians we'll need. Let's put our young people where the jobs will be. Let's fill our training curricula with programs that are relevant!

Now my third key word is profit. Before you tune me out, let me assure you I do not propose to turn vocational education into a hymn in praise of capitalism. I do not suggest we can resolve the issue of prayer in the schools by substituting quotations from Adam Smith.

I believe an understanding and appreciation of the driving power of profit in business will raise our topic of the day to an even higher level—that it will lead to a partnership that includes not only business and the schools, but also the workers who come out of the schools and into business.

In reality, as you and I know, nobody operates a business for the sole purpose of providing jobs. Businesses exist for the purpose of filling needs or wants—and doing so at a profit. If the needs or wants change, if the profit disappears—so does the business. And with it disappear the jobs that existed solely to help satisfy those needs or wants.

One wise man said that the quickest way to impress people with the role of profit in business would be to ask whether—in times of economic stress—they would rather be working for a company that makes a good profit or one that does not. I sincerely believe that one of the most valuable lessons a teacher in a vocational program can convey is a healthy respect for profit. I would suggest a program under which a guest lecturer would come into the classroom and talk about profit and its place in the world of work.

Let these business men and women tell how all costs affect that well-known "bottom line"—and how the bottom line affects jobs and pay. Let them point out that profit is not exclusively the concern of the boss.

Those are the elements, ladies and gentlemen, of one businessman's message to those who fund, those who administer, and those who teach our vocational education programs.

I can sum it up in three short sentences built upon those three key words. Rigor is a vital need, relevance is a crucial concept and profit is the driving force.

Together, they add up to a prescription which can help America's vocational educational programs achieve the goal of preparing people for satisfying productive careers. Let the schools follow this prescription and they will find business walking right beside them—in a strong and creative partnership—a partnership that works for the schools, for the students and for the community.

Reference: (C.R. 6/8/83, Pg. S-8005)

Embassies
• • • • • • • • • • • • • •
U.S. Embassies Abroad: We Mean Business
Excerpts from Speech
in the Congressional Record
by
Ambassador Charles Gargano

For the past two years, I have been privileged to be the American Ambassador in the Caribbean island-nation of Trinidad and Tobago. Being an Ambassador involves one in a whole variety of activities: negotiating bilateral agreements, reporting to Washington political and economic conditions, fighting drugs, protecting American citizens, promoting American business.

All these activities are important, and I have found all of them challenging. But since I have been a businessman my entire career, it was natural for me to pay special attention to the business and commercial aspects of the job.

I want to talk to you today about how our embassies are promoting United States business abroad, and, specifically, what we have been doing in Trinidad and Tobago to make life easier, and more profitable, for the business people who come to us for help.

First, let's look at the dramatic way the world is changing around us, and what this means for American business. Not since the end of World War II have we been shaken up so profoundly.

The destruction of the Berlin Wall is a symbol of the disintegration of trade barriers everywhere.

The single European Market, the U.S.-Canada Free Trade Agreement, the brand new agreement between the United States and Mexico as well as the fresh free market spirit that is sweeping the world from the Soviet Union to South America—such changes are radically altering the world business environment.

Fortunately, American business has been getting in shape for these challenges for at least a decade. The Japanese made us realize that the United States market could no longer be isolated from the rest of the world.

As a result, American firms today are more aware of international competition and international opportunities, and they are more aggressive in meeting them. More companies than ever are exporting to increase sales. More companies are sourcing their inputs from abroad to cut costs and stay competitive. And more companies are looking at joint ventures with foreign firms to penetrate new markets, acquire new products, land new technologies, and get further financing.

But we still have a great struggle ahead of us if we are to out-distance our foreign competitors in the coming years. In the past, United States companies have not always gotten the service they want from our embassies. Our missions abroad were sometimes criticized for paying too much attention to geopolitics and to maintaining smooth relations with the host government, and not enough to furthering U.S. commercial interests.

Things have changed. Today, most United States ambassadors would list support for American business as one of their top priorities. Just as American companies have learned to be more aggressive in the international marketplace, so too have American embassies changed the way they view their responsibilities.

Since this changing role for our embassies may not yet be fully understood by our business people, let me explain the kinds of service we offer.

First, for individual business visitors, the embassy can be a valuable first point of contact. We provide information and advice on local market trends, import regulations, and product standards, as well as on the credit worthiness of local firms. We can give visitors a feel for current political and macroeconomic trends which affect their business. Most important, we have lists of potential buyers, and can make referrals to vital government contacts.

Secondly, we devote plenty of attention to organized business groups. Embassies are often called upon, for example, to assist trade delegations sent to our country by State governments or industry groups. Just last week my embassy assisted a delegation of business people from Florida. We made all the necessary local arrangements and provided each delegation member with a schedule of meetings tailored to his or her special interests.

A third kind of service, embassies are continually alert to major projects or government tenders that offer opportunities for U.S. exporters. Many local firms call us first when they are look to buy products.

With an increasing number of American companies taking advantage of our willingness to assist, one of our main problems is finding the resources to do the job. Our Eastern European missions in particular are being swamped with business visitors. Commercial offices that used to average only ten visitors a week are now expected to cope with 50 or 60, with no increase in resources.

Eastern Europe is a difficult place to do business, and United States companies are having trouble coping with nonconvertible currency, inadequate property safeguards, and rapidly changing commercial climates. This points to a critical need to beef up our support for U.S. firms in Eastern Europe if we are to hold our own against the West Europeans, with their natural advantage, and the energetic Japanese.

Of course, it is in Trinidad and Tobago that I have had my own experience as a United States ambassador assisting American businessmen. So perhaps the best way to show how embassies support business is to describe further how my embassy has gone about it in Trinidad, an oil-rich democracy of 1.3 million people, located at the end of the Caribbean island chain, near Venezuela. Let's start with the Mobil Oil Company.

In July 1988, Mobil was awarded oil exploration rights by the government of Trinidad and Tobago in a newly opened offshore block. For the next 14 months top Mobil officials engaged in strenuous, often frustrating negotiations on the terms of a joint operating agreement with a local, state-owned oil company.

Throughout, Mobil negotiators worked closely with me and my embassy staff on all aspects of the talks. We advised Mobil on who to see and how to present arguments with maximum effect. We kept Mobil appraised of developments that affected negotiations—like debt restructuring efforts that make the government reluctant to take on large new debt obligations.

I myself made personal calls on ministers on Mobil's behalf. The end result was an agreement which, while tough, was one Mobil felt it could live with.

The completion of the Mobil deal allowed three other U.S. oil companies to finalize their negotiations. This meant strengthened opportunities for our oil companies, a major injection of United States capital for Trinidad and Tobago, and, if more oil is found, an increased oil supply for the U.S. from a close, stable, democratic neighbor.

Let me give you another example. The Continental Oil Company, or CONOCO, wanted to enter a joint venture with Trinidad-Natural Gas Company to build a world-class liquid gas separation plant. The negotiations were hard, and, for the Americans, strewn with obstacles, such as an early requirement by the government that CONOCO accept an unwelcome European joint venture partner. We started to meet with CONOCO executives, and were able to provide continuing commercial intelligence as well as advise on how to deal with the government.

The final result was that last November, after months of negotiations, CONOCO and the U.S. engineering firm Pan West signed a joint venture agreement with the local company to build Trinidad's $95 million Phoenix Park plant.

Another example involves the new international airport that is projected for Port of Spain, estimated at the moment to be a $250 million venture. The airport project may not only make Trinidad a regional air hub, but has major implications for the development of the country's tourism industry.

Our embassy played an instrumental role in obtaining a U.S. government grant for an airport development study, helping to ensure that a U.S. management firm landed the long-term development contract. We also arranged for a USIA grant to allow the head of Trinidad's Airport Authority to travel throughout the United States. This allowed him to make key contacts in the industry and has given U.S. suppliers the inside track for procurement of equipment and services.

Those are real life cases from Trinidad. They show how an embassy can assist business, and they show some other things as well. First, they give the lie to what used to be the standard excuse for embassy passivity—the contention that "the big guys can take care of themselves, they don't need us." That's wrong—they do need us.

An embassy can be of real assistance at those important junctures where a joint venture negotiation is in danger of breaking down. A U.S. company feels it is being squeezed unfairly by the host government, or crucial authorizations are being denied or delayed. At such times an ambassador and his staff can often cut through the red tape, speak directly to the people that count, and deliver a vital message.

Second, these examples sound a warning—that an embassy can play a facilitative role only. In the cases involving American companies, it is not the American embassy but the companies themselves who were primarily responsible for the success of their efforts.

These examples show that Embassies can only help firms which show that they want to be helped. The companies involved briefed us on their strategies, kept us up to date on developments and solicited our advice and intervention when they thought these could be helpful.

Let me now share with you one last way in which a U.S. embassy abroad can help U.S. business. An American embassy can be an influential institution in a foreign country, especially a small to medium-sized country. In such a situation, an Embassy can help U.S. business by voicing the American viewpoint when local economic policies are being decided.

In Trinidad, for example, I have spoken out on the need to remove unreasonable restrictions on foreign investment if the country indeed wants to attract investors from abroad. Last month the Trinidadian Senate passed new legislation which represents a major step toward an open investment regime. The result is, that from now on, American investors in Trinidad will meet fewer obstacles than in the past. Both countries should benefit.

The United State government is making a major new thrust to assist American business to hold its own in a world that will be sharply more competitive than in the past.

The State Department, whose front-line units are U.S. embassies, is determined to play a strong role in this effort. Ambassadors and their embassies can be of assistance to American companies who show that they want our help by keeping us informed of their problems on a routine basis. If businessmen do that, we'll show them that we, too, mean business.

Reference C.R. 6/22/90, Pg. S-8577)

Energy
·········

National Energy Policy

Excerpts from Speech
in the Congressional Record
by
Donald Paul Hodel
Former U.S. Secretary of Energy

Our Nation's national energy policy consists of a goal, and strategies and programs to achieve that goal.

Our goal is an adequate supply of energy at a reasonable price. To realize this goal, our strategies are (1) to minimize federal control and involvement in the energy market while maintaining public health and safety and environmental quality, and (2) to promote a balanced and mixed energy resource system.

We seek a balanced and mixed energy resource base ranging from essential conventional sources such as oil, gas, coal and nuclear, to renewables such as hydro-electricity, solar, wind, geothermal and biofuels, and new emphasis on conservation as a resource.

If available, petroleum is the fuel of choice. But the burning questions are: how much is available, how much can be produced and at what price?

Our estimates are that only 3 percent of our known recoverable fossil fuels reserves are in the form of natural petroleum. In 1983, oil represented 43 percent of our nation's energy consumption, and when the closely related natural gas is thrown in, these two resources supplied more than 60 percent of our energy for at least the next ten years. Much of it will be imported. We are still net importers of almost 30 percent of our oil needs, and our imports are rising.

This year, we remain, along with Japan, the largest importer of oil, not in terms of percentage, but in terms of volume. So what are we doing to reduce our reliance on imported oil and achieve a more balanced and mixed energy resource base? We have made substantial progress.

As a result of conservation, improved energy efficiency and increased domestic production, we are less dependent on foreign resources today. U.S. consumption of oil in 1983 was down 11 percent compared to 1980 levels. Consequently, our oil imports were down 33 percent. We have also diversified our suppliers. In 1983 none of the top four countries from which we imported oil shipped through the Strait of Hormuz.

The United States can take comfort in the fact that only 2-3 percent of our oil requirements come from the Persian Gulf, but 20 percent of the free world's total oil supply moves through the Strait of Hormuz. So even if we took no oil from that area, we must be concerned about the reliance of our allies on Persian Gulf oil.

The Administration views conservation as an essential component of our mixed and balanced resource system. I believe that Americans do have a conservation ethic. As a nation, we have already made significant progress in conserving energy:

• Residential and commercial buildings in the United States today consume 20 percent less energy per square foot than 10 years ago;

• Energy consumption per capita has declined by 14 percent in the last 10 years;

• Energy input per unit of industrial output has declined by 23 percent since 1973; and

• Energy consumption per dollar of gross national product has declined by 11 percent for the past four years.

These are important steps in the right direction. However, the time for additional conservation is now. In addition, we must continue to develop renewables, which will play an increasingly important role in complementing our conservation efforts.

Projections indicate renewables will contribute over 9 percent to our energy mix by 1992 and over 10 percent by the year 2000. A one percent increase may not at first sound like much, but when you consider what a large and growing energy system we have in the United States, you begin to realize that a very high rate of growth is occurring in the renewable areas.

Some key developments in renewable energy technology include:

• The cost of photovoltaic-generated electricity decreased by 57 percent from 1980 to 1983. Worldwide photovoltaic sales have increased 400 percent and are expected to more than double by 1990.

• In wind energy, the number of small communities producing wind machines more than doubled from 1980 to 1983.

• The number of active solar building installations in operation in this country has more than doubled since 1980; and the number of new homes incorporating passive heating and/or cooling technologies has increased by nearly 100 percent since 1980.

In addition to renewing our conservation commitment and expanding our renewable resource base, there are other actions we as a nation must take to change the way we have traditionally dealt with our conventional energy resources.

We must deregulate natural gas pricing—one of the ways we are seeking to minimize federal control of energy markets. We believe that decontrolling the price will bring consumer costs down. Natural gas regulation is forcing consumers to pay for high-cost and imported gas.

Nuclear power is also an important alternative to our continued reliance on oil. But the nuclear industry has been severely damaged in recent years. No new plants have been ordered since 1978. Many currently under construction are in financial distress. I believe that a primary reason for this distress is the licensing process. Other nations can build nuclear plants in five or six years; it takes 12 to 14 years to build the same plant in the United States.

We must address this critical problem if America is to have a nuclear component in our energy future. In addition, the Department of Energy will take a series of specific actions to help ensure quality construction of safe nuclear plants.

Coal is another essential component of our energy mix. It is one of the resources that makes us an energy rich nation today, and can make us more energy secure in the future. It can be fairly said that we are the Saudi Arabia of coal. It accounts for over 85 percent of our estimated recoverable fossil fuel reserves—yet contributes only 20 percent of our energy today.

The Administration is dedicated to expanding use of coal and stimulating increased exports of all types of United States coals. We are researching ways to burn coal cleanly. Tremendous opportunities exist for coal to play an increasing role in our energy mix without compromising our environmental objectives.

All the resources I have outlined contribute to our balanced and mixed energy resource system, and thus to our energy security and non-dependence.

As I mentioned earlier, the conflict in the Middle East continues to escalate. Despite the fact that a minimal amount of our oil requirements come from the Persian Gulf, some of our Western European allies range from 20 to 40 percent dependent and Japan is about 60 percent dependent on oil moving through the Strait of Hormuz. As a result, the President has said that the free world must keep the strait open.

The Gulf states themselves would probably be the most seriously impacted by closure of the Strait of Hormuz. Virtually their entire income would be affected by their inability to reach the market. The "threat" of such a closure is among those energy emergencies for which we must be, and are, prepared.

Contingency planning remains fundamental to our goal of ensuring an adequate supply of energy.

Our contingency plan realizes the important fact that market forces—millions of American consumers making individual choices—are the most efficient allocators of energy supplies. Individuals and firms can make their own decisions on how best to cope with an energy shortage—whether it be through conservation, use of alternative fuels and by other means.

We have, therefore, focused our efforts on filling and maintaining the Strategic Petroleum Reserve (SPR); removing or reforming economic and technical barriers; fostering a closer government-industry partnership; promoting public understanding of the need to prepare for energy emergencies; and gathering and disseminating accurate and timely information.

At its present level, the Strategic Petroleum Reserve could provide more than 80 days supply if all imports to the United States were cut off; more than 800 days if the Persian Gulf only were cut; and more than 200 days if OPEC supplies were halted.

This supply of oil provides a cushion I hope we will never need to use. That is, I hope we will never have a serious oil supply disruption that would necessitate its use.

Let me emphasize that the decision to activate the SPR is the President's. We at the Department of Energy in making a recommendation are not working in isolation. We have a continuing interagency effort involving the State, Treasury, Commerce and other departments to monitor and analyze any interruption of supply.

As I have indicated, we believe wholeheartedly in the marketplace. If we are to be energy non-dependent, we must not resort to techniques of the past such as price and allocation controls or more regulation.

We are committed to providing timely and accurate information to the public prior to and during any interruption that may occur. By doing so, we will enable industry, business and American consumers to exercise the judgment and common sense that will prevent "panic" reactions that otherwise could unnecessarily drive the price of oil to levels beyond what is necessary to balance supply and demand.

I believe you and I must together begin elevating public awareness of the United States' energy situation, and that is why I am here today. We have no choice but to care and be involved. We have no choice but to move America toward energy non-dependence. Our lifestyles, our economy, our national security depend on it.

Reference: (C.R. 8/2/84, Pg. S-9644)

Energy and Geopolitics in the 21st Century
Excerpts from Speech
in the Congressional Record
by
James Schlesinger
Former Secretary of Energy

At this annual gathering of the World Energy Conference I have been asked to discuss energy and geopolitics in the 21st Century. One is, no doubt, flattered by the suggestion that he may possess the requisite gift of clairvoyance to foretell long-range energy development, let alone their perspective impact on geopolitics.

So I shall make my task somewhat less difficult by limiting it in two ways. First, my comments shall not extend beyond the early decades of the next century. Even in the course of 25 years new technologies could radically alter the shape of the future and one's judgments about it. But the probability that such new technologies might emerge, and on a vast scale be introduced commercially, is mercifully lower than it is over a century or longer.

Second, I shall confine myself to delineating those major trends likely to affect developments in the decades immediately ahead. In this way I can avoid the pitfalls of prediction or the rather beguiling ambiguities of the Delphic Oracle.

One cannot, of course, measure with any precision the strength of such major trends or the pace at which they may influence future developments. The 17th Century English political operative, the Marquis of Halifax, stated: "The best qualification of a prophet is to have a good memory." Quite right—for as we peer into the future, it is certain to be influenced by the re-emergence of past tendencies which, for one reason or another, have been temporarily submerged. Among such tendencies is the intimate association between energy security and the strength of nations or, more broadly, the strength of alliance systems. That association—which in the past has led to military conflict to establish control over fields of coal or oil, has been partially obscured since World War II. But those days during which one could take energy security for granted and focus on other issues came to an end in 1973. Since then, the rise of nationalism, the rebirth of religious fundamentalism, and the weakened cohesion of the major power blocs have all contributed to renewed attention to the issue of energy security.

Without doubt, the most significant, indeed the dominant, trend in energy is the rapidly growing dependency on OPEC and producing nations of the Persian or Arabian Gulf. In just four years time, the call on OPEC crude has risen by some 35 percent—largely eliminating that atmosphere of desperation, instability and cutthroat competition that marked OPEC behavior in the middle of the decade. The call on OPEC will continue to rise—gradually eliminating whatever surplus capacity presently exists. In large measure this change in the market has been driven by developments in the United States, the reputed leader of the free world. Many of the trends marking the American developments apply elsewhere in the free world. But I shall concentrate initially on the United States, which in this matter has truly forged into the lead.

(1) America's appetite for oil is once again growing. In four years time it has rebounded by some 15 percent from the comparatively low level of 15 million barrels a day in 1985 now approaching the peak reached before the second oil shock. At the same time her ability to satisfy that appetite from her domestic resources has been shrinking. The result has been a growth in imports. By the end of 1990, they will have grown by some 4.5 million barrels per day, roughly doubling in the five-year period. By the mid-90s, imports will again have grown by a similar volume.

(2) There is nothing that compels import growth to occur at this pace, yet, despite the persistent political rhetoric, not to say hand-wringing, regarding national security, nothing has been done to arrest the growth of imports. In this era, the United States appears wedded to reliance upon "free market forces." To be sure, there exist the usual possibilities of enhancing domestic oil production or achieving fuel substitution and limiting oil consumption through a variety of fiscal and regulatory measures. Discouraging all consumption or directing usage to other fuels through regulatory devices is highly suspect—save for motives of environmental protection. Thus, in brief, imports will continue to grow and grow rapidly—because the measures required to restrain such growths are not in accord with prevailing national psyche.

(3) Despite the continuing declamations regarding the villainy of the OPEC cartel, the United States has now become the best ally that OPEC has. The growth in United States import requirements has done far more to remove excess slack from the market than any force. The United States has become the main engine for the restoration of OPEC power. A friend in need is a friend indeed. The United States has been such a friend.

(4) What is true for the United States is, to a lesser degree, true elsewhere. World consumption continues to rise, perhaps most markedly among third world nations.

(5) As the market tightens, excess availability declines and, ultimately, prices rise, other nations will pay attention to the rapidly expanding role of the United States in international oil trade. There will be renewed criticism for its propensity to squander energy.

(6) It should also be noted that the United States will by the mid-90s be facing

foreign exchange requirements of over a $100 billion a year just to finance its oil imports. Particularly in light of the present health of the U.S. balance of trade, these additional out payments for oil imports will detract both from the U.S. economy and from the strength of its geopolitical position.

As the outside world becomes steadily more dependent upon Gulf crude, the Middle East will become the focus of a revived and ever-increasing external interest. Even without such outside attention, its internal passions and rivalries have turned that region into something like the world's cauldron. Add to those rivalries, an ever-growing dependency and an ever-rising stake, and the Middle East becomes something akin to the Balkins before 1914, a potential tinderbox. Any spark must draw the immediate attention of outside forces.

However, what is happening to those outside forces—those changes in military capabilities, political goals and attitudes, the cohesion of alliances, and the relative strength and weakness of economies which together provide the structure of geopolitics?

(1) Perhaps the greatest uncertainty in determining what the geopolitics will be is the evolution of the Soviet Union, which is as yet unresolved. Under Mr. Gorbachev the Soviet Union, at least temporarily, has placed less stress on military intimidation. Moreover, since the Afghan adventure, the Soviet Union has faded as a threat. But its future remains uncertain. Right now one must judge that there will be, at a minimum, an extended armistice in the Cold War; nonetheless, in assessing the geopolitical future of the Soviet Union, it does remain, as Churchill called it, an "enigma."

(2) As the perception of the Soviet threat fades, the nations of the West will gradually relax. U.S. military power will be substantially reduced—with the changed appreciation of the threat with environment re-enforcing what had already become inevitable because of budgetary pressures. The power of the West will decline as it has been doing in some sense since 1939 and 1945. In the 21st Century the population of the Western bloc will have fallen to less than 10 percent of the world's population—in contrast to the 30 percent that it was prior to World War II.

(3) The spread of sophisticated military capabilities is likely to continue. The perceived decline of the Soviet Union—and a less bipolar world means that the number of ready suppliers of military equipment is likely to rise. The Middle East will continue to be a major and growing repository of such sophisticated military equipment.

(4) One should not be misled by the ease of United States intervention in the Gulf Tanker War during the late 1980s, to protect Kuwaiti tankers and generally to offset Iranian power. Those conditions were unique. Iran, through its own follies and through the course of the war, had largely eliminated its own air and naval capabilities. The flow of events had led it to a point of substantial exhaustion both militarily and economically.

(5) Soviet capacity for military intervention is likely to increase relative to the West, assuming that the Soviet Union can surmount its current "time of troubles." Western military forces will be reduced—along with the inclination, and perhaps the will, to become militarily engaged in the region. At the same time, Soviet conventional forces will remain immense. The Soviet Union is near at hand; the United States is far distant.

Thus, if there were a sudden introduction of outside forces—it becomes increasingly plausible that the outsider would be the Soviet Union.

(6) What about the Gulf Region itself? As the outside world becomes increasingly dependent upon the Gulf, the principal nations of the region will become far more influential than today. Their financial difficulties will rapidly or gradually come to an end. They will become increasingly cocky. They will also become more tempting as a target.

(7) The Middle East will likely continue to be marked by disunity. It is possible, of course, that the producing states may become more unified. Given the present conditions and particularly the historic rivalry between the Persian and the Arab this appears implausible. If such unity could be achieved, it would further enhance the economic and political power of the region relative to the outside world.

(8) Concern about the Soviet Union may at some point revive among the nations of the region—as the memory of the failed Afghan adventure recedes. Although the Soviet Union has proved to be a far weaker competitor than was generally believed in the 1970s, its capacity for local intervention will certainly not diminish and may grow substantially.

What I have outlined are the major forces that will be at work. No one can precisely gauge the strength or the interactions of these specific forces. That will vary with time and circumstances. No one can predict the future with any confidence. But where does this all lead us?

We can foresee a world that has grown increasingly dependent on the Gulf region for its energy resources and for the performance of its economies. The Middle East will thus become the cockpit of contending world forces—a potential tinderbox. If there is a major conflict, the Middle East is likely to be its vortex. "If there ever is a World War III," as one oil industry analyst observed, "it will be fought over the Middle Eastern oil reserves."

Let me close with two final observations. First an early student of geopolitics, Karl Haushofer, reached his ultimate conclusion with the pithy observation: "Who controls the Heartland, controls the world." That does provide food for thought. It might now be said that whichever great power may come to control the world's oil tap in the Gulf region will to a large extent control the world.

Second, you will recall the beatitude: "The meek shall inherit the earth." Reportedly it was amended by the late J. Paul Getty to the effect that the meek may inherit the earth but not the subsoil rights. Whatever else, those crucial subsoil rights in the Middle East are not now, nor are they likely to be, controlled by the meek.

Reference: (C.R. 11/7/89, Pg. S-15192)

Environment

• • • • • • • • • • • • • • • • • •

Not in My Backyard: Institutional Problems in Environmental Protection

Excerpts from Speech
in the Congressional Record
by
William D. Ruckelshaus, Administrator
Environmental Protection Agency

The last time I had the pleasure of speaking with you was in 1971. I would like to use the perspective afforded by that meeting to reflect on some of the changes that have taken place in the environmental protection field and to focus on what I consider quite serious problems that still remain to be solved.

In 1971, the dominant environmental issues were pollution from cars and sewer systems. Mobile source control problems took up most of my time then and shortly before I gave my first speech here, the Environmental Protection Agency had filed a 180-day notice against Detroit's pollution of Lake Erie.

In 1984, I find that the 1971 issues, while still important, are no longer consuming, for the simple reason that we have achieved much of what we set out to do. Auto exhaust controls have reduced carbon monoxide 96 percent, hydrocarbons 95 percent, and nitrogen oxides 76 percent from the uncontrolled state. Despite a substantial increase in the number of cars, urban air quality has shown a steady improvement and an almost continuous decline in the number of exceedances of air quality standards for pollutants associated with mobile sources.

With respect to controlling sewage, the city of Detroit has made steady progress in meeting its responsibilities; it achieved full secondary treatment and phosphorous removal late in 1981, which represents a significant contribution to improving water quality in the Great Lakes.

Along with these changes we have seen an accompanying change in attitude among industrial leaders. Environmental controls have been accepted, like taxes and employee benefits, as part of the price of doing business in this industrialized society. And here it is fair to say that both industrial and political leaders have simply followed the clear preference of the American people. For the past decade, Americans of all classes and conditions have time and again indicated their willingness to pay higher prices for goods and to face the prospect of fewer jobs in order to keep the environment clean and public health protected.

But despite these achievements and that kind of public support, we are beginning to see an increased level of contention over environmental issues. As if, having swept our stables, we cannot agree about dusting the piano. We appear, in fact, to have lost much of our ability to turn environmental consensus into practical action. We

Americans have always prided ourselves on pragmatic idealism, but we now appear less capable in this regard than we were in the recent past.

Part of the explanation lies, of course, in the vexed nature of the environmental issues that dominate the current decade. It was relatively easy to act against smoggy air and clouded waters, but in dealing with such problems as acid rain or toxic chemicals, the smog is in the data; what is clouded is the association between the presence of pollutants and the incidence of disease, or between proposed remedies and the damage we want to fix.

This quandary springs from a peculiarity of American political life. It has been noted that the American people are ideologically conservative and operationally liberal. In theory, they are against too much government until the elimination of a particular program affects their own well-being. In practice, we demand that our political system do the wide variety of tasks we think are necessary to preserve our personal position in modern America. That often means a "liberal" governmental response. In the environmental area, in contrast, I believe we are ideologically liberal and operationally conservative.

This position has led to some difficulties in the formation of an effective national environmental policy. While it is a fine thing to embody high ideals in legislation, laws should be written so that mortals can put them into effect without either torturing the language or prescribing nonsense. Environmental protection is an enormously compli-cated technical process; that it now shows the aura of motherhood and the flag makes it less, rather than more, likely that we will do a good job of it.

This is because we encourage public officials to strike extreme postures as defenders of the environment, while we shy away from requiring the hard decisions implied by such postures. As a result, in the typical environmental statute, concern for protection tends to overwhelm careful thinking about precisely how such protection will be accomplished. This passes the buck to the executive agency. Moreover, there is ample provision for judicial review, which passes the buck to the courts. Many statutes have state discretion built in—another set of bucks to be passed. Harry Truman's famous desk sign said, "The buck stops here." The trouble today is that the buck stops nowhere.

Unfortunately, the ordinary solution proposed, when hard decisions have been deferred, is for the Congress to order EPA to perform certain specified actions, usually within a strict timetable. The agendas of the agency during much of its recent history have been set not by any sort of ordered, explainable, rational analysis, but by the press of public outcry and resultant political response. The public appears to be demanding immediate but not very painful solutions to long-standing problems that we don't know how to fix. Congress appears to believe that the way to satisfy this public demand is to load the statutes with specific constraints and directives. Motion is its own reward, whether or not it is in the right direction.

Think of what it takes to site a major industrial facility. A firm often must obtain agreement from perhaps dozens of agencies and authorities at each of the three levels of government, not to mention the courts. And it doesn't help to satisfy a consensus, or a majority of the interests involved, a single "no" anywhere along the line at any time in the process can halt years of planning, effort and investment.

Similarly, we have begun a major national commitment to properly dispose of hazardous wastes. Everyone is in favor of safe disposal, but not in their backyards or anywhere close. In some parts of the country we are running out of places to put the stuff. It stays in improper places, piles up on the loading docks of the generators of waste or has to be shipped around the country. The additional risk this may represent to the nation at large does not bother the local groups who resist disposal facility siting. This is the way to run a railroad only if you like what happened to the railroads.

The key problem in the environmental area is trust. As I noted, mistrust and a tradition of encouraging maverick opinion are built into our system. The Vietnam War and Watergate, in which government appeared to fail the public, have simply exacerbated what has always been present in American thought. But from the standpoint of an American governmental agency charged with protecting human health and the environment, trust is the oil in the gearbox. That is, the public can object to what a regulatory agency does, or believe that it is going too fast or too slow, but when it ceases to believe that the agency is trying to act in the public interest, that agency cannot function at all.

I don't believe that's the situation at EPA today. Our agency, with its wide scope of responsibility, is especially vulnerable to failures of public trust. Can you imagine what would have happened if the decision we made recently about allowable levels of ethylene dibromide (EDB) in food had not been broadly accepted? Each state would have set its own protective standards, many foods would have vanished from the marketplace and the food production and distribution industries would have been thrown into chaos. But EPA was trusted enough, its judgment did prevail, and we avoided such needless disruption.

I don't believe that EPA must be whipped into doing its job, but it is undeniable that many people do, and the Congress often agrees with them. In my view, that is not the way to establish a sensible environmental policy. We need a better way, we need to find some means of converting the broad societal consensus on the government into a practical system for solving environmental problems. It can be done.

Somehow we have to create institutional frameworks that will buffer our country's environmental commitment from the two-year and four-year cycles of the political world. It is sad that, although many knowledgeable people agree that our environmental laws need recasting to reflect scientific and practical realities, there is almost no chance of accomplishing this in the current political climate. But that climate must someday change, and in that hope we are actively and aggressively exploring ways of making our environmental statutes more consistent and effective.

When I spoke to you last, the message I tried to convey was that the EPA did not represent merely a red light for industrial growth, but that it served a green light's function as well, in directing movement toward the kind of society we all wanted, one in which a healthy economy and environmental values coexisted. The metaphor is, I think still apt across more than a decade, except that now we find ourselves at one of those infuriating intersections where the red, green and yellow lights are all on at once. We must develop more efficient ways of coming to a practical consensus in response to new problems, or we are heading toward a sort of societal gridlock. Nations that can force the requisite social unity will have the road all to themselves. We must get back on that road or be out of the race.

Reference: (C.R. 4/25/84, Pg. S-4767)

Chapter 6

Free Enterprise
•••••••••••••••••••••

Going Public for the Private Enterprise System

Excerpts from Speech
in the Congressional Record
by
Willard C. Butcher, Chief Executive Officer
Chase Manhattan Bank

It is a pleasure to be in Des Moines amid the most efficient and productive agricultural land of the world, and among the many thriving business and financial institutions of mid-America.

I would like to share with you today a major marketing opportunity. If diligently pursued and professionally implemented, it will raise your productivity, supply your energy needs and boost your profits. What's even more important, it will help secure jobs, economic growth and prosperity for all Americans.

I recognize that's a mighty impressive claim. But I am talking about something far more powerful and profound than any chemical or machine. I am suggesting we market an idea—specifically, the idea of private enterprise. Any successful marketing effort requires good timing, and I believe the best time to promote free enterprise is now.

It is the challenge of the business community to help channel growing public discontent with U.S. economic performance into constructive action—proposals for greater capital investment, improved productivity and a return to stable growth— concrete measures that will restore confidence in our system of private enterprise. To succeed we must obtain greater public understanding and active public support.

For two centuries, economic expansion and growth provided increasing numbers of Americans with a better life. Yet, today we hear from a number of different sources that economic growth is unattainable or even undesirable. In essence, many Americans have lost faith in the institutions—the system—and the process that have generated our prosperity.

It is disturbing to see a sizable American movement that advocates surrender and retreat from the major challenge of the day. Instead of seeking new oil, we are told we need to rigidly allocate what oil we already have. Instead of working toward even safer nuclear power, we're told we must abandon nuclear power altogether. Instead of eliminating the disincentives that make it difficult for the small entrepreneur to thrive, we are asked to hobble our most efficient and competitive large companies.

Yet, I don't really believe that you, or I, or for that matter the vast majority of Americans, are prepared to deny our children of tomorrow, the privileges that we enjoy today.

I believe we have one critical task: To go public. We must take our message directly into American homes, to the people—to the ultimate deciders of our society's fate. We need nothing less than a major and sustained effort in the marketplace of ideas. As Judge Learned Hand noted, "Words are not only the keys to persuasion but the triggers of action."

I believe this is a top management concern. Speaking out is a constitutional right under the First Amendment and a duty in our representative democracy. The framers of our Constitution created a system where citizens responsibly, yet aggressively, pursuing their self-interests are what determines the public interest.

Business must have more than a casual commitment to the idea marketplace. Indeed, it seems to me that as individual companies and industries, we have succeeded in carving out our own deserved piece of the "economic pie." What we must now address collectively is preserving the pie itself.

We must apply the same sophistication, discipline, resource commitment and courage in the marketplace of ideas as we apply in the marketplace of products. This implies an obligation to use all the opinion avenues open to us in our democracy: meetings with the media, customers and suppliers; issue advertising; congressional testimony; trips to campuses; and meetings with community groups.

Participation in associations such as the Chamber of Commerce, the American Enterprise Institute and the National Association of Manufacturers. In short, participation in the idea marketplace should be a living, breathing part of everything we do in our everyday business lives.

In the past few years, many large corporations have begun to take a more active and visible role in communicating the private enterprise perspective on a variety of critical public issues. I believe the public has been surprised and generally pleased to see business step forward to defend, report and explain its activities and positions. These efforts, although useful, are only a toe in the water. We will need wider and more sustained efforts.

Small business may not command the same resources as a Chase or Mobil, but it plays an equal, or perhaps even more critical, role in the public arena. The individual entrepreneur enjoys personal contact with his customers, employees, elected officials and fellow citizens in his community. Opinion polls have shown that despite the battering business in general has received, the public holds small business in higher esteem than nearly any other American institution.

The independent businessman is the embodiment of the competitive and entrepreneurial spirit of our country. Reflecting the esteem in which he is held, the small business executive has proven to be highly effective in the halls of Congress.

The media have a major role in reporting and explaining the dynamics of our economy to their audience. This is not a matter of serving as a mouthpiece or even an advocate of business. I recognize that one purpose of a newspaper is to "comfort the afflicted and afflict the comfortable." Yet, the outstanding newspapers of our nation have always served as communicators, interpreters and educators as well as advocates and watchdogs.

While the press has not always been as accurate or fair as it might have been, the fact is that business has not done all that it can to keep the media informed and accurate. And the result, most often, has worked to our detriment.

We can reverse this situation by accepting, as former AT&T Chairman John DeButts once put it, "a sufficient openness to public inquiry—and a sufficient readiness to respond to public challenges." Stated in another way, in the public arena, we must be bold not bland, forceful not fearful, courageous not cowardly, and productive not reactive.

When I travel on business throughout the United States, I make an effort to meet with business and financial writers and editors of the local press. I've found from these visits that the majority of the business press is conscientious and responsible. But they do need information and that's where you and I can play a role. We can't withdraw and whine over biased reporting. We have a right and an obligation to hit back. We must effectively rebut inaccurate or distorted media coverage through letters to the editor, advertisements or other communications. This encourages dialogue.

Communicating the case for private enterprise in the electronic media is a far more difficult task. It's difficult to articulate the complex workings of our economic system within the brief flashes of TV or radio newscasts. But I think we must find new and better ways to use radio and television to communicate our position. Effectively communicating in the electronic media requires preparation, experience and agreement over fair ground rules. It is not easy going before a camera and not all of us may be well-suited to it. But it must be done, professionally and on a regular basis.

Oliver Wendell Holmes Jr. once said, "The best test of truth is the power of the thought to get itself accepted in the competition of the market." We must bring the public into the forefront of the idea marketplace. We must openly and vigorously debate with our opponents the critical issues of our day. We must stand for freedom of the press but insist on a responsible and fair press. We must speak out for the system that we believe safeguards our freedom—generates our prosperity—and provides for the greatest common good. We owe it to ourselves and the enterprises we represent. But far more importantly, we owe it to our children.

Reference: (C.R.2/21/80, Pg. E-719)

Fiber Optics
. . . .
The Synergy and the Future
Excerpts from Speech
in the Congressional Record
by
Reese Schonfeld, President
Opt in America

When I was a young student of the law, I was taught principally by the Socratic method—repeated questioning to pull the truth out of, or pound the truth into, the unsuspecting student.

Using this technique, one of my best law professors made me an offer I couldn't refuse, although later I wish I could have.

He said he would let me give any answer I want. At that point, I thought I had a pretty good deal in the making. But then he stated his condition: as long as he got to phrase the question. And that is where he had me, because both Socrates and my professor knew that he who controls the question controls the show—the answer, the agenda, the outcome.

Unfortunately, in the fiber-to-the-home debate, we are letting someone else control the show, because we are letting them control the questions.

And the questions they have chosen are narrowly framed, trivial and incidental to the real debate. They are saying that the cable-telco struggle is really over who gets to transmit old movies to the American home. It is depicted as a battle for entertainment profits, not technological progress. These are the old and tired ideas.

The fundamental questions are: will America have a great all-purpose network in the 21st Century, and will all Americans have access to it?

This turf-struggle interpretation—unfortunately so common to Washington public policy debates—totally misses the real point about fiber-to-the-home: its incredible potential to affect our lives, values and public services.

The "Batman" rerun debate is a case of the tail wagging the dog. It pits an industry struggle against the real interests of the American people.

You have heard the litany of fiber's capabilities: long distance health care, distance learning, distance shopping, smart buildings, smart houses, smart cities; a whole new range of jobs not restricted by geography; to say nothing of strengthening our values of speech, press and the family.

We are not talking about who is going to bring us "Batman." We are talking about how you and I are going to get medical treatment, education, jobs and all the bits of knowledge and information that it will take to sustain life in the 21st Century.

How will we remain competitive in an increasingly technologically sophisticated world economy? How will we educate our children to prepare them for the 21st Century? How will we care for our increasingly aging population? These are some of the critical questions that must be asked—of the Congress, of the Federal Communications Commission (FCC) and of the American people

The only group that I know of that is really asking those questions is Opt in America, a public interest organization I belong to that is dedicated to bringing fiber optics to the American home.

It is our view that in the history of communications we have come to one of those benchmark times when a truly historic step forward is at hand. I refer to the opportunity to move from a period of scarcity to an era of abundance in video communications.

We have arrived at this stage of our communications development because it is now possible to provide a future of abundant video channels into every American home, thanks to fiber optic technology.

I worked for years to get the phone companies to open their video lines to non-network users, cable and independent stations, and we were eventually successful.

I worked to get the FCC to permit domestic use of satellites, and we were successful there.

Both of these ideas—cable and satellites—turned out to be big ideas, two of the biggest in the history of communications. But what I am describing here is bigger than both of these.

A nationwide public fiber optic network is the next big idea of our time. It is a destiny that this technology suggests and even demands. It is big not just in engineering terms, it is big also because it touches the bedrock of values upon which our nation rests—speech, press and assembly, family cohesion, community problem-solving, how we raise our children and how we spend our old age. This is a clear case where the whole of this technology is much greater than the sum of its parts.

This is because dated federal rules and regulations unnecessarily restrain competition, thereby restricting companies which are ready to install the fiber technology.

We have a $13.8 billion-a-year cable industry based on the scarce availability of a finite number of cable channels. Fiber optics offers a different challenge: not the problem of allocating scarcity, but of managing abundance.

Just as there are no limits now on the number of cameras, VCRs, telephones, televisions or computers that are produced, there will be no practical limits on the number of channels that fiber optics can provide—one-way, two-way, mini-networks, even global networks.

The development of this network is being held back largely by the opposition of the cable industry, which is itself virtually a monopoly in many markets. That industry misperceives fiber optics as a threat to its economic welfare.

They are wrong. With fiber, there are enough channels for everyone, cable and non-cable alike. The opportunity to produce and distribute video information will be there for everyone. This is like candle-makers holding back electricity, or printers holding back copiers.

One measure of a smart industry is its ability to adopt and to turn change to its advantage, not to suppress it.

Has the movie industry died because of television? No, although it once fought television. Today, the studios flourish, in large part because of television.

And this will be the case with fiber optics. Programmers and distributors alike, cable and non-cable alike, will flourish. Fiber is a technology of abundance, not scarcity, and there will be enough to go around for everyone.

Since there is enough to go around, we must see that it does go around. This is another undertaking of Opt in America: to ensure a full and fair and an equal access of all Americans to the benefits of this technology.

A century ago our leaders made a commitment to public health and public education. This century, our leaders made a commitment to public power and public transportation. Now we must make a commitment to public telecommunications, to a public fiber optic network that goes from the inner city to the farm.

We are talking about much more than old movies. We are talking about something on the scale of public education and public power. Indeed, fiber optics is so unique, so powerful, that it deserves a special place in our communication policies.

Twice in my lifetime Congress has favored a technology, and it has worked. They did this with the two big communication ideas of our time: satellites in the 60s—and cable in the 80s.

The technology of the 90s will be fiber optics. Congress should begin by lifting the restrictions on competition for the delivery of video signals to the home. Telephone and other non-cable companies should be allowed to compete. The market would respond dramatically to a most-favored technology policy. When the genius of the American people is combined with the genius of this technology, uses and needs we cannot imagine will emerge.

Let's get on with the job, so history can be made.

Reference: (C.R.. 11/17/89, Pg. S-16114)

Foreign Policy (Europe)

Congressional Views of Europe '92

Excerpts from Speech
in the Congressional Record
by
Hon. Lee H. Hamilton of Indiana

Congress' perspective on the European Community revolves around trade issues. The key issues for members of Congress concern U.S. exports, the trade deficit and the future of U. S. competitiveness.

First, Congress pays attention to the "hot spots" in the world. Places like Nicaragua and El Salvador at that time were more important to members than Brussels, Bonn or Madrid. European integration was simply not a question on the agenda.

Second, because of the enormous internal disputes in the European Community (EC) about the budget and agricultural subsidies, Members frankly doubted at the time whether Europe would make progress on the 1992 plan.

The subsequent pace and intensity of European Community integration caught everyone, including the Europeans, by surprise. Beginning in 1987, members of Congress heard constituents and low-level officials complain that 1992 would hurt U.S. access to European markets.

This crescendo of concern grew through 1988 and early 1989, and became expressed in the phrase "Fortress Europe." The fears of constituents that European Community '92 was protectionist, exclusionary and discriminatory came through load and clear.

Today, there is an acceptance in the Congress that Europe '92 will take place. Members' fears have been partially addressed. They no longer assume that EC '92 means protectionism. But they will want to look carefully at the development of the nearly 300 European Community directives guiding the 1992 process, of which more than half already have been adopted. Access by American high technology firms will be particularly important. For now, the overall attitude in Congress remains one of caution, and wariness.

Today, Members of Congress are watching developments in Europe to see how they will affect the United States and the post-war world as we have known it.

First we realize that the EC is becoming an increasingly important institution and its power will only grow as 1992 draws near.

The EC will play a key role in the new European order. In addition to promoting the process of economic integration, the EC will serve as an all-important anchor in the West for a new unified Germany. It will be a central action in coordinating Western policies toward the newly emerging democracies in Eastern Europe and toward a reforming Soviet Union.

Closer EC coordination in the political and security areas presents a challenge for the United States. Increasingly, the Europeans are consulting among themselves on matters previously left to NATO. In many respects, this process has short-circuited trans-Atlantic cooperation. The U.S. is being brought into key decisions now after the Europeans have decided among themselves what course they will take.

This trend away from NATO coordination is likely to be exacerbated in the current transition to a new security regime in Europe. The nature of this new regime is still uncertain. It may be based on the Conference on Security and Cooperation in Europe (CSCE). It is important that the U.S. take steps to guarantee its role in whatever new security framework emerges.

Second, we recognize that European integration can be a potentially positive-sum game with advantages for the U.S. and for American businessmen. By removing existing barriers to the movement of goods, capital, technology and labor between the 12 EC member-states, Europe '92 should lead to new investment, more jobs and faster growth throughout the EC. In fact, high expectations for 1992 have already produced an investment-led economic boom in the European Community.

As the Community's largest trading partner, the U.S. stands to benefit from this process, too. With 320 million consumers, a unified EC will have the largest single market in the world. If you include the rest of Europe, we are talking about a "European Economic space" of some 500 million generally middle income and well-educated consumers with a total economic output of $6 trillion—twice that of Japan and the four Asian tigers (South Korea, Hong Kong, Singapore and Taiwan) combined.

In addition to greater trade opportunities, European integration holds out the promise of new technology for U.S. firms to acquire. The EC is committed to a strong program of technology development and collaborative research and development. These efforts, combined with corporate research and development performance by European firms fortified with such a strong domestic market, should enrich the international storehouse of technology on which all of us can draw.

Third, there is a growing uneasiness in the Congress that the U.S. is being left behind in Eastern Europe. The West Europeans, led by the Federal Republic of Germany, are moving aggressively to take the initiative in Eastern Europe.

German, French, Italian and British businessmen and bankers, building on historic ties between their countries and the East, are pursuing joint ventures and extending new credits in East Germany, Hungary and Czechoslovakia. The perception is that U.S. firms have been slow to follow and that the U.S. has lagged behind its European allies in offering trade and investment incentives to companies interested in doing business in the East.

Fourth, we are focusing attention on the impact of German reunification on the European Community and the EC '92 program. There is some danger that Bonn's new focus on the East will slow the pace of European integration. Such a development would not be in the U.S. interest. European integration must keep pace with the process of German unification. In recent weeks, this has become a tall order, because of the accelerating pace of change in the Germanies. We are already beginning to see the jitters that German unity can give its neighbors. Unity within an integrated EC will be a key to future stability in Europe.

Fifth, we note the issue of the future depth and breadth of the European Community and the importance to the United States of how this question is resolved.

As the major economic force on the continent, Brussels will serve as a magnet for all countries on the continent interested in trade. The neutral countries and the emerging democracies in the East are already setting their domestic economic agendas to Brussels' tune. Austria and Turkey have applications for EC membership pending, and Hungary, Czechoslovakia and Poland are likely to be close behind.

The European Community has not yet decided how it will proceed on these applications. For the time being, Brussels has said there will be no more expansion until after 1992. But the pressure to open its doors to new members will only build in the coming months or years.

Sixth, we are aware that the new developments in Europe are shifting U.S. relationships with our European allies. There is a growing recognition within the Administration of the need to work more closely with Brussels on political, as well as economic, matters. In addition, the pace of developments in Germany has increased the urgency of close U.S. cooperation with Bonn.

While knowledge of the EC and opinions about it vary, most of us in Congress had genuine concerns about the impact Europe '92 will have on American firms. Let me give you a flavor:

The EC's standard-setting process does not allow sufficient participation by U.S. exporters. For example, the EC mandated a battery cable standard for forklift trucks to which only European manufactured cables were able to conform.

Government procurement rules favor EC products and services in certain sectors. As a result, U.S. exporters of telecommunications and electrical equipment cannot sell to European governments.

Local content requirements may result in American movies and television programs being taken off the air, to reserve program time for "European works."

Approval to market biotechnology products may involve a "fourth hurdle," in addition to the normal criteria of safety, efficacy and quality. This fourth hurdle would take into account whether the product would cause economic harm to segments of the European society, such as small farmers, that have received special concessions from national governments.

To many members of Congress, these practices appear to add up to fairly strong encouragement that U.S. firms manufacture in Europe.

Congress is less worried about large American multinationals. Most members believe that the giants of American industry are well-positioned to benefit from a single market. But we are concerned that exporters—particularly small and medium-sized firms—could be hurt by a change in the rules. Until their access to European markets and technology is assured, Congress will remain skeptical.

Congress is also concerned about U.S. policy toward the EC. The sweeping changes in Eastern Europe as well as the EC have underscored the need to update our own governments policies and priorities for a world in which economic strength is increasingly more important to our nation's security than military strength.

We are concern about the inadequacy of resources assigned to EC '92. The U.S. Trade Representative has only one person assigned to the U.S. mission in Brussels; the Treasury and Commerce departments have no one. Because of this staff structure, we rely heavily on U.S. multinational companies for economic intelligence and information. Their information is important but the private interests of these U.S. multinationals may diverge from United States national economic interests, including the interest of U.S.-based exporters.

We also suffer from a common problem of who's in charge. On any given issue, it's often not clear who's in charge. Fragmentation of executive authority leads to turf battles. This tension between departments may be unavoidable and even healthy.

But it reflects the lack of overall direction from the Administration concerning Europe '92. Those of us in Congress don't know whom to call on E.C. policy. Industry officials, perhaps more than congressmen, have been frustrated by this problem.

Finally, we are concerned with the dominance of military interests over economic interests. In the case of EC '92, many embers are concerned that the U.S. is not getting the leverage it should from the Memoranda of Understandings (MOVs) that the Department of Defense maintains with European nations. Although these MOVs are the major bargaining chip we have in the EC '92 negotiations, DOD has been unwilling to let our U.S. Trade Representative use these as a bargaining tool.

Congress is watching EC '92 developments carefully and members are concerned. My own view is that the U.S. has benefited from the past expansion of the European Community. These benefits have not been automatic, however. We were vigilant in the mid-70s and again in 1981, and our vigilance was met with success in the form of trade barriers lower than they otherwise would have been. We need to approach Europe '92 with the same vigilance.

Reference: (C.R. 3/19/90 Pg. E-707)

Foreign Trade
· · · · · · · · · · · · · · · · · · · ·
2001: A Trade Odyssey
Excerpts from Speech
in the Congressional Record
by
U.S. Trade Representative Carla Hills

I want you to take a short journey into the not too distant future. The date: January 1, 2001. The place: Dallas. You are president of a manufacturing firm with 100 employees, annual sales of $15 million and big problems. That's because your company did very badly last year. You finally gave up trying to market your products in Europe and the Pacific Rim; there was just too much protectionism, too many trade barriers. You were forced to lay off a third of your employees and take a huge write-off on new equipment you purchased in anticipation of the extra business, which now sits idle.

Then some of your most important product designs were stolen by a gray marketeer in India who is making cheap knockoffs and is selling them in our markets. You spent $1 million in legal fees trying to stop it, but now your lawyers tell you that there is nothing you can do about it.

Is it you? Are you such a bad manager? No, your other friends in business are telling similar horror stories. So you wonder: How did things ever get this bad? What went wrong? When did it start? Who's to blame?

It all began in 1990 when, after four years of hard-nosed negotiating in Geneva, the United States was unable to get its trading partners to agree to sweeping new rules for the General Agreement on Tariffs and Trade or GATT.

Funny, but you had never heard of GATT until recently. Just the other day the newspaper did a story about the decline of world trade in the decade since the GATT's demise. The writer said that for the latter half of the 20th Century, the GATT was the most important trade agreement, involving nearly 100 countries and covering better than 80 percent of world trade.

You learned that after the GATT was signed in 1947, seven successful rounds of tariff cuts by the world's great trading nations permitted trade to soar from $60 billion to break the $3 trillion mark in 1990. As a result the global economy grew faster in those 40 years than in any four decades of world history.

But 1990 was a turning point for the GATT. World trade had outgrown the rules that had served so well for so long. Areas inadequately covered by GATT rules, like agriculture, or not covered at all, like services, investment, and intellectual property, had taken on much greater importance in global trade.

To make matters worse, many developing countries claimed exemptions from the rules already in place. No longer at the margin of the trading system, they accounted for half a trillion dollars in trade.

Thus in 1990, more than $1 trillion in goods and services was not adequately covered by internationally agreed rules of fair play. That trillion dollars of trade, in industries vital to America's future prosperity, amounted to a third of world commerce.

That was why the U.S. pushed hard to launch the new round of GATT talks in 1986, and why President Bush made the successful conclusion of the GATT negotiations in December 1990, America's No. 1 priority.

That is why President Bush, who fervently believes in the economic and social benefits that flow from open markets, has us in a full-court press in our trade negotiations around the world. Our orders from the President: unlock once-sealed markets so that trade can expand, and negotiate a clear set of enforceable rules that will curb unfair trade practices.

We seek to implement that policy in three ways:

First and foremost, we are laboring very hard to achieve a successful conclusion of the current round of international trade talks on-going under the auspices of the GATT. We believe that a good agreement could transform an aging trading system of international trade rules into a passport for free trade.

Second, we are conducting market-opening negotiations with our key trading partners. These negotiations cover the entire range of American enterprise—from avocados to zincography.

Lastly, we are using our own trade laws to pry open the markets of recalcitrant nations.

As I said, a successful completion of the Gatt talks in Geneva is our first priority. We seek to:

• Expand market access for trade in goods, achieve fundamental reform of agriculture, cut the $72 billion of income lost annually from world protection of agricultural markets.

• Rein in the hundreds of billions of dollars of trade-distorting government subsidies with which governments bribe the market instead of letting entrepreneurs win share on the basis of price and quality.

• Create a swift and effective means to resolve our trade disputes.

• Ensure that the rules that we have and those that we are negotiating apply to developing countries, and finally

• Develop equitable rules for the new areas of services, investment and intellectual property.

Opening markets will benefit all business, but particularly small businesses, which now account for 20 percent of our exports and create four out of five new jobs.

Improving protection of our intellectual property will shield our producers of fine chemicals, pharmaceuticals, films and textbooks from the $60 billion theft of their basic know-how that occurs each year.

Eliminating the protectionist policies that exist worldwide in agriculture will put $11 billion in the pockets of American farmers—that's an extra $3,400 for each and every one of them.

The vision underlying all these efforts is our belief in the benefits that will come from an integrated global trading order.

We see the negotiations under GATT and our talks with individual nations as an important force to maximize each nation's prosperity and security, while broadening and strengthening its economic ties to the world.

A solid agreement coming out of this round of GATT talks can be the unifying for integration from Budapest to Brasilia. Only through such an agreement will each nation alone, and the world as a whole, gain the assurance that can come from a strong set of fair and enforceable global trade rules.

If we can achieve a solid agreement, then we could enthusiastically concur with those who suggest that we go beyond the current round of the GATT and create a new institution to govern our trading system—a World Trade Organization.

For a World Trade Organization to succeed it will require the confidence of all it serves that it will safeguard their national interests. We believe that such confidence will be inspired if ember nations know that they can rely upon clear and enforceable rules.

Some may view this new organization with apprehension. Indeed any further elaboration will require close consultation with our trading partners, as well as with Congress and American industry. But, I challenge anyone to name a single country that has been economically dominated through free trade.

Furthermore, a World Trade Organization could be a positive vehicle for cooperation between the United States, Europe and Japan by keeping trade channels open and thus aiding the growth and progress of both the developed and the developing world. It could also enable smaller countries, who fear that the world is fissioning into trade blocs, to find a forum for raising issues of concern.

A successful GATT agreement can fuel the engine of growth for the 21st Century; a World Trade Organization could be the engineer who helps keep the throttle wide open.

I began today with an ominous trip into the future. Let me take you on a more pleasant one. Again, the year is 2001, and the place is Dallas.

You are feeling good. You are the chairman of the board of a large manufacturer. Last year, your 1,000 employees could barely keep up with the orders from your sales reps in Tokyo, Brasilia, Berlin, Moscow and Warsaw, your Delhi office was able to swiftly stop a knockoff manufacturer from making cheap imitations of your hottest product by using new intellectual property rules negotiated in 1990 at the GATT talks. And, your accounting department says sales look like they are going to top $150 million for the first time.

1990 is a pivotal year for the world economy. Down one path lie open markets, expanded trade, economic growth and prosperity. Down the other lie closed markets, nations turned inward and gravely diminished prosperity for all.

You and I need to heighten public awareness that the rules we are negotiating in the GATT to curb unfair trade practices and to open markets mean more revenues for our industries and more jobs for our people.

So when you leave here, talk to your suppliers, buyers, employees, friends and neighbors. Ask them to urge their Congressmen and Senators to support our positions sat the GATT trade talks. Tell them that open markets mean revenues for our industries and more jobs for our people.

And if GATT sounds too much like jargon, tell them that it means Growth, Access and Free Trade Today. That is good for America.

Reference: (C.R. 4/19/90 Pg. H-1596)

Foreign Relations

Relations Between United States and Canada

Excerpts from Speech
in the Congressional Record
by
Hon. Brian Mulroney
Prime Minister of Canada

I come here today to celebrate the historic friendship between Canada and the United States. On the border between our two countries, there are no fences and no barricades; there are no soldiers and no arms. That 5,000-mile frontier, spanning a continent between two oceans, is, of itself, a remarkable historical fact. It symbolizes neighborliness between two free and peace-loving nations. It signifies leadership not only in the conduct of our bilateral relations, but for the international community as a whole.

History requires us to provide for our common security on the North American continent, through NORAD and in the NATO alliance. Geography obliges us to preserve and protect our environment, to pass on intact to future generations what providence and our forebears have so generously bequeathed to us. Economics and geography together present us with a unique opportunity to further enhance our prosperity through trade. We begin from a common heritage of democratic traditions and a common defense of liberty.

There are reminders of that—from the trenches of one war to the beaches of the next—places inscribed in the history of valor where Canadians and Americans have stood together, where Canadians and Americans have died together, in the defense of freedom. Canadians and Americans can and always will be proud of their commitment to democracy and freedom.

As we made common cause in two world wars and in Korea, so do our young men and women now stand the first watch of liberty in Western Europe. In peacetime, as in war, the United States and Canada have shouldered and shared heavy burdens in our common commitment to freedom. Together, we have maintained our presence in Europe for two generations, at considerable expense to both nations. The importance of our defense capabilities now lies not so much in projecting power as in deterring war. The INF agreement, which has the full support of Canada and all NATO members, addresses the collective security of East and West, not just the United States and the Soviet Union; ultimately, it deals with the survival of the human race. Canada, more than many countries, and Canadians, perhaps more than many peoples, are aware of the somber of nuclear realities of our world. For we live in the shadow of nuclear arms, situated as we are directly between the world's superpowers.

We live between the two superpowers, but did not and we do not see them as morally equivalent in any way. The United States is a bulwark of democracy, a beacon of liberty. The United States and its NATO allies stand for freedom; they exemplify human rights and individual dignity.

We are two independent nations, each with its own national interests and unique character. You have one official language; we have two. Your system of government is congressional, our is parliamentary. Neither of our countries is without its inequities nor its imperfections. But we are, each in our own way, building caring societies that give our citizens remarkable opportunities for education and employment, enabling them and our countries to make dramatic social and economic progress. We each have sovereign interests to assert, national interests to uphold. And we can have different views of the world, just as we have different responsibilities in the world.

It is fashionable in some circles to suggest that America is growing weary of its role in the world. The evidence to the contrary is all about you—in the Silicon Valley of California, in the Sun Belt of the South, in your great agricultural heartland, in the new high technology corridor of the Northeast, in the towers of Manhattan and throughout this splendid capital.

The world still looks to America not only as a model of liberty, but as a source of persuasive international leadership. The world counts as well on the strength and independence of this Congress, a legislature of unprecedented influence and capacity for good, which has endured for over 200 years and which stands proudly as a cornerstone of this impressive democracy.

Our common democratic values and our shared commitment to defend them is but one worthy example of neighborliness and leadership. The protection of our environment is another. As President Reagan has said:

"Our two countries should work together on all matters of environment, because entrusted to us is the care of a very unique and a very beautiful continent and all of us share the desire to protect this for generations of Canadians and Americans yet to come."

For more than 75 years, since the creation of the International Joint Commission, the United States and Canada have demonstrated both sensitivity and effectiveness in environmental protection and wildlife conservation. The flow of nature is rarely constrained by boundaries. The Canadian goose winters in the United States—and the American bald eagle nests in the forests and soars in the skies of British Columbia.

In the newly updated agreement signed by our two countries last November, we agreed not only on the nature of toxic wastes that have polluted the Great Lakes, but on a process for action to restore them.

Together, the United States and Canada are taking the first steps to arrest the deterioration of the ozone layer that shields the Earth from the most damaging effects of the sun. The Montreal Accord is but one example not only of what we can achieve together, but of leadership for the world.

This is not to say that there are not issues of great moment between us, you are aware of Canada's grave concerns on acid rain. In Canada, acid rain has already killed nearly 15,000 lakes, another 150,000 are being damaged and a further 150,000 are threatened. Many salmon-bearing rivers in Nova Scotia no longer support the species. Prime agriculture land and important sections of our majestic forests are receiving excessive amounts of acid rain.

We are doing everything we can to clean up our own act. But you know that is only half the solution—because the other half of our acid rain comes across the border, directly from the United States, falling upon our forests, killing our lakes and soiling our cities.

The one thing that acid rain does not do is discriminate. It is despoiling your environment as inexorably as it is ours. It is damaging your environment from Michigan to Maine, and threatens marine life on the eastern seaboard.

It is a rapidly escalating ecological tragedy in this country as well as ours. Just imagine the damage to your tourism and recreation, to timber stands and fishing streams, to your precious heritage—if this is not stopped.

We acknowledge responsibility for some of the acid rain that falls in the United States, and by the time our program reaches projected targets, our export of acid rain to the United States will have been cut by an amount in excess of 50 percent. We ask noting more than this from you.

We invite the Administration, and the leadership of Congress, to conclude an accord whereby we agree on a schedule and targets for reducing acid rain that crosses our border. I will admit without hesitation that the cost of reducing acid rain is substantial, but the cost of inaction is greater still.

Canada will continue to press fully its case to rid our common environment of this blight—and we shall persevere until our skies regain their purity and our rains recover the gentleness that gives life to our forests and streams, and we hope the United States Congress and the American people will respond in exactly the same manner.

In terms of resources, Canada plays a major role in the world. With the seventh largest economy in the free world, Canada has had, since 1984, the strongest growth rate of the economic summit countries. We are the world's largest exporter of metals and lumber, the world's second largest exporter of wheat, and we supply fully one-third of the world's newsprint. Canada and the United States conduct vital energy trade—Canada is your most important foreign supplier of oil, gas and electricity.

The Free Trade Agreement presents our two countries with an historic opportunity to create new jobs and enduring prosperity. The agreement is not everything either side would have wanted, but as Franklin Roosevelt once observed: "Nations are co-equals, and therefore any treaty must represent compromise."

We stand at the threshold of a great new opportunity for all our citizens. This is more than simply a commercial agreement between two countries. The Free Trade Agreement for you and for me is a call to excellence. It is a summons to our two peoples to respond to the challenge of comparative advantage in the 21st Century.

Mr. Speaker, Mr. Vice President and members of the Congress, succeeding generations of Americans have known the wisdom of the philosopher Ralph Waldo Emerson, who wrote: "The way to have a friend is to be one."

Our two peoples, our two countries, have met that test in the past. We do so today, and I know that we shall in the future. I am confident—there is not the slightest doubt in my mind—that the relationship between Canada and the United States of America, we will know difficulties, we will know moments of strain, we will know moments of crisis and tension, but there is not the slightest doubt in my mind that rooted as we are in fundamental values and democratic traditions that this relationship will always be, as Winston Churchill described it more than a half century ago, "an example to every country, and a pattern for the future of the world."

Reference: (C.R.4/27/88, Pg. 2620)

A Vision for the West Ascendant

Excerpts from Speech
in the Congressional Record
by
Margaret Thatcher
Former British Prime Minister

We have before us today the opportunities created by two great victories: President Reagan's victory over communism in the Cold War and President Bush's victory over aggression in the Gulf.

Both those victories were hard won. They required courage, the vision to see what was possible when others could not, and the persistence to fight through to a full and final conclusion.

Very few leaders possess that combination of qualities. But in the Gulf War, President Bush has showed leadership of the very highest order.

He built a grand coalition of 28 allies; he assembled overwhelming force from around the world; he gave full backing to a brilliant military concept which produced one of the greatest feats of arms with the fewest casualties in history; and he helped lay the foundations of future stability in the region.

But that victory was not won solely in the last six months. It was the culmination of a decade's achievement. The military buildup of the 1980s. The recovery of America's and the West's self-confidence. Through technological advance that created the Patriot missile and the Apache attack helicopter. And the revival of our economies that made these miracles possible.

It is difficult today to conjure up the despairing and defeatist atmosphere of the post-Vietnam '70s. But in those days, the West was on the decline and the defensive. Our defenses were neglected. The Soviet Union steadily reinforced its military superiority. Our allies felt abandoned.

In the battle of ideas we had all but ceased to aim at furthering freedom and had settled for containing communism. We knew we had lost time, lost nerve and lost ground.

So, as the 1980s began, we in the United States and Britain set out in a new direction.

We wrestled with the challenge of reviving our economies. We rebuilt our shattered defenses. We faced up to the threat of a Soviet empire at the peak of its military might.

We made it clear that arms control would proceed on the basis of genuine equality of weaponry between East and West—or not at all. The Soviet Union built up its SS-20s. We deployed cruise and Pershing missiles. The result—the first-ever agreement to reduce nuclear weapons.

When the Soviet Union said that Germany could only be united if it left NATO, President Bush and I stayed firm. The result, a reunified Germany fully within NATO.

At home we liberated enterprise and cut taxes, producing higher living standards, more jobs and the spread of ownership. Capitalism made our peoples prosperous at home and enabled us to feed the hungry abroad. Socialism, by contrast, proved the road to poverty and serfdom.

As Eastern Europe emerges from the darkness, the truth is now fully known, and told even by communists:

• Behind the statistics boasting of bumper crops, food rotted.

• As economic growth rates soared on paper, people queued for hours to buy goods that a Western supermarket couldn't even give away.

• As five-year plan followed five-year plan, command economies turned out products that no one wanted to buy and created an environment in which no one wanted to live.

But the world was strangely reluctant to observe these factors.

In the decade of the 80s, Western values were placed in the crucible and they emerged with greater unity and strength. So much of the credit goes to President Reagan. The world owes him an enormous debt and it saddens me that there are some who refuse to acknowledge his achievement. For the whole world has changed.

The Cold War was won without a shot being fired. Eastern Europe regained its freedom; its people elected democratic governments and they announced their intentions to leave the Warsaw Pact.

The Berlin Wall came down, and Germany was reunited within NATO. A weakened Soviet Union was compelled by the West's economic and military competition to reform itself; a new, more realistic and clear-sighted leadership came to the top.

Glasnost was launched, perestroika was started and we saw the beginning of democratic politics.

And the United States once again became the pre-eminent power in the world. These are great and, for the most part, beneficial changes. A new world means new problems and the need for new approaches. How do we deal with the crisis in the Soviet Union?

How do we reshape NATO in the post-Cold War world? How do we preserve and strengthen the economic foundations of the Western Alliance? How do we defend Western interests elsewhere and extend stability beyond the West in the aftermath of the Gulf War?

In my view, we shall tackle all these problems more effectively by the tested policy of Western unity based on the firm United States leadership of sovereign nations in alliance.

But not every change in recent months has been for the better. In the Soviet Union there is evidence that progress toward reform has been slowed, possibly halted. Dark forces of reaction are on the rise.

How do you persuade people brainwashed by egalitarian propaganda for years that inequities are the side effect of rising prosperity for all? How do you tell them that higher living standards can only be attained at the short-term price of higher unemployment? And how do you do any of this while the demoted bureaucrats, the discredited politicians and all those who flourished under totalitarian mediocrity are out to undermine everything you do?

I am often asked: Can we do business with Mr. Gorbachev? We should not underestimate the future reforming zeal of a man who allowed Eastern Europe to grasp its freedom; who has begun the withdrawal of Soviet troops; and who cut support for communist insurgencies across the world. We have to go on doing business with him. In the same way, he has to do business with the democratic reformers if he is to succeed.

So what kind of reform should we be seeking for these people who have rejected a false ideology but have not yet learned the ways of freedom?

Any assistance to the Soviet Union must be granted only in response to practical economic reforms. We must encourage the dispersal of power from Moscow to the republics.

Second, we have to stress to the Soviets just how essential private property is to freedom. History teaches that human rights will not long survive without property rights; nor will prosperity be achieved without them.

Nor is freedom secure without independent courts and a rule of law. We must also draw the Soviet Union closer to the institutions of the international trading and payments system. Associating the Soviet economy more closely with these, will, over time, help to transform that economy internally. Their rules will help promote sound money, competition and genuine trade. No economy will prosper if it is strangled by regulations and bureaucrats.

There are signs that the Soviet Union is failing to fulfill either the letter or the spirit of the terms of the treaty for reduction of conventional forces in Europe. And there are signs of pressure from the Soviet military to reassert its position.

Moreover, the re-emergence of tension and uncertainty on Europe's eastern border ought to remind NATO's continental European members both that international dangers can rarely be predicted and that sustained commitment is necessary to deal with them.

We must never forget that it is NATO—because it is a strong defense which underpins that peace with freedom and justice that we in the West enjoy and now have the opportunity to extend to others.

NATO has been a great success. We should be wary of creating new institutions to replace or complement its unique and indispensable role. Perhaps the most extraordinary suggestion is that the disunity and halfheartedness of most European nations during the Gulf crisis demonstrated the need for a united European foreign and defense policy. A new structure, even if it were necessary, can never be a substitute for will.

For many years, successive American governments believed that progress toward a United States of Europe would relieve America of the burden of defending freedom. That hope turned out to be greatly exaggerated. This kind of geopolitical strategy should be regarded with the greatest skepticism. If a European superstate were to be forged, it would almost certainly develop interests and attitudes at variance with those of America. We would move from a stable international order with the United States in the lead to a more dangerous world of new competing power blocs. This would be in no one's interest, least of all America's.

So NATO must remain the principal defense organization of the West. Instead of seeking to supplant it, we should aim to adopt and extend it to meet the challenges of the post-Cold War world.

Our first step should be to enlarge its political role. This great trans-Atlantic partnership should not confine itself to matters of defense but should extend its discussions into other political and economic areas. This would be of benefit to countries on both sides of the Atlantic.

Second, those Eastern European countries which have left the Warsaw Pact should be given a new, special status in NATO—something short of full membership but well beyond mere observer status.

Third, I believe NATO's role should be extended to threats which are out-of-area. There is no guarantee that threats to our security will stop at some imaginary line. With the spread of sophisticated weapons and of military technology to areas like the Middle East, potential threats to NATO territory may originate from outside Europe.

By the year 2000, more than two dozen developing nations will have ballistic missiles, 15 of those countries will have the scientific skills to make their own, and half of them either have or are near to getting nuclear capability as well. Thirty countries will have chemical weapons and 10 will be able to deploy biological weapons.

This means that NATO countries, under America's leadership, must be in a position to deter aggression by these countries and, if it occurs, to make a swift and devastating response.

But no less important is the second means—the maintenance of world prosperity, founded upon an open system of free trade. And if there are risks to our security, the risks today to the open trading system are just as great.

Let us remember that the West's post-war prosperity could never have been achieved without the orderly framework of free trade provided by the GATT (General Agreement on Tariffs and Trade). But the dangers to free trade are now greater than for 40 years. And paradoxically, they have been increased by the end of the Cold War.

It would be a tragedy if the GATT talks were to fail because the United States, the Cairns Group and the European Community could not reach an agreement on cutting farm subsidies. We cannot expect the Third World to agree to what the West wants—

protecting the intellectual property rights and liberalizing services—when we deprive them of their main export market, agricultural commodities, and hence of the funds to improve and diversify their economies.

The stakes are high. If GATT should fail, we would gradually drift into a world of three powerful protectionist trade blocs—based on America, Europe and Japan—engaged in mutually destructive trade wars. That would not only threaten world prosperity, but it could also damage the common sympathy vital to defense ties across the Atlantic.

The Gulf War is now over and we are working to build a secure and lasting peace. I believe that six items among others must be on our agenda for peace in the Middle East.

First, the Gulf must be protected as an international seaway.

Second, military equipment and supplies may need to be prepositioned in the area, both to deter aggression and to enable rapid deployment of Western troops should that deterrent fail.

Third, arrangements must be made to safeguard the security of Kuwait.

Fourth, there is the question of biological, chemical and nuclear weapons. We must be satisfied by observation that Iraq's have been destroyed.

Fifth, countries which engage in aggression should not be allowed freely and quickly to build up their military strength.

Finally, there is the Palestinian question, so long encased in suspicion and hostility. It can only be tackled by direct negotiation with the representatives of the Palestinian people.

Today, I have suggested how to create or adapt political structures for prosperity and peace—in NATO, in the GATT, in the Soviet Union, in Europe and in the United Nations. But true statesmanship in a free country must be measured by more than that. It requires an unswerving commitment to make the sovereignty of justice prevail. It requires an ability to inspire others with the rightness of a cause. It requires strong arms and great hearts.

We look to America for these things. And we do not look in vain. After victory in the Cold War and in the Gulf, we face a still nobler task—to advance the reign of freedom and free enterprise throughout the world. It is now—more than ever—America's destiny, supported by her faithful friends—and no friends are truer than her friends in Britain—to press ahead with that endeavor.

In the words of President Abraham Lincoln: "Let us strive on to finish the work we are in."

Reference: (C.R. 3/14/91, Pg. S-3313)

Germany—The New Economic Challenge

Excerpts from Speech
in the Congressional Record
by
Congressman Robert G. Torricelli

A month ago a speech on Europe could have been titled "Europe, Germany and the Next Century." We aren't talking about the next century anymore; we are talking about tomorrow. Things are moving so fast it's almost impossible to provide an accurate analysis.

Americans were surprised when they turned on their televisions the evening of November 9 and saw people walking and celebrating atop the Berlin Wall. But the seeds of change had long been there, sown in the fertile ground of the dynamic West German economy. Before the Berlin Wall crumbled, we saw Europe only in terms of 1992 and the consolidation of the European Community. In discussions about global economic challenges, the focus was solely on Japan.

The importance of economic development in Europe has been building for years. However, they were slow to be recognized and were overshadowed by seemingly more dramatic changes along the Pacific Rim. The changes in Europe have been driven by a re-emergence of West German economic power and the rise of West German technology. As we were watching issues in other places and thinking about other things, our vision of West Germany remained fixed by images of the Berlin airlift and a divided, weakened country. That vision has been transformed before our eyes, West Germany now has nearly a $1.5 trillion economy, the third largest market economy in the world.

West Germany today presents an entirely new set of facts. New patterns are developing in the political and economic relationship between the United States and West Germany. The British and the French have maintained their traditional roles of debating about how the European Community would be structured, its central bank, currency, trade policy and other points, but the balance of power seems to be shifting to Bonn.

We think of the European Community as a great combination of states. In fact, its structure is similar to that which analysts ascribe to OPEC. OPEC in many ways functions as a cover for Saudi policy. Germany, in turn, may soon occupy the same position in the Economic Community. Given West Germany's predominant economic position, and the remarkable opportunities available to it because of events in the Soviet Union, its ascendancy is clear.

The mix of mounting West German economic power, new feelings of self-confidence, a generational shift in power, and the opening provided by the Soviet Union gives us a set of facts which raise some very interesting questions.

What is not sufficiently understood is how well West Germany is itself positioned to take advantage of the fluid European situation. First, there is an enormous economic opportunity opening up for West Germany that is not being sufficiently discussed.

People in Washington and New York are talking about the West German role in the Economic Community acknowledging that Germany will be making decisions for the EC in the 1990s. But that misses a crucial point! What happens now that the Soviets are reducing their financial responsibility for Eastern Europe? Gas may not flow at the same prices, currencies may not be supported, products may not be purchased, and aid may not be provided. An enormous and historic vacuum has been created unlike anything we have seen since the end of the war. An entire sphere of influence is now open.

This is not to suggest that strong Soviet interests won't remain, including a military presence. But somebody is going to make up the economic difference. Consider what happened when China was opened. That policy was determined by American diplomatic and military security needs, but it opened the world's largest potential market. At the time, we failed to anticipate that the Japanese would take advantage of this new market.

A similar situation is now taking place in Eastern Europe. A market with a combined economy of nearly $1 trillion is now opening up in the Eastern European states, and that may be expanding into the Soviet Union. This isn't simply a question of what will happen, but how much has already happened. German exports to Poland are $1.6 billion, compared to the United States' $304 million; German exports to Hungary are $1.5 billion, U.S. exports to Hungary are $78 million; German exports to Czechoslovakia are $1.5 billion, those of the U.S. are $55 million. The West German economic sphere of influence has now opened in Eastern Europe.

West Germany, therefore, has not only taken control of new markets, it has provided substantial aid to the countries in those markets. In addition, it has begun to integrate Western and Eastern infrastructures. Almost unnoticed a few months ago, the electric power grids of West Germany, East Germany and Czechoslovakia were partially joined. In the next few years, natural gas for homes and factories will flow through West Germany. These factors assure that West Germany is extremely well placed to capture an obvious and enormous market.

Finally, German economic influence has spread beyond Eastern Europe. West Germany has a $6 billion, one-way relationship with the Soviet Union. West Germany provides the USSR with its largest western trading partner, its principal access to Western technology, its biggest provider of industrial credits—more than every other Western nation combined—and its largest Western investor.

West Germany can use this leverage to promote reunification and to reverse political attitudes in Moscow. The leverage that Germany has is not simply on East Germany alone. It is far greater.

It is interesting to note the variety of questions that these issues provoke. Do borders move to meet people or do people move to meet borders? What of the millions of Germans who live in areas now that are designated as the Soviet Union? What of the several million ethnic Germans living within the borders of Czechoslovakia or Poland. All of this obviously raises far more questions than answers, but that is typical of this year.

In fact, 1989 will long be remembered as one of the most extraordinary years of this century. As suggested earlier, there isn't a great deal about these changes that the United States can alter. Decisions made in Moscow will probably be more important than decisions made in Washington, and decisions made in Bonn will perhaps be more important than decisions made in either. But these decisions will redefine the world in which the United States operates and will dramatically change the challenges we face, both militarily and, perhaps even more fundamentally, economically.

In these changed circumstances, the United States has a basic choice to make. Germany will provide a challenge for the American economy and future equal to the Japanese challenge. The West Germans are saving money at four times the rate of Americans, and their students are testing among the third and fourth highest in the world, while American students rank 18th.

Germany has decided upon a structure of government and private industry, a trade policy, and a philosophy of export promotion that have served it well. Germany might now be on the road to having the one advantage that it has not possessed in the past—a market, or potential market, as large or larger than that of the United States.

The issue for Americans is to understand the challenge of the multipolar economic competition in the next century and meet it. Someone recently said that the Second World War was really no more than an interruption of the economic ascendancy of the Japanese and the Germans. That is proving to be true.

Reference: (C.R. 11/21/89, Pg. E-3998)

Relations Between the U.S. and Ireland and Northern Ireland

Excerpts from Speech
in the Congressional Record
by
Former Ambassador Sean Donlon

I congratulate those involved in setting up the Washington/Baltimore Chapter of the University College Dublin Graduate Association. It not only serves the obvious functions of supporting (UCD) and providing an attractive social platform but, hopefully ,it will also serve in some way to keep Irish graduates and others here in the United States in closer contact with Ireland and what is happening there.

While the ties between Ireland and the United States and particularly those between Ireland and Irish America are very close, we cannot assume to understand one another unless we make an attempt to keep in regular contact. Even those of you who have been in this country for, say, 20 years must now regard yourselves in some measure as being out of touch with what is happening in Ireland. I say this particularly because I think all of us, even those of us who live in Ireland, underestimate the pace as well as the nature of change in Ireland today. Let me illustrate what I mean by drawing attention to some haphazardly selected developments in the fields of population, education, the economy and the Northern Ireland situation.

In 1954, a commission established by the Irish government to report on emigration projected that the population of the Republic of Ireland in the 1990s would, at best, be two and a half million. In fact, it is just over three and a half million. Even with the current relatively high figure of emigration again, our population continues to grow but not necessarily conforming to patterns of previous generations.

For example, 50 years ago only 30 percent of the population of Ireland lived in urban areas. Today's figure is about 60 percent—not very far short of the United States' figure of 65 percent. Another interesting development relates to the age of marriage. Up to 1977, the average marriage age in Ireland continued to drop. Since then, however, it has come back up again and the average age of marriage is now close to what it was in the mid 1950s. The birth rate, however, is much higher but, significantly, fully 10 percent of all births in Ireland are now extramarital. This compares with a figure of 1.6 percent as recently as 1960.

In relation to education, let me draw attention to two interesting statistics. First, five years ago, almost no Irish Leaving Certificate student contemplated going to Britain for third level education (college). Of the 52,000 who did their Leaving Certificates in Ireland three months ago, 15,000 applied for places in British third level institutions and, while obviously most of those 15,000 did not end up registering in British third level institutions, quite a significant number did. Twenty years ago, 80 percent of those who took third level education did so at universities. Today the figure is less than 40 percent. The majority of our third level students are now at institutions such as the nine regional technical colleges and other institutions. Relatively speaking, the universities are less popular than they used to be.

An important instrument of change in Ireland remains, of course, the development of the economy. As with most economic development, there is good news and bad news but, in general, it is fair to say that the Irish economy is back on a healthy track and continues to grow at an impressive rate. Public spending is being brought under control. The balance of payments is in surplus. Exports will exceed imports by almost two thousand million Irish pounds this year. Inflation and interest rates continue to fall even when the international trend is otherwise. The major distressing statistic is that relating to unemployment which remains at 18 percent.

The Irish economy is, however, very different from the one we knew 30 years ago. In 1958, we exported a mere 17 percent of everything we manufactured in Ireland. The figure today is 66 percent. The Irish economy is now driven not by Irish market demand but by the demands of the world market. Every major Irish company is now more heavily dependent on its external activities than on its domestic activities.

Another indication of change is in the agricultural sector. As recently as the 1960s, 380,000 people worked on farms. The figure today is 190,000 and it continues to drop. Since we joined the EC (Economic Community) in 1973, l00,000 people have left farming and a recent forecast suggests that within the next ten years, a further 45,000 will also leave.

Perhaps the most dramatic change that is taking place relates to the Northern Ireland situation. Obviously, it is not an area of change which lends itself to agreed analysis and many Irish people would dispute elements of my analysis. Before commenting on change, however, let me remind you of one set of figures which we should never forget and on which we are all agreed—the number of fatal and non-fatal casualties in Northern Ireland over the past 17 years is now just over 2700 dead and 25,000 maimed. To put that in a historical Irish context, the 1916 Easter Rising was brought to an end by its leaders to avoid further bloodshed when just over 400 people had lost their lives. And, in the subsequent war of Irish independence, the total number of fatalities was about 750. I sometimes feel that outside of the immediate area of Northern Ireland, there is not enough consciousness of the extent of death and destruction.

That level of violence in Northern Ireland and our general reaction to it has obviously had an impact. On the one hand it has widened and made it enormously more difficult to bridge the gulf between Nationalists and Unionists within Northern Ireland. It has, I believe, also inhibited the development of a relationship based on respect by the Unionists, who make up one million of the Northern Ireland population and the rest of us who live on the island of Ireland.

Clearly, we have a long way to go, but I think it is accurate to say that we have embarked on the road of change. The major change is that in the 1985 Hillsborough Agreement the British government has declared that, if in the future a majority of the people of Northern Ireland clearly wish and formally consent to a United Ireland, the British Government will introduce at Westminister legislation to give effect to that wish. Simply translated, the British no longer have a vested interest in Ireland. It is now up to us who live in Ireland, Nationalist and Unionist, to come to terms. As I will explain in a moment, the burden of change so far has impacted on Unionists and has created some pain for them. As we look ahead we should not underestimate or hesitate to accept that our own attitudes as Irish Nationalists may also have to undergo some change, some of which may be painful.

Three times in the last 16 years Unionists have had change forced on them. In 1972, their corrupt and selfish 50 years of one-party rule was brought to an end when London was forced to rule Northern Ireland directly.

In 1974, a short-lived set of arrangements under the Sunningdale Agreement brought on the one hand Unionists and Nationalists together in a government in Northern Ireland and on the other hand North and South together in a proposed Council of Ireland. The failure of British will in the face of Unionist industrial action brought that arrangement to an abrupt end.

The third change forced on Unionists was in 1985 when the Anglo Irish Agreement, signed at Hillsborough, gave to the Irish government for the first time an internationally recognized role in relation to the affairs of Northern Ireland. The Hillsborough Agreement has had a very big impact on the situation, not because of anything it has done to improve the position of Nationalists in Northern Ireland but because of the impact it has made on Unionists' consciousness.

Unionists have been forced to re-evaluate their relationship with the British government, with the Irish government and with the Nationalist community in Northern Ireland. Obviously, the full consequences of this process have not yet emerged. Those of us who are in the Irish Nationalist tradition can afford to be generous. Let us show our generosity sooner rather than later.

All of these changes taking place in Ireland are difficult enough for those of us who live in Ireland to understand and absorb fully. How much more difficult it must be for people living outside Ireland to keep abreast.

There are times when external assistance is badly needed and I have no doubt that the constructive role played by successive United States Administrations in recent years has been an important element in bringing the British and Irish governments together to bring about the limited progress that has been achieved. I am also satisfied that the generous dollar contributions by the United States to the International Fund for Ireland is making an important contribution to economic and social development in particularly deprived areas of Northern Ireland and along the border.

These external influences can in the last analysis be constructive and sustained only by informed leadership role here in the U.S. of people such as yourselves. Long may your interest be maintained and our efforts rewarded.

Reference: (C.R.4/5/89, Pg. S-3314)

United States and Japan: Relationship at a Crossroads
Excerpts from Speech
in the Congressional Record
by
Senator John D. Rockefeller
United States Senate

Ambassador Mike Mansfield is fond of describing the relationship between the United States and Japan as "the most important bilateral relationship in the world, bar none." Today, I would like to talk about that relationship, which stands at a dangerous crossroads.

In many respects, the relationship has never been stronger. Japan is one of our key allies in the world and plays a vital role in the Western Alliance. A strong, democratic, stable and friendly Japan forms the basis of our strategic and geopolitical policy in Asia. Military cooperation has never been better.

Japan, at our urging, has started to reach out to the world politically. The number of people moving between our countries—students, tourists, businessmen, scholars— is at an all-time high. More Americans today study Japan and learn Japanese than ever before.

There is no shortage of admiration in this country for what Japan has accomplished.

We buy superb Japanese products in abundance, study the Japanese education system, and try to learn from Japan's management techniques. Most Americans recognize that in a world economy, it is natural that Hitachi and Toyota would come to do business in the United States, just as IBM and Schick went to Japan decades ago. Virtually all our states see Japanese investment as a catalyst for economic growth and job creation, rather than as a threat.

Yet at the same time, tempers are rising on both sides of the Pacific. In a very real sense, the relationship faces a crisis.

Here in the United States, when Fujitsu threatened to acquire Fairchild Semiconductor, a hue and cry was heard that a major company in the critical semi-conductor industry was being taken over by foreigners—even though Fairchild was already owned by a French firm! Anger about Japan's closed market and a one-sided trading relationship is probably the principal force driving the trade legislation through Congress. The number of Americans who defined U.S.-Japan relations as friendly declined by 13 percentage points in a single year.

In Japan, there is increasing anger at what are perceived to be American "demands" on Japan: for market access; for more yen evaluation; for a restructured economy; for more defense spending—demands that frequently change, but never end. More dangerously, one finds a widespread belief that the U.S. is using Japan as a scapegoat for our growing economic impotence and the inability to face up to our problems.

It is worth remembering that our trade problems with Japan are not new. We last ran a bilateral merchandise trade surplus with Japan in 1964. In 1971, our $4 billion trade deficit with Japan constituted enough of a threat to our economy to cause President Nixon to devalue the dollar and abandon the gold standard. Japan's economic system and its effect on trade have troubled us for many years. But until recently, those concerns stayed below the surface. In my view, this was the heritage of the Cold War. After China went Communist in 1949, and the Korean War erupted in 1950, it became American policy that a strong, free Japan was absolutely vital to our national security. Through the leadership of Douglas MacArthur, we rebuilt Japan as surely as we rebuilt Europe through the Marshall Plan. If anything, what was accomplished by Japan was more miraculous: with no democratic traditions, a modern, democratic, free industrial giant emerged.

Times—and conditions—have changed radically. Japan is no longer the "weak sister" of the Western Alliance; instead, it is the second largest economy in the world. Fueled by capital earned from trade surplus, Japan is now the world's leader in many industries and technologies, and is making heavy investments in the science and technology needed to build future world leadership.

What Japan has accomplished is truly an economic miracle; a tribute to what a nation can do by tapping the talents and energies of its people, driven by a sense of urgency and national commitment. If every nation behaved as Japan has—maximizing exports, minimizing imports, practicing what amounts to mercantilism—the international system would have collapsed years ago. Moreover, the U.S.-Japan relationship has been essentially one-sided, lacking reciprocity in almost every area, from products and services to the flow of scientific and technical information.

The truth is that Japan is still an essentially closed market. While many in Japan deny that serious barriers to trade exist, the facts suggest the contrary. We are not alone in our inability to crack the Japanese market. The sale of 170,000 Hyundai Excels in the United States last year versus fewer than a dozen sold in Japan reminds us that virtually every major trading company is stymied by Japan's trade barriers. Korea, Taiwan, the ASEAN nations, and the European Community all share our problems with access to the Japanese market.

As long as Japan approaches world trade in a totally unbalanced manner, the rising tempers in this country, reflected in the mood of Congress, are just beginning.

Increased animosity toward Japan around the world is one consequence; the anti-Japan aspects of the trade bill are another. If the world falls into a spiral of protectionism and retaliation, Japan will bear a large part of the blame. Japan will also be one of the principal victims of any protectionist wars, given its continued great dependence on the export market.

There are many in Japan who understand the changes that must take place. The Maekawa Commission, appointed by Prime Minister Nakasone, spelled out a clear and unmistakably sound blueprint for opening the Japanese economy to the products of the world, and restructuring the economy to depend more on domestic growth, and less on export-driven growth.

The commission's recommendations included changes to promote housing construction and stabilize land prices; tax cuts to increase disposable income; a shorter work week; more money for infrastructure developmen; improved conditions for foreign investment in Japan; and strict enforcement of the antitrust laws.

But the Japanese political system prevents far-sighted leaders from implementing the changes they know must be made. As long as the Liberal Democratic Party, which dominates Japanese politics, derives disproportionate financial support from the construction industry, Kansai Airport is likely to stay off limits to American companies that have built superb airports all over the world. As long as the Liberal Democratic Party politicians derive disproportionate votes from agricultural districts, land around Tokyo will remain stunningly scarce and staggering costly, while Japanese consumers pay five or ten times the world's food prices.

Some of the changes Japan must make require a reversal of patterns that extend back 40 years; others relate to the habits and customs of a century or more. However, change is in the air. But change may not spread as quickly as the fissures in our relationship. That has been the dangerous reality to date.

The Japanese system does not have the ambivalence about government intervention in the economy as our's does. Politicians like to talk, demanding "a level playing field" in trade, but given how much our approach to trade and industrial questions differs from Japan's, it is worth asking if we are even playing the same game.

I see no alternative than to exert sustained pressure on Japan to change. Not because their system is unfair, but because it is inappropriate given the size of their economy, level of development and responsibility they must assume in the international system. We need true reciprocity and equivalent access to their markets; if their market does not open, we really will have no choice but to deny access to ours.

If the closed nature of the Japanese economy poses a threat to the international trading system, so does the American budget deficit. If Japan is guilty of exporting too much and importing too little, we are surely guilty of exporting too little and importing too much. If Japan has saved too much and consumed too little, we have saved too little and consumed too much. No amount of changing by Japan—or beating on Japan—will strengthen our schools, retrain our workers or rebuild our factories.

Lastly, both countries must not lose sight of the overriding importance of the relationship, and an economic and political interdependency that makes solving problems jointly essential.

Our frustration with our trading partners, particularly Japan, must always be tempered by the reality that they are indeed partners, not adversaries. The new interdependence in the world economy will not disappear—it is a permanent fixture. We need to handle our problems with Japan without tearing the fabric of an international system that is stretched to the breaking point.

The size of our economies gives the United States and Japan a special opportunity and a special responsibility. Together, our nations represent 35 percent of the world's GNP, 32 percent of the exports of the industrialized countries and fully 45 percent of all the foreign aid provided bilaterally to the third world. We will deal with debt crisis, avoid global recession and accelerate world economic growth together through cooperation and coordinated action—or not at all.

Reference (C.R. 10/21/87, Pg. S-14756)

Relations Between the U.S. and the Soviet Union

Excerpts from Speech
in the Congressional Record
by
Hon. Bill Bradley
United States Senate

In 1985 you are Mikhail Gorbachev and you become the Secretary General. You looked out at your country and you saw the following things: you saw a country where the infant mortality rate and the adult mortality rate were rising. You saw a primitive health system where hospitals routinely reused needles and bandages. "The Soviet physician today is a soldier armed with a bow and arrow, and it is not within his power to fight against complex diseases" said a leading Russian doctor last year. You saw water supply systems no better than many developing countries. For example, 13 percent of the deaths in the Soviet Union were caused by bad water.

You saw a corrupt system at the core. Corrupt not only in terms of criminality, which was rampant, but corrupt in the sense that people believed it would not deliver a better life for themselves and their families.

You looked out and saw a society that had a massive need for capital: in agriculture, in industry, in energy development, in the consumer sector and of course in the military.

After surveying the state of your nation, you decided that unless there were dramatic changes, you would remain a second rate economic power in the 21st Century. You might even become a second rate military power. So you embarked on a course which would either destroy you or make you the most significant Soviet leader since Lenin.

I believe Gorbachev has decided to take the risk. I believe he has decided that leading a society that is falling behind and dominated by the military was not enough. He has instituted massive reforms characterized by three words: perestroika, glasnost and democratization.

Perestroika means economic decentralization: taking power away from the central bureaucracy in Moscow and giving it to the enterprise managers in the field. It means letting prices reflect true costs. It means paying workers based on effort and production.

What do these changes imply for the average Soviet citizen? They imply much higher prices for everything from bread to housing. They also imply much less job security. In the last 18 months, 130,000 workers in the railroad sector in the Soviet economy have lost their jobs.

How can this leadership keep support if the result of perestroika is going to be higher prices and less job security? Soviet reformers give you several very clear answers. One way to keep the population on board is to give them more and better housing. In two of the last three years, Gorbachev increased the housing targets contained in the five-year plan. By 2000, everyone is supposed to have an apartment.

Second, they say they are going to provide better quality food. As a friend of mine in the Soviet Union said, "What we need is more fruit, vegetables and meat being brought to the market."

They have established truck cooperatives and a variety of other mechanisms to achieve that objective. But they have not reformed agricultural production by dismantling collectives, the way the Chinese have.

Third, if you do have a job, you may be making more money. Some workers have said they are making 30 to 40 percent more this year.

So in order to keep the average citizen on board in support of perestroika, you expect to offer better food, better housing, higher wages and, fourth, more leisure time activity. As for people who lose their jobs in the overmanned industrial sectors, they are supposed to be moved into the service sector where many cooperative small business activities, ranging from coffee houses to dry cleaners, will be established.

Finally, glasnost helps keep support for perestroika. Now it is very important to understand what glasnost is and what it is not. Glasnost is not freedom of speech guaranteed as a right under the law as we know it. Glasnost is permission to speak. Permission granted because Gorbachev and the reformers know that without more and easier information flow, without debate and criticism, the economy cannot hope to improve much.

So in order to keep people on board for perestroika, for the higher prices to come and for the lessened job security, Gorbachev is planning on better housing, better quality food, higher wages, more leisure time activity and glasnost.

The question is will perestroika work? Last winter after spending two hours with the head of the price commission and with any number of economists, I concluded they haven't thought it through. They have not yet confronted the need for the price system to reflect supply and demand as well as cost.

They also have not thought through the labor mobility problem caused by industries shedding workers. They have not designed the worker retraining or relocation polices. They haven't figured out how they're going to do joint ventures. They haven't begun to offer foreign companies terms and conditions that are competitive with investment opportunities elsewhere. Foreign ownership is limited to a minority share. Rights to hire and fire do not exist. Prices are set arbitrarily. Even office space and housing require special approval. In short, every detail must be negotiated.

And who are the real opponents of perestroika? They are the bureaucrats who want to keep their jobs. The plan is to cut the bureaucracies in Moscow by 50 percent. They are the privateers, the people who illegally obtain goods and sell them on the black market. They are the workers who don't work. There is a saying, "We pretend to work and you pretend to pay us." And finally, they are the local party officials. Under peristroika, the local party leader has less responsibility for economic decisions.

So what are the odds of success? What does that mean to us? What are the implications for the West? The main implication is that economic criteria could become more influential in allocating the resources of the Soviet Union: its labor output, energy, capital, land and skills.

The military and the security folks in the Soviet Union receive a disproportionate amount of resources. They do so, they argue, because they need it to protect the Soviet citizens from external threats. Until now, they have succeeded in that argument. But the capital and investment that follows to the military in the Soviet Union is capital not available for agriculture or energy or health care. Moreover, the Soviet Union does not have need for such a large conventional army in central Europe. Third world adventures and selling weapons that are never paid for do not serve Soviet economic interests, and the Soviet's new attitude toward Afghanistan is but one example that they may be beginning to recognize that.

If the internal logic of perestroika works as I have described it, we can expect the Soviets to propose dramatic reductions in conventional forces in Europe and to withdraw from various third world adventures, not only Afghanistan.

How should we relate to the Soviets on economics? To begin, I think we should be who we are. We are cold, calculating capitalists who maximize profit, and that is how we should relate to the Soviet Union. We have an unprecedented opportunity, because the Soviets are now more receptive than ever before. Gorbachev knows he is in trouble and is prepared to take bold initiatives. But to capitalize on this opportunity, the United States must see it clearly and not mistake it for more than it is.

The United States must forge a common, as well as a clear, view of this strategic opening with the leading economic powers of the West, namely Japan and Germany. We should look at an investment in or trade with the Soviet Union and apply the same criteria we would apply to an investment in New Jersey or Belgium or Brazil.

By being national capitalists, we will do the most to promote reform in the Soviet Union by clearly identifying for them what it takes to be part of the dynamic world economic system. Above all this means the Soviets must level with the West, and also their own people. A complete accounting of the civilian and military uses of the Soviet gross national product, valued at its true cost, will be necessary for the normalization of East-West economic relations. In this way, we will give the reformers in the Soviet Union the greatest leverage to implement the reforms that they know must be achieved if they are to use Western trade and technology effectively.

So on the military side, perestroika challenges Americans to remain strong and to look for opportunities to reduce arms together with the Soviet Union. On the economic side, perestroika challenges us to remember who we are. But there is another challenge. Perestroika challenges us to remember what we believe about human rights and freedom.

When I was in Russia last January, I asked some Soviets what they liked about the United States. They said, "We like the standard of living, the freedom, America's stand for human rights."

I asked, "What don't you like about the United States?" They said, "The existence of homelessness, joblessness and crime."

So when we think about Gorbachev and the challenge perestroika poses for us, we can't just think about it in terms of military challenges or economic challenges. We have to think about it as a challenge to the United States to live up to our own ideals and to make sure that the charges of homelessness and joblessness and violence are no longer valid. It is our obligation to address those problems so that we can look Gorbachev in the eye, as well as ourselves in the mirror, and say, "We are a special society."

Reference: (C.R. 5/27/88, Pg. S-7115)

The Democracy Movement in Mainland China

Excerpts from Speech
in the Congressional Record
by
Dr. Shaw Yu-Ming
Director General of the Government Information Office
of the Republic of China in Taiwan

I am truly impressed and honored that so many of you found the time to attend this gathering and discuss issues relating to China.

You all know about the shocking events that took place in mainland China in early June; the Chinese Communists mobilized tanks, armored personnel carriers and other weapons to massacre unarmed students and others who were demonstrating peacefully in Tiananmen Square in Peking. This was a rare tragedy in the history of mankind, in which a government massacred its own people. As news of the incident spread, the world responded with rage and condemnation, and the international news media launched an unbridled attack against the Chinese Communists' brutal actions. Chinese both at home and abroad have through this incident not only reached a consensus to do away with the Chinese Communist regime, but have also achieved a high degree of solidarity based on shared nationalistic feeling. This has profound and far-reaching historical significance.

Regarding the reasons behind this democracy movement on the mainland, there is no doubt that the political corruption, cultural isolation and economic backwardness accumulated over 40 years of Communist rule has resulted in a high level of popular dissatisfaction. This has caused a feeling of disillusionment and hopelessness in mainland youth, students and intellectuals, those most sensitive and attuned to events, those with the sharpest sense of justice and mission, to the point where they were ready to risk their own lives for what they believed in. But there was also another important reason; they were influenced by Taiwan's success story and by the Republic of China's open policy toward the Chinese mainland. Taiwan's success story has been disseminated across the mainland and was one of the motivating factors behind the mainland democracy movement.

The mainland democracy movement was launched by youths and students. To avoid giving the Communist authorities an excuse for suppression, they staged sit-ins and hunger strikes to win the support and sympathy of the general population and the people of other countries. Throughout the whole process, they did not use slogans voicing opposition to communism or socialism. They had good reason to stage such a mature and restrained demonstration. In 1956, Mao Tse-tung launched the so-called "Hundred Flowers" campaign, whose slogan was "Let the hundred flowers bloom, and the hundred schools of thought contend." Mao used this campaign to get those with anti-communist sentiments to spill out their true feelings so that they could be readily identified and dealt with in one blow. They believed the "promises" of the Chinese

Communists that those who spoke out would not be incriminated, and that what they said would be received as constructive criticism. Soon after, however, these intellectuals went from being "fresh flowers" to "poisonous weeds" and were subsequently purged.

This is why students in this democracy movement attempted to use the most peaceful methods possible, and avoid the possibility of trumped-up charges against them. Ultimately, however, they did not escape the Chinese Communists' purging of dissidents through brutal suppression. For 40 years, the greatest tragedy of mainland China's intellectuals has been how they have repeatedly been the offerings sacrificed on mainland China's political altar, and how they have been unable to realize their ambitions and goals.

I personally believe that this student democratic movement can be considered a revolution to overthrow the Communist system, and that it is not an effort at reform within the Communist system. Although those demonstrating in mainland China did not call for the overthrow of the Chinese Communists, in no case did they voice support for the Chinese Communists. It is reasonable to assume that the true demands of the students and others in mainland China are in fact the same as the mainland Chinese living abroad, namely, to overthrow the Chinese Communist dictatorship. Thus, this is a revolutionary movement outside of the Communist system and that is the reason why the Chinese Communists had to suppress it with heavy weapons, something the Chinese Communists openly admit.

Some people in other countries, as well as some overseas Chinese, have expressed that the statements issued and actions taken by the government of the Republic of China (ROC) on Taiwan during the period of the democratic movement came too late and were not strong enough. I would like to respond to this. The ROC has from the beginning followed this movement closely and studied various counter strategies. However, in order to avoid giving the Chinese Communists a pretext to suppress the movement and bring harm to the mainland Chinese students and others, we had to take an extremely cautious attitude. For this reason, our government did not make its first formal statement until May 21, one day after the Chinese Communists declared martial law in Peking and sent in troops. Our government initiated a series of measures to support the Mainland Chinese Democracy Movement. These measures included using every means available to break through the Chinese Communist blackout on news regarding the Tiananmen massacre, providing aid in kind for mainland Chinese students and scholars presently in foreign countries who have been deprived of their passports or stipends due to their anti-communist activities.

The ROC government's mainland policy will proceed as in the past, continuing to disseminate the "Taiwan Experience" under the premise of protecting our national security. It is our hope to use Taiwan's model of development as a basis for our goal of eventually achieving China's reunification under a free and democratic system with an equitable distribution of wealth.

I believe that, in the wake of the Tiananmen massacre, the Chinese Communists' "four modernizations" program faces a very gloomy future. When the Chinese

Communists declared over a decade ago that they could "realize the modernization of agriculture, industry, national defense, and science and technology within this century," the ROC government pointed out that the basic condition for the realization of the "four modernizations" was political democratization. Without it, the Chinese Communists would never be more than an oppressive, tyrannical regime. Without the cooperation and support of the intellectuals and other angry souls, along with the tightening of foreign investment and technology transfers, plus the nearly unanimous contempt and implementation of sanctions toward the Chinese Communist regime by foreign governments, we can safety predict that the future of the "four modernizations" is a dismal one, and the victory the ruling stratum has now temporarily claimed for itself will in the end be reversed.

When at critical moments in history Chinese people come to a consensus and resolution in their thinking and actions, the common wishes of the people will be realized. In 1905, for example, when Sun Yat-sen founded the Revolutionary Alliance, a predecessor of the Kuomintang in Tokyo, Chinese intellectuals in China and abroad resolved to overthrow the Manchu government. Seven years later, the Manchu government was overthrown and the Republic of China established. Again in 1919, Peking's students and intellectuals made up their minds to bring down the northern warlords. Nine years later Generalissimo Chiang Kai-shek led a successful campaign against the warlords, and set up the National Government in Nanking. When the Japanese militarists invaded China in 1937, they incurred the hatred of all the people. Eight years later China was victorious in the Sino-Japanese War.

Chinese in Mainland China, Taiwan, Hong Kong, Macao, the United States, Canada, Europe and the Asian-Pacific have all, in the wake of the Tiananmen massacre, come to a consensus, namely, to do away with the Communist Chinese tyranny. Based on historical experience, I personally believe that through the efforts of all the Chinese people, China will eventually be reunited under a free and democratic system.

As I mentioned earlier, the democracy movement in mainland China traces its beginnings to the "Hundred Flowers" movement of 1956, after which the democracy movement continued an unbroken development, wave by wave. Another climax in this movement that occurred before the Peking massacre was the Tiananmen incident of April 5, 1976, when students and scholars from all over China expressed their resolution to fight the fascist Communist Chinese regime to the bitter end.

The Chinese Communist revolution has devoured its own children, but it has also produced countless fighters who have vowed to fight to their deaths to overthrow the Chinese Communist tyranny. The future history of China will be written by these heroic fights, and democracy will in the end conquer tyranny.

I believe that because both the American and Chinese people possess countless fighters like these, democracy has a brilliant future ahead of it. Let us all salute our fighters for democracy.

Reference: (C.R. 8/4/89 Pg. E-2858)

Chapter 7

Geography
· · · · · · · · · · · · · ·

National Gallup Geography Test
Excerpts from Speech
in the Congressional Record
by
Gilbert M. Grosvenor, President
National Geographic Society

The humorist S. J. Perelman once told of a conversation he had with a young lady in which he suggested she take a trip around the world. "Oh I know," said the young lady, "but there are so many other places I want to see first."

Yet that sort of ignorance is not just the domain of humorists. There is a shocking lack of geographic knowledge in this country.

It's a good thing our ancestors found their way to America, because 24 million American adults, one in seven, can't even find the United States on a map of the world.

It's fortunate our pioneer fathers and mothers knew the way west across the prairies and the deserts and over the mountains, because 43 million American adults, three in ten, couldn't follow N.S.E.W. directions on a map. Yet, 70 percent of these same people assert that map-reading skills are essential—a higher percentage than the same people placed on the importance of writing a business letter or using a calculator.

These are but a few of the findings from an international survey conducted for the National Geographic Society by the Gallup organization. We believe this survey is the most comprehensive study ever done of adult geographic knowledge.

The television network anchors will find this hard to believe, yet approximately one out of two Americans could not even locate South Africa on a world map.

At one time we could afford insular thinking. Distance and vast oceans protected us. Yet these natural protections mean nothing in the age of ICBMs, satellite television and computerized money transfers across continents. National boundaries mean nothing in the age of holes in the ozone, the greenhouse effect and nuclear accidents.

We're part of a global village. We're all interconnected. We all share the same world, not only environmentally but economically.

Clearly this nation wishes to be a major player in the future decision-making process. If we are to be influential in resolving atmospheric and ocean pollution, deforestation, global hunger, nuclear arms control, population balance—and a whole host of other issues, we must be geographically literate. Gone are the days when American dollars could override international ignorance.

A professor at the Wharton School of Business said during October's stock-market crash, "This is one financial world today." Well, it's one economic world in all sorts of ways.

Consider world trade. I was in Jordan a few weeks ago when I spotted an open van full of boxes of fruits and vegetables. I was interested in what was written on those boxes so I jumped up on the truck. I found onions and avocados from Spain, bananas from the Windward Islands, Honduras and Belize, strawberries from Kenya, fruit from Cyprus, tomatoes from the Netherlands, grapes and pears from South Africa—nothing from the United States. After reading the Gallup Poll, I'm not surprised. Twenty percent of Americans could not name a single country in Europe!

We face an increasingly competitive world. Europe is preparing for a revolution in how it functions in terms of trade. By the end of 1992, all border barriers and other impediments to the flow of people, goods, services and money among the 12 nations of the European Economic Community are scheduled to fall. If this happens it will create the world's largest single market with a greater gross national product (GNP), greater number of consumers and greater economic clout than the United States.

Americans apparently don't carefully follow current events. Take the Persian Gulf. Our ships have been attacked, and we have lost men. Tensions are so high we accidentally shot down an Iranian passenger jet. And yet three out of four Americans cannot identify the Persian Gulf on a map.

The same geographic ignorance abounds at home. We have experienced a disastrous drought in the American farm belt, but would you believe that one-half of our adult population can't find Illinois on a map.

Ladies and gentlemen, geographic ignorance has dire consequences. Our adult population, especially our young adults, do not understand the world at a time in our history when we face a critical economic need to understand foreign consumers, marketers, customs, opportunities and responsibilities. If we don't understand place and location, then the consequences of events lose meaning. Many Americans don't even know where they themselves are. And as I have often said, if you don't know where you are, you're nowhere.

One in four Americans could not find the Pacific Ocean. Now that's 33 percent of the planet's surface. Earth's combined land masses would comfortably float within the boundaries of the Pacific Ocean.

Yet we must know these people inhabiting the Pacific Rim. New Zealand, Australia, the Philippines, China, Taiwan, Korea, Japan—just to name a few—wield tremendous economic clout. To increase our trade, we must understand those who are to buy our products.

Bankers don't like to hear this, but any decent economic geographer could have warned bankers that those massive loans to the Third World were gravely at risk. Most of these countries don't generate enough harvestable natural resources to pay off the interest on these loans, much less support a reasonable repayment schedule. Let me say again: geographic ignorance has dire consequences.

Let's turn to the flip side of geographic knowledge. I am reminded of Governor Lamar Alexander's spectacular success in promoting Tennessee as an ideal environment for Japanese investment. How did he do it? He sold the very thorough Japanese Mission Autosearch Committee on Tennessee's geography. He preached central location, easy access by sea, rail and interstate highway networks; stable labor force, favorable climate; excellent local engineering schools; available land and water resources; and favorable economic conditions. The Governor steeped himself in Japanese culture and business practices. He consulted at length with Ambassador Mike Mansfield about trade, business and cultural factors that are important to Japan. Pure geography!

Our competition understands the world much better than we do. Internationally, the Swedes scored higher than anyone else; over 90 percent of them said they had taken at least one class in school devoted exclusively to geography. Only 25 percent of our students have had a geography course in elementary, junior or senior high school. When you compare American adults generally to adults in other countries surveyed, we are in the bottom one-third. In the nine nation standings, Sweden is No. 1; followed by West Germany; then Japan, France and Canada lumped together; then Great Britain and the USA; followed by Italy and Mexico.

We've heard why Johnny can't read, why Johnny can't add. The reason why Johnny doesn't know where he is, is very simple. Geography simply isn't taught in the schools any more.

Charles Kuralt once said, "Thanks to the Interstate Highway System, it is now possible to travel from coast to coast without seeing anything." And really, that's what geography became—a bland monotonous blur of memorized names and places.

We cannot allow the planet to be a blur to our people. The world is too dangerous, too competitive, too immediate a place. We at the National Geographic Society are throwing everything we have into the fight against geographic illiteracy because we believe this country's future depends upon it. We are putting our reputation, our money, our relevancy on the line.

We are committed to restoring geography to the American classroom. Here's how:

(1) Create a public awareness. The President's page in the magazine, which reaches 40 million readers each month, will carry periodic accounts of our programs and the progress to solve the problem.

We must create a dialogue with the American people, elected officials, educators, and parents, stressing the importance of teaching geography in our K-12 schools.

(2) An intensive and aggressive training of our geography and social studies teachers in every state. Teachers are the key—the heart—of our effort. I have great confidence in the ability of our teachers to respond, but they need our support nationally. We are establishing regional alliances throughout the country on university campuses

(3) We are building—or funding others to build—creative, modern, high-tech,

visually driven curricula materials. For example: (a) the National Geographic Kids Network, a $5 million equally funded project with NSF working with TERC (Technical Education Research Center) in Boston; (b) an exciting joint project with Apple Computer, Lucas Films and National Geographic Society; and (c) a well-funded research program to develop laser disc capability.

After six years of work, we will soon publish the first atlas of United States history from a geographic perspective to be published in 50 years. It's full of wonderful maps, photographs, artists' renderings. As one way to show our commitment to the effort of geographic literacy, today we are also announcing that we are sending a copy of this atlas at no cost to 35,000 public, private and parochial schools across the United States. A $1 million National Geographic Centennial gift to our nation's schools.

The purpose of education is to prepare our children for the world, to give them perspectives in which to view the world and to participate successfully in it. I don't believe we are currently doing that. As today's survey results indicate, we've already lost a good number of young adults to geographic illiteracy. They lack knowledge and curiosity about the world. This is limiting to personal fulfillment and national progress. I grew up in a family that has been associated with the National Geographic Society since its founding. Geography was the adventure of exotic locations, the mystery of ancient excavations, the thrill of an African plain bursting with wildlife.

Konrad Adenauer once said, "We all live under the same sky, but we don't all have the same horizons." Ladies and gentlemen, America's children must have the broadest horizons possible.

Reference: (C.R. 7/28/88, Pg. S-10318)

Gun Control
• • • • • • • • • • • • • • • •

Why the Police Need Handgun Control
Excerpts from Speech
in the Congressional Record
by
Patrick V. Murphy, President
The Police Foundation

I appreciate the invitation to be with you tonight. I had the privilege to serve for more than 20 years as a member of the New York Police Department and those years have given me many wonderful memories.

Memories of the valor, decency and dedication of the vast majority of New York police officers. Memories of thousands of instances over the years when citizens like yourselves gave their police department cooperation and support.

Memories of the tremendous opportunities for growth and advancement which the New York City Police Department provides.

But all my memories of service in policing here are not happy ones. The worst memory concerns 11 brave and dedicated men, sworn officers of our Department. In one year, as police commissioner, I helped bury them. They were felled by handguns.

Those police officers believed in the dignity and worth of their fellow citizens. I sometimes wonder if a good number of their fellow citizens reciprocate in that belief.

I am not speaking solely of the assailants of those officers and the hundreds of other officers who have been attacked with handguns throughout the years. I refer also to those millions of citizens who claim that they have the so-called right to enjoy the indiscriminate possession of unregistered handguns.

The minority of Americans who lobby against gun control demean the memory of police officers slain with handguns. No one can claim to support the police and oppose handgun control, because the continuing, uncontrolled proliferation of handguns in America makes the police officer's job increasingly dangerous and stressful. The danger lies in the ever-increasing possession of handguns by citizens who use them in law-breaking or in conflicts with others or under the influence of drugs or alcohol.

No police officer wants to use the revolver. Police officers are sworn to protect life, not take it. But the tidal wave of handguns engulfing American society contributes to situations where officers may have to use deadly force.

The perverse disregard for the police of handgun advocates has reached an incredible extreme. Gun advocates are fighting legislation at the state and federal levels which would ban the sale and possession of armor-piercing handgun bullets. These armor-piercing bullets are made with hard steel or brass and usually have a teflon or plastic coating. They have penetration power five times as great as that of lead bullets.

This penetration power means they easily can pierce bullet-proof vests which, I am sad to say, many police officers are forced to wear. The gun lobby's string of victories over the last few years has led to the wild proliferation of handguns on the nation's streets and in its homes—to the extent that police officers, like medieval warriors, must wear special armor, the bullet-proof vest.

On Capitol Hill, proposals to ban the manufacture, sale and distribution of armor-piercing bullets have been introduced with the support of conservative and liberal congressmen alike.

It appears that at least 52 senators and 120 members of the House have co-sponsored the McClure-Volkmer Gun Decontrol Act. The effect of this Act would be to make the already tough work of law enforcement all the more difficult.

The legislation would effectively repeal existing federal gun control laws. First, the prohibition on mail-order gun sales would be lifted. Next, anyone, not just federally licensed dealers as is now the case, could make interstate gun sales.

Third, the term "gun dealer" would be redefined in such a way that anyone could sell handguns without keeping a record of gun sales. Finally, some local and state laws concerning gun commerce would be nullified in a way that would pre-empt state and local laws prohibiting the carrying of guns.

What does this mean for the police?

For one thing, the successful work of the Bureau of Alcohol, Tobacco and Firearms in tracing guns used in crimes would be undermined.

Thus, it would become more difficult for local police and prosecutors to detect and convict offenders in crimes involving guns.

It would be even easier for the criminals and the unstable to obtain guns, thereby increasing the number of gun crimes with which the police must deal.

In short, the proposed legislation would enhance opportunities for Americans to blow each other away and kill and wound the police if they try to intercede.

I have emphasized for a reason the effects on police of the lack of effective gun control laws and of the attempt to repeal the laws we have. I have emphasized the police because the gun lobby seeks to pose as a valiant friend of law enforcement and as its concerned ally in the fight to control crime. You know the slogans:

"When guns are outlawed, only outlaws will have guns."

"Control criminal, not guns."

"Without handguns, citizen will be defenseless."

Actually, police officers will tell you that all too frequently guns are what otherwise law-abiding citizens use in fits of passion or drunkenness or derangement to kill others or themselves, thereby literally becoming outlaws.

As for "controlling criminals, not guns," guns are the principal weapons that give street criminals the sense of warped empowerment which encourages muggings, rape and other violent crime.

As to the notion that "without handguns, citizens will be defenseless," the police know that the handgun in the innocent citizen's nightstand is many more times likely to be used accidentally or in suicide or in family or other disputes than in defense against intruders. The same gun in the nightstand is also one of the most frequently sought-after prizes of the burglar.

To summarize: There is no valid law enforcement reason to justify the position of the gun lobby. Guns possessed by citizens for reasons of self-protection are far more dangerous to themselves, their loved ones and neighbors, than to criminals.

Further, the easy availability of handguns poses a continuing threat to the police and to the goal of safe streets and neighborhoods.

Thus, it is clear that those citizens interested in the welfare and success of their police are the ones who support gun control efforts. They are the citizens with a true dedication to law and order—a very useful descriptive phase which deserves rehabilitation.

For the police, law and order is a phrase describing their mandate to control crime and maintain order, two goals of every civilized society.

In my opinion, Americans who champion gun control champion law and order. They are the real allies of police.

At a minimum, Americans interested in law and order should support legislation that:

• Bars the sale and manufacture of Saturday Night Specials;

• Requires a 21-day waiting period and background check for handgun purchases;

• Requires mandatory jail sentences of at least two years for using a handgun in the commission of a felony;

• Tightens restrictions on handgun dealers and manufacturers; and

• Limits the number of handguns a person may purchase to two guns per year. My preference would be for legislation that concentrates on more than Saturday Night Specials. Police Foundation research has shown that the famous Saturday Night Specials, the cheapest of handguns, play no dominant role in the commission of violent crime.

On the contrary, the Foundation study demonstrates that higher priced brand-name handguns are used as crime weapons every bit as frequently as the cheaper guns.

I would like to see federal legislation strictly controlling all handguns, regardless of their price tag.

In the best of circumstances, possession of handguns would be limited to those who have a good reason to hold them: the police, the military, registered and trained private security personnel, and, perhaps, some retail merchants, sportsmen and others who can show a valid need.

However, because 50 to 60 million handguns already are in circulation and because the gun lobby's strength in Congress is still so pervasive, support of gun control legislation is the least Americans can do as a first step toward eventual federal gun control.

It also might help prevent police chiefs from having to attend funerals of slain officers.

Reference: (C.R. 1/25/84, Pg. S-152)

Chapter 8

Health
● ● ● ● ● ● ● ● ●

Health Care Issues
Excerpts from Speech
in the Congressional Record
by
Edwin R. Werner, Chairman
Blue Cross and Blue Shield of Greater New York

Good health, in my judgment, is the most important ingredient in the recipe for human happiness. Without it, little else really matters.

You honor me because of my accomplishments and that of our company in providing services for others in that most important area of life—health. But I also assume that your interest in me also speaks to the interest of the academic and business community in answering the question of how to secure the best health care system without bankrupting society. To try to answer that question, it seems only appropriate to address my comments to the rapidly changing aspects of health care, how to improve it and contain its costs, and the role Blue Cross and Blue Shield is playing in that regard.

A recent study among leaders in the health care field and those concerned with it, including providers, corporate executives, top executives in the health insurance industry, government officials, union leaders and authorities on health public policy at universities, confirm that our American health care system is undergoing major changes, and relates these changes to various historical developments in our society during previous years.

To gain perspective on the current problems, it is appropriate to examine several trends of the past decades and how values have shifted in the American social environment.

Following World War II, the United States became very prosperous with its technological developments. The majority of people accepted the ethic of hard work and reaped its awards. Our economy made rapid strides and middle-class lifestyles became the norm. Moral standards prevailed as the accepted form of behavior, and in most families, the husband was still the sole provider.

By the end of the 1950s, optimism was so high that most Americans felt our economic growth was limitless. They also came to believe that affluence should no longer require struggle and hard work.

The decade of the 60s, in response to change in social attitudes, focused on worker happiness instead of worker productivity, and emphasis was placed on the responsibility business had to society. If business was not willing to meet certain standards, the government was ready to step in and regulate. The civil rights movement began with activists aggressively attacking the inequalities between blacks and whites.

Medical care was viewed as inequitable because the poor and many aged could not afford it. America began to change this inequity and accepted the notion of universal health care programs such as Medicaid and Medicare.

The new style of American life during the 60s and 70s began to change from materialism and upward mobility to self-fulfillment. The traditional values of hard work, moral standards, money and success were replaced with self-expression, enjoyment and freedom from moral and financial constraints, all based on the assumption of the permanence of our economic strength.

But toward the end of the 70s, doubt began to set in about the economy. Inflation and unemployment could not be ignored. Massive government spending programs, which were intended to repair the inequalities of poverty and to end racial discrimination, did not do so.

As we confront these new facts in the 80s, there is a certain decline in optimism. We are witnessing ideas of entitlement being replaced with recognition of merit. There are new thoughts about cost consciousness, rather than fulfilling ideal wishes, regardless of price.

We are living and working in a society that has many fears and frustrations. While we are all interested in progress, legitimate concerns about the impact of our technology have been raised. Concern about world peace, concerns about toxic waste, concerns about unemployment, our international monetary situation, the crumbling infrastructure of our cities, alcoholism, drug addiction and changes in nuclear energy are just a few of the issues confronting us today.

My business, health care and its financing, must also be re-examined. The nation's health care bill last year reached $325 billion, health care costs jumped 11 percent in 1982, while overall inflation was reduced to 4 percent. Health care providers are no longer just a part of the ever-increasing inflation in all areas of the economy. With inflation under control, they now stand out and must defend their increases to a public that demands reassurance that what they receive is worth what they pay for it. Containing health care costs requires delicate balancing. On the one hand we need to cut or curtail expenditures, while on the other we need to protect the high quality of care to which we have become accustomed.

Regulatory agencies of the government have exerted tremendous pressures on providers and payors to contain health costs. At the same time, legislative bodies mandate broader coverage for specific categories of people, resulting in greater administrative and benefit costs.

The challenges faced by physicians, hospitals, insurers and employers are for the most part generally the same, but their responses to these challenges can differ to such an extent, that the solution for one group may well result in the creation of additional issues for another.

A theory which is in the forefront today is the question of the consumer's role in holding down health care costs through "competitive" shopping for medical care.

How much control can a consumer exert? Illness is not a state which is freely chosen, and it often arises unexpectedly in emergency circumstances. The consumer is usually under stress and is not likely to search for or haggle over competitive prices for health care.

Due to the complexity of medical treatment, the average consumer is hardly able to judge the degree of expertise of one physician over another, or why one doctor's fee may be higher than another. In truth, the patient is ill-equipped to really judge either the quality of care or the appropriate quantity essential to a good result.

Another question which arises in controlling costs is the technological developments in the medical field, which now make it possible for us to prolong lives to an extent that was impossible 20 years ago.

These developments have indeed prolonged life, but at a great cost. An additional issue is the condition of the life that is prolonged. Given these two difficulties, are we going to deny access to treatment? Regardless of our position on competition or on government regulations or our concern about cost, it is not likely that there will be serious proposals to limit treatment, thus selecting who shall live and who shall die.

To solve these and other problems of health care nationwide, Blue Cross and Blue Shield recognizes the need for an effectively coordinated strategy across the country to meet the demands and needs of the marketplace.

Blue Cross-Blue Shield has been a pioneer in developing responsible cost controls. We are proud of our accomplishments. In one year alone, a savings of $134 million was realized by:

• The prevention of duplicate collection of benefits for claims covered by more than one insurer;

• The monitoring of physicians' claims to detect those who abuse benefits by charging excessively high fees and perform services not medically necessary;

• The medical evaluation of hospital claims, which are reviewed for contractual limitations and exclusions;

• The tracking of fraudulent claims for services not performed;

• The encouragement of second surgical opinions for elective surgical procedures; and

• Pre-admission outpatient testing before admission.

Another important way that we contain costs is through alternate care programs. Many surgical procedures can be safely performed on an outpatient basis, and this saves the expense of inpatient hospital care.

What can we expect as the emerging health care patterns and prospects for the future?

Technology, both operational and professional, will expand.

The number of alternate and less costly delivery facilities will grow.

Benefit programs with deductibles and co-insurance features will increase.

Innovative and creative reimbursement methods will emerge to change the current mode of demand and practice.

Highly competitive pricing will occur in all areas of health care service.

These are but some of the directions that the health care system will be taking in the ensuing years.

While the responses to new challenges may differ from one group in society to another, it is our united efforts which are important. By working together for mutually agreeable goals such as good health for all, at an affordable price, we will arrive at results which will guide us safely through to a sound future for all.

We fully recognize our responsibility as the largest single private sector purchaser to use our economic power to influence the system to assure that the high quality health care we enjoy is not weakened but that every dollar spent for it is used wisely. This is our corporate philosophy. We will work that philosophy for all it's worth.

Reference: (C.R. 5/23/83, Pg. S-7272)

Needs of the Mentally III

Excerpts from Speech
in the Congressional Record
by
John A. Talbott, M.D., President
American Psychiatric Association

At our annual meeting in California 26 years ago, Harry C. Solomon, president of the American Psychiatric Association, called our large mental hospitals "antiquated, outmoded and obsolete." He noted that a recent reduction in the census of such facilities had been coupled with a rise in the number of psychiatric wards in general hospitals, outpatient clinics, halfway houses, home care services and day hospital and night hospital facilities. He cautioned that "liberalization of insurance plans" might encourage increased use of new facilities by acutely ill patients rather than the chronically ill— necessitating the formation of homes or colonies for the chronically ill who were "less readily recoverable."

He urged us to "liquidate our large mental hospitals" as rapidly as can be done and move toward a two-tiered system of "community-oriented intensive treatment" for the acutely ill and moderate-sized homes or colonies for the chronically disabled.

Today, with the end of the century staring us in the face, we seem no closer to Solomon's dream than he was. Our public facilities are deteriorating physically, clinically and economically; our chronically ill either transinstitutionalized to nursing homes or deinstitutionalized to our cities streets, lost in the vast army of the homeless; and our "liberal" insurance plans a thing of the past.

Psychiatry, so full of promise, so expectant of cure, so flush with excitement just 26 years ago—now seems mired in a multiplicity of problems. It is these problems, which constitute our unfinished business for the remainder of the 20th Century, that I wish to address today.

Harry Solomon's call for an end to the antiquated large mental hospital was not done in isolation—the World Health Organization, the Joint Commission on Mental Illness and Health, lay and professional leaders throughout this nation made similar suggestions. Ironically, while we have experienced the de-emphasis on the large state hospitals, we have seen neither any provision for funding the homes or colonies for the "less readily recoverable" chronically ill nor have we witnessed any widespread implementation of an integrated community care system for the more "readily recoverable." In addition, while crippled and cracked, our state hospitals have not withered and blown away.

It is time we called for a reappraisal of the policy of depopulation of state hospitals. It is time to face the facts that, as of now, we have no cure for dehabilitating psychotic illnesses, that not all schizophrenics are amendable to our current therapeutic armamentarium, that no community in America has an adequate number or array of psychiatric services, and that no fiscal ledger in the world can make our "system" cost-effective as long as 297 state and county mental hospitals continue to consume the lion's share of money spent by our states nationwide.

Dr. Solomon in 1958 noted the beginning liberalization of insurance plans to fund care for the mentally ill, currently over 98 percent of Americans are covered by either government or private health insurance plans. However, there are gigantic blotches in this seemingly rosy picture. First, coverage for treatment of mental illness has always been less than for other medical illnesses. Second, fears of increasing health costs have prompted both government and business to suggest drastic measures for cutting costs.

From an economic standpoint we have cost-containment measures; insurance construction, through increased co-payment, deductibles, and outright elimination of benefits. Business coalitions formed for the purpose of reducing health care costs for employees, reduction of benefits through increased claim review, demands for documentation and administrative harassment.

From a regulatory standpoint, the increased constraints are similarly restrictive:

• Attention by the accrediting bodies to quantitative rather than qualitative or outcome measures;

• Strangling regulation by an incredible number of governmental and "voluntary" agencies, which in New York State number 164;

• A zealous effort by PSROs and their competitors to disallow or "carve-out" patient days;

• Competition from other mental health professionals seeking parity of reimbursement, admitting privileges and licensure; and

• Introduction of "new" forms of practice, such as HMOs, IPAs and PPOs, designed to provide less expensive packages of care.

But it is self-defeating to complain and bemoan the loss of the good old days, to blame the bearer of bad news. Or to act as if there were no abuses, problems or substance to the charges of overspending. If we are to ensure our patients' future, we must lay aside our misguided notions that our legislators will do what we want merely because of our medical degrees, that the public on their own will fight for mental health benefits and that the introduction of money, advocacy efforts and old-fashioned politics are unbecoming scientist-physicians.

We must spend time getting to know our federal and state legislators, be available to discuss pending legislation, journey to our capitals to testify on bills, and agree to appear or speak on the record to the news media.

We are this profession's most precious resource, and we must be willing to spend a sizable amount of our professional time in what I call legislative-lobbying overhead— if we are to survive and our patients are to receive the care they so desperately need.

Since time immemorial, the mentally ill have been ridiculed, discriminated against and stigmatized. While alcoholism is now accepted as a "medical disease" and mental retardation a "physical affliction," the mentally ill are still considered by many to be responsible for their illnesses and penalized for them.

What we need is a serious, concerted and professional effort to educate the public about the prevalence of serious and chronic mental illnesses, about the necessity of funding research for the prevention and treatment of these illness and about the limitations and efficacy of psychosocial and biological treatments.

This association must also find some way to protect the seriously ill from being punished for acts committed while incomprehensibly psychotic, while eliminating the spectacles that occur all too frequently between our so-called forensic experts that tarnish all of us and our patients.

For years, public mental hospitals have utilized foreign medical graduates (FMGs) because they could not attract qualified American medical graduates. The psychiatric training, cultural education, language preparation and professional socialization of most FMGs has been second-class. In addition, they perform more clinical service than they are rewarded for educationally.

We can no longer continue to encourage the importation of FMGs as cheap labor for the public facilities, we can no longer continue to offer those now in the country such substandard cultural, linguistic and didactic experiences, and we can no longer countenance the gap between those graduate psychiatrists who are foreign born and those who are not.

Throughout psychiatry's relatively short history, enthusiasm and personal conviction have frequently determined what patient receives which treatment in what setting. Only recently have we begun to look at differential therapeutics with a scientific eye. To some extent, our current outcome research is prompted by the same cost considerations I have enumerated above. While awaiting the results of all the important investigations into the etiology of mental illnesses, the critical research questions that should occupy us for the remainder of this century include:

What treatment works for which patients in what setting?

What is the best system of care for the mentally ill?

How do we ensure the provision of the most appropriate treatment for care for each individual?

Let me re-emphasize that our relationship to the rest of medicine and organized medicine is at a critical phase. Through the hard work of our members on national, state and local levels, we are once again being seen as "real doctors" who are interested in not only our own specialty but in the problems, challenges and actions of all our medical colleagues. Our continued reintegration into medicine must proceed vigorously.

Psychiatry, along with the rest of medicine, can thrive only as long as it maintains the public's trust. That trust, in our case, is frequently shaped by events and developments we may have little or no control over. Whether we like it or not, our social status, our income level and our public image as an ethical profession depend less on our therapeutic effectiveness, individual integrity and scientific knowledge than on publicly visible problems such as deinstitutionalization, homelessness, sexual abuse of patients, criminal acts by patients, and the psychiatric underservice of the poor, minorities, severely and chronically ill, etc.

As many of you know by now, my primary goal as president will be to focus attention on the patients we have the responsibility for treating. Whether we are talking about public policy decisions, clinical decisions, research questions or training issues, we will only be able to address the issues appropriately if we start with the patient.

If we start with the patient, that is where we will also end up. For the next 15 years, I expect we as a profession will try to settle the issues I've spoken about today. But as a starting point, for the next year, I hope you and I will concentrate our attention on the ultimate purpose of all our work, whether clinical, administrative, research or teaching: our patients.

Reference: (C.R. 7/23/84, Pg. S-9004)

The Trauma of Living with AIDS

Excerpts from Speech
in the Congressional Record
by
Michael Callen
to the New York Congressional Delegation

I am a gay man with AIDS and I have been asked to speak to you today to personalize the tragedy of AIDS. Each person's experience with AIDS is different. I can only tell you my story. I was diagnosed with AIDS in December 1981, although I believe I was immune depressed for over a year before.

I have been hospitalized twice since then and continue to have my health monitored by my physician and by a number of privately funded research projects.

Although I believe I will beat this disease, I am continually confronted by media reports telling me that no one has recovered from this syndrome, and that my chances of living past a year are poor.

My life has become totally controlled by AIDS and my fight to recover. I begin each day by checking my body for Kaposi's sarcoma lesions and other signs of serious health complications. I am subject to fevers and night sweats and an almost unendurable fatigue. I live with the fear that every cold or sore throat or skin rash could be a sign of something more serious.

Whenever I am asked by members of the media or by curious healthy people what we talk about in our support group for AIDS patients, I am struck by the intractable gulf that exists between the sick and the well: What we talk about is survival.

We talk about how we're going to buy food and pay rent when our savings run out.

We talk about how we are going to earn enough money to live when some of us are to sick to work.

We talk about how it feels to get fired from our jobs because of unjustified fears of raging and lethal contagion—fears based on ignorance and unfounded speculation—fears which are being fanned by the Centers for Disease Control's endorsement of the view that we may be carrying and spreading a lethal, cancer-causing virus—fears that AIDS may be spread by casual, non-sexual contact.

We talk about the pain we feel when our lovers leave us out of fear of AIDS. We talk about the friends who have stopped calling.

We talk about what it feels like when our families refuse to visit us in the hospital because they are afraid of catching that "gay cancer."

We compare doctors and treatments and hospitals. We share our sense of isolation—how it feels to watch doctors and nurses come and go wearing gowns, gloves and masks. We share our anger that there are doctors and health care workers who refuse to treat AIDS patients.

We share our tremendous sense of frustration and desperation at being denied treatments such as plasmapheresis because many hospitals fear that our blood may "contaminate" the machines.

We share our fears about quarantine—the rumors that separate wards are being created to isolate us from other patients—rumors that certain hospital workers' unions have threatened to strike if forced to treat AIDS patients or wash their laundry—rumors that closed hospitals are being readied for the quarantine of AIDS patients and maybe even healthy members of at-risk groups.

We talk about our fears that the personal data we have volunteered to the Centers for Disease Control to help solve the mystery of AIDS may be used against us in the future. We are asked if we have had sex with animals. We are asked to detail sexual practices which are illegal in a number of states. We are asked to trust that the confidentiality of this information is being safeguarded—only to find out that the CDC has already made available its lists of AIDS patients to the New York Blood Center.

We try to share what hope there is and to help each other live our lives one day at a time. What we talk about is survival.

AIDS patients suffer in two basic ways. We suffer from a life-threatening illness, and we suffer the stigma attached to being diagnosed with AIDS.

The end to both aspects of this suffering depends on finding the causes(s) and cure(s) for AIDS. And that can only happen if research money is released in amounts proportional to the seriousness of this emergency. In order to confront and challenge the ignorance and insensitivity which we, as AIDS patients, must face on a daily basis, we need answers to the pressing questions of course, cure and contagion.

The political context in which AIDS is occurring cannot be ignored. AIDS is affecting groups which remain disenfranchised segments of American society: homosexual men, heroin abusers, Haitian entrants and hemophiliacs. This so-called 4-H club has risk groups who are also victims of poverty.

As a gay man, I could never decide whether I should be pleased with how far the gay rights movement has come in recent years or whether I should be disgusted and angry at how far we have to go. The government's non-response to the AIDS crisis has answered this question for me.

Not only is my government unwilling to grant my right to love whom I choose— my right to be free from job discrimination—my right to the housing and public accommodation of my choosing, this same government—my government—does not appear to care whether I live or die.

Prejudice and oppression are words often bandied about too freely. But the tragedy of AIDS has made many gay men take a new look at the situation of America's other disenfranchised groups. We are beginning to see that homophobia and racism are not, as some of us thought, totally unrelated. We are beginning to see that America's fear and ignorance of homosexuals and its hatred and bigotry toward black and brown people are not just coincidental. We are beginning to see that a Haitian infant dying in poverty in the South Bronx and the death of a white, middle class gay man in Manhattan are sadly, but undeniably, interconnected.

These are the politics of AIDS. When the history of this country's response to this health crisis is written, it will stand as yet another appalling example of American apathy, indifference and inaction.

History teaches that such prejudice and bigotry ultimately poison the whole society—not just those at whom it is directed. If the personal suffering of human beings is not enough to motivate you to fight for increased AIDS-related funding, let me offer you another way to justify to your constituents the release of federal research funds.

Newsweek recently called AIDS "the medical mystery of the century." Solving this mystery will surely benefit all Americans—indeed all humankind. Finding the cause of AIDS may well hold the key to cancer—maybe to all diseases.

Whatever you and your colleagues do or don't do, whatever sums are or are not allocated, whatever the future holds in store for me and the hundreds of other men, women and children whose lives will be irrevocably changed—perhaps tragically ended by this epidemic, the fact that the Congress of the United States did so little for so long will remain a sad and telling commentary on this country and this time.

Surely, when you first dreamed of holding public office, you did not, in the furthest reaches of your imagination, foresee that your duties would include having breakfast with a homosexual facing a life-threatening illness. You can be sure that 10, five, even a year ago, I could not have imagined the possibility that I would be up here begging my elected representatives to help me save my life. But there you are. Here I am. And that is exactly what I am doing.

Reference: (C.R. 5/19/83, Pg. E-2404)

Why Nurses Leave Nursing

Excerpts from Speech
in the Congressional Record
by
Mabel A. Wandelt, Patricia M. Pierce,
and Robert R. Widdowson

"As they said in the book 'Nurse,' it's a wonder nobody died."

The supervisor of labor and delivery in a Texas hospital offered the above comment during an interview. She is a good nurse, but she is frustrated and angry with her practice.She doesn't have time to provide the kind of patient care that she was prepared to give; she feels trapped and alone with overwhelming responsibilities. Like many of her colleagues, she may leave nursing.

In Texas, about 18,000 registered nurses are licensed to practice and are not currently working in nursing; yet some hospital beds cannot be used because there are not enough nurses to care for the patients who might occupy those beds.

In a study of the nursing shortage, the staff of the Center for Research at the University of Texas at Austin set out to identify factors associated with nurse unemployment and to suggest ways to attract non-working nurses into the work force. Thirty-five hundred nurses responded to the study by filling out a questionnaire; 30 hospital nurses in six small-group interviews supplied reasons for working/not working in nursing and things that would encourage nurses to return to work; and in a day-long conference of interested persons, including consumers, nurses, physicians, administrators, educators and legislators, produced innovative suggestions for attracting nurses back to work.

In a sense, the data from the questionnaire add to the stockpile of information about nurses' perceptions of the job of nursing; those from the interviews add to the raw materials for understanding nurses' feelings about patient care and about opportunities for professional practice. The findings show that nurses leave nursing and remain outside the work force because of conditions in the job setting that interfere with the practice of nursing.

The questionnaire asked for opinions from both employed and unemployed licensed registered nurses about a variety of factors associated with the job of nursing. The employed nurses were asked to rate the importance of each factor and then to rate how satisfied they were with that factor in their present job. Unemployed nurses were asked to rate the same items by importance of each item in influencing them to leave nursing and then to rate the importance of each item in keeping them out of nursing.

The rank order of the 10 job conditions with which the largest percentage of employed nurses were dissatisfied was as follows:

(1) Availability of adequate salaries.

(2) The amount of paperwork.

(3) Support given by the administration of the facility.

(4) Opportunity for continuing education.

(5) Adequacy of laws regulating the practice of nursing in Texas.

(6) Support given by nursing administration.

(7) Availability of acceptable child-care facilities.

(8) Availability of inservice education.

(9) Availability of fringe benefits.

(10) Competence of non-registered nursing staff.

High percentages of non-employed nurses listed many of the same items as their reasons for leaving nursing. Additional highly ranked items included:

(1) Family responsibilities.

(2) Unavailability of desired work schedule.

(3) Environment that does not provide a sense of worth as a member of the health care team.

(4) Lack of positive professional interactions with physicians.

(5) No emphasis placed on individualized patient care.

Of the factors which foster dissatisfaction and contribute to withdrawal from practice, all but family responsibilities are directly related to employment conditions common to the hospital setting. Data from the interviews reinforced the conclusion that dissatisfaction stems from the work setting rather than nursing practice.

Nurses believe that the tasks they perform constitute a meaningful part of health care delivery. Regardless of whether a student attends a four-year baccalaureate program, a two-year associate degree program or a three-year hospital diploma program, the nursing care plan is emphasized as an integral part of the total therapeutic regimen.

As licensed professionals, nurses expect to be able to exercise some discretion and choice over work methods. Yet, nurses respond that they are seldom asked to participate in hospital policy decisions. This inability to exercise control over their clinical practice produces feelings of career stagnation.

Nurses need to have occasional recognition for a job well done. They need a timely "pat on the back" and not only negative evaluations.

Conditions on the structure of the hospital organization often inhibit the process of professional nursing. A conflict results because nurses perceive themselves as professionals engaging in nursing practice while administration views them as employees carrying out the job of nursing.

The nursing job encompasses nursing practice, but it also includes setting the work schedule, coordination of patient activities and interactions with other departments, visitors, new employees and students. The data show that nurses are dissatisfied with employment when job conditions do not allow them to administer professional nursing care to patients. These conditions are due to hospital policies and administrative attitudes that fail to accommodate the following professional prerogatives:

• Autonomy of practice and respect for the judgment of the professional.

• Determination of standards of quality of care and determination of staff needs and work schedules to achieve the standards.

• Educational programs and support (financial and time) for updating knowledge and skills.

• Participation with full vote in establishing policy related to patient care, personnel benefits and working conditions.

• Work responsibilities that are nursing related, with elimination of requirements for nurses to perform tasks that are the responsibility of other services.

• Recognition and personnel benefits comparable to those accorded other health care professionals.

Failure to recognize these professional prerogatives creates a disparity between the nurse's job expectations and the nursing care that can actually be provided within the hospital structure. Nurses report that a major area of dissatisfaction is administrative support. This is a misunderstanding of the most fundamental nature, one that has major impact on whether nurses are satisfied with their jobs and satisfied with the care they provide to patients.

In hospitals where nurses are dissatisfied because of limitations in the amount of input and influence they have in matters of concern to themselves and to the patient care program, the introduction of a quality assurance program would allow them to become involved in matters with which they are most familiar and in ways in which they would feel most competent to contribute. From the beginning, with a quality assurance program, nurses could move to participate in assessment, planning, development and decision-making at all levels of program functioning within the hospital.

Staff nurses can assume a large responsibility for changes in situations that cause distress. They need to document episodes of unsafe or inadequate care in specific detail, particularly when job conditions are responsible.

Head nurses should take the lead in organizing such documentation. Staff can also outline, for administration, plans for change and offer to be involved in implementing the plans. Proposals should include a rationale, precise steps for implementing a plan, and a way to evaluate its impact.

Nursing education has a responsibility to provide education programs that will accommodate registered nurses who wish to update their own formal education. Also, nursing faculty need to recognize staff nurses for the experts they are and allow them greater interaction with students.

Nursing faculty members need to maintain their clinical skills and encourage student nurses to consider direct patient care in a hospital setting as a long-term career, rather than a stepping stone to a different career.

Nursing service administration, registered staff and head nurses, and nurse educators can all take action to improve job conditions and promote professional nursing practice. There must be collaboration and compromise among these three groups to effect work conditions conducive to providing good nursing care for patients.

To summarize, nurses who leave nursing and choose to remain outside the work force do so because of work conditions which interfere with the practice of professional nursing.

There is overwhelming evidence that what nurses complain about and report as reasons for leaving and staying out of nursing does exist; it is real. There is also evidence that the distressful conditions need not exist. Where they do not exist, there is no shortage of nurses, and nurses judge the quality of care provided patients as good.

Nurses are concerned about the quality of care they are able to render patients; when quality is compromised because of the work environment, nurses become dissatisfied with the job of nursing.

Concerted efforts are needed by hospital and nursing administrations to grant autonomy and recognition to staff nurses. The description of nurses working and not working in this report is derived from what nurses think, feel and believe about the job and professional practice of nursing. Those who seek to attract nurses into the work force would do well to attend to what nurses themselves are saying.

Reference: (C.R. 2/27/81, Pg. S-1698)

Housing
Putting Commitment to Work

Excerpts from Speech
in the Congressional Record
by
Hon. Nancy Pelosi
U.S. House of Representatives

The federal commitment to housing was codified in the Housing Act of 1949—to provide a decent home and a suitable living environment for every American family—and we must once again focus our efforts on attaining that goal.

Over the last eight years, this goal has not only been ignored but, unfortunately, many steps that had been taken by prior administrations to house all Americans have actually been undone. For example, the 1980s have seen a serious and rapid decline in both the federally assisted construction of new housing and the substantial rehabilitation of existing housing for use as low-income housing. In fiscal year 1981, the federal government provided funds for 110,231 housing units; by fiscal year 1987, only 14,500 housing units were assisted.

There is in Congress a growing belief that housing must once again be made a priority on the national agenda. The severity of the housing crisis has been elevated to a national level by the sight of homeless individuals and families wandering city streets. The American people want the federal government to work for them in developing effective programs which will provide decent, safe and affordable housing for all Americans.

Over the past decade, real incomes have decreased, rent burdens have increased and the supply of affordable housing has been disappearing at an alarming rate. Between 1974 and 1983 alone, the number of units renting for less than $300 per month dropped by nearly 1 million. At the same time, federal policies have resulted in an increase in the number of low-income households . Between 1974 and 1987, the number of households earning incomes of $5,000 to $10,000 and not receiving rental assistance grew from 3.8 million to 4.5 million.

The federal commitment to housing must be long term and it must be flexible. If we have learned anything from the past 40 years of housing programs, it is that local participation in the development of successful housing programs is essential. It is clear as one looks at housing problems across the country that what works in one market may not work in another one. Urban and rural areas face very different problems, and even within urban areas, the problems of cities differ widely.

San Francisco, for example, has a critical shortage of land, as well as a critical shortage of housing units. In San Francisco, there are 6,800 public housing units with another 240 under construction. Houston, meanwhile, is a metropolitan area which has between 10,000 and 35,000 homeless families annually, no public housing units available and a waiting list of 23,000 families. At the same time there are 70,000 vacant apartments and an undisclosed number of foreclosures on houses. Clearly, any federal policy which tries to assist low-income housing in San Francisco and in Houston, to name only two cities, must be flexible enough to address their very different needs.

The federal commitment must also be long term. We must make a commitment to develop new low-income housing and to maintain that housing, as well as to rehabilitate the housing stock we currently have. The housing crisis we face right now will seem small if we allow the current low-income housing stock to disappear.

Another problem with which many of you are familiar is the economic difficulties caused by the fact that operating costs for projects are rising, while tenants' wages and subsidies are not. Unless the federal government makes the commitment to save the several million units of public housing we have in existence now, it is unrealistic to add more.

In fact, it is cost effective for the federal government to put resources into the "modernization" and rehabilitation of current public housing stocks. The estimated $20 to $22 billion needed to bring housing projects up to decent standards is manageable. The replacement value of these units would run about $70 billion. It would be penny-wise and pound-foolish not to invest that money for modernization.

The importance of a long-term federal commitment to housing must also be reflected by a commitment to funding operating costs. Construction costs are not the only costs associated with public housing projects. I am sure most of you have faced the problem of how to continue to operate housing projects in the face of rapidly escalating energy and general maintenance costs. Funding for operating subsidies is a continuing battle which we will have to fight over and over again.

Some of us in Congress have started the fight to place housing back in the priority position it merits. Part of the so-far limited success is a result of the growing awareness of the national disgrace of homelessness. Passage of the Omnibus Housing Bill in 1987 was significant; it was the first major housing bill passed by Congress and signed into law by the President in seven years.

Yet, those of us concerned about housing must always remember that authorizing legislation is only one step in the process. Without appropriations to back it up, the authorizing legislation is of limited value. This year, I worked with other members of the Housing Subcommittee to try to reprogram $400 million from space programs into programs for the homeless, other housing programs and the Environmental Protection Agency.

My colleagues and I worked for this amendment because we believe it is time for us to make a clear statement of our priorities. We support the space program, we also believe it cannot and should not be funded at the expense of the poor of this nation. As we make our long-term plans for high technology, we have to recognize that we have some very low-tech emerging needs that must be addressed. A balanced budget means more than just making revenues and outlays equal, it also means that we must promote future goals without ignoring the needs of our citizens today.

The housing crisis is more than a lack of available housing units and an inability to rent or purchase them; it is a deeper crisis which affects our community. The solution involves programs offering mental and physical health services, education and job-training, literacy programs and child care. Community development funds play a vital role in the development and operation of these kinds of programs.

We must rededicate ourselves to the task of building strong and viable communities, of strengthening local resources and small business, and of providing excellent educational facilities to train people for the needs of the future. We must look for solutions to the devastation of drugs on our youth, and we must strengthen the safety net for the growing number of people who are falling through the cracks in our society.

This task cannot be accomplished by the federal government alone. It requires a partnership of government, private industry, financial institutions and non-profit organizations. As we struggle to develop solutions at the federal level to the many problems facing us, we are turning to those of you with hands-on experience for your advice and expertise. I believe that we can solve the housing crisis, but that it will take the creativity, the energy and the commitment of all of us to do it.

Reference: (C.R. 7/26/88, Pg. E-2484)

Human Rights
• •
The Semantics of Human Rights
Excerpts from Speech
in the Congressional Record
by
Hon. Richard Schifter, Assistant Secretary of State
for Human Rights and Humanitarian Affairs

In the last few decades an international debate has raged over the various classifications of human rights. We have heard discussions of what have often been referred to as "civil or political rights," which have been either bracketed with or juxtaposed to what are called "economic, social and cultural rights." Some theoreticians in the field of human rights have also spoken of a first, second and third generation of human rights.

The first generation has generally been viewed as encompassing civil and political rights, the rights so clearly enunciated by the writers and thinkers of the enlightenment in the 18th Century.

The second generation of human rights is generally assumed to include the aforementioned "economic, social and cultural rights." In learned discussions of the subject it is said that these are the contributions of the Marxist-Leninist societies.

The third generation appears to be a concoction of issues developed during the last quarter century, including what has been referred to as the right to a clean environment, the right to die, and other relatively new matters of social concern.

As a footnote to this introduction of the three so-called generations, let me point out that the attribution of the second generation to Marxist-Leninist thinking is historically and substantively inaccurate. If you take a good look at the rights spelled out in the Universal Declaration of Human Rights and the Covenant on Economic Social and Cultural Rights, you will find that they fit into the programs of Franklin D. Roosevelt rather than Karl Marx or Lenin. And that should not be surprising. After all, it was Eleanor Roosevelt, the President's widow, who, in her capacity as chairwoman of the United Nations Human Rights Commission, played a very important role in the framing and ultimate adoption of the Universal Declaration, whose text served as a basis for the framing of the Covenants.

The point I would like to make to you today is that a good many of us have fallen into a semantic trap. Rather than getting to issues of substance, we often debate the question of what does or does not constitute a human right. It is a debate which has become extraordinarily sterile.

I would suggest that we try to deal with these topics by using different terminology. The bundle of issues with which we are concerned focuses on the relationship between government and the individual citizen. Let us divide that bundle between , on one hand, the limits imposed upon government to safeguard the integrity and dignity of the individual and, on the other hand, the affirmative programs and policies to be conducted by government to achieve the same ends.

And let me say further that the fact that we are dealing with one large bundle of relationships between government and the individual does not mean that the entire bundle must at all times be discussed jointly, nor that the same persons are qualified to discuss every single issue that comes up in this context.

In my country, at least, the typical expert on the right to freedom of expression is not normally an expert on the delivery of medical care to the elderly.

Nor is there value in debating the question of which set of relationships is more important than the other. Let us simply say that all are important. The point is well illustrated by a story of two dogs meeting at the Czechoslovakian-Polish border. One dog, seeking to cross from Czechoslovakia to Poland is slightly on the fat side and well-groomed. The dog seeking to cross from Poland to Czechoslovakia is bedraggled and scraggly. The dog leaving Czechoslovakia asks the other one, "Why are you going to Czechoslovakia?" The other dog answers: "To eat," and continues. "But why are you going to Poland?" The first dog answers: " To bark."

This story is not only political commentary on comparative conditions in Czechoslovakia and Poland. It is also a profound observation about the instinctual character of the drive to express oneself.

It follows that the desire to be free, to be able to express oneself, to write as one pleases, to worship God in accordance with one's conscience or not to worship God— all these are not the inventions of Western civilizations. They reflect natural human aspirations and that is indeed why an ideology based on them has worldwide appeal and, understandably, served as an underpinning for such international stand-setting instruments as the Universal Declaration of Human Rights.

But then there are those who argue that persons who are starving are not concerned about freedom of speech. That may very well be true. But what we of the West say is that the choice before humanity is not one of starving in freedom or eating in slavery. On the contrary, as we look around the world, we can see that freedom and prosperity go hand in hand. The ideal solution is one in which we, unlike the dogs in my anecdote, can both eat and bark.

What we frequently hear at international gatherings is that one of the principal differences between the two major options of governmental systems offered the world today is that one pays attention to the special concerns of a few individuals and the other cares about the welfare of the masses.

I submit to you that if one really cares about the masses, one must also care about each and every individual that makes up the mass. Otherwise, as is often the case, "caring" becomes an abstraction, a vague promise that is not sought to be realized.

What we who profess the democratic ideology believe is that, as Thomas Jefferson put it when he wrote the U.S. Declaration of Independence, we are all endowed with unalienable rights, including the right to life, liberty and the pursuit of happiness. These rights, we believe may not be subordinated to any allegedly higher objective, as determined either by a single potentate or a collective, self-perpetuating leadership group.

In countries in which principles of individual freedom are now well-established, the basic precepts of individual freedom are not even the subject of argument. Such debate as still continues deals with what we might consider marginal questions, such as what are allowable restrictions on pornography, how serious must be a person's mental illness before such a person can be involuntarily committed to a psychiatric institution, what may government do to restrict freedom of assembly if demonstrators interfere with access to a public building?

We are then told that with all the attention paid to these freedoms to speak, publish or assemble, we neglect the unemployed, the homeless, the sick. "Is anyone paying attention to these issues of public policy?" is the challenging question to us in debates.

My response is that precisely because the issues of basic freedoms have become so non-controversial, public debate and election campaigns in the democratic world do indeed revolve around questions of economic and social policy, not because anyone has called them "rights" or outlined them in a constitutional document, but because they are often in the forefront of the thinking of our ultimate decision-makers, the voters. Voters choose among candidates on the basis of who, in their opinion, advocates better solutions to the problems that we face in the economic and social sphere. It is in that context that the issue is not one of promise, or writing guarantees into constitutions and other basic documents, but one of delivering results.

Since the beginning of the century one of the principal arguments in the political arena has been the question of which system of government can deliver the best solution to the problems we confront in the economy and social sphere. By now, it appears the verdict is in. With all the problems that we in the democratic world still face, that we continue to grapple with day by day, the private-incentive system has proved itself better capable of delivering the goods than the various collectivist experiments.

We need to gather at conferences such as this and to gather those expert practitioners and thinkers who are prepared to discuss the dignity and the limits which must be imposed upon the powers of government to assure respect for those principles internationally.

And there is nothing wrong with holding meetings for the purpose of discussing ways and means of dealing with the problems of unemployment, as well as vocational training, the advisability or inadvisability of subsidizing uneconomic enterprises, of the creation of make-work jobs, etc. We could also discuss differing approaches to the encouragement of the construction of housing, the furnishing of quality medical care, and provisions to be made for the elderly.

This conference, devoted to the themes which relate to the limits of government, should, therefore, appropriately deal with the major threats to individual dignity and freedom which are posed by the authority of the state. It is appropriate, I suggest, to go through the relevant articles of the Universal Declaration of Human Rights which were thereafter incorporated into the Helsinki Final Act and determine where shortfalls can be identified and how steps could be taken to encourage correction in these shortfalls.

For today, almost 40 years after the adoption of the Declaration and 12 years after the signing of the Helsinki Final Act, the limitation imposed on government to protect the individual's liberty, security of person, freedom of thought, conscience and religion, freedom of expression and similar freedoms are in many places consistently and deliberately violated. These violations must not be ignored, for ignoring them means betraying the heros and heroines throughout the world who take great risks and make major personal sacrifices, endangering their life and personal security so that the cause of freedom may live. It is to them that we all owe a debt of gratitude. And we must continue to discharge that debt by speaking up on their behalf wherever and whenever we can.

Reference: (C.R. 2/25/88, Pg. E-385)

Chapter 9

Intelligence
. . . .

The Traditional Functions
of National Intelligence

Excerpts from Speech
in the Congressional Record
by
Robert M. Gates, Deputy Director
Central Intelligence Agency

Over the years, public views of American intelligence have been shaped primarily by movies, television, novels, newspapers, books by journalists, hearings growing out of Congressional inquiries, exposes by former intelligence officers and essays by "experts" who either have never served in American intelligence or who have served and still not understood its role. The Central Intelligence Agency (CIA) is said to be an "invisible government" yet it is the most visible, most externally scrutinized, and most publicized intelligence service in the world. While the CIA is sometimes able to refute publicly allegations and criticism, usually it must remain silent.

Let me describe briefly the three basic functions of national intelligence—of the CIA—as set forth in the 1947 National Security Act.

The first is the collector of intelligence worldwide. U.S. intelligence gathers its information from a variety of sources. Our information comes from satellites, from newspapers, periodicals, radio and television worldwide, from diplomats and military attaches overseas and, of course, from secret agents. All of this information flows to Washington where it goes to the analysts. Much of our most valuable information comes from the voluntary, overt cooperation of businessmen, academicians and others who are willing to share with the United States information they acquire when traveling overseas.

Our dependence on different sources of information varies from issue to issue. On some, such as Soviet weapons development, we depend heavily on satellites and spies, on others, such as international economic affairs, we depend on open literature and mbassy reporting. In all cases, what clearly distinguishes information as suitable for intelligence exploitation is its relevance to U.S. national security policies and interests.

The second function, the correlation, evaluation and dissemination of intelligence, or analysis, is the only function of the CIA specifically authorized by the 1947 National Security Act. CIA's creation derived from determination to prevent another Pearl Harbor; to ensure that all available intelligence would be collated and evaluated in one place and provided to those who need it.

As information flows to Washington, analysts with expertise in scores of disciplines collate and try to make sense of it. It is the comprehensiveness of the CIA'S collection and analysis that make the intelligence valuable to the policy-maker.

This information finds its way to the policy-maker in several ways. Early each morning a written briefing is delivered to the White House for the President. This analysis is also shared with the Vice President, the Secretaries of State and Defense, the National Security Adviser and the Chairman of the Joint Chiefs of Staff.

Second, the CIA contributes analysis to policy papers by describing both current events and potential opportunities or problems for the United States.

Third, national intelligence estimates can play an important role in the making of policy. An estimate provides a factual review of a subject and forecasts future developments. In recent years a high premium has been placed on the presentation of diverse points of view and alternative scenarios—the different ways even this may play out, and with what likely consequences.

Fourth, the CIA's assessments and research papers are the products of the largest intelligence analysis organization in the world. The range of issues is breathtaking—from strategic weapons to food supplies, epidemiology to space, water and climate to Third World political instability, mineral and energy resources to international finance, Soviet laser weapons, chemical and biological weapons and many more.

The third function of national intelligence—of CIA—is the implementation of covert action. Covert action is an instrument for protecting or advancing American national security interests in those cases where it is essential that American involvement be hidden or at least not officially acknowledged. The first and most important thing to understand about covert action is that it does not represent some sort of independent CIA foreign policy. The decision to use covert action is a policy decision made by the National Security Council—the President, Vice President, and the Secretaries of State and Defense. And it is CIA's responsibility to implement such decisions.

Under the law, the President must sign a document known as a "Finding" to authorize such covert action. These Findings are shared with the two intelligence oversight committees and the funds for their implementation are approved by Congress. Contrary to popular impressions, the congressional intelligence committees have been broadly supportive of covert action. With a very few exceptions—most obviously in Central America, there has been broad bipartisan support for most of the covert actions undertaken in recent years—most of which have become known publicly. Finally, it is CIA's responsibility to be scrupulous in keeping our oversight committees informed about covert action. If there is to be controversy, let it be about the policy, not how CIA carried out its responsibility to the committees.

There is a fourth function of intelligence that is relatively new and that is its relationship to and support of the Congress. Since the mid-1970s, virtually all CIA assessments, as well as those of other principal intelligence agencies, have gone to the two congressional committees. I regard the distribution of intelligence reports to Congress as an important added protection for the objectivity and integrity of our assessments.

I might add that the oversight process also has given Congress far greater knowledge of and influence over the way CIA and other intelligence agencies spend their money. Congress has been immensely supportive over the past ten years in providing the resources to rebuild American intelligence.

I have focused my remarks on traditional functions of national intelligence. Before closing, I would like to mention several trends that dominate our work now and almost certainly in the future.

As we contemplate the strategic relationship with the Soviet Union, a dominating reality is that the margin for error of U.S. intelligence is becoming narrower. The costs of miscalculating will be high. This is at a time when Soviet weapons are produced with greater secrecy, higher technology and more effort to mislead us than ever before.

Intelligence for some years has been marked by a growing diversity of the problems and issues it is expected to address. Today, the Soviet Union and China together probably account for no more than half of our overall work. The diversity of issues that we cover is expanding every day.

The growing diversity of issues has been accompanied by a growing number of the users of intelligence. We now supply intelligence to nearly every department and agency of the government as well as to the Congress.

Intelligence increasingly is becoming central in policy deliberations. The capacity of U.S. intelligence to monitor and verify Soviet compliance with arms control agreements is increasingly driving the negotiation process. Agreements that cannot be independently verified by the United States probably cannot be ratified.

Finally, intelligence is the only part of the American government that is looking ahead—what I call "scouting the future." We are increasingly alone in identifying problems and opportunities this country will encounter overseas five or ten years from now or even well into the 21st Century.

The real intelligence story in recent years is the significant improvement in the quality, relevance and timeliness of intelligence assistance to policy-makers—a story that with rare anecdotal exceptions cannot be publicly described, in contrast to the publicity surrounding controversial covert actions, problems between the CIA and the Congress, and spy scandals.

The fact is, the CIA cannot advertise better collection or intelligence analysis. CIA officials understand this political reality, but it is imperative that Americans know that the CIA's primary mission remains the collection and analysis of information. This is the CIA's principal role in the making of American foreign policy. The President, the policy community and the Congress depend upon the CIA.

The United States has the finest global intelligence service in the world. Faithful to the Constitution and the law, it helps to safeguard our freedom against our adversaries and helps the policy-maker understand and deal with the often dangerous world around us. Intelligence is America's first line of defense—its eyes and ears—and, at time, its hidden hand. And, just possibly, America is at peace tonight because around the world, from shadowy streets to the depths of space, America's intelligence services are on guard—keeping the watch.

Reference: (C.R. 8/13/88 Pg. E-1009)

International Aviation

The Condition of International Aviation

Excerpts from Speech
in the Congressional Record
by
Bob Crandall, Chairman and CEO
American Airlines

Good afternoon, ladies and gentlemen. To begin a dialogue on international aviation, let me offer this proposition—the international aviation system is in chaos, and it's getting worse! Today, I'd like to suggest some alternative approaches which—utopian as they may sound—are in my judgment perfectly practical and would offer all of us—and the world's travelers—a far better future than today's policies seem likely to yield.

In one respect, at least, the aviation story is a good-news tale: Demand for airline seats is strong—very strong! All over the world, more and more people want to fly.

In a service-oriented world hungry for growth, jobs and wealth, you'd think governments would be going all out to exploit that demand by promoting aviation growth—but just the opposite is true. Around the world, aviation is hobbled. Capacity is short. Competition is constrained—and growth is stunted.

There's a distinct similarity between where we are today in international aviation and where we were a dozen or so years ago in domestic aviation. I am sure many of you remember that world—before we got the regulation monkey off our backs. Carriers would send the Civil Aeronautics Board (CAB) pound after pound of specious exhibits, diligently argue points of minutia—and hope against hope they'd win a little something.

It took American Airlines 10 years to get the right to fly to Des Moines—back in 1976!

International aviation is still in what I call the Des Moines mode. Despite the fact that on many of the world's air routes load factors run in the 70s and 80s, new competition can't add service. Governments tell airlines where they can fly, when they can fly, what equipment they can use and what they can charge. And more often than not, they say "no" to any new idea!

In today's international aviation world, the really intense issues of competition are things like—whether we will or will not put teeny TV's in each seatback; whether we should or should not put aftershave in the amenities kit; and whether our business-class seat is or is not two inches wider than yours!

Our government says it likes competition—but those things do not constitute competition! Competition is frequency—competition is price—competition is daily service, everywhere. Competition drives the market, overcomes restraints, tests the limits of the possible—and creates opportunities galore!

To some considerable extent, we are in a mess because the world's political leaders do not understand aviation's immense economic promise and have failed to provide the physical environment needed to accommodate growth. The United States of America has no national aviation policy. This lack of government policy—around the world—has had many adverse consequences, not the least of which is an acute and growing shortage of aviation infrastructure.

Take the issue of air traffic control. The United States has had, until recent years, a first-class air traffic control system—it doesn't anymore. Ours is still better than most, but it's woefully inadequate for today's traffic demands—and certainly inadequate for future growth.

There are other constraints as well. There are far too few airports and runways—and the result is that slot controls, and rationing, are in place at many airports around the world.

Huge areas of the Southwest are off limits to civilian aircraft—to accommodate a very few military planes whose use of the space is non-intensive to say the least. In West Germany, our military's extensive use of Frankfurt International Airport is a terrible hindrance to civil aviation, is dangerous, and is a growing diplomatic concern.

With these and other problems so blatant, have the world's political leaders ever sat down to discuss—let alone solve—the aviation infrastructure crisis? Not to my knowledge. Most senior political leaders seem blissfully ignorant of the entire subject—which can only mean they haven't focused on aviation's growth potential—and the lost opportunities that untapped potential represents!

Our problems are also partially the consequences of the fact that international aviation still operates under terms of a complex web of agreements stemming from the International Civil Aviation Conference at Chicago in 1944—and I think we all must admit that 45 years ago, no one could possibly imagine the world of the 1990s.

There are lots of agreements that are anything but in the United States' interests, which are, in fact, heavily weighted in favor of our trading partners.

Like it or not, today's agreements are there—and if we want to change, we must start from the base they represent. We must find a way to reach new agreements—and we must have a new policy framework to hang them on.

As a first step toward creating that new framework, the United States should launch a real effort to achieve a consensus among our aviation partners—a new consensus tipped toward liberalization and growth. Such a consensus is, first, in everyone's long-term interest, and, second, consistent with the competitive orientation of the deregulated aviation marketplace we advocate domestically.

Consider, if you will, just one of the many current discussions. Alitalia would like new U.S. routes, but is unwilling to let any U.S. carrier compete with its monopoly between Chicago and Rome/Milan—despite the fact that our bilateral explicitly permits it. The Italian government is taking its advice from Alitalia and is clearly worrying more about its flag carrier than about the vigor of the Italian economy. If more people could conveniently travel to Italy, more dresses and shoes would be sold, more hotels would open, more restaurants would spring up, more gondoliers would be employed—and the entire Italian economy would benefit.

In my opinion, we can't get agreement because neither side understands the overall impact of more service between Italy and the United States. Creating such an analytical model is not a trivial task—but neither is it impossible. The impacts are known—it's time they were quantified.

Second, we should urge all governments—our own included—to worry less about achieving perfectly "balanced" agreements. In any good business deal, all parties are winners—but not necessarily equal winners. The truth is to be sure no one loses. We ought to stop worrying about a perfect balance of direct aviation benefits in every negotiation. In my view, if economic studies show that both countries will benefit, the deal ought to be done.

Those who argue that cabotage should be granted as a way of redressing ancient wrongs would be unlikely, in their personal lives, to make a voluntary second payment for an asset acquired years ago. And those who argue that cabotage—or any other subject—is non-negotiable have clearly forgotten that the best way to end a discussion is to begin with the word "never."

The point is that by either making unrealistic demands or starting with an automatic "no," aviation leaders preclude progress.

Let's consider two current situations. First, if we are ever to have a fully developed North American aviation market, we must give the Canadian carriers broader competitive opportunities. Would some limited form of cabotage really be worse than the absurd limitations which constrain us today?

Second, we cannot seem to make any progress in the long-running U.S.-UK discussions—the two sets of negotiators say they can't find a balanced agreement. Yet what we have today is anything but balanced. British Airways is getting substantial benefits by using its many points of entry in combination with a code sharing deal with United—but since it refuses to bless entry by United States carriers, and since the United Kingdom government takes its cues from British Airways, United States carriers aspiring to serve Britain are left with no recourse.

There is another step I think the U.S. should take which is a fundamentally different character—and that's to insist that other governments honor the agreements they've already made.

Two years ago the U.S. made a deal which gave Swissair access to Atlanta in exchange for the Swiss government's agreement that U.S. carriers would have the right to do their own ground handling and have their own customer service counters at Zurich and Geneva. Last year, the U.S. promised the Swiss an additional gateway in exchange for a number of things. One of those things, strangely enough, was the Swiss government's agreement to let U.S. carriers do their own ground handling and have their own customer service counters in Zurich and Geneva! Swissair hopes to launch service to its new gateway, which is Los Angeles, and we still don't have our people or counters in Geneva.

Competition—a free marketplace—creates far more opportunities for all than monopolies ever will. To maximize those opportunities, the Administration must convince other countries to live up to the aviation agreements already on the books, and to accept its leadership in working toward a far more liberal international aviation regime.

As I said at the outset, airline seats are in great demand—but our marketplace is out of kilter. The aviation industry has far more to offer than it now provides. If the world wants what we can give, the system simply must change—and change dramatically.

To summarize, the Administration should take the lead.

First, to create the air traffic control, runway and airport capacity we need to accommodate a truly competitive system.

Second, to revise—slowly but surely—today's constraining agreements in favor of a broadly liberal regime built on a framework of macro-economic analysis—balanced but not necessarily equal agreements and practical rather than theoretical underpinnings—in short a market-driven, deregulated international aviation system.

And finally, to assure strict compliance—by every government—with both the letter and the intent of existing and future aviation agreements.

These steps will, over time, create new opportunities for all.

Our country—our industry—and the world—deserve no less!

Reference: (C.R. 5/10/89 Pg. E-1635)

Terrorism in the Air
Excerpts from Speech
in the Congressional Record
by
Samuel K. Skinner, Secretary of Transportation
to the International Civil Aviation Organization

It is truly an honor and unique opportunity to visit with my distinguished counterparts from other countries and members of the International Civil Aviation Organization to discuss immediate steps we can take to eliminate terrorism in the skies.

I look forward to working closely with all of you here today and in the future to enhance the safety and security of international civil air transportation. First and foremost, let me stress the obvious—many can be proud of the world community's efforts to keep our skies safe. The dedicated men and women who screen the passengers, check the baggage, handle the cargo and evaluate the threat are to be commended for their vigilant efforts in carrying out their important mission. Generally, air travel continues to be one of the safest forms of transportation. But we are not here to rest on our laurels. We can and must do more to counter the despicable acts of terrorism.

There is no question that citizens and carriers from all of our countries are potential targets of these barbaric acts of terrorism. Over 1,000 passengers on civilian aircraft from 14 different ICAO (International Civil Aviation Organization) member states have fallen prey to sabotage in the last 10 years. None of us here today knows which carriers or airports will become targets next year, or the year after. No one country or carrier should have to stand alone in matters of security. It is only by joining together, in the finest traditions of ICAO, that we can secure international civil aviation from acts of terrorism.

Over the past decade, we have experienced a disturbing increase in international terrorism for which civil aviation seems to have become a favorite target. This problem has unquestionably become an international concern. Since 1979, there have been 21 explosions resulting in 867 deaths and 174 injuries.

In the last four years there have been four acts of sabotage against international flights: Air India Flight 182 was destroyed in 1985, with the loss of 329 passengers and crew; Trans World Airways Flight 840 suffered an explosion in 1986 resulting in the deaths of four passengers; and Korean Airways Flight 858 was destroyed in 1987, with the loss of all 115 passengers and crew. The destruction of Pan American World Airways Flight 103 on December 21, 1988, which resulted in the deaths of 259 passengers and crew and 11 persons on the ground, was the fourth and most recent of these tragic incidents. It has demonstrated with shocking clarity the sophistication of terrorist capabilities, and has focused the attention of the world on the problem of terrorist and criminal acts directed against international civil aviation.

The United States is determined to assume its share of the burden in the struggle against terrorism. In the wake of Pan American Flight 103, our Federal Aviation Administration took decisive action to tighten security requirements on U.S. air carriers operating out of airports in Western Europe and the Middle East. We also have enhanced security at U.S. airports. We are also examining further measures to increase security while respecting sovereignty. It is our hope, however, that ICAO, as it has in the past, will take a leadership role and adopt a unified approach to aviation security. There must be a coordinated international effort to increase aviation security. While each country must bear its own burden, we must recognize that the terrorist threat is a global one, and that alleviating the problem in one place will only cause it to appear in another.

Many countries, airports and air carriers are periodically faced with situations of greater security threats that require measures beyond those appropriate for normal international operations. We believe it essential that once a high-risk situation has been identified by members, either individually or in concert, all carriers and facilities subject to these higher threats should be uniformly subject to strengthened security requirements. We therefore urge that a set of standards and recommended practices be developed for uniform application to operations assessed as being subject to high risk.

It is the view of my government that the Council should take specific action now to develop an effective response to this critical problem. We should specify where improvements in existing standards and recommended practices might be considered, particularly to prevent acts of sabotage, and particularly for operations assessed as being subject to high risk. Some of the more important improvements should be:

• Additional and comprehensive screening for passengers and carry-on articles;

• More thorough screening of checked baggage, through X-ray and other techniques;

• Better reconciliation of passengers and checked baggage;

• More comprehensive screening of cargo and mail;

• Expedite development and implementation of state-of-the-art screening technology;

• Tighten control of access to areas where aircraft, cargo and baggage are handled; and

• A review of the problems posed by allowing electronic devices, such as computers and radios, on board aircraft.

Of course, the success of this organization depends on the will of its members. I therefore urge member-nations to intensify their efforts in implementing the existing standards and recommended practices in Annex 17 and to commit themselves to implement any new or strengthened provisions and to cooperate in applying uniformly any of those additional measures designed to deal with operations assessed as being subject to high risk. We appreciate fully that addressing increased security threats may require additional resources. The United States is committed to working with our fellow ICAO members to this end.

I urge member-nations to review the current situation and consider in cooperation with other states what appropriate interim measures could be imposed immediately and uniformly to operations subjected to high degrees of threat.

We concur in the need for urgent future action which would rededicate the efforts of this organization to ensure international civil aviation security. People around the world are calling for leadership and decisive action to eliminate the gruesome, common threat of terrorism in the skies. We owe it to them, and to the families and loved ones of all who have suffered from these despicable and cowardly acts, to meet this problem head on by raising civil aviation security standards. That is why this gathering is a unique event in ICAO's history, and is a unique opportunity for us to all stand together in the fight against terrorism and against unlawful acts against international civil aviation. I look forward to working with all of you to bring about quick and concrete action to achieve that end.

Reference: (C.R. 2/28/89, Pg. E-540)

Chapter 10

Jews
• • • • • • •

United States-Israel Relations
Excerpts from Speech
in the Congressional Record
by
Hon. Chaim Herzog, President of Israel
Before a Joint Meeting of the U.S. Congress

Mr. President, how pregnant with significance is this occasion, as I, the head of a state of an old people, and yet a young democracy, have the privilege to address this august assembly. An assembly representing the leadership of the free world. This Congress is often a shining beacon of hope to the hundreds of millions in a dark world who suffer bondage, inhumanity, poverty; are deprived of freedom of speech, of expression of movement; who live in societies in which hundreds of millions have never known and do not experience the gifts of human freedom.

I stand here proudly before this great assembly and think back to the years of struggle and sacrifice which have led to this occasion which will be a milestone in the age-old history of our people—that of a first state visit of the President of Israel to its closest ally and friend—the United States of America.

I come to you in the year of the 40th anniversary of Israel's independence. When I recall the enormous sacrifice that we made for our independence—when I recall how the flower of our youth gave its life so that we should live—when I recall how as we struggled for our existence we opened our gates and absorbed five times our original population including those refugees who had emerged from the ashes of the Holocaust.

We have achieved peace with the largest Arab state, namely, Egypt, and are advancing slowly but inexorably along the road of the ultimate goal of comprehensive peace in the Middle East. We have become in our area a major center of technology, agricultural, scientific and medical advancement. Like you, so did we make very painful sacrifices in order to achieve the celebration of our 40th birthday with all the accomplishments of which we are so proud and with all the problems we have to face.

Seventy years ago, world Jewry was electrified by the Balfour Declaration in which the British government acknowledged the Jewish people's right to a homeland in Palestine. This was at a vital stage in World War I. The content of the letter sent by Lord Balfour to Lord Rothschild was incidentally approved by President Wilson.

Forty-nine years ago, Nazi Germany's major onslaught against Jews and Jewish culture, assumed its most brutal expression in the terrifying Kristalnacht—the Night of the Crystals, when Jewish synagogues, homes and schools were set ablaze throughout Germany, and our Hebrew Bible and our holy books were burnt in bonfires across the land.

Forty years ago, the United Nations, with the support of the U.S. government and the Soviet Union, voted for a resolution which determined the establishment of a Jewish State in Palestine. We were thereupon attacked by seven Arab armies bent on our destruction. We fought literally for our lives, sacrificing 1 percent of our population in bloody battle, and achieved our independence.

Ten years ago, President Sadat made his historic trip to Jerusalem and addressed the Knesset. This visit marked an historic watershed in our region which was to lead to the first peace treaty between Israel and an Arab state—indeed the leading Arab state. That peace treaty was signed here in Washington by the late President Sadat, by Menachem Begin, the former Prime Minister of Israel, and was witnessed by President Jimmy Carter.

I stand here representing a democracy aged 40 years, in the heart of the greatest democracy in the world, celebrating the 200 anniversary of its Constitution. I represent an ancient people and a young state, but what binds us is not our age but our values. Israel represents the belief in man and in his right to the basic freedoms and to peace. We believe that man must help his fellow man. We believe that prosperity comes only to those who share it with other fellow men. We are a society that has made enormous strides in agriculture, in industry, in science, and as such see ourselves as a bridge between the developed world and the developing world. Our great ally, the United States, unselfishly supports other nations in the world. So do we, as a matter of national policy, aid, support, and share our experience and our progress with developing countries who require it.

We live in a world in which a minority of the members of the United Nations are democracies. We live in a world in which hundreds of millions of people wake up every morning hungry. We live in a world in which the scope of ignorance exceeds that of education, in which helplessness exceeds ability. We live in a world in which insensitivity is greater than enlightenment. We live in a world a great part of which believes in violence and the solution of problems by force. We live in a world of holy wars, racism and prejudice, a world which experienced two world wars, and has been incapable of putting an end to war. A world which believed in the League of Nations and has been frustrated and disillusioned by the United Nations. It is a world which is in dire need of hope and of aid and which instinctively turns to this country, the powerful keeper of the seal of democracy in the world, a fortress that no upheaval, political or economic, can move from the basis which was created by its Constitution 200 years ago.

Mr. President, as I stand here there flash upon my inward eye the images of great leaders of the world who stood here in times of challenge and tragedy to the world and expressed their gratitude to the American people and its leaders for their generosity and support. Never in the history of man has there been such an unselfish approach to the less fortunate countries of the world than that of this great nation.

We note that the aid provided to Israel is extended as a function of the vital interests of the United States. Today in the Near East the longest war in this century is being waged—a brutal bloody war motivated by fanatic religious fundamentalism on the one hand, and the ambitions of a megalomaniac dictatorship on the other hand. An unconventional weapon, poison gas, has been introduced, and the world has stood by in mute helplessness. The figure of those killed has gone well beyond the million mark. A war which threatens one of the vital arteries of the Western world, with all that this implies for the freedom of the world, a lifeline which you are so valiantly defending today.

Let me emphasize to the distinguished members of these two houses that the world has in many ways been misled into viewing the Israel-Arab conflict as being the main issue in the Middle East. You know as well I do that if the Israel-Arab conflict were to be resolved and to disappear, as I certainly hope and pray that it will, all the centers of bloodshed, war, instability and fundamentalistic religious fanaticism from the Atlantic Ocean to the Persian Gulf would persist. It is against this background that we must view the sole bastion of democracy in our region—Israel. A glance at the map of the Middle East must surely emphasize the vital significance for the security of the United States and the free world of this solid island of stability, loyalty and friendship to the United States.

We see as our major challenge the achievement of peace between us and our Arab neighbors, including the Palestinian people. In our Declaration of Independence we held out our hand in peace to our neighbors. After the Six Day War in 1967, a week after the sounds of battle receded, the government of Israel called on the Arab states to open negotiations for peace. The reply given us by the Arab world at that time was the three "no's" of the Khartoum Conference—no peace, no recognition, no negotiations.

A great man arose in the Middle East—President Anwar Sadat. His dramatic offer was matched by the no less dramatic response of Prime Minister Menachem Begin and the warm and enthusiastic welcome accorded him by the people of Israel. The President came, spoke and negotiated, and thanks to the active involvement of the President of the United States at that time we achieved a peace treaty. Since President Sadat's visit to Jerusalem, not a single Israeli or Egyptian soldier has fallen along the border. What greater recompense can both of our countries ask for?

Mr. President, since World War II, you have borne the burden of Western civilization and guaranteed the forces of democracy. You have experienced a difficult period and may be facing further trying problems. This nation produced the greatest and most powerful economy on earth. Your achievements in science and technology, your advances in arts and culture have opened up new vistas for mankind and for the world. You are strong, great and dynamic people which has given the world a constitutional system which has weathered the storms of 200 years and has maintained your freedom as a nation. It is particularly at times such as these when clouds hover in the skies that the ordinary individual, wherever he may be, realizes in his heart what the United States means to the world.

Thanks to your aid my small country is capable of defending all that you stand for in terms of human freedom and dignity in an area buffeted by the winds of extremism and fanaticism. It is proper and just that on this occasion we utter a reminder of what free people owe to this great nation and of what hopes this mighty country keeps alive in the hearts of people in bondage wherever they may be.

Never in history has a nation given to mankind in so unselfish a manner what the American people have made available to the world. Mindful of the unique role that Providence has bestowed upon you, I stand before this great assembly today, in the year of our 40th anniversary, and extend to you the greetings of a grateful nation and a staunch ally. God Bless America.

Reference: (C.R. 11/10/87, Pg. 9916)

Holocaust Memorial Day, 1984
Excerpts from Speech
in the Congressional Record
by
William R. Perl

I am sometimes referred to as a survivor and so is my wife. I believe that there are no real survivors of the Holocaust. Anyone who experienced any facet of that unimaginable horror can have survived partially only. One who saw the mother, father, brother or friend murdered or knew of one's beloved shipped in cattle cars not to be just killed but to be "exterminated" like vermin is bound to remain captive in the grip of such experience.

In a few days it will be 39 years since Nazi Germany collapsed, yet the real dynamics of the Holocaust remain widely misunderstood. I am often asked: "How did you get out?" and it is this very question that shows the abyss of misunderstanding regarding what made the Holocaust possible. The fact is that up to the almost final stages the problem was far less of how to get out than how to get into another country.

The guilt of the Nazis is irreducible. They developed the idea; they put it into action; they were the executioners. But to view them as the sole responsible ones is an oversimplification which has lived in the minds of too many too long. The so-called free countries closed their doors to those who tried to escape or admitted nominal numbers only. The Nazis set the house afire, and the nations of the world locked the doors of escape.

It has been described in detail how Britain abused the power vested in her by the League of Nations, which accepted Britain's promise of the Balfour Declaration and made its statement (Britain's obligation to aid in the establishment of a Jewish homeland in Palestine) the preamble of the mandate with which the League of Nations entrusted the British.

But when we look at the other nations, we find a related pattern of brutally sabotaging rescue efforts. Though my presentation lasts only a few minutes, I have to provide a few figures to substantiate my accusations that the nations of the world must share in the guilt of having made the Holocaust possible.

During the 12 years of the Hitler era, American immigration remained ruled by an anti-quota system dating back to 1920. Visas were assigned according to the ethnic distribution in 1920, thus reserving huge percentages to natives of Ireland, Britain and Russia, although by the time of the Hitler emergency, immigration from Ireland and Russia had come to an almost complete standstill. All Jewish pleas to have these unused visas transferred to the desperate natives of countries in need of them were denied.

And worse than that, from July 1, 1932, to July 1, 1938, only 26 percent of the available German quota visas were issued, and of those 31 percent were not given to Jews. And from 1938-1942, when persecution was in full blast, this period including the Kristallnacht and Babi Yar, less than half of the total of available visas were issued.

Another example of how these cruel statistics worked on the individual level is the one of the S.S. St. Louis, of the Voyage of the Damned. Shortly before the outbreak of the war, in the seventh year of Nazi persecution, 907 mostly German Jews obtained visas to Cuba. When their ship arrived in Havana, the Cuban government had changed its mind. Desperate pleas for rescuing admission went to several countries in the Americas. All of them, including the United States, refused. Rabbi Steven Wise, accompanied by other Jewish leaders, met with Mr. Roosevelt and pleaded to admit the 907 ex quota. Denied. He asked to mortgage the German quota for future years. Denied. So Rabbi Wise and his entourage went home. And the 907 escapees went home too— to Europe. The ship's captain delayed the return by sailing along the Florida Coast. His ship, a German liner flying the Nazi flag, was shadowed by a U.S. gunboat to make certain that nobody tried to save himself by trying to swim to the free shores. And life on Collins Avenue went on as usual as the 907 sailed back to Europe, most of them to their deaths.

Canada behaved even worse than its large American neighbor. The infamous answer of a key Canadian immigration official to the question of how many admissions he would think acceptable became the title of a recent book. The answer was, "None is too many."

And let nobody claim that the respective governments did not know exact details of the persecution from the day Hitler came to power. Particularly the British and the American governments had first hand intelligence on the Jewish condition. The horrors of the Kristallnacht were even widely reported in the press and on radio, and as the persecution increased, incoming reports grew more numerous, more detailed—and more gruesome.

The statement I am going to make is quite strong, but it is based on facts which we so far refuse to face clearly. In making it I am, of course, not speaking for the Wiesenthal Center, but I do speak on behalf of historical facts and in the name of those whom we are commemorating today, those who could have been saved but found the saving doors barred.

History shows that the Holocaust was not committed in Berlin and in Auschwitz only, and in Treblinka, Maydenek and the other places of slaughter but also in London, Washington, Rio, Ottawa, Pretoria and the other capitals that refused to admit those trying to escape the massacres.

It is a truth hard to swallow, but the Nazis operated the factories of death and by their policies, the nations of the world made certain there were ample supplies.

Only if we have the courage to face even the most repugnant facts, can we avoid falling victim to the principle that those who do not learn from history are condemned to re-experience it.

Today's situation of the Jewish people shows frightening similarities with the antecedents of the Holocaust. Again a substantial percentage of the Jewish people, three and a quarter million, is openly, even challengingly, threatened with annihilation. Again the nations of the world, when dealing with the countries which openly proclaim this annihilation threat, choose, for reasons of expedience, not to acknowledge it. And again, too many Jewish groups minimize its deadly seriousness.

Almost unnoticed in its meaning, the psychological preparation required for the unimaginable brutality of such mass murder has been set into motion. Barbarity against humans, the Nazis had recognized, is best achieved by first delegalizing and dehumanizing the victims. The American slave holder could pray with full devotion in the morning, yet in the afternoon buy, sell or otherwise mistreat slaves—they were outside the law. The Nuremberg laws and the media painting the Jews as depraved, vicious, and satanic preceded the mass brutalities. Systematically, the propaganda of the avowed mideastern annihilators tries to delegitimize Israel and to dehumanize its citizens. Ousting of Israel from this or that organization, persistent refusal to acknowledge even her existence, slaughter of her diplomats, athletes, and just plain citizens goes together with fabricated claims of Israeli inhuman behavior.

Certainly many of those who write or send such distorted reports are not consciously working toward another genocide, they simply follow the pro-Arab line of their paper or stations. But it is our duty to point out to them what kind of game and what game they are playing.

We must also tear the mask off the faces of those who try to convince the public that some of those who have sworn to destroy Israel are "moderates." Who was more moderate: Hitler or Eichmann? Dr. Mengeles or Borman? And who is more moderate: Arafat or the rulers of Saudi Arabia who, as almost a matter of routine, proclaim the existence of Jihad, the Muslim holy war with one aim only, the total elimination of Israel. They also have been bankrolling the PLO for decades and are still financing them to spread terror in Israel and against Jews outside of it. And how moderate is King Hussain who in 1967, when every inch of what he now calls the West Bank had been under his rule for 19 years, though Israel pleaded for peace with him, invaded Israel and who still refuses to accept even its existence, bound as ever on its destruction.

It is not a popular task those are facing who have the courage to stand up and to say: So many of the previous generation kept quiet while every day from sunrise to sunset alone in Auschwitz, 8,000 of their brothers and sisters were marched into the gas chambers. Let us vow as follows: I shall not keep silent. I shall keep faith with the martyred ones who are honored here today. Through my organization devoted to that purpose but also by utilizing all my personal connections and possibilities, I vow to do my utmost to expose the pattern that is being employed for yet another bloodbath, one that if it did, God forbid, succeed, would make the cruelties of the Hitler era pale, I promise to myself, to the victims of the Holocaust, to my children—in fact to mankind, that I will do everything in my power to make certain that anything near to what happened to Europe's Jews between 1933 and 1945 will happen never, ever again.

Reference: (C.R. 6/29/84, Pg. E-3222)

Journalism
• • • • • • • • • • • • • • • •

A New Look at Journalistic Responsibility
Excerpts from Speech
in the Congressional Record
by
Daniel Schorr
Cable News Network

Not many people say nice things to journalists any more. Jody Powell has just come out with a scorching book about the press, and he is only the latest press secretary to blame the press for most of what went wrong with his President's tenure.

When the Reagan Administration forgot to take reporters along on the invasion of Grenada, the press protested, but many Americans cheered. One wit said that on the next invasion, President Reagan will send reporters. Only reporters. No soldiers.

What has gone off the tracks between Americans and their press? Why do juries sock us with big libel judgments? Why do so many groups resent us, from the left wing to the right wing; from Jesse Jackson to the Moral Majority, which, forgetting the Bible, will not forgive us our press passes? Why is "power of the news media" a synonym for manipulation of people where "power of the press" used to be a synonym for serving people?

One reason is the growth and pervasiveness of television. Television is coming to replace government as an authority figure and, therefore, a target of public resentment. The epithets once reserved for government—unresponsive, insensitive, arrogant—are not applied to the media. Many resent the influence of the media, which they perceive as more powerful, and more intrusive, than the government it professes to monitor.

The media are perceived as willing to sacrifice national security to rating and circulation, and willing to intrude in private lives and personal tragedy in the search for audience-building titillation. I need mention only the reaction to the way some television people sought to exploit the grief of next of kin informed of loved ones lost in the Beirut bombing.

Anchor persons for the big networks are perceived as overpaid superstars. Something went out of the perception of the reporter as a dedicated servant of the public with a press card in his greasy hatband when word got out about million-dollar contracts for reading news from a teleprompter.

With the growth of television, journalism has become part of a vast entertainment industry—dragged along with entertainment in the fierce competition for ratings—influenced by television's addiction to drama and confrontation.

Television news is driven to seek villains—a lot of them—and heros—a few of them. The pursuit of stardom encourages some half-baked investigative reporting by video journalists nurtured on post-Watergate cynicism and looking for shortcuts to fame and fortune.

One ominous aspect of all this is the perverse incentive that television offers to the unstable and the fanatical. Because television goes to town on a hostage crisis, some are encouraged to plot hostage crisis.

The Washington Monument siege in December 1982 was apparently staged as a media event. Norman Mayer made clear at the outset that it was the media, not the police, he wanted to deal with and he apparently spent part of his last day on earth watching, on a TV set in his van, the live coverage of his siege. Then he started moving toward the White House, to be met with a hail of police gunfire, at 7:30 p.m.—by coincidence, just as the network news ended.

Then there is John Hinckley Jr., addicted to movie and television violence, who set out to crash the media hall of fame by shooting President Reagan before the cameras. His first question to the Secret Service that evening was, "Is it on TV? Hinckley may be legally crazy, but he is not stupid. He wanted to get on television to prove he was a somebody. He surely succeeded. And television taught him how.

Why do I throw stones at the glass house I live in? Why do I, a reporter, criticize the news media? Because I fear that if we don't find the way to self-restraint, then others will find ways to restrain us.

I believe that news should be covered, not exploited. A hostage incident should be reported, but not turned into a round-the-clock circus. I believe that we must learn again that people are persons, not generic footage. We must not trample on privacy, even if we risk losing a dramatic bite of tape.

We can no longer pretend that what we do doesn't matter. Television has profound effects on the lives of persons and on the life of the nation. It is the great arbiter of importance, even of identity. Because this award ceremony is a special time for introspection, let me tell you of two experiences of my own in this ill-charted trouble zone between journalistic and other identities.

In 1957, working on a "CBS Reports" documentary in Poland, I came across Jewish families in a town with their possessions piled high on carts, as in a scene from "Fiddler on the Roof." They explained in Yiddish that they were on their way to Israel. I had my camera crew film this unexpected vignette of post-Stalin Poland.

When I returned to Warsaw, I asked the Israeli minister whether there was some new policy that made this emigration possible. Staring at me in silence for a full half-minute, he said, "All right, I will tell you, and then you decide what you will do."

The diplomat explained that a secret arrangement permitted Jews to be "repatriated" from the Soviet-annexed region of Poland with the understanding that they emigrate to Israel. But the Soviets, anxious not to offend the Arabs, had warned the Polish regime that the arrangements would be canceled the moment it became publicly known.

"So," he concluded, "your knowledge of Yiddish has enabled you to discover that Jews are leaving, and whether a few thousand more of these pitiful people can leave is in your hands."

I did not consult my superiors on the open telephone or cable to New York, but simply made my own decision to forget the story.

Another experience I had was when I was working in the Netherlands and learned of Queen Juliana's attachment to a faith healer. Under the influence of this strange woman, the Queen wrote pacifist and neutralist ideas into speeches planned for delivery on a state visit to the United States. The Dutch government, which was committed to the Atlantic Alliance, balked at the speeches. Unknown to the public, a constitutional crisis threatened.

I know my way around the Netherlands and spoke its language. One of my stories had won the first William the Silent prize for fostering Dutch-American understanding, and my reporting from flood-stricken south Holland in 1953 had won me a royal decoration. So I had no trouble in developing the story of the Queen and the faith healer. After several months of investigation, I wrote a long article, which Life magazine accepted for publication.

The government undertook frantic measures to have it suppressed. I was summoned to the foreign ministry in The Hague and warned that publication would cost me all government contacts and possible expulsion from the country. I said I would not be intimidated.

Then I met a good friend outside the government who undertook to dissuade me from publication. The government had been stupid to try intimidation, he said. The Queen's bizarre attachment and the resulting conflict with her government, was a legitimate story, almost certain to come out eventually.

"But it cannot come from you," he added. "You are no ordinary foreign correspondent in the Netherlands. You are known, accepted and trusted. You could not have gotten this story if people did not think they were talking to a family friend."

I agonized and temporized. I agreed to cable Life asking for postponement while I considered my course. Then the decision was taken out my hands. Henry Luce gave orders to kill the article in response to an appeal from the Dutch Government citing the danger of destabilization of a NATO ally. But I made no effort to have the article published elsewhere.

How do I justify killing two stories after a lifetime dedicated to "the people's right to know"? I have no answer, other than that a reporter cannot live by catch phrases alone. We have other connections. We have human responsibilities, which become greater as the power of our industry becomes greater.

I love being a reporter. I am proud that, in moments of crisis, like Watergate, when other institutions were muzzled, the press may have saved our democratic institutions. I have lived in too many countries, including totalitarian countries, not to appreciate how great our press is, with all its faults.

I believe that, if we are not to be vulnerable to demagogues who would limit our freedom, we must win back the confidence of the people. That means not overdramatizing what is already dramatic. It means respecting the privacy of the private. It means occasionally being willing to pass up a story if the human cost of that story is too high.

Reference: (C.R. 5/14/84 Pg. S-5679)

Chapter 11

Labor
• • • • • • • •

America in the 21st Century
and the Demographic Imperative

Excerpts from Speech
in the Congressional Record
by
Professor Vijaya L. Milnick, Ph.D.
University of the District of Columbia

Today we stand in the twilight of the 20th Century and at the threshold of the 21st Century. It is a crucial time for taking stock and to prepare for the future. How we do it will decide what we want for this nation and where its place will be among the world community of nations.

Scholars and crystal gazers alike warn us that if we, as a nation, do not want to commence our "ride into the sunset," along with that of the 20th Century, then we have some serious thinking and work ahead of us. Fundamental change is required in the way we look at ourselves, in the way we plan to compete in the new economy, in the way we plan to preserve and invest in our resources, most significantly in our most valuable asset—the human capital.

The global leadership, power and prosperity that America has enjoyed in the past and hopes to continue into the future will largely depend upon how successful we are in reordering our national investment strategies and priorities.

America has an enviable position among the great nations of the world—it stands almost alone in that it cannot be defined in terms of religion, race, language, ethnic origin or ancestry. Instead we define ourselves by the vision that is spoken of as the "American Dream." A dream that welcomes all who share its ideals to participate and to prosper.

We must treasure that ideal. We know that for many that dream is not yet a reality. We must therefore strive for opportunities to make it possible for all.

It's against this backdrop that I wish to examine the demographic imperative in America's role in the 21st Century. The United States has been experiencing profound demographic and economic changes over the last two decades.

As the baby boom generation reached maturity more women entered the work force. During the same time there was a large influx of immigrants into the United States—most of them from Latin American and Southeast Asian countries. During this time, we experienced an increase in foreign trade, followed by a large trade deficit. We saw more and more foreign manufactured goods entering the United States, triggering, in turn, the demise of industries at home that manufactured similar goods.

Computers became common place and automation changed employment patterns. New jobs required higher skills and educational qualifications. More than ever we became part of the global economy. Changes occurring on faraway shores had a direct effect on the American wage earner.

These changes are so profound that they have begun to assert, and will continue to have, an ever-increasing effect on the political, social and economic future of this country, including its very survival.

At the end of World War II, white men constituted almost two-thirds of the labor force. They comprised over one-half of the labor force up until the early 1980s. Latest available statistics show that in 1985, the labor force was comprised of the following: 47 percent, U.S. born white male; 36 percent, U.S. born white female; 5 percent, U.S. born nonwhite male; 5 percent, U.S. born nonwhite female; 4 percent, immigrant male; and 3 percent, immigrant female.

But if we look at new entrants to the labor force between 1985 and 2000 we find that it is projected to be 15 percent, U.S. born white male; 42 percent, U.S. born white female; 7 percent, U.S. born nonwhite male, 13 percent, nonwhite female, 13 percent, immigrant male and 10 percent, immigrant female.

These demographic changes indicate that the new workers entering the work force between now and the year 2000 will be very different from those reflected in today's work force.

The Labor Department has devised a method for measuring on a scale of 1 to 6 the levels of reading, writing and vocabulary needed to perform a wide range of jobs. The Hudson Institute, a conservative think tank, matched the new jobs that the economy will create against these scales. They found that new workers with limited verbal and writing skills (Levels 1-2) will be able to compete for less than 40 percent of the new jobs.

Most new jobs will require solid reading and writing skills. In retail sales, for example, the employees will have to write up orders, compute price lists and read catalogs. But only 22 percent of the new workers, it is estimated, will be able to function at this level.

Level 4 and above, will require more than a high school education, ability to read journals/manuals, write reports and understand specialized terminology. Examples range from nursing to management jobs. Only 5 percent of new employees will be able to do this.

The most challenging task before us is to appropriately educate and train the young work force entrants. To meet future demands, current workers will also have to be retrained. Estimates are that in the next 12 years, 21 million new workers and 30 million current workers will have to be trained or retrained.

Coupled with this is the decline of the number of 21 to 25 year olds. Larger proportions of the new workers will be immigrants and minorities who currently have less education and few skills. Very few among these groups currently hold jobs in the growth industries.

Let's focus specifically on science and engineering since most of the projected "Job growth areas" will demand this background. Blacks account for 12 percent of the American population but only 2 percent of all employed scientists and engineers are black. They earn 4 percent of the baccalaureates and 1 percent of the Ph.Ds in science and engineering.

Hispanics comprise 9 percent of the U.S. population and are the fastest-growing minority group. They account for 2 percent of all employed scientists and engineers. They hold 2 percent of the bachelor's degrees and 1 percent of the Ph.Ds in science and engineering.

American Indians make up 0.6 percent of the U.S. population and 0.7 percent of all employed scientist and engineers. They hold 0.3 percent of all bachelor's degrees and 0.16 percent of all Ph.Ds in science and engineering.

Women are now 51 percent of the total U.S. population and 45 percent of the nation's work force. They comprise 11 percent of all employed scientists and engineers. In 1986, they earned 30 percent of all bachelor's degrees in science and engineering; 34 percent of the Ph.Ds in life sciences; 16 percent of the Ph. Ds in physical sciences and 7 percent in engineering.

The federal government is the leader in the nation's research and development enterprise. The Task Force on Women, Minorities and the Handicapped in Science and Technology found in its report of 1988 that "federal agencies have neither recognized nor begun to address the demographic issues that will affect the conduct of research and development in the 21st Century. Until now the role of minorities, women and people with disabilities in science and technology has been widely seen only as an equity issue, not as the key to future national security and economic competitiveness."

At the doctoral level only 30 percent of the Ph.Ds earned by U.S. citizens were in quantitatively based fields. In this case, whites earned Ph.Ds at equal the national average; Asian Americans at twice the national average; Hispanics and Native Americans at two-thirds, and blacks one-third the national average. What this indicates is that a major problem confronting the nation, and more acutely minorities, is that most of the graduate degrees that are earned are in disciplines that are related to "low growth" rather than "high growth" industries.

In summary, if we are to preserve the competitive edge of the United States in the world economy, we must take major steps to improve and enhance our scientific and technological talent pool. All labor force projections indicate that basic knowledge in science and mathematics will be a requirement for the work force of tomorrow.

Especially acute is the under representation of women and minorities in science and engineering. In light of the demographic data presented, it is imperative that we develop national strategies to attract, involve and develop these potential human resources. Encouraging women and minorities to participate in science and engineering can no longer be regarded as a matter of affirmative action, but it must be seen as an action for national survival.

White males are a rapidly decreasing proportion of our population and, therefore, cannot shoulder the responsibilities in the work force to the degree they did in the past. Women and minorities must be prepared to move in and take their rightful place, they must work shoulder to shoulder, along with others, to keep this nation flourishing and in the forefront of world economy.

The investment we make in our children so that they will be healthy, well-educated and motivated to become the leaders of tomorrow—is an investment that this nation cannot afford not to make.

The investment in developing the untapped minority pool so that they can fully contribute toward building this nation is an investment we can ill afford not to make.

The investment in women who will become a major sector of tomorrow's work force by providing them with needed support and opportunities to become full partners in tomorrow's economy is an investment which has no viable alternative.

These investments will no doubt be costly—but not to make them will be far costlier for the nation and its citizens. Taking needed action is our passport into the 21st Century. It is our only recourse to preserve our strength, creativity and leadership. Doing this will prepare us, as a nation, to take on the challenges that lie before us and carry the promise of the American dream into the 21st Century.
Reference: (C.R. 6/6/89, Pg. E-1989)

America Works When America Works
Excerpts from Speech
in the Congressional Record
by
Jackie Presser, Former President
International Brotherhood of Teamsters

As I have stated repeatedly since becoming General President of the International Brotherhood of Teamsters, it is time to break with the past. Time to develop a new American partnership that can lead this nation into a progressive new direction that benefits the individual working man and woman and the economic system as a whole.

The many weighty questions that confront the labor relations community in America—bankruptcies, layoffs, trade deficits, productivity and technological innovation—boil down to a simple issue of job security. By job security I'm talking about more than just the retention and creation of jobs today. I'm talking about the adaptation of business, labor and government to the demands of the future. That future is staring us directly in the face and the prospect is not a happy one.

We can appreciate the magnitude of the challenge that lies before us by a quick glance at the past. Our union is a little over 80 years old.

Eighty years ago, nearly half of America's workers were farmers. Eighty years ago, the steel industry was an infant, and the automobile industry not yet born. Computer technology lay a full two generations in the future.

The transformation of our work force, the movement of our people and the improvement in their skills and standards of living since then have been staggering. Just imagine the changes in American society an 80-year-old man or woman has witnessed in his or her life. And yet, hard as it may be to comprehend, the changes of the final years of this century will likely surpass those of the last 80. It means that all the displacements, all the technological innovations of 80 years will be compressed into 16.

Look at what has happened in just the first three years of this decade. There are one-third fewer auto workers today than there were in 1980;

For the first time in our history, more than one-half of the work force is female;

Home computers sales have topped $1 billion;

A generation of school children have grown dependent on calculators and video games; and in business circles, teleconferencing and fully automated offices are no longer novelties.

The question is: can the three major economic institutions—labor, management and government—keep pace with this change in order to improve employment opportunities for the people of this nation?

I don't know the answer to that question—but if we don't, America will not have much of a future, and we will have squandered the glorious inheritance our forefathers left to us.

I have been in the labor movement all my life, and I have witnessed first-hand the evolution of labor-management relations in this country. I well remember the early days of deep mistrust and mutual threat. I rose through the labor ranks during the so-called "golden-years" when America's postwar economic boom calmed fears and reduced strife. And finally, I have watched in recent years, at first, inflation and then recession rekindle the distrust and anger of those early years and threaten to rip the fabric of stable labor-management relations.

Of course, our economic growth, if we can sustain it, will expand employment opportunities. But that will not be enough. We need an employment policy that will make sure that our workers can fill the job openings that this growth will create.

The sad fact of life is that we have millions of laid-off workers whose jobs are likely never to return.

How do you tell the steel worker, the auto maker, the truck driver that the mill, the factory, the truck terminal is closed forever? As a union leader who talks with other union leaders, I see and hear that every day. The worker, in his frustration, blames his union. We blame management. And management blames the government, and all that finger-pointing accomplishes absolutely nothing.

We need an employment policy in this country that emphasizes prevention of unemployment rather than one designed merely to soften its impact. We need a plan that not only offers remedies for today, but hope for tomorrow. We need a program that anticipates displacement, not one that reacts to it. And we need to put job security on the same level of priority as national security.

In my opening remarks, I referred to the possibility of a new American partnership between labor, management and government. It is time to make that possibility a reality.

I have proposed the establishment of a tripartite policy-making body that would meet on a regular basis to develop long-range plans for labor relations in America. I am not talking about just another paperwork commission. I'm talking about a committee comprised of labor, management and government officials that would have broad authority over employment and training programs.

The need for a new structure is obvious at a time when, just in Congress alone, eight committees must deal with even minor changes in the unemployment insurance law.

I genuinely believe that such a tripartite body could get this country moving again. The experiment of labor-management cooperation committees has worked and continues to this day. Why not add the third integral partner in the labor relations system in America and start to get things done on a large scale?

I have no doubt that carrying out a comprehensive attack on the employment crisis will be very difficult. But winning the right to collective bargaining was no picnic either. At the time that legislation was posed, many forecasters predicted doom for the American economy. Instead, the collective bargaining process brought dignity and hope to the American worker and markets and opportunities to American industry.

It is time for another "labor revolution," one based on courage, cooperation and concern for the future. There's no turning the clock back. We're engaged and must compete in a global economy. The industrialization of newly developed countries will continue, as will technological progress.

The important point is that we are all in this together. Unions, management and government must all be concerned with how to make enterprises more effective and efficient, and how to best make use of our manpower.

As the spokesman for the largest labor union in the free world, I welcome that challenge and I urge you to join me in helping to shape a future in which the American family has the opportunity to make tomorrow better than today.

Let's remember the words of the wise philosopher who wrote, "The essential things in life are the things we hold in common, not the things we hold separately."

Reference: (C.R. 4/24/84, Pg. 1710)

Labor Day Rally

Excerpts from Speech
in the Congressional Record
by
William W. Winpisinger, International President
International Association of Machinists and Aerospace Workers

We gather here on Labor Day in a festive spirit of camaraderie and solidarity. For those of us here in this assemblage, that's as it should be. Individually and selfishly we may have good cause to celebrate. We are free. We are employed. We are fully fed, clothed and housed. We may even have money in the bank and IRA accounts beckoning us toward secure retirements.

We can say we have arrived. The promise of America has been fulfilled for us. We can celebrate our political freedom and economic and social security. Today—this one day—belongs to us—and the world is ours.

But let us not get carried away on the fanciful wings of festive merriment. Outside our own tight knit cadre of activists present here—and in those trade union enclaves celebrating in 150 other cities across this land—we are surrounded by the jungles of contempt, hostility and indifference.

The world is not ours for the asking.

Corporate America mocks us on this Labor Day. In its day of leisure, it snickers at us. For it believes it has us in retreat and on the run. The multinational corporate animus represents a new sovereignty in the global economy, that, it believes, can be reached or haltered by either sovereign nations or the collective bargaining contracts of trade unions. They owe no duty of loyalty to their workers or patriotism to their home nation. They believe themselves supreme in the new world order.

From his summer palace in the Pacific Cascades, the President of the United States takes time out from his Star Wars cinema and war against the weak and oppressed in Central America, to perfunctorily extol the virtues of the work ethic and the success of his grand economic design to make this nation one percent rich and 99 percent poor. And he looks down his nose at our gathering here as an interference with his game plan to achieve corporate America's dream of a union-free environment, he thinks he's almost won.

Congressmen and senators, unified in the unisex politics of the corporate states are flocking back to our shores from their vacation retreats and global junkets to praise the virtues of labor in one contrived forum after another. They believe their rhetoric inspires us, regardless of their contrary words, and deeds and votes. They take us to be economic and political illiterates, while they practice their politics of deceit, with the money and lucre of corporate PAC slush funds.

Backing them up is a vast indifferent and ill-informed citizenry, that doesn't hold membership in our trade unions, doesn't know what a trade union is, and in a preponderant number of cases, doesn't care what a trade union is. They only know that in times like these, the "smart money" goes into the coward's crouch, hunkers down, looks at the floor, surrenders to the boss, and dares not speak of the noble causes of humankind. It's enough to look after one's own well-being.

Each of these adversaries, from the corporate quarterback of Reaganomics to the mental midgetry of the President himself, to the glib and unprincipled politics of Congressional and Senatorial neuters, to the unwashed ignorance and unabashed selfishness of four out of five workers in this country—each of them is taking the day off to watch us—assuming we are making funeral arrangements for our own demise.

Well, we're here to say, "Shove it!" We're here to say, "We shall be heard!" We're here to say, "Half-fast economic recovery is not recovery at all!"

This land is our land! We will fight for our piece of the rock. In Arizona and Montana, the copper mine workers are fighting for their piece of the rock. In Colorado and Texas, the airline workers are fighting for their piece of the rock. In the Great Pacific Northwest, the shipyard workers and loggers are fighting for their rights and livelihoods.

All across this land workers are in revolt against the politics of greed, meanness and retrenchment. We've had enough of this ship-of-fools running our lives aground. We've had enough of the assumptions and theories of the free market and free trade. We've had enough of trickle-down economics. We've had enough of Ronald Reagan's reincarnation of Harding, Coolidge and Hoover.

Beginning here, now, today, we are determined to rebuild America to fulfill the promises of America.

If President Reagan wants to live by the merit system, then he's going to die by the merit system. He promised full employment and delivered over 20 million people into unemployment. He promised prosperity and gave us a depression. He promised economic and social equality and gave us class warfare. He promised peace and gives us a war. He promised us a dream and gives us a nightmare.

President Reagan's politics is the politics of economic recovery. We must ask, recovery for whom?

Recovery of 26.5 million American workers who experienced some duration of unemployment in the early 1980s?

Recovery for a permanent standing army of unemployed of 15 million, marking time in the ranks of idleness and despair?

Recovery for 34.4 million people dwelling in the hole of poverty?

Black people in this country make up 12 percent of the population, but they constitute 28 percent of the poor. Hispanics are no better off.

Women make up nearly half of the work force in America. And nearly half of the nation's poor families are headed by women. One out of every five children under the age of 18 in America lives in poverty.

Tell them that economic recovery is here.

Those gratuitous tax cuts President Reagan likes to brag about haven't brought about that great capital investment boom they were supposed to beget either. Corporate America has used its billions in tax cuts to cannibalize each other; shut down operations here at home and open up shop in some oppressed third or fourth world country; or to hire management consultants to bust unions. None of that activity adds a single productive job to the economy.

Any new equipment corporate America has ordered with its income tax cuts is labor-saving equipment—new technology—which may show up as a productivity gain on the corporate balance sheet, but shunts more workers to the end of the unemployment line at the local level.

If we in the trade unions are going to rebuild America along fair and just lines, we have to set out clear and unmistakable objectives.

Rather than dismantle the federal system of government, we must remake that system so that it serves the needs of the people.

The New Deal structure and programs have served this nation well for the better part of 50 years. It built our bridges and highways, it built our water supply and electric energy systems; it gave us public ground transportation and airway services; it brought the crass and callous behavior of big businesses under some form of public control.

If we are going to rebuild America, the way we want America to look, then we cannot go back to the old economics of the pure free market and free trade. We cannot rebuild America by tearing down the New Deal and all the rest. We cannot rebuild America by instituting the law of the jungle's survival of the fittest code, for that means might makes right and the King of the Beasts is the greedy Corporate Cat.

In order to rebuild America, we must go beyond the New Deal, go beyond the Fair Deal, the New Frontier and the Great Society. Our objectives must be these: (1) the right of each individual to rewarding employment in a full employment economy; (2) an equitable distribution of wealth, income and the political power derived therefrom; (3) industrial democracy in the workplace, with the absolute right of employees to form trade unions, bargain collectively with employers over terms and conditions of employment, including the right to participate at the highest enterprise and national planning levels in investment decisions which may impact upon our lives and livelihoods; (4) the pursuit of peace as a primary and complementary goal of all of the above.

We can no longer rely on those private interests to act in the majority of the people's interests. They cannot be trusted to do the people's business. It is time to go beyond the Great New Deal and restructure our political economy and begin the redistribution of jobs, income, goods and services on the basis of a shared materialism.

This will require a leveling of the economic pyramid and making the crooked straight. It will require hacking out of the free market jungle a road toward peace and prosperity for all.

That's the American Dream. And that's what trade unionism on this holiday is all about: commencing the urgent task of rebuilding America.

Reference: (C.R. 10/5/83, Pg. 4787)

Libraries
. . . .
A Nation of Readers
Excerpts from Speech
in the Congressional Record
by
Daniel J. Boorstin
Librarian of Congress

The pundits in every age have been quick with premature obituaries. When the printed book spread across Europe, learned men forecast the vulgarization of knowledge and the decline of culture. The Renaissance followed. When people from all over came to the United States, our English friends forecast the corruption of their language. When radio appeared, David Sarnoff had difficulty persuading his business colleagues that anybody would want to send messages that were not directed to a specific addressee.

Every new movement, every new technology, spawns predictions of cataclysm or disaster. In the United States, the most changeful, technologically innovative nation in history, we have had our share of Cassandras. The telephone, some confidently predicted, would soon abolish the mails. The human body could not stand the breathtaking speed of the railroads. Automobiles, Henry Ford was warned, would cause chaos on the roads by frightening all the horses. The obvious example in our time is the common prediction that television and the computer will displace the book, that a nation of watchers will cease to be a nation of readers.

When we Americans speak of a nation of readers, we are describing opportunities, risks and experiences different from those anywhere else or at any other time. For reading is not simply a skill or a consumer activity. It is an experience and it has been part of our whole national experience.

The American public school, in its New England beginnings, taught children to read their "New England Primers," which eventually sold 5 million copies. In the mid-19th Century, readers prepared by William Holmes McGuffey dominated American elementary schools for decades, taught reading along with morality and patriotism and sold 125 million copies. American public schools, especially in the cities, were a crossroads of peoples, where pupils learned to read the American language, which they taught to their immigrant parents. The United States became a nation as it became a nation of readers.

For the diffusion of reading matter across our nation, no institution was more powerful than the mails. It was 1851 before books were admitted to the mails, and given special postage rates. In the very next year, 1852, when "Uncle Tom's Cabin," was published and then carried by the mails all across the North, the postal service helped bring on the Civil War. By 1885, new laws for mailing printed matter simplified the collection of postage on newspapers and created a new third class for books. This so effectively promoted the publication and circulation of reading matter that in 1891, Postmaster General Wanamaker calculated the annual weight of dime novel paperbacks at more than 50,000 tons. In the 1890s, Rural Free Delivery widened the flood of printed matter. In 1911, more than a billion newspapers and magazines were delivered to farm homes over rural mail routes. RFD was christened, with only slight exaggeration, "the great university in which 36 million of our people receive their daily lessons from the newspapers and magazines of the country.

The history of how we, a people spread across a continent, have become a nation of readers is, of course, a history of the U.S. mails. It is also a history of transportation in our United States where technologies of transportation have been remarkably precocious. This new nation by mid-19th Century had more railroad mileage than all of Europe. The automobile grew with similar suddenness, and millions of Model T's were being produced before the roads were there. The rise of the quick lunch (now fast food) was only one symptom of an America preoccupied with speed—a nation in a hurry, eager for change, anxious for the latest word about everything. The history of the mails and the growth of reading in the United States, then, is largely a drama of our bias for speedy useful information.

Of course, other agencies have promoted and spread reading matter across our nation, and these too have grown with great speed. In 1875, there were only 188 public libraries in 11 states, but in the next quarter century the public library became one of the most characteristic American educational institutions. By 1900, they numbered 5,000, today there are some 9,000 public library systems with countless branches and outposts.

In this century a newly characteristic American institution for the diffusion of books has been the book club . The Book of the Month Club, founded 1926, and the Literary Guild, founded about the same time, were pioneers. The nine book clubs in 1928 multiplied until today there are 113 adult book clubs and 21 juvenile book clubs large enough to be listed in "The Literary Market Place."

Meanwhile, of course, retail book outlets—in wholesome competitive rivalry with the books clubs—have multiplied and taken new forms. The neighborhood book store which we all love and need, has had problems of survival. But there have been growing outlets in department stores, supermarkets, drugstores and airports—in addition to the large chains of Dalton, Waldenbooks and others. The familiar statistics of book publishing show an increase in new titles from some 11,000 in 1950 to about 40,000 this year.

Tonight, as we celebrate what are or might be the benefits and delights of a nation of readers, I would like to suggest some of our peculiar temptations. Do we as a nation of readers find refuge from the narrowing biases of our time?

First, the bias of presentism. Modern communications—from telegraph and the telephone to television—have increased the emphasis on our daily experiences on the recent and the present—on news—scoops and newsbreaks, on the latest words and images. Most of what we learn from day to day is certified by its immediacy. We learn more and more before anyone has reflected on whether it is worth knowing. By the time it is put into print, it would be obsolete or proven false. But this is an old story in our country. The whole American experience from colonial times—when the current and the useful almanacs, the latest laws and newspapers and pamphlets and how-to-do-it manuals dominated the presses—through the many decades of the postal rates which have almost always preferred newspapers and magazines to books—American institutions have been biased toward the recent and the up-to-date, toward information rather than knowledge.

This bias of American printed matter was reinforced by the gargantuan enterprise and spectacular growth of American daily newspapers in the 19th Century—and it has been reinforced a hundredfold by the rising electronic media. A nation of watchers has its eyes focused on yesterday and today. But book readers have a window to the whole past. Every book has its roots at least six months ago. The full stock of all past books is available to all of us without special programming. Every good reader can find momentary refuge from the present.

Second, the bias of publicity. Just as we are more than ever flooded by images and sounds of the present, so we are dominated by publicly spoken words. Public utterances are more numerous, more frequent and more public than ever before. The sunshine laws make the private conferences of our highest officials a new kind of public word. When the President and the Secretary of State have a private conversation it is presented verbatim in the day's newspapers. The public word and the public speaker reach us vividly and continually, aided by large expenditures of capital, by large organizations, on channels regulated from within and without.

Third, the bias of statistics. Not the least of the special charms for a reader today is refuge from the quantifiable. Of course we have our best-sellers, but who can say what books are the best read? While the TV audience is increasingly Nielsen-rated, the reader and his ways remain delightfully secret and mysterious. We have heard the boast that on one evening of John Gielgud's "Hamlet" on TV, more people saw Shakespeare's play than all the audiences together since 1604. But who can count Hamlet's readers? A book read is not consumed. And surely some of the best read books do not enter into this year's or last year's publishing figures. The reader continues to "consume" models from the horse and buggy days, or before, from the Model T era, or from last year, sometimes without noticing which. For each of us our reading remains a private, uniquely qualitative nook of our life.

To have the benefits of a nation of readers we must have citizens who can read. Our first assignment is not to allow the published electronic image or the public word to deter us in the primary effort of our education. We must raise a citizenry who are qualified to choose their experience for themselves, from the books past and present, and so secure the independence that only the reader can enjoy.

When we think of the role of words in our nation's political life, prominent in our minds are famous utterances—Burke's Speech of Conciliation, Patrick Henry's "Give Me Liberty or Give Me Death," Webster's reply to Hayne, Lincoln's Gettysburg

Address, Bryan's "Cross of Gold," or Franklin Delano Roosevelt's, "We have nothing to fear but fear itself." Representative government, universal suffrage and a host of technological forces, especially in the United States, have focused our political interest on the public speaker. The building across the street from this Library of Congress has reverberated with many of the nation's great public utterances.

It is symbolically appropriate, and even necessary, here on Capitol Hill that we find two grand buildings, one a temple of the spoken word, another a temple of the read word. One is a symbol of the publicity essential to a free government; the other a symbol of the privacy essential to a free people.

Reference: (C.R. 6/17/82, Pg. S-7057)

Chapter 12

MIAs and POWs
· ·

National League of Families of POWs and MIAs
Excerpts from Speech
in the Congressional Record
by
George Herbert Walker Bush
to the National League of Families

Earlier I was reflecting on the magnitude of what you have endured through so many years of uncertainty. Despite your burdens, you have brought about a change in our nation that will never be reversed. Your organization provides us all with a stirring example of how citizens working together can help craft sound policy.

As you know, Barbara and I returned from Central and Eastern Europe two weeks ago. And in the faces of the brave workers of Gdansk and the hopeful students of Budapest, I saw a truth that cannot be denied—the democratic ideal is winning the hearts of people around the world.

It is this ideal that we honor when we fly the flag. And it is for this ideal that so many Americans were ready when their country called.

Today, we see the symbol of this commitment, the League's POW/MIA flag, on permanent display in the Rotunda of the Nation's Capitol. It stands in a position of tremendous honor. And it will not come down until we have the fullest possible accounting of your missing loved ones.

Your flag can be seen across the land—over the state houses, fire stations, schools, military installations and stadiums—even on ships at sea—a stirring reminder that America's sons are still missing.

The ideals for which your loved ones fought may finally be coming to pass—the failure of totalitarian and repressive communist regimes. The evidence is clear through recent events in China, the Soviet Union and even in Cambodia, where Vietnam appears to be withdrawing its troops.

Some of our finest young men and women were lost during the many long years of the Vietnam War. And the divisions that resulted from our involvement there shook our country to its core. But as tragic as the loss of a loved one is, even more difficult to endure is the uncertainty, which, for you, has extended over so many years.

Now we are coming to a time when the divisions of the Vietnam War are healing, we have let go of the bitterness of the past. But with this reconciliation comes a temptation to forget those who served. Yet we will not forget, and we'll never break ranks.

When I sought the Presidency, I renewed President Reagan's pledge that we would write no lost chapters, we would close no books, we would put away no final memories until your questions about missing and possible prisoners of war have been answered.

And it is as your President that I repeat this pledge. Let me simply state the policy of this new Administration. The fullest possible accounting remains a matter of highest national priority.

We will do everything that a government can do to recover the missing, and if we discover proof of captivity, we will take action to bring our men home.

And as long as you must live without knowing the fate of your loved ones, the United States will insist, in the name of humanity, that the governments of Indochina give the fullest possible accounting.

Frustration on this sensitive issue is very understandable. I hear those who say more must be done. If more can be done, then it will be. Understand this—I do not counsel a timid patience, I counsel a bold persistence.

The task of learning more is daunting, but we can count on some powerful allies.

First are the nation's veterans organizations, those who have stood side-by-side with us through the long years. It was these veterans groups, supporting you, which protested government indifference to the POW/MIA issue in earlier years.

Other partners in our quest are the men and women in government who are dedicating their careers to learning the truth about our POWs and MIAs. These public servants are not uninspired bureaucrats just going through the motions. They have a deep and abiding commitment to their task. This is a commitment shared by people in the military services, in the Defense Intelligence Agency, in embassies throughout the world and among those American pilots who bring our fallen soldiers out of Hanoi, to at long last come home.

You also have many friends in both parties in Congress. To keep this issue at the forefront, they have passed resolutions establishing National POW/MIA Recognition Day, this year on September 15.

In Southeast Asia, there are Americans who are unaccounted for. As I said in my inaugural address, "Assistance can be shown here and will be long remembered. Good will begets good will."

We look forward to normalizing our relations with Vietnam, once a comprehensive settlement has been achieved in Cambodia. That settlement must include genuine power sharing with the non-communist Cambodians led by Prince Sihanouk and an internationally verified troop withdrawal. But Hanoi must clearly understand that, as a practical matter, the pace and scope of this process will be directly affected by the seriousness of their cooperation on POW/MIA and other humanitarian issues.

In Laos, so many questions remain, and so few answers have been received. In light of the difficulties involved, their agreement earlier this year to a year-round program of cooperation is encouraging.

To the families of those missing in Cambodia, I must tell you that our efforts to gain Phnon Penh's humanitarian cooperation on resolving the fates of your missing loved ones have thus far been unsuccessful. Despite their public claims to be holding remains of some Americans, officials there have been deaf to our appeals. I call on Phnon Penh to act responsibly, humanely, and return these remains. Failure to do so will surely hinder their efforts to gain international respect and support.

The policies pursued during the past eight years have shown some success. Incomplete? Yes, but progress is being made because our government is giving it high priority.

As we proceed, we will continue to search for ways to improve the process. We will continue to assemble the best resources, technology and, most of all, qualified people to interview refugees, evaluate intelligence information and negotiate with foreign governments.

In closing, I want you to know that in my frequent travels to cities and towns across America, I see many heartfelt demonstrations of support for your cause. Americans know that across our land, every Thanksgiving, there are families that still set an empty chair at the table. We know that faded photographs and school mementos are still being lovingly kept in scrapbooks.

And questions remain, and will remain, until answered.

Now the mothers, fathers, wives, children and friends of another great power share the same kind of grief, share with you lingering doubts about missing loved ones. That this power, the Soviet Union, backed the North Vietnamese; and the United States backed the Afghan freedom fighters, is an irony. But there is no room in the American heart for a mean-spirited and petty indifference. Far from it.

I am pleased to note that Soviet General Secretary Mikhail Gorbachev recently made a humanitarian appeal for our help in obtaining the fullest possible accounting for Soviet citizens still prisoner and missing in Afghanistan. Let me answer him today— we will do everything we can. And in return, we confidently expect the Soviets will do all they can to encourage more serious and timely cooperation from their allies in Indochina.

Working together we can resolve the anguish of many families in two lands. And we can do something more—we can build a new spirit of peace.

In Ecclesiastes, it is written that there is a time for war, a time for peace and a time to heal. We will never forget those who served our country. And when we receive final answers about their fate, then this will truly be a time for healing.

Reference: (C.R. 8/4/89, Pg. E-2836)

Moral Responsibility
Product Liability Case
Excerpts from Speech
in the Congressional Record
by
Miles W. Lord
Federal District Court Judge

Mr. Robins, Mr. Forrest and Dr. Lunsford: After months of reflection, study and cogitation—and no small amount of prayer—I have concluded it perfectly appropriate to make to you this statement, which will constitute my plea to you to seek new horizons in corporate consciousness and a new sense of personal responsibility for the activities of those who work under you in the name of A. H. Robins Company.

It is not enough to say, "I did not know," "It was not me," "Look elsewhere." Time and time again, each of you has used this kind of argument in refusing to acknowledge your responsibility and in pretending to the world that the chief officers and the directors of your gigantic multinational corporation have no responsibility for the company's acts and omissions.

You, Mr. Robins Jr., have been heard to boast many times that the growth and prosperity of this company is the direct result of its having been in the Robins family for three generations. The stamp of the Robins family is upon it. The corporation is built in the image of the Robins mentality.

You, Dr. Lunsford, as director of the company's most sensitive and important subdivision, have violated every ethical precept to which every doctor under our supervision must pledge as he gives the oath of Hippocrates and assumes the mantle of one who would help and cure and nurture unto the physical needs of the populace.

You, Mr. Forest, are a lawyer, one who upon finding his client in trouble should counsel and guide him along a course which will comport with the legal, moral and ethical principles which must bind us all. You have not brought honor to your profession, Mr. Forrest.

Gentlemen, the results of these activities and attitudes on your part have been catastrophic. Today as you sit here attempting once more to extricate yourselves from the legal consequences of your acts, none of you has faced up to the fact that more than 9,000 women have made claims that they gave up part of their womanhood so that your company might prosper. It is alleged that others gave their lives so you might so prosper, and there stand behind them legions more who have been injured but who have not sought relief in the courts of this land.

If one poor young man were by some act of his—without authority or consent—to inflict such damage upon one woman, he would be jailed for a good portion of the rest of his life. And yet your company, without warning to women, invaded their bodies by the millions and caused them injuries by the thousands. And when the time came for these women to make their claims against your company, you attacked their characters. You inquired into their sexual practices and into the identity of their sexual partners. You exposed these women—and ruined families and reputations and careers—in order to intimidate those who would raise their voices against you. You introduced issues that had no relationship whatsoever to the fact that you planted in the bodies of these women instruments of death, of mutilation, of disease.

Gentlemen, you state that your company has suffered enough, that the infliction of further punishment in the form of punitive damages will cause harm to your ongoing business, will punish innocent shareholders and could conceivably depress your profits to the point that you could not survive as a competitor in this industry. When the poor and downtrodden in this country commit crimes, they too plead that these are crimes of survival and that they should be excused for illegal acts which helped them escape desperate economic straits. On a few occasions, Courts will give heed to such a plea. But no court would heed this plea when the individual denies the wrongful nature of his deeds and gives no indication that he will mend his ways. Your company in the face of overwhelming evidence denies its guilt and continues its monstrous mischief.

Mr. Forest, you have told me that you are working with members of Congress to ask them to find a way of forgiving you from punitive damages which might otherwise be imposed. Yet the profits of your company continue to mount. Your last financial report boasts of new records for sales and earnings, and all the while, insofar as this court is able to determine, you three men and your company still engage in the self-same course of wrongdoing. Until such time as your company indicates that it is willing to cease and desist this deception and to seek out and advise victims, your remonstrances to the Congress and to the Courts of this country are indeed hollow and cynical. The company has not suffered, nor have you men personally. There is as yet no evidence that your company has suffered any penalty whatsoever from these litigations.

You gentlemen have not been rehabilitated. Under your directions, your company has in fact continued to allow women, tens of thousands of them, to wear this device—a deadly depth charge in their wombs—ready to explode at any time. The only conceivable reasons you have not recalled this product are that it would hurt your balance sheet and alert women who have already been harmed that you may be liable for their injuries. You have taken the bottom line as your guiding beacon and the low road as your route. This is corporate irresponsibility at its meanest. Rehabilitation involves an admission of guilt, a certain contrition and acknowledgment of wrongdoing and a resolution to take a new course toward a better life.

Mr. Robins Jr., Mr. Forrest, Dr. Lunsford: I see little in the history of this case that would deter others from partaking of like acts. The policy of delay and obfuscation practiced by your lawyers in courts throughout this country has made it possible for you and your insurance company to delay the payment of these claims for such a long period that the interest you earn in the interim covers the cost of these cases. You, in essence, pay nothing out of your pocket to settle these cases.

You gentlemen have consistently denied any knowledge of the deeds of the company you control. Mr. Robins Jr., I have read your deposition. Many times you state that your management style was such as to delegate work and responsibility to other employees in matters involving the most important aspect of this nation's health. Judge Frank Theis noted this phenomenon in a recent opinion. He wrote: "The project manager for Dalkon Shield explains that a particular question should have gone to the medical department, the medical department representative explains that the question was really the bailiwick of the quality control department, and the quality control department representative explains that the product manager was the one with the authority to make a decision on that question. Under these circumstances, Judge Theis noted, "It is not at all unusual for the hard questions posed in the Dalkon Shield cases to be unanswerable by anyone from Robins.

Your company seeks to segment and fragment the litigation of these cases nationwide. The courts of this country are now burdened with more than 3,000 Dalkon Shield cases. The sheer number of claims and the dilatory tactics used by your company's attorneys clog court calendars and consume vast amounts of judicial and jury time. Your company settles those cases in which it finds itself in an uncomfortable position, a handy device for avoiding any proceeding which would give continuity or cohesiveness to this nationwide problem.

In order that no plaintiff or group of plaintiffs might assert a sustained assault upon your system of evasion and avoidance, you time after time demand that able lawyers who have knowledge of the facts must, as a price of settling their cases, agree to never again take a Dalkon Shield case nor to help any less experienced lawyers with their cases against your company.

Another of your callous legal tactics is to force women of little means to withstand the onslaught of your well-financed, nationwide team of attorneys, and to default if they cannot keep pace. You target your worst tactics for the meek and the poor.

Despite your company's protestations, it is evident that these thousands of cases cannot be viewed in isolation, one at a time. These litigations must be viewed as a whole. Were these women to be gathered together with their injuries in one location, this would be denominated a disaster of the highest magnitude. The mere fact that these women are separated by geography blurs the total picture. Here we have thousands of victims—present and potential—whose injuries are from the same series of operative facts. You have made no effort whatsoever to locate them and bring them together to seek a common solution to their plight.

If this were a case in equity, I would order that your company make an effort to locate each and every woman who still wears this device and recall your product. But this court does not have the power to do so. I must, therefore, resort to moral persuasion and a personal appeal to you. Mr. Robins Jr., Mr. Forrest and Dr. Lunsford: You are the people with the power to recall. You are the corporate conscience. Please in the name of humanity lift your eyes above the bottom line. You, the men in charge, must surely have hearts and souls and consciences.

Reference: (C.R. 8/24/84, Pg. 3256)

Chapter 13

National Defense
· ·

Our Choice: National Power or Paralysis

Excerpts from Speech
in the Congressional Record
by
Adm. James D. Watkins
Chief of Naval Operations

Let me take you back 25 years to 1958, when President Dwight D. Eisenhower told a tense nation he was sending 5,000 marines into Lebanon. Their mission was to preserve peace in the Middle East. His steps were tough, courageous and successful. Peace was preserved without firing a single shot.

Four years later, in 1962, President John F. Kennedy told us that the Soviets were preparing to introduce offensive, nuclear-tipped missiles into our hemisphere.

That was the beginning of a showdown between this nation and the Soviet Union—the Cuban Missile crisis. Again, an American President took quick steps to turn a crisis around by implementing a strict naval quarantine on all offensive military equipment under shipment to Cuba.

These actions were summarized by President Kennedy, not with a threat, but with a promise. "Any hostile move anywhere in the world against the safety and freedom of peoples to whom we are committed—will be met by whatever action is needed."

And again, aggressors understood the message. It was clear—we were standing ready to defend our national interests. They backed down and dismantled their missile sites in Cuba. Peace was preserved without firing a single shot.

In Lebanon in 1958, and off Cuba in 1962, we had the willpower to stand tough. Proper use of diplomacy, fused with military power, stemmed each crisis.

But would a belligerent nation believe us today. Could we take quick action and keep peace. Some students of government sincerely doubt it. They say—at best any similar action by a President today would cause full-scale debate, not only in Congress but by armchair strategists as well, thereby dulling our reaction time. Our resolve would be doubted.

Why? Because something about us has changed they say; a metamorphosis occurred between the 1950s and the early 1970s.

First there was Korea, then the pain of Vietnam. Later, we saw fellow citizens taken prisoner and humiliated in Iran, and a daily parade of media criticism which made it sound like we couldn't do anything right.

Vietnam, more than any other single event, epitomized this change in America. For us in the military, Vietnam was a confusing and ever-changing maze of rules engagement and policy. The Vietnam conflict—which I don't even call a war because we lacked a national commitment to win—was like an exercise in how to fight by public opinion poll.

So a creeping national malaise began to infect this nation's spirit, drive and determination. Many individuals have questioned our self-worth, doubted our dignity, and with that every American value we had always nourished and cherished. Some have rejected principles which worked for us in the past, which helped to make us great. One important principle that has been rejected was the principle which allowed a President to use military force judiciously in support of national policy and security.

This basic principle of our Constitution was clouded by passage of the War Powers Resolution of 1973. This resolution was caused by a series of events—starting with the hotly contested, much-debated "police action" in Korea—and culminating in the Vietnam experience.

But today, America has changed. We are on the move again. Our military strength, once decimated, is building anew. Our economy is improving, and people are going back to work. But most importantly, Americans are again feeling good about themselves and this great nation.

Still, some symptoms of that era of defeat remain, causing us to falter a bit as we step forward. I see some symptoms remaining in my area as uniformed head of our Navy, and member of the Joint Chiefs of Staff. Case in point—recently in Lebanon, we executed a mission called "Presence." Presence is supposed to signal our interest in an area or situation. But this signal was weakened by time limitations imposed under the War Powers Resolution. This influenced our military mission in Lebanon, and hampered our President from carrying out national objectives in a well-planned manner.

Much has happened over the past 10 years. Perhaps now it is time to factor in the lessons we learned. Reviewing the War Powers Resolution could help us develop better ways to meet the needs of a dynamic, effective foreign policy. I am not a constitutional scholar, and must judge this Resolution's effects through my experience as a military leader. For this reason, I believe that while the intent of this legislation is good, the result is not as clear.

This Resolution was born out of controversy, fathered by an uneasy Congress over the veto of a politically wounded President. It directs a President to consult whenever possible with Congress prior to introduction of U.S. forces into any hostilities or situations where imminent hostilities are clearly indicated; it requires a President to report to Congress within 48 hours after the introduction of U.S. Armed Forces into those situations and to terminate the use of Armed Forces in hostilities, or situations of imminent hostilities, within 60 days.

When bound by the Resolution, the only alternatives then available are: Congress subsequently declares war, extends the 60-day time period or authorizes use of force as the President feels necessary—alternatives announced to the adversary for him to manipulate by counter-political strategies.

Although drafted to limit what was seen as limitless power of an imperial Presidency—an answer to "no more Koreas" and "no more Vietnams," the Resolution's ability to keep us out of future Vietnams is questionable. Some forget—Vietnam, in its early stages, was a veritable cause celebre.

The war powers resolution has had a far-ranging impact on our President's ability to exercise, and to implement, foreign policy in the world's trouble spots. His ability to act decisively and effectively is hobbled, because the military arrow in his quiver of responses, the most effective symbol of resolve in executing a strong American foreign policy has been blunted. This is not to say military solutions are the best or only solutions available to this nation. I have never proclaimed employment of military power as an option, except as a last resort. Military options are no panacea, and should never be substituted for aggressive diplomatic efforts or other measures to implement national policy and strategy.

This nation uses military force to prevent escalation of conflict, to force a diplomatic settlement. In other words to keep peace, with the least possible loss of life. But to accomplish this objective, military force must be sufficient, sustainable and credible. It is up to our President, as Commander-in-Chief, to use military power carefully—in this regard.

But military force, which is easy to call upon, because we are ready to go on a moment's notice, is difficult to use, particularly when there is no commitment to win. Military missions quickly grab headlines, national will begins to falter, self-doubt and self-criticism set in.

Unfortunately, because of restrictions like the War Powers Resolution, we sometimes end up preventing our President from effectively using the tool of military force.

This is dangerous, for when our intentions and capabilities are questioned, so is our ability to prevail if directly challenged. And when this is lost, deterrence—the foundation of our national strategy and what has helped avoid global conflict for about 45 years—is placed in jeopardy.

I am not speaking out against consultation between executive and legislative branches. I am not speaking out against Congress' established constitutional role in foreign policy and military operations. What is needed, however, is not a constitutional power sharing debate, not political maneuvering required to avoid such a debate, but a search for a solution to the tough global problems we must face.

This nation must be ready, and must be seen as being ready, to use military power when forced to do so by our adversaries. We must be able to show American power—not American paralysis.

I am not here to apologize, for any past actions, military or otherwise. I am proud of this nation. I am proud of our Navy's capability to carry out missions assigned to us by our President. Our actions in Grenada are an example of how well we can do when we act quickly with identifiable goals.

So in answer to whether or not we could take action to stem crisis, as we have in the past, I know the military capability exists, and when directly challenged, this Nation will come to its feet. But we need to guarantee more. We need to prevent crisis from turning to war. This is no easy task, but it can be accomplished by early use of all tools—diplomatic, economic and military—which are part of this nation's coherent national strategy of defense.

The President has brought together all underpinnings of a national strategy. Now it is up to this nation to let the President use the tools at his disposal. All our resurgent military strength or diplomatic undertakings will be of no use, if our national leaders do not have the freedom to act in accordance with constitutional powers. As a nation, we have not done everything we can to ensure our leaders have the freedom to act with strength. So we must clear the decks of Vietnam-era debris—we must allow our leaders to lead.

To paraphrase William Pitt, America can save herself by her own exertions and help save the rest of the world by her example. Our historic mission of preserving peace and freedom requires no less.

Reference: (C.R. 4/5/84, Pg. E-1451)

A War About Peace

Excerpts from Speech
in the Congressional Record
by
Former President Richard Nixon

In his book, "Great Contemporaries," Winston Churchill described Lord Rosebery, a 19th Century British Prime Minister, as a man who had the misfortune of living in a time of great men and small events. Our leaders today do not have that problem. There is no question but that we live in a time of great events.

1989 even more than 1945, which marked the end of World War II, will be remembered as the year of the century for the forces of freedom in the world. Nineteen forty-five marked the defeat of fascism. Nineteen eighty-nine marked the defeat of communism, an even greater threat to peace and freedom.

As a result of what happened in this historic year, we hear today: The Cold War is over. The United States and the Soviet Union are no longer adversaries but allies as we were in World War II.

We are witnessing the end of history—a time when great strategic issues no longer divide us and when we will compete economically rather than militarily and when we can direct our attention to the environment, global warming, world poverty and other issues where we have common interests.

We are told that we can rely on the United Nations to deal with aggressive nations.

We see an alliance developing between isolationists on the right and the left who for different reasons say that the United States should withdraw its forces from Europe and Asia and concentrate on solving our problems at home.

Conventional wisdom inside the Washington Beltway is that we are on the brink of forging a new world order in which all nations will be dedicated to justice and international law.

Before going that far, let us see what has changed, why changes have occurred, what has not changed, and what America's role should be on the world stage now that the Cold War seems to be over.

The changes in 1989 have been breathtaking. The Berlin Wall came down. Germany was united. Communist governments were driven from power in all of the countries in Eastern Europe and, except for Romania, this was accomplished peacefully.

The frosting on the cake occurred in our own hemisphere early this year when Violetta Chamorro defeated Daniel Ortega in a free election, the first time this has happened to a communist leader in 70 years.

The most significant changes have occurred in the Soviet Union, symbolized by the award of the Nobel Peace Prize to Mikhail Gorbachev. Consider what he has done:

• He withdrew the Red Army from Afghanistan.

• He did not use his Red Army to keep his communist clients in power in Eastern Europe.

• He has allowed West Germany to unite with East Germany.

• He has negotiated arms control agreements.

• He has adopted political and economic reforms which are so revolutionary that some observers have speculated that rather than be a dedicated communist and a Russian nationalist, he may be a closet Democrat and closet capitalist at home and a sincere partisan of peace and freedom abroad.

Before reaching these conclusions let us see why he acted as he did. Look at what he confronted when he came to power six years ago. Everywhere he looked, communism was suffering from terminal illness.

His third world communist colonies were all liabilities costing huge subsidies from Moscow and in Afghanistan costing lives as well as money.

In Eastern Europe, forces of revolution against Soviet-supported rulers were ready to explode at home, the Soviet economy was a basket case plagued with corruption, alcoholism and inefficiency.

Abroad, he saw that his major adversary—the United States—had recovered from the malaise of the late 70s, was restoring its military strength and was embarking on a new weapon system—SDI—which the Soviet Union lacked the resources to match.

Gorbachev had no choice. He had to retrench abroad and reform at home. His first priority was to restore the health of the Soviet economy.

He withdrew the Red Army from Afghanistan not only because it was costing men as well as money, but primarily it helped create a peaceful image for Gorbachev which opened the door for good relations with the West and the economic assistance he needed for his sick economy.

He let East Germany go because he needed financial aid from West Germany.

In the Gulf, he had to choose between Iraq and financial aid from the nations allied against Iraq. He chose the allies.

Let us take a look at the Soviet Union after six years of Gorbachev's leadership. His political reforms have been revolutionary. Where there was no freedom of the press, there is now some. Where there were no free elections, there are some now. Where there was no freedom to criticize Soviet leaders, there is now some.

While he deserves credit for his bold political reforms, we must face up to the fact that his economic reforms have been a total failure. For example, while China's per capita income has doubled in the past ten years, Soviet per capita income under Gorbachev has gone down. Bread lines have replaced vodka lines. To get through the winter, Gorbachev has had to go hat-in-hand to get assistance from his friends in the West. The shopping list he gave Prime Minister Mulroney included pork, beef, flour, powdered milk and peanut oil.

The results of Gorbachev's policies in the Soviet Union are now clear. The Soviet economy is collapsing and the Soviet empire is disintegrating. Fourteen of the 15 Soviet republics have declared independence from Moscow. As has been the case in Eastern Europe, instead of a reforming communist as their leader, the people of the Soviet Union want reforms without communism.

Because of his more benign foreign policy, should we help Gorbachev with his problems at home? The answer is that except for humanitarian aid we should help him only if it serves our interests as well as his. His economic reforms do not meet that test. He is trying to combine a command economy with a free market economy. It won't work. There is no halfway house between communism and capitalism.

In foreign policy, we should applaud his withdrawing the Red Army from Afghanistan. But except for Nicaragua where the people voted out their communist leader, every one of Gorbachev's communist clients in the third world is still in power subsidized by as much as $15 billion a year by the Soviet Union.

Let us now turn to Europe. Isolationists on the right and left are now urging that since the Cold War is over, we should withdraw all our forces from Europe. But what would Europe be without an American military presence. Great Britain and France are minor nuclear powers. Germany is an economic superpower without nuclear weapons. The Soviet Union even without Eastern Europe will still be a nuclear superpower with the world's largest conventional army. No one can suggest that the British and French would use their nuclear force to deter a Soviet attack on Germany. With the United States forces gone from Europe and NATO dissolved, Germany would have the option of going nuclear or neutral and would be strongly tempted to become a political and economic ally of the Soviet Union. Either of these options would be bad for Europe, bad for Germany and bad for the United States.

Let us look at Asia. There are some who say that because there is no longer a Soviet threat, we should bring our forces home from Japan and Korea. They are wrong. Keeping an American military presence in Asia is indispensable if we are to have peace in the Pacific. Let us look at Asia without the United States.

You have the Soviet Union, a nuclear superpower which has strengthened its naval and nuclear forces in Asia. You have China which will be a nuclear superpower within 10 to 20 years. You have Japan, an economic superpower without nuclear weapons and without a U.S. defense guarantee. Japan would have no choice but to go nuclear or to make a deal with the Soviet Union. Japan can afford to massively increase its defense forces.

Let us look at China. We should continue to deplore the tragedy of Tiananmen Square 18 months ago. But the Bush Administration is right to restore diplomatic and economic cooperation with the Peoples Republic of China. This is in our interests and the interests of the Chinese people.

The restoration of a cooperative relationship between China and the United States is without question in the interest of human rights for the Chinese people. As we saw in Korea and in Taiwan, economic progress leads to political progress.

Let us look at the crisis in the Persian Gulf. It is time for some straight talk as to why 400,000 young Americans are spending Christmas in the deserts of Saudi Arabia. We are in the Gulf for two major reasons.

Saddam Hussein has unlimited ambitions to dominate one of the most important strategic areas in the world. Because he has oil, he has the means to acquire the weapons he needs for aggression against his neighbors, including at some future time, a nuclear arsenal. If he succeeds in Kuwait, he will attack others and will use whatever weapons he has including chemical and nuclear to achieve his goals. If we don't stop him now we will have to stop him later when the cost in the lives of young Americans will be infinitely greater.

There is an even more important long-term reason for turning back his aggression. The whole world is heaving a collective sigh of relief as the Cold War appears to be coming to an end. But if Saddam Hussein gains from his aggression against Kuwait, there are other potential aggressors in the world who will be tempted to wage war against their neighbors. If we fail to roll back his aggression—peacefully if possible, by force if necessary—no potential aggressor in the future will be deterred by warnings from the United States or by United Nations resolutions.

If we have to resort to force, it will not be just a war about oil. It will not be a war about hostages. It will not be a war about democracy. It will be a war about peace—not just peace in our time but peace for our children and grandchildren for generations to come. That is why our commitment in the Gulf is a highly moral enterprise.

This brings us to America's major role in the world today. It is not military or economic. It is ideological. Communism has been rejected because it didn't work. Freedom is now on trial. Will freedom provide the economic and political progress the communists promised and did not produce?

The United States is the oldest and most successful democracy in the world. Our challenge is to provide an example for others to follow.

If we are to provide that example we cannot tolerate a permanent underclass. We cannot tolerate second-class education. We cannot tolerate poor productivity. We cannot tolerate political gridlock. There are some who say that the answer to our problems is to give more power to government. We reject that proposition.

America is a great country. We have become great not because of what government has done for people but because of what people have done for themselves and their country. Only by policies which make our economy sound, protective, compassionate and free can we provide an example for others to follow.

What is our great enterprise? Exactly 49 years ago today, the attack on Pearl Harbor plunged the United States into World War II. Fifty-six million people lost their lives in that war, making the 20th Century the bloodiest in history. Our challenge is to make the 21st Century a century of peace and to leave as our legacy not just the defeat of communism and fascism but the victory of freedom.

That is truly a great enterprise worthy of a great people. Only by meeting that challenge can we be true to ourselves.

Reference: (C.R. 1/24/91, Pg. E-298)

National Holidays
The Origins of Christmas
Excerpts from Speech
in the Congressional Record
by
Mrs. Julia N. Moore
Aiken, South Carolina

Surely there can be no season of the year more filled with beauty and joy than Christmas: its roots run deep in the long tradition of Western culture. Through the ages it has gathered unto itself a rich heritage of customs and folklore from many lands and peoples, all transformed by the spirit of love enshrined at the heart of the Christmas story. Intangible and indestructible, Christmas survives among men as a symbol of light and life, the gracious gifts of God.

Scholars tell us that to find the origins of the Christmas feast as we know it today, we must go back to the very earliest days of Christian history.

An almanac of ecclesiastical events at Rome, compiled by an unknown writer, tells us that December 25 was observed in Rome by 336 A.D. as the anniversary of Christ's birth. The custom gradually spread from Rome to all parts of the Western Church, but in the East, Christians celebrated January 6, the Feast of the Epiphany, which became associated also with Christ's Nativity. In Jerusalem, the Christian Churches observed January 6 as Christmas until the 6th Century, and it is still so observed in the Armenian Church.

The popular observance of the Christmas feast was marked early by the joys and merry-making which had been characteristic of the old Roman feast of Saturnalia, a time of carnival and wild revelry in honor of the field god Saturnus. Houses were decorated with lights and greenery, as today, and the opening of the festival was celebrated by processions, the ancient version of the modern Christmas parade.

In Northern Europe lights and fires were also associated with the Yule, the December Celebration of the Winter Solstice, marking man's struggle against the darkness of winter, and his affirmation of fertility, life and light.

So the evergreen tree, which had symbolized life among pagan religions, came to signify Christ bringing new life to the world after the longest dark, cold day of winter. In the 16th Century, Martin Luther is believed to have begun the practice of decorating the Christmas tree set up in the home as the center of the family circle. It is said he was taking a walk and saw a star shining through the branches of an evergreen tree, which was the inspiration for putting candles on the tree. The use of the tree spread very slowly in Northern Europe and was introduced into Vienna in 1816, and into Paris in 1840. The greatest influence in shaping our present day Christmas celebration, however, emanated from the examples of Prince Albert, Queen Victoria's German-born consort, and Charles Dickens, the greatest English novelist of the Victorian era. In 1841, Prince

Albert set up a Christmas tree at Windsor Castle, and the custom was taken up rapidly throughout the English-speaking world.

Apparently it spread to America in 1832 when Charles Fallen, a German professor at Harvard, provided a tree for his son. In 1851, in Cleveland, Pastor Henry Schwan placed the first Christmas tree in a church. Today, the Christmas tree is probably the most popular custom of the season in homes, churches and communities. There is even a National Living Christmas tree lighted each year by the President near the White House.

The first hymn of the Nativity was written in the 4th Century. The earliest German Christmas lieder dated from the 11th Century. The French songs and the English carols were first sung in the 13th Century.

The use of fireworks on Christmas is common in Italy, France and Spain. The French settlers in Louisiana introduced this custom in America and it spread to many other Southern states. The Northern states shoot fireworks on the 4th of July instead of on Christmas

The wassail bowl, the forerunner of the punch bowl, was filled for Christmas in England, and the English brought it to America where it frequently serves its ancient purpose.

It was the Christmas revels of the Hessians in the British army at Trenton in 1776 which made the victory of Washington easier than it would have been. Washington crossed the Delaware on Christmas night, found the British army sleeping off the effects of the celebration and took it by surprise.

The Christmas card is purely an English invention. In the early 1800s, it became the custom for English school children to write and decorate "Christmas pieces" for their parents. The custom of exchanging Christmas cards soon spread to America.

The use of mistletoe is without doubt traced to the Druids who considered it magical and mysterious—a bestower of life, fertility, healing and protection. The Druid priests cut it from oak trees with a golden sickle. It was placed on altars and hung in homes. Whenever enemies met under the mistletoe, they would drop their arms, forget their enmities and embrace. From this grew the custom of kissing under the mistletoe.

The poinsettia originated in the Spanish countries of the new world where it was known as the Christmas Flower. Americans cultivated it as the flaming Star of Christmas that we know today. It is named after Dr. Joel Poinsett, our first minister to Mexico who brought the plant to the United States in 1836.

In the "old days" it was customary to pray: "Peace on earth; good will to men." In 1973, according to the women's "lib" movement, we must pray: "Peace on earth; good will to people."

Christmas cards, the Yule log, the atmosphere of festive cheer, family reunions, the exchange of gifts—all of these were forever associated in the public mind with the keeping of Christmas by Charles Dickens, thanks to his "Pickwick Papers" in 1836-1837 and, above all, to the fame of "A Christmas Carol" in 1843.

The mythic figure of Santa Claus took his present shape from mingled Dutch, different names such as Father Christmas, Pere Noel and Kriss Kringle. The history of Santa Claus goes back to a real Saint Nicholas, the bishop of Myra, a city in Asia Minor. This saintly figure was devoted to children and, on Christmas Eve, carried a basket of gifts for good children and birch rods to punish the naughty ones. The Dutch contracted his name to Sinter Klaas and brought his tradition with them to the new world. The Dutch legend of Saint Nicholas, patron of children was adapted by Washington Irving and transformed in the jolly, chubby fellow riding his reindeer-drawn sleigh through the air. This was celebrated and immortalized by Dr. Clement Moore, an Episcopal clergyman in New York City, in 1822, in his "A Visit from St. Nicholas," also known as "The Night Before Christmas".

Innumerable are the ways in which Christmas has been observed by people of good will in every age and throughout the world. The origins of Christmas as we know it are lost in the mists of antiquity. But its central and abiding message is the unfailing good news of God's loving and redemptive purpose in Christ. Beneath the merrymaking and festivity, there is ever heard the angelic chorus heralding the blessed birth:

"What babe new born is this that in a manger cries? Near on her lowly bed his happy mother lies. Oh, see the air is shaken with white and heavenly wings. This is the Lord of all the earth, this is the King of Kings." —R. W. Gilder.

References: (C.R. 12/1/75, Pg. 20843) and Faith—The Origins of Christmas, Walter Jarrett; Mankind Vol 4. No.4

Thanksgiving Celebrations
Excerpts from Speech
in the Congressional Record
by
Mrs. Julia N. Moore
Aiken, North Carolina

The Pilgrims, who in 1621 observed our initial Thanksgiving holiday, were not a people especially enthusiastic about the celebration of festivals. In fact, these austere and religious settlers of America would have been dismayed had they known of the long and popular history of harvest festivals, of which their Thanksgiving was only the latest. It seems that whenever man has tilled the soil, he has paid homage to the heavenly being who has permitted him such good fortune.

When they chose exile from England rather than persecution for their beliefs, the Pilgrims escaped to Holland. They took their religious difficulties with them, divided into quarreling sects, and even found fault with doctrines of the Dutch Reform Church. Their religious and financial problems drove them to the decision to leave Holland. They voted on a destination and considered South America, but the prosperity brought to the Virginia Colony by the new commodity tobacco led them to select North America.

Forty-six "Saints," as those who held to their religious beliefs were titled, sailed from Holland in July 1620 on an old ship named Speedwell. At Southampton, England, they joined up with their other ship, the Mayflower, and met the English immigrants who had been recruited by the Joint Stock Company.

After sailing for three hundred miles, the Speedwell began to ship water. Plymouth was the port of call and it was necessary to leave her there. The Mayflower was not big enough to accommodate the passengers of both ships and some had to return to their homes. The Mayflower, however, was a good-sized ship of 180 tons. There were 102 passengers, of whom 41 were Saints. The other passengers were called "Strangers" by the Saints. They were not religious dissidents, but rather economic opportunists who found the Church of England quite to their liking. The three most famous, posthumously, on the Mayflower—John Alden, Priscilla Mullens and Myles Standish—were "Strangers."

On November 11, 66 days out of Plymouth, 98 days out of Southampton and almost four months out of Holland, they came into what is now Provincetown Harbor. Before landing, the Mayflower Compact was drawn up, and a governor, John Carver, was selected by vote of the free men. The site which the Pilgrims chose for colonization was Plymouth, named in 1614 by Captain John Smith who was exploring the coast for Plymouth Company.

By most standards, the first harvest was very mediocre. But the only meaningful standard in Plymouth was whether there was enough on which to survive. A holiday was decided upon in the small town which now numbered seven private houses and four communal buildings.

The first Thanksgiving lasted for three days and was celebrated with enthusiasm. Captain Myles Standish paraded his group of soldiers in a series of maneuvers. Massasoit, chief of the Wampanoags was invited and came with 90 braves who competed against the settlers in racing and jumping games. The Indians showed their bow and arrow marksmanship, and the white men exhibited their skill with firearms.

While Thanksgiving day got off to a glorious start, it could easily have been a one-time celebration. The winter of 1622-23 did not see such wholesale death as the first one, but a two-month drought destroyed the meager crop. A day of fasting and prayer was set and for nine hours the people prayed for relief. Rain fell the next morning. Shortly after this, Myles Standish brought news that the ship, Anne, laden with supplies, was nearing port and carrying as passengers many of the Saints who had returned to Holland from England when the Speedwell proved unseaworthy.

For the blessings of supplies and rain and the arrival of their friends, Governor Bradford issued a proclamation naming July 30, 1632, as a day of thanksgiving and prayer.

The first national Thanksgiving proclamation was issued by George Washington in 1789, the year of his inauguration. President Washington called for another Thanksgiving in 1795, the same year that John Jay, a governor of New York, endeavored to have the day observed throughout his state. The ancient problem of coordinating the season of the herdsman with the season of the farmer made it difficult for various communities to accept a common date. And the Puritans refused to recognize even a civil judgment which tried to set the date, for they believed in a more spontaneous show of thanks, prompted by tangible and immediate signs of well-being.

New York officially adopted Thanksgiving Day in 1817. In other states the day continued to be celebrated according to regional preferences. It was still largely a religious observance, and in the early 19th Century, some governors considered it an example of state interference with religion and so avoided it.

On October 3, 1863, President Lincoln issued his Thanksgiving Proclamation, after which Thanksgiving became a national holiday observed on the last Thursday of November. Lincoln's document is a clear reminder of the great North-South conflict which prevailed when it was written.

Officially, each President has, by proclamation, set the Thanksgiving Day date each year, the last Thursday in November. There have been two exceptions— November 23, the third Thursday, was celebrated as Thanksgiving in 1939 by order of President Franklin D. Roosevelt. The reason given for the change was that the store owners, wanted to extend the time between Thanksgiving and Christmas to better prepare for the Christmas shopping rush. The following year the third Thursday was also set as Thanksgiving. However, the people of the country were not about to let a long-standing custom slip by so easily and they protested with vehemence.

A Congressional Resolution in 1941 settled the dispute and now Thanksgiving Day is always the fourth Thursday in November. It is proclaimed by both the President and the Governors of the states. It is a legal holiday in all states and possessions.

Various customs have through the years become associated with Thanksgiving Day. Some have died out while others have flourished. Thanksgiving was once a more religious holiday than it is today. The urbanization and swift industrialization of our country, in removing the majority of the people from a farm-oriented life, must have had much to do in secularizing the day.

In Plymouth, Massachusetts, there is still a full dress re-enactment of the First Thanksgiving. The quaintly attired citizens march to Burial Hill, the resting place of the victims of that first dreadful winter and there hold a Memorial and Thanksgiving service.

Schools and church classes around the country use the Thanksgiving scheme as a basis for plays and episodes put on to educate the children in American history.

In some of our cities, long and elaborate parades are held, not only to portray the spirit of Thanksgiving but also to welcome in the Christmas season. Since 1924, the most famous of these parades, Macy's of New York City Thanksgiving Day parade, has made its way down Broadway on Thanksgiving morning.

In recent years, Thanksgiving has become an even more popular holiday, as a prelude to the Christmas season, as a gala sports occasion and as a time for families and friends to enjoy getting together for what is often a long vacation weekend.

Reference: (C.R. 12/1/75, Pg. S-20843)

Natural Resources

Our Own Natural Resources

Excerpts from Speech
in the Congressional Record
by
William Perry Pendley, Member
Secretary of the Navy's
Advisory Committee on the Naval Postgraduate School

As I have traveled around this country in the weeks since the end of the Persian Gulf War, in every city, large and small, in every village and hamlet, in every airport, I have seen the signs, "Welcome home." To those brave men and women who served in the Middle East, "Welcome." To those who supported them here and abroad, throughout the Fleet, "Welcome Home."

We have learned, and are yet to learn, many lessons from the War in the Persian Gulf. We learned that American technology, ingenuity, know-how and creativity work. We learned that our weapons worked. Just ask Saddam Hussein.

We learned that our men and women can fight and win a war. We are yet to learn if our diplomats can win a peace.

We have learned how to deal with the press. First, it is ironic that censorship in the Persian Gulf War came first from the media. It was the media which demanded that the military cut short the daily briefings and go on "background," so that the media could be the conduit for information on the war.

Today, as we welcome home our fighting men and women, I want to discuss yet another lesson we must learn from the war in the Persian Gulf. That lesson is that political decisions made here at home will determine if the sons and daughters of America will fight on foreign shores.

For there is something unique about the war in the Persian Gulf other than the swiftness of our victory. That is, it was the first war America has ever fought over resources.

America, on whom God has surely shed his Grace, America, blessed with rich farmlands and forests, with ore and oil, has fought a foreign country over energy. Yes, we fought to rid the world of a despot. But we also fought, in President Bush's words, because, "we cannot allow control of the world's oil resources to fall into Saddam Hussein's hands."

It may be the first war America has ever fought over resources, but I fear that it will not be the last, unless we change our policies. Before I discuss what we must do, I need to discuss where we are today.

I must go back 14 years to the Administration of President Jimmy Carter. After his election, his Administration engaged in policies that were widely perceived of as a war on the West: a war on our water projects, a war on our water laws, and a war on our mining, timber and other natural resource policies.

His policies yielded opposition. It was called the "Sagebrush Rebellion," and it catapulted the man who called himself a Sagebrush Rebel, Governor Ronald Reagan, into the Presidency in a landslide.

What is happening now is yet another "War on the West." The grassroots uprising that we are seeing all across the West, from the 100th meridian to the Cascade Mountains, is what John Lancaster in *The Washington Post* calls "an honest-to-goodness phenomena."

It all began in 1988 when Vice President Bush said, "I am an environmentalist." When I heard that I worried because for 20 years or so, westerners have been at odds with the leaders of the environmental groups as they have sought, so it would seem, to shut us down.

I worried even more when President Bush, in his first State of the Union address, said two very important things about natural resources issues. First he said he wanted to increase the National Park Service's land acquisition budget from zero to $200 million a year. That is the budget the federal overnment gets to take property out of private hands, off the tax rolls, and put into federal ownership.

Second, President Bush placed three Outer Continental Shelf (OCS) sales off limits to exploration and development. Those sales were supposed to bring into the Federal Treasury more than $450 million in bonus bids alone, not to mention jobs, revenues, taxes and, yes, even oil and gas.

Taken together, these two initiatives reduced revenues to the federal government by more than $650 million. You should know that there is enough oil in the OCS to replace all of the oil we get from the Persian Gulf for the next 25 years. We are not running out of oil in America, we are running out of the will to develop it.

Exploration for oil and gas on U.S. Forest Service lands has dropped by 60 percent in the last five years. The OCS is largely unavailable for exploration. The Arctic National Wildlife Refuge—an area the size of South Carolina in which we need to explore an area the size of Dulles International Airport—is off limits.

Our country is 80 percent dependent on foreign sources for the fuel we use to create nuclear power.

There is oil to be found in America. Recently, a major new find was announced in the Gulf of Mexico, the largest find in the last 20 years. It may be as large as the North Sea.

For nearly 100 years the people of Colorado have looked to an area called Two Forks—the two forks of the Platte River—as our source of water for the future. Forty units of local government—no federal or state money was involved—spent $47 million performing the environmental studies to build the water project. They agreed to spend $90 million in mitigation measures to make local environmental groups happy. But that was not enough. National environmental groups went to the Environmental Protection Agency, and the agency said, "Veto the Project."

I hope you have been following the tragedy that is unfolding in the Pacific Northwest, as 60,000 men and women face the loss of their jobs due to the Northern

Spotted Owl. Imagine what would happen to your hometown if 40 percent of the people lost their jobs. That is beginning to happen in Washington, Oregon and Northern California at a cost of $475 million per spotted owl.

President Bush traveled to Wyoming and announced a national "no net loss of wetlands" policy to protect bird habitat. That sounds great at the levels in which the President and his duck hunting buddies operate. But in the bowels of the bureaucracy where even the deserts are "wetlands," it is a problem primarily because of the definitions lawyers use.

In California, in the desert, the Desert Tortoise is in danger of becoming extinct. The U.S. government has determined that the cause is predation by the common raven. According to the government document, "Raven predation will lead to the extirpation of the tortoise population." The government decided to get rid of some 1,500 ravens. But the American Humane Society filed a lawsuit saying that would be inhumane to the raven. The government settled the lawsuit but it did not act quickly enough, and the Humane Society added another condition. The government could only kill ravens it could "positively identify as habitually preying on tortoises."

So what did the government do? It took action against the miner, and the rancher, and the off-highway vehicle enthusiast, and it shut down the fastest-growing city in the country, Las Vegas, Nevada. In exchange for the ability to build on 22,000 acres in downtown Las Vegas, the people of Las Vegas must set aside 400,000 acres in the county (Clark) for a tortoise habitat on which no ranching will be permitted, from which miners will be evicted and on which no off-highway vehicle activity will be permitted.

In Southeastern Arizona, the University of Arizona and a number of other institutions are attempting to build a world class observatory. Originally, they wanted to build 17 telescopes but they "negotiated" with the U.S. Forest Service and reduced the number from 17 to 15 to 10 to 7 telescopes. The University of Arizona still could not build due to environmental objections so a law was passed by Congress to cut the red tape. However, the Sierra Club filed a lawsuit on behalf of the red squirrel and the project is on hold at a cost of $25,000 a day.

Last year the Justice Department concluded that it did not have a good enough case against Exxon, so the Justice Department lawyers went to the U. S. Fish and Wildlife Service to ask permission to kill several hundred birds, dip them in oil, and throw them into Prince William Sound (Alaska) so lawyers could calculate how many birds were killed in the Exxon spill. The Fish and Wildlife Service agreed and killed several hundred birds from two Alaska wildlife refugees, dipped them in oil, and threw them into Prince William Sound. This is the same Fish and Wildlife Service which recently fined a mining company $500,000 for accidentally killing 25 birds in Nevada.

This is not just a Western phenomenon. It is happening all across the country. Government regulation regarding "threatened" and "endangered" species is stifling critical economic development and the utilization of resources and facilities nationwide, from the Northern Spotted Owl in Washington, Oregon and California to the Sea Turtle in Louisiana, to the red-cockaded woodpecker in Texas. "Wetlands" designation has stopped legitimate development activities all across the country and has subjected landowners, farmers and ranchers to heavy fines and imprisonment.

The Environmental Protection Agency has vetoed vital municipal water projects from San Diego to South Carolina and from Florida to Denver, Colorado.

There is an environmental passion in this country that the media is exploiting. While much good has come over the past 20 years from our concern with being good stewards of the planet, I am concerned about this passion, as I fear any passion which acts without regard to Constitutional liberties, without regard to the Fifth Amendment of our Constitution, without regard to the rights of the individual.

On the fringe of these environmental organizations are the terrorists—those who "spike" trees, "spike" trails and attempt to topple ski lifts—and the animal rights advocates, those who say, "A rat is a pig, is a dog, is a boy."

What we see from so many environmental leaders is a dangerous elitism, an elitism that ignores the needs of most people; an elitism that ignores the needs of our high technology civilization, our need for energy, for ore, for timber. These elitists don't have the answers for where we get what we need. They are just in the business of stopping activity.

The question in this country is where do we get the resources that we need, the energy, the minerals, the timber—if we don't develop them here. The answer is that we get them from foreign countries, countries like Iraq, South Africa and Russia. Yet if we are truly global citizens we should recognize that the Soviet Union doesn't just have a terrible human rights record, it has an abysmal environmental record. It is America that has an outstanding record on wisely developing our forests.

One of the major problems we face in America today is what I like to call weird or political science. There are two bodies of scientists today. On the one hand are those who know what they are talking about, who seek peer approval, who publish in scholarly journals and who do not talk to the press. On the other hand are those who don't know what they are talking about, who do not seek peer approval, who talk to the press and who publish in People magazine.

Unfortunately, the latter are helping to make or influence major decisions in this country, including critical issues of environmental policy.

(C.R. 6/5/91, Pg. S-7230)

Nuclear Proliferation
• •

Nuclear Proliferation:
Our Shared Responsibility

Excerpts from Speech
in the Congressional Record
by
Hon. Richard T. Kennedy
Special Representative for Non-Proliferation Policy

In 1976, David Lilienthal, the first Chairman of the U.S. Atomic Energy Committee gave a chilling personal view of nuclear proliferation. "If a great number of countries come to have an arsenal of nuclear weapons," he said, "then I am glad that I am not a young man and I'm sorry for my grandchildren."

Around the world today, nuclear industries face a dearth of domestic orders for new facilities. Thus, there is a natural tendency by supplier nations to reach out for foreign orders to support their domestic industries and to sustain the infrastructure they have developed at great expense over so many years. They want to keep that industry healthy so that it will be available to meet the anticipated future domestic demand. New suppliers are also coming on the scene, anxious to generate business on their own.

More is at stake, however, than the natural and understandable quest for markets. This is what I want to speak about this evening: Our shared responsibility to prevent the spread of nuclear explosives.

Thirty years ago, President Eisenhower took a historic step which, in a sense, created the worldwide civilian nuclear industry. He inaugurated the Atoms for Peace program in 1953. By this generous act, the United States volunteered to share the nuclear technologies it had developed so that they could benefit all mankind. In the intervening years, American policy has sought to assure that nations could benefit from the peaceful application of nuclear technology under a system which prevented the misuse of that technology. Atoms for peace, not war, has been our objective.

We have no pangs of conscience about nuclear power. We think it is a clean, efficient and reasonable way to generate electricity. As far as we are concerned, it is not a choice of last resort. We see it instead as a key element in our domestic energy future, and, we see nuclear generated energy as important for the economic development and energy security of many nations around the world. For resource-starved developing countries, as well, nuclear power will not be a choice of last resort. Some of the most prosperous nations on earth—Japan, for example, or some of the nations of Western Europe—have not been blessed with abundant sources of domestic energy. There, too, nuclear power is critical to their well-being and energy security.

We believe strongly that the United States must be—and must be seen to be—a predictable and reliable supplier of nuclear materials and technology. For only in that event can we reasonably expect to exert the influence which our technological experience and competence could rightly be presumed to yield.

We stand by the idea, too, where the necessary nonproliferation conditions are met, all nations can and should enjoy the benefits of nuclear energy—to power their industry, to hasten their development, to light their cities, to contribute to the health and well-being of their people, to curing and diagnosing their illnesses. The peaceful atom can do all that if we let it.

There have been departures by the Reagan Administration from the polices of our predecessors on questions of how we set out to accomplish our goals.

Let me be specific. We recognize that plutonium is an inherently dangerous substance. It is a basic element of nuclear weapons. How to control it is a very real and substantial challenge for any non-proliferation regime. Thus, our policy seeks to inhibit the spread of sensitive technology, facilities and material, which could lead to production of weapons—usable material, particularly where there is a risk of proliferation.

At the same time, the leaders of Japan and of many European countries believe that plutonium fuel is both economical and necessary to their long-term energy security. Our approach to this situation would be to conduct a series of metaphysical meditations on the nature of the so-called plutonium economy. We are not doing that. Instead, we are seeking to work with Japan and Euratom to achieve our shared goals of rigorous standards, controls and safeguards for the reprocessing and use of plutonium. At the root of this more flexible approach is our conviction that such nuclear activities pose no risk of proliferation in Japan and Euratom.

There are some nations whose views on safeguards and nuclear supply, or on the Nuclear Non-Proliferation Treaty, differ from our own. Not every nation in the world agrees with our policy and all its ramifications. But rather than cutting off contact with those nations or treating them with stony silence, we are trying to open a dialogue with them. If we are to have any influence, if our views are to be understood, if there is to be any hope of having our views prevail, we must talk with one another and try to find ways to resolve the issues which divide us.

So, if our policies and their concrete applications on occasion depart from those of former times, it is not because we are insensitive to the dangers of nuclear proliferation. It is not because we are prepared to put commerce ahead of global security. Rather, the changes we are making are based on judgments about how best to win the necessary support of other countries and to create the consensus needed to further a sound non-proliferation regime.

In other areas, continuity is the hallmark of our policy. There are standards for nuclear commerce and supplier guidelines in place today. These are the rules of the game and, as such, are part of the technical basis for nuclear commerce. In the future we expect those standards to become even more specific and more complete. No list of sensitive items can be immutable; over time it must be elaborated as new technologies develop, new uses for old technologies are devised.

As I have said on many occasions before, both here and abroad, everyone should know that this Administration will never sacrifice non-proliferation goals for commercial gain or economic advantage. We have set this high standard for our own conduct, and we believe it should be the universal norm.

A few weeks ago, I addressed a group within the State Department and my theme that day was that non-proliferation is a fundamental and pervasive element in American foreign policy, and a key national security goal. My statement was that non-proliferation is everybody's business. It is our shared responsibility.

We, of course, recognize that a policy of technical denial can't do the job alone or forever. No one has a monopoly any longer. Nuclear technology and industrial expertise are increasingly widespread.

Why should we even bother then with trying to strengthen nuclear export controls? The answer is simple: Our efforts to create a consensus behind rigorous rules of nuclear trade are aimed at buying time. And if we can buy time, we can lessen the danger for a time. But we must use that time wisely. We must use it to eliminate, or at least reduce the threats, real or imagined, which can spur countries to seek the bomb. We must ask the leaders of other countries that may be toying with the idea of "going nuclear" to think through the whole proposition soberly and dispassionately. They must ask themselves whether "going nuclear" will truly serve their national interest or promote their national security.

We think the answer is clearly "No." Twenty years ago, American policy-makers seriously talked of a world with 25 to 30 nuclear weapons states by the 1980s. They were wrong.

Instead of 25 to 30, we have today only five declared nuclear states. On the other hand, 116 nations, the vast majority of the nations on earth, for their own reasons and in their own interests, have become parties to the Nuclear Non-Proliferation Treaty of 1970. That is very encouraging.

On the negative side, we must realistically acknowledge that with the passage of time more countries can reach the threshold: with time and money—and a political will to do so—they could probably produce nuclear weapons. Our task is to deflect them from such a self-defeating course. The proliferation of nuclear weapons is not inevitable. Preventing it is not impossible. And to prevent it will benefit every human being on earth.

In the final analysis, non-proliferation has to be everybody's business, everybody's concern, everybody's priority. Each of us can help set a tone, and can lead the way. This is truly a great responsibility, but it is also a great opportunity. The task is formidable, but I am convinced that we can succeed. This responsibility that we share demands our best, our most careful, our most thoughtful efforts. With those efforts, we can—we will succeed. For succeed we must.

Reference: (C.R. 2/15/83, Pg. S-1183)

Chapter 14

Organization of American States

Prospects for Latin America:
The Multilateral Dimension
Excerpts from Speech
in the Congressional Record
by
Ambassador Robert M. Sayre

When we discuss Latin America it has to be done in the context of the overall world situation, and, with respect to the United States, in the context of the overall interest and objectives of the United States. "What is it that we want to see?" President Bush asked in a speech on May 24, 1989.

It is a growing community of democracies anchoring international peace and stability, and a dynamic free market system generating prosperity and progress on a global scale. America looks forward to the challenge of an emerging global market. These values are not ours alone: they are now shared by our friends and allies around the globe—the opportunity for peace—world peace—lasting peace has never been better. Our goal—integrating the Soviet Union into the community of nations is every bit as ambitious as containment was in its time"

To a meeting at the Carter Presidential Center, the Secretary of State (James Baker) characterized changes in Latin America as truly historic. "The United States does not stand aloof from the historic changes which are transforming our hemisphere—in fact quite the opposite. We are proudly rediscovering our shared heritage with Latin America."

After four decades of a highly successful strategy based on nuclear deterrence and massive retaliation, the United States has a new agenda. The United States has decided to join the world and work with our friends and others as the leader among equals. The emphasis is on Democracy and the economic, trade and financial relationships based on the free market idea. It is in this context of new relationships and a new agenda that we need to look at Latin America and the Caribbean, the Organization of American States, and relations with individual countries in this hemisphere.

More than a century ago, on May 24, 1888, the Congress authorized the President to invite the independent nations of this hemisphere to a meeting in Washington to address eight agenda items which broke down into two broad topics: peaceful settlement of disputes and a customs union based on uniform customs rules and a common medium of exchange. The meeting convened on October 2, 1889. The conference itself gave more emphasis to peaceful settlement and arbitration because our Latin America neighbors did not believe that the hemisphere was quite ready for a common market.

The first international conference in the Americas was a meeting to discuss broad issues and hopefully arrive at a consensus. The international organization that emerged—first the Union of American Republics and today the Organization of American States—is the creature of the member states. The meeting in 1889 set the pattern for future international organizations, including the United Nations. These international organizations have no independent status and are designed to provide the meeting place to perform the function of open covenants openly arrived at.

The major issue confronting this hemisphere is the economic crisis in Latin America and the Caribbean, which the United Nations has characterized as of "dramatic proportions." Inflation, on the average, has doubled, and real salaries and wages have decreased. Transfers of capital out of the area continue to be alarming, with the net transfer now running at an annual rate of $20 billion. The deteriorating economic situation has taken on a life of its own with scarce foreign exchange, a weakened investment climate, and declining possibilities of growth.

The debt crisis in Latin America, has been exceedingly costly to the United States in financial terms. Our sales to Latin America which were running at the rate of $42 billion annually in 1981 have fallen to $30 billion today, a drop of 30 percent. Sales of steel and automobiles fell 50 percent. Construction equipment by 80 percent, farm machinery by an even larger percentage, and agricultural sales were especially hard hit. Overall, this loss has cost the United States about one million jobs. If we had been able to maintain and increase our market in Latin America at even a reasonable rate of 10 percent annually, we would be selling $40 billion more this year, i.e. close to $80 billion, or $40 to $50 billion in lost sales.

When we look at this issue on trade, we see that after a century of effort we have come back to square one. We debate our trade with Japan and Europe, but the fact is that since 1982, Latin America was our most important trading partner—more important than either the four largest trading nations in Europe combined, or Japan. As we contemplate a genuine common market in Europe in 1992, we must ask ourselves about our competitive position and whether a common market with Canada alone is an adequate answer.

What role can the Organization of American States play? It includes all the countries in the western hemisphere except Canada. So we have a multilateral forum in which to pursue more cooperative trade relationships with the other independent countries in this emisphere. The OAS is making a major effort to provide the basic data and other information on the trade situation. The OAS is also managing a multimillion dollar study to update the telecommunications system in Latin America and the Caribbean and tie it together with the United States and Europe. The mere existence of the OAS has brought pressure for better solutions. And the persistent pressure from the member countries of the OAS has promoted a new approach in Latin American debt, which has some possibility of assuring a more positive growth rate in the hemisphere in the 1990s.

Another major issue affecting the hemisphere is drug trafficking. For many years, the United States said that it was a supply problem, and the Latin American countries said that it was driven by demand from the United States. Finally, in 1986, the OAS met in Rio de Janeiro at a special conference on the drug issue. There was agreement that it was both demand and supply, and the member countries agreed to work together to resolve the problem. They agreed that there had to be a vigorous effort on drug awareness in the education systems encouraged by the OAS. They also agreed that stronger efforts had to be made on harmonizing legal efforts. They alsoworked out an agreement with the United Nations that the programs of the two international organizations would be fully coordinated.

I do not want to suggest that this hemisphere program will solve the problem. What I do want to say is that the hemisphere is now working together more effectively on the drug issue and that we are pursuing a strong multilateral initiative through the OAS. This program will get us closer to a solution. Stronger efforts are needed, as well as more funds for a broader and more effective program.

Another issue is the environment. Much is said about the protection of the huge Amazon region and the effect of what happens there on the air we breathe and the life we live. This huge area which is larger than all of the United States west of the Mississippi, is divided among eight sovereign states. They have a compact among them. They have asked the OAS to help them, and the OAS has been doing so. In effect, the OAS has been establishing the standards on the development and protection of the Amazon. The United States has been contributing about $600,000 annually to this continental-size effort. If the United States wants to do something about the environment in the western hemisphere, and wants to help avoid disputes in the future, then it would be well-advised to make a serious financial contribution to the work of the OAS.

Democratic government has historically been a major foreign policy objective of the United States. Crucial to democracy is respect for human rights. From its very inception promotion of democracy and respect for human rights have been key objectives of the OAS. It should surprise no one that democratic government has grown in this hemisphere over the past decades despite economic adversity. Panama stands out today because it is so inconsistent with this long-term effort.

But democracy can stand only so much strain as we have seen repeatedly throughout history. If we really believe in political democracy, then we must also insist on and support economic democracy, including policies that make economic democracy work.

Let me say a word about Central America. The issues there are democracy, economic development and security. After the meeting of the OAS in Nicaragua in 1979, the tactics of the United States to achieve its policy objectives became unilateral. The vital concern was the security of the United States. This was a genuine concern, given the level of arms the Soviets were pouring in directly and through Cuba, and the military facilities being constructed. A side effect was the flight of people northward seeking refuge in the United States from the warfare and economic depravation.

In pursuing its policy, the United States unfortunately overlooked, or decided not to use, its treaty rights in the Rio treaty and the OAS charter. That unilateral approach was not consistent with these rights. But the United States strategy is now headed in a direction that its allies in Central America say they want, and also is one that its own long-term interests require.

In working more closely with its democratic neighbors in Central America, the United States is now on the right road. It is pursuing its objectives consistent with its rights and international law and its own principles and values, which more and more are becoming the values of the international community.

The broad issues then are reducing debt, stopping drug trafficking and drug abuse, development on an efficient and national basis and democracy.On each, the OAS can make an essential contribution, sometimes leading, sometimes handling key elements, and sometimes playing a supporting role.

Let me turn to Brazil and Mexico. Brazil and Mexico are two of the key players in the hemisphere, indeed in the world. It is not possible to have an effective inter-American system unless the United States, Brazil and Mexico are working together. A major difficulty over the past two decades is that their relationships have not been working well.

Mexico is making major adjustments in its domestic, political and economic systems as well as its relationships with the rest of the world, especially the United States. On the economic side, it has joined the General Agreement on Tariffs and Trade—a clear sign that it is prepared to play a larger role in international trade. There is a consensus that Mexico is trying to do everything that it can to get its economy functioning effectively, including resolving the debt crisis. In doing so, Mexico has had to try to overcome a lot of history such as the century of difficult relations with the United States before World War II. It is also adjusting its political arrangements to keep pace with its political and economic growth.

Brazil stands somewhat in contrast both as to the past and future. Brazil is a member of the "Big Ten," one of the ten largest countries and economies in the world. Brazilians are seeking to resolve problems associated with their remarkable success from 1945 to 1982. They, too, seek to open up their political and economic systems.

On the economic scale, Brazil also needs to broaden the base among its people. The so-called informal economy is spreading and really cannot be controlled by existing restrictive rules. The Brazilians are a creative, imaginative and hard-working people. So I am confident they will do it.

There was a breakdown beginning in the late 1960s of the historic working relationship with United States and Brazil. The involvement of the United States in the Vietnam War and the political turmoil in the U.S. was a major contributing factor. The United States had been the first to recognize Brazilian independence in 1822, and Brazil and the United States had the closest of relationships in World War I and II and in between those two wars. Trade and financial relationships were also especially close.

But both the United States and Brazil have had trouble adjusting to Brazil's major role in the world since the 1960s. At the moment Brazil is focused inward on a very murky political situation as well as a most unsettled and deteriorating economic situation. More than any other bilateral relationship, this one with Brazil must move to the top of the United States international agenda because a failure to put it back in good working order, based on equality and mutual respect, portends serious consequences for both countries.

Latin America needs priority attention. The situation there has deteriorated badly since the 1980s. Events there have been extremely costly to the United States, whether it is the few billions spent on Central America, or the tens of billions taken each year since 1982 by Adam Smith's "invisible hand," through the collapse of our trade relationship.

The 1990s and beyond must be a time for rededication to cooperation and growth. The long-term interest of the United States is bound up in the well-being of our neighborhood.

Reference: (C.R. 10/17/89, Pg. E-3456

Chapter 15

Patriotism
4th of July, 1989
Excerpts from Speech
in the Congressional Record
by
Hon. George E. Sangmeister
U.S. House of Representatives

It is with great pleasure that I join you and all Americans in celebrating the birth of our nation, Independence Day.

In the immortal words of Lincoln's Gettysburg address, we find the reason why all Americans should celebrate July 4th as a national holiday. "Fourscore and seven years ago our fathers brought forth on this continent a new nation, conceived in liberty, and dedicated to the proposition that all men are created equal." And it was another famous American, Daniel Webster, who in 1830, described our democracy as "the people's government, made for the people, made by the people, and answerable to the people." It is most appropriate, therefore, that once every year we, as a nation, take time to remember the birthday of this great republic and to remind ourselves and our children of why this nation was born.

It was sheer boldness (and some would say even madness) for 56 representatives of 12 colonies to sign the Declaration of Independence on that July 4th in 1776. They were like Little David facing the Giant Goliath, their Goliath being England! They were, in essence, telling a powerful King George III that since his government was tyrannical "it was the right of the people to alter or abolish it, and to institute a new government." And as if to underscore that they knew the dire consequences of their actions, they added as a conclusion: " For the support of this Declaration, we mutually pledge to each other our lives, our fortunes and our sacred honor."

It is indeed fitting that we remember these heroes: John Hancock, John Adams, Benjamin Franklin and Thomas Jefferson, among others. Yet, who were these revolutionaries? Professor Waldo Braden describes them thus: "They were mainly farmers, planters, merchants and lawyers. Some were rich. Many were self-made men who had to work hard for what they had; one had actually been a bond servant." Of the original 56, more than half paid dearly. They lost homes and property, were taken prisoner, lost sons and their own lives. They lost much, but never their sacred honor.

Shakespeare once asked, "What's in a name?" The names that fill the proud pages of our history ring like the liberty bell: Concord, "where the embittered farmers stood and fired the shot heard round the world," Valley Forge, where Washington's ill-clad soldiers left bloody footprints in the snow; Bunker Hill and Yorktown, sacred to our memory; Independence Hall, where the Declaration of Independence was adopted and the Constitution drafted; Patrick Henry, who demanded liberty or death; Nathan Hale, who regretted he had but one life to give. And during the terrible years of the Civil War, there were the names of Grant and Lee, of Gettysburg and Chancellorsville, and Abraham Lincoln, who wept that the union was being rent asunder.

Unhappily, many of the names that remind us of the gift of freedom are a litany of battles: Verdun, Bastogne, Normandy, Iwo Jima, Guadalcanal, Heartbreak Ridge, and Pork Chop Hill. What's in a name? For an American, a stark reminder of the price of loving freedom, and honor above life itself.

When we watch the accounts of anti-American demonstrations in foreign countries on TV, what is the first thing we see? The burning of the American Flag, an act of contempt toward the democracy and freedom in America which it symbolizes. We are outraged and rightfully so. Should we be less outraged when it happens right here at home? The answer is no. And I believe that those who endangered their lives by courageously and boldly signing our Declaration of Independence would weep if they were here today to witness the desecration of our beloved flag which is taking place under the protection of the first amendment to that Constitution.

But is it only with picnics, parades and fireworks that we remember each July 4? During the height of the Nazi threat, President Franklin Roosevelt reminded all citizens that, "It is simple—I could say simple-minded—for us Americans to wave the flag, to reassert our belief in the cause of freedom—and to let it go at that." He was reminding us that our vision of freedom must embrace the whole world. It was the same sentiment that John F. Kennedy expressed when he said that we should "regard any threat to the peace or freedom of one as a threat to the peace and freedom of all."

Today, we hear repeated the phrase, "people power." In recent months the students of China reflected "people power" in Tiananmen Square, and the world applauded their courage. But freedom is never cheap; it is purchased with the blood of martyrs. The butchers of Beijing may have temporarily crushed a people's peaceful demonstration with brute force, but they forget that no army is stronger than an idea whose time has come. That for one brief shining moment, a replica of our Lady Liberty and cries of "freedom and democracy" were present in the very heart of Communist China and should remain a symbol that freedom is both contagious and fragile. It was Thomas Jefferson who warned that "the price of freedom is eternal vigilance."

As Americans, it is our duty to hold high the torch of liberty to the world. We work with head and heart and hands to keep the original American dream alive. We are legion, and we are diverse, but we are Americans, all. We are the judges and the lawyers whose duty is "to establish justice." We are the law enforcement officers and the firefighters who "ensure domestic tranquility." We are the teachers who touch eternity and the students who ask for truth. We are the children who trust that they will continue to live in America, the beautiful. We are the doctors and nurses and health-care professionals who "promote the general welfare." We are the National Guard and the conventional armed forces who protect this land "from sea to shining sea." We are the journalists who expose corruption even in the highest places. We, the people, are workers; we build the skyscrapers, the homes, the roads and bridges. We are the farmers who put bread on our tables, here and abroad. We are the scientists and the inventors; and we walked on the moon! We are the musicians and the poets who sing of "the blessings of liberty." We, the people, inspire, we are the ministers, the priests, and the rabbis who teach the glory of goodness and the shame of evil. We are the elected officials who represent us and make the laws "for ourselves and our posterity."

A melting pot of different colors, creeds and classes, we awaken to an alarm clock and go to our work because, to paraphrase Robert Frost, "we have promises to keep and miles to go before we sleep." We endure, but we will survive because, as the great novelist William Faulkner put it, "we alone of all creatures, are capable of pity, and compassion and sacrifice."

As a people, we were not defeated by Pearl Harbor, or Watergate or Irangate, and we will survive and ultimately defeat the scourges of drugs, AIDS, pollution, discrimination and corruption. But we must be ever-vigilant against the abuse and arrogance of power, whether it be on Wall Street or on Main Street—whether it be by big business or by big government. To fail in our vigilance would mean the death of "people power."

And so, on this July 4, 1989, let us, as a united people, "highly resolve that this nation under God shall have a new birth of freedom. And that government of the people, by the people, and for the people shall not perish from the earth." For this noble cause, let us, too, as did our forefathers, "pledge our lives, our fortunes, and our sacred honor."
Reference: (C.R. 6/29/89, Pg. E-2414)

Patriotism
Excerpts from Speech
in the Congressional Record
by
Ralph J. Brooks, State Commander
Maine American Legion

As I was preparing my speech for today, I asked myself, "What brings us together? What common bond do we have? We come from all walks of life."

The one thing we all have in common is that we are patriots. The same patriots that were at Bunker Hill, Concord. The same patriots in France during World War I. The same patriots that were in Italy, Germany and Japan during World War II. The same patriots that were in Korea and Vietnam. Sure the faces are different but the patriot is the same.

As American citizens we truly are members of the greatest society on Earth, the society of free men, and while we sometimes think our freedoms are limited, we should remember that all things are relevant. All who hold citizenship in this land of the free can say without reservation that we have greater freedom than any other citizen of any other nation in any period of history.

Patriotism and the willingness to sacrifice for those principles we hold dear have made us what we are—and adherence to those principles will ensure that our children and their children will enjoy the blessings that are ours.

This nation, conceived in liberty and dedicated to the proposition that all men are created equal, is a leader in the world and has been for nearly a century. This nation, that transformed the ideals of the Western world from colonialism to freedom for all, must be ever vigilant to guard and protect the freedom that we enjoy.

Perhaps we should review our own Americanism. Just what is Americanism? Reduced to its simplest terms it is simply an inspirational, sacrificial and unselfish love of country. Americanism and patriotism are synonymous. Both stem from a belief in and love of God.

Americanism is a vital, active, living force. Americanism means peace, strength, the will and the courage to live as free men and women in a free land. It means a friendly hand to people everywhere who respect our institutions and our thinking. It is not a word, it is a cause, a way of life, a challenge and a hope in a world of turmoil.

Americanism is complete and unqualified loyalty to the ideals of government set forth in the Bill of Rights, the Declaration of Independence and the Constitution of the United States. It is respect for, and ready obedience to, duly constituted authority and the laws of the land. It is freedom without license, religion without bigotry, charity without bias or race hatred, love of flag, and a readiness to defend that for which it stands.

To us today, this ideal of government seems natural. We ask, "What other basic idea of government can there be?" But we must realize that a large part of the world today subscribes to a form of government that is unalterably opposed to our own philosophy.

They say that the state, not God, is the author of our rights. This is totalitarianism, which appears under the guise of Communism, Naziism, Fascism and many other kinds of isms. Often it is presented under a patriotic guise that fools those who do not see its basic evils.

Whether we view democracy as a system of popular self-government, or as a way of life in which the equality of individuals is generally recognized, America approaches true democracy more closely than any other country in the world.

But these privileges will not be maintained unless we create for ourselves, and among the youth of this country, a renewed faith in our system of government.

We need a rededication of American faith, clearly defined and acted upon. Each one of us should say in his or her mind and heart, "This country belongs to me and I must cherish it. I believe in the right of human beings to life, liberty and the pursuit of happiness; in government by the consent of the governed; in freedom of the press, speech and assembly; and in the right to worship according to one's own conscience. I believe in the rights of all to justice and in the other rights declared in the Declaration of Independence and in the Constitution. I believe that these rights belong to others as well as to me, and that I have not only the privilege to enjoy them, but the obligation to cherish and maintain them.

To be a good American is the most important job that will ever confront us. But essentially, it is nothing more than being a good citizen, helping those who need help, trying to understand those who oppose us and doing each day's job a little better than the day before.

I am sure all of you will agree that America does have some serious problems. I am sure you will all agree with me that we must do more to meet the needs of our people. We must commit ourselves to the fight against poverty, crime, drugs, pollution and the other social and economic ills of this nation.

We owe it to ourselves and to our children to dream new dreams, to have pride in the past and faith in our future. For without such dreams, such pride, such faith, we will have no future.

We work constantly to bring about a renewal of faith in and love for the principles that founded our great nation. We believe that to "stand and wait" while others serve is not enough. We must take up the challenge before us—to recapture the values which made us a great people—and rise up to a new sense of love for our country.

So I say to all of you people out there, you great veterans, for whom this day, November 11, was set aside, this is your day. You and your fallen comrades earned it. Let no one take it from you.

Reference: (C.R. 6/22/82, Pg. S-7302)

Memorial Day, Arlington National Cemetery
Excerpts from Speech
in the Congressional Record
by
Hon. James H. Webb Jr.
Secretary of the Navy

It is an honor to be among you on this very special day of remembrance. It is a tribute to all who have ever served our country that so many of you chose to gather in this historic place and collectively honor our fallen comrades from so many battlefields in too many wars.

The ceremony at the Tomb of the Unknown Soldier is, I think, the most touching and appropriate way of remembering sacrifice that one can imagine. By honoring the nameless Americans whose branch of military service we do not know, whose unit we cannot discern, whose rank and whose manner of death will always remain a mystery, we honor the greatness of the sacrifice of all Americans who have faced terror and died young so that others might live in peace.

Listening to the reading of Gen. John Logan's General Order, which created Decoration Day, filled me with mixed emotions, which as a Son of the Confederacy, it always has, but it also gave me an appreciation for the paradox that so often attends the aftermath of war. General Logan had in mind a day that would honor the soldiers of the Union after the War Between the States. We continue to carry out his custom, properly broadened on the family grounds of the most revered soldier of the Confederacy.

And how ironic it must have seemed in 1950, when in May the Congress passed a law asking the President to proclaim Memorial Day, a day of prayer for permanent peace, and then scarcely a month later our soldiers were dying on the battlefields of Korea, and that irony continues. Every year on this day we pray for permanent peace, and yet we know, even as we pray, that the time given us on this earth, has been, at its most optimistic, one of volatility and frequent violence.

And so on this day when we remember the valiant dead from the battlefields that scar our history, we should also contemplate what it has been exactly that Americans have fought and died for over the course of our existence. In this context, it is hardly a day for remembering old enemies. We fought the British, now a major ally. We fought the Mexicans, now our friends. We fought each other, and, in fact, the greatest takers of American lives in all our wars have been other Americans. We fought the Spanish, now our allies, and the Germans, and the Italians and Japanese, now close friends whom we help defend. We fought North Koreans and the Chinese to a stalemate that our country has wrongly forgotten, and the North Vietnamese in a war where our soldiers were too frequently criticized by their own countrymen for their efforts.

These fallen men and their compatriots fought for something, rather than simply fighting against an ephemeral foe. They fought, rather, for the values that have made our country pre-eminent in the world. We are not a country that seeks war, and we are not a country that seeks enemies.

We are a society founded on the greatness of individual effort, whose power has been used so that other powers might flourish; the power of the unfettered mind. The power of a multicultural society in free debate. The creative power of the dynamic entrepreneur. The inner power of spiritual belief.

And in a society which treasures the individual, there can be no greater tragedy than the loss of individual life. The markers which surround us on these rolling hillsides remind us that weakness, miscalculation, failed diplomacy, and naive isolationism can ask a costly price.

This is not a new dilemma. Alfred Thayer Mahan, the principal architect of American naval strategy, used to worry about our democratic system's lack of foresight and unwillingness to pay the price of the very naval power that would guarantee its international stability. He once wrote that "it behooves countries, whose people, like all free people, object to paying for large military establishments, to see to it that they are at least strong enough to gain the time necessary to turn the spirit and capacity of their subjects into the new activities which war calls for."

And I would say to you that, unlike in Mahan's day, time is what we no longer have. Today, in this era of what we call "violent peace," there are no other countries between ourselves and our obligations. The lesson that should be apparent from the very magnitude of the names surrounding us, the names that speak to us from the silence of their graves, is that it is better spend dollars for readiness than it is to spend lives, because unpreparedness invites the hostile acts of an aggressor.

In the aftermath of the tragedy abroad the USS Stark last week, it is important for all of us to remember that those serving today exhibit the same dedication, sacrifice and love of country as has been found in any war-time period. Their lives are at risk every day, on the cutting edge of America's security needs around the world. While their peers languish in college or pursue carefree careers, these young, dedicated soldiers, sailors, airmen and Marines have become the quiet heros of their generation.

One of our first duties on Memorial Day is to remember. William Gladstone, the former British Prime Minister, once said, "Show me the manner in which a nation or a community cares for its dead, and I will measure exactly the sympathies of its people, their respect for the laws of the land, and their loyalty to high ideals." Those of us who have seen war's ugliness know that a battlefield does not honor its dead. It devours them without ceremony. Nor does a battlefield honor heros. It mocks their sacrifice with continuing misery and terror. It is for those who survived to remember sacrifice and to honor our heros.

The second duty is to keep this country strong. Wars are not prevented, nor are dreams preserved, because one side is more logical, more illuminated, or more kind. This country is great because it has been strong. It has been strong because its individual citizens have believed in its uniqueness so strongly that they have been willing to provide for the common defense and, if necessary, to take up arms on its behalf. So has it always been—so must it ever be.

Today, as we remember those who have fallen let us also remember that peace is bought, not with a wish, but at the price of dedicated service. And let us on this special day, be thankful for the dedicated service of those who are at this moment, quietly and without fanfare, defending our interests throughout the world.

Reference: (C.R. 5/27/87, Pg. S-7146)

Peace and Prosperity
America's Commitment to Peace and Prosperity
Excerpts from Speech
in the Congressional Record
by
Hon. Dan Quayle
Vice President of the United States

It's good to be here in Chicago, the Mid-America Committee is celebrating its 25th anniversary. You have always provided a forum to discuss the great issues facing our nation. Today will be no exception.

We meet at an extraordinary moment in world history. The United States and it allies have just won one of the most stunning military victories. The movie Henry V reminds us that our Persian Gulf victory has parallels to Agincourt. You'll recall that English forces killed 10,000 French troops in that epic battle, while losing only 25 men themselves, and in Desert Storm we destroyed an Iraqi army of over half-a-million troops, while suffering slightly more than a hundred fatalities.

Operation Desert Storm is going to be studied in military academies for years to come. But it holds important lessons for the rest of us as well. This afternoon I would like to examine some of these lessons.

My first visit to Chicago as Vice President was in April 1989 to address the American Newspaper Publishers Association. My speech zeroed in on America's so-called "declinists." America's declinists are a group of pundits who were predicting America's imminent fall from world leadership. America's best days, the declinists argued, were behind us. We had better accept this fact, and resign ourselves as graciously as possible to our diminished role in the world. The declinists predicted defeatism, low growth and an America unable to sustain its status of world leadership.

For me and happily others, the Persian Gulf war has once and for all slam-dunked our declinists. Other nations made impressive contributions to Desert Storm, but it was America's leadership and contribution that were decisive. Today, as in the past, the world looks to America for leadership in times of crisis. And today, as in the past, only America is capable of providing world leadership.

But the stunning victory achieved by coalition forces against Iraq has refuted the declinists in yet another respect. As one pundit put it on the eve of the war, "All those precision weapons and gadgets and gizmos and stealth fighters are not going to make it possible to reclaim Kuwait without many thousands of casualties."

Well, it turned out he got it exactly wrong. The quality of our people was the key to our victory, and our military technology saved thousands of American and allied lives, and provided us with the decisive edge. Let me give you a few examples.

I'll begin with the Patriot missile. The idea of a bullet hitting a bullet was proven a reality. Scores of Saddam's scuds were blown out of the sky by the Patriot.

Another example was the M-1 Abrams tank. Although some in Congress have criticized the M-1 tank as "vulnerable" and a "questionable buy," it showed its capability in Desert Storm. Going up against the Soviet-made T-72 tanks of Saddam's Republican Guard in the largest tank battle since World War II, the M-1 tanks destroyed hundreds of their adversaries. Throughout the course of the battle, the Soviet-made T-72s were able to knock out only two M-1s.

A final example of the effectiveness of American technology was the Stealth Fighter in Desert Storm. The F-117 constituted less than three percent of the total aircraft. Yet it accounted for more than 40 percent of the Iraqi targets we hit.

All in all, smart weapons, in the hands of smart people, made all the difference in Desert Storm. Indeed, the U.S. technology skills won the war. American quality triumphed over Iraqi quality. And American brainpower triumphed over Soviet hardware. As the President said, "The America we saw in Desert Storm was first-class talent."

In the aftermath of the Vietnam War, armed forces were badly demoralized. Veterans who came home after serving in Vietnam were often shunned by the rest of society. Parts of the country turned their backs on the military. Today is a different story. Today our military wear the uniform proudly. Yes, there has been a dramatic change over the years. There have also been some profound reforms which have changed the qualities and character of servicemen and women.

Perhaps the most important reform was replacing the draft by an all-volunteer force. This means that the only people who are serving in our armed services today are men and women who have chosen to serve. But while our armed forces no longer rely on the draft, they have not abandoned their high standards. For they understand that no one signs up to join a third-rate organization. To attract the best, you've got to be the best, and our armed forces are the best!

A final reason for the superb performance of our armed forces in Desert Storm was that they were allowed to do their job. Washington didn't try to "micro-manage" this war. The President set the war's broad objectives. He carefully defined the military's mission and after having done all that, he let the military itself carry out that mission. He treated our servicemen and women like professionals, and our soldiers responded as he knew they would: With skill, courage and dedication.

But our military is not the only American institution that should be second to none. Our schools, our industries and our productivity should also be second to none. And while I would not argue that techniques that work in the military are directly applicable to the domestic sector, I would argue that the military's emphasis on our people is a lesson that does carry over into other walks of life.

President Bush knows that our future competitiveness depends as much on the intangible currency of our people's skills and motivations as it does on the dollars and cents of financial capital. He knows that as we move into the 21st Century, we must continue to improve our competitiveness, and that means using our moral and intellectual resources as effectively as possible. That's what President Bush's domestic agenda is all about.

For example, the President is committed to restructuring our educational system by promoting greater educational choice. You can't solve the problems of our educational system simply by throwing more money at it, any more than you could have solved our military problems in the wake of Vietnam through financial means alone. You had to change the system. You had to change the atmosphere. You had to change people's motivation and that's what educational change is all about.

But along with education choice, the President is dedicated to maintaining standards of educational excellence. His goal is for our students to be No. 1 in the world in math and science by the year 2000.

We will also achieve another goal of the President's—becoming a truly color-blind society. And you don't do that by discriminating in favor of one group and against another. You do it by treating all groups equally. That's what the President's civil rights agenda is all about: Equality. All Americans of all races desire fairness and equal opportunity.

The President is also committed to promoting America's progress in science and technology. Smart weapons in the hands of smart people won the war in the Gulf. And the finest technology in the hands of a skilled people will keep America competitive in the world of the future.

That is why the President's budget calls for a 13 percent increase for research and development.

But along with record levels of federal investment in research and development, we are committed to working with American industries. We want to make it easier for companies to capitalize on the discoveries of basic science. We want businesses to develop new products and processes. One way to meet these goals is to remove the roadblocks of overregulation. For just as federal micro-management undercuts our military effectiveness, so federal overregulation undercuts our economy's effectiveness.

And the President remains committed to reducing the tax rate on capital gains to unleash the power of the marketplace—the power of ideas and free enterprise. Despite what the critics try to argue, the facts are in: A reduction in the capital gains rate creates jobs and promotes economic growth. We saw it happen in 1978. We saw it happen in 1981. We'll see it happen again.

All the domestic initiatives that I've just outlined have a single underlying goal. They seek to enlarge the scope of individual freedom, to liberate the power of the American mind and the potential of the American spirit. For when it comes to the military, when it comes to politics, and when it comes to economics, we know this: Freedom works, and we know how freedom works—by enabling every individual to put his or her talents to full use.

Speaking nearly 150 years ago in Illinois, Abraham Lincoln looked forward to the day when "mind, all conquering mind, shall live and move the monarch of the world." My friends, that day is fast approaching. In the 21st Century, success will go to the nation that utilizes its intellectual resources most effectively.

And as Desert Storm demonstrates, that nation will be the United States—provided we are wise enough to learn its lessons, and determined enough to apply those lessons.

Reference: (C.R. 3/19/91, Pg. 979)

Politics
· · · · · · · · · ·
The American Political System
How It Works — And Why
Excerpts from Speech
in the Congressional Record
by
Hon. Robert W. Kasten Jr.
United States Senate

As a legislator and a politician, I have had occasion for many years to reflect on the principles and practices of the American form of government, and I am very grateful for this opportunity to share with an audience of Soviet students and intellectuals both my understanding of the philosophical foundations of our system of government and my appreciation of how that system works to improve the lives of the American people.

The people of the state of Wisconsin elected me to represent their interests in the national capital of Washington, D.C. In maintaining contact with those I represent, I have frequently addressed groups of young people in these or similar words: "The kind of America we have depends on your efforts. It's up to you to build the America of the future."

In America, these sentiments are so commonplace that they have almost lost their meaning. It's taken for granted that the role of young people is to build up their country in their own image, so that they can spend their adulthood in a society of their own creation.

The Gorbachev reforms—political glasnost and economic perestroika—have confronted the young people of Russia with fundamental choices about the kind of Russia they want to inherit, and the kind of Russia they want to bequeath to their children.

I think President Gorbachev discovered the correct path when he called for a Russia reintegrated into Europe, and a Soviet Union reintegrated into the global community of nations. Many in the Communist Party media will try to convince you that America seeks a hegemony in Europe, and is therefore threatened by a new European Russia. But the truth is just the opposite.

America welcomes Russia back into its European heritage, because only through rediscovery of that heritage can the liberty and prosperity of the Soviet peoples, and a future of peace and security for all nations, be assured.

In the late 18th Century, my country, America, was a colony being exploited by an imperialist power, Britain. The exploitation had been under way for over a century and a half, and the colonists were finding it increasingly difficult to reconcile the denial of political and economic rights to the colonists with the traditional system of liberties enjoyed by British subjects. The rights they were denied—among them the rights of life, liberty and the free pursuit of happiness—were held sacred by British tradition. This philosophical system was the foundation for the successful revolution of the American colonies, as well as for the establishment of the Constitution by which today's American government is organized and controlled.

After the Revolution, America for a brief time was a loose Confederation of States. The weakness of the central government during this period prompted Americans to draft a new system of government organization—a new Constitution.

In 1787, the several states that made up the American Confederation sent delegates to a national convention in Philadelphia. The purpose of the convention was to establish a system of government for the newly liberated colonies which would avoid the extreme centralization and denial of rights which marred the British administration, while at the same time possessing adequate power to meet the needs of the new nation in a democratic-pluralist way.

The answer that emerged from the convention was that men and women are indeed capable of constructing good government based on reason, and that they could devise a system that took sufficient account of all factions and interests while denying the rights and legitimacy of none.

Some argued that all of these factions would irreparably weaken the government, and that it might be better to limit liberties in order to decrease the factional conflict and thus provide for a stronger government. The new government, after all, had a lot of serious problems to confront—why strangle it with a lot of unnecessary restrictions.

Instead of curtailing liberties in order to make the government strong, the Constitution divided and limited the power of the government so that no faction could hijack all of the power even if it controlled part of the government. It didn't make the government weaker; it made all the several factions weaker as they each sought to divert government to their particular economic, regional or ideological ends.

I would like to describe briefly how that Constitutional system works, my own role in it, and how my vote interacts with the role of others.

At the core of the American democratic system is the separation of powers. The legislative function in the United States is exercised by the Congress, which comprises two popularly elected branches. The Senate has two members from each of the 50 American states. The entire population of a state votes on candidates running for election to the Senate. Senators are elected for six-year terms.

The House of Representatives has 435 members, and these are distributed among the states according to population. For example, my own state of Wisconsin sends nine members to the House; the largest state, California, sends 45; and the very smallest states send only one each. To win a seat in this body, a candidate must contest and win an election in one of the geographic districts in his state.

Because members of these two chambers of the legislature are directly elected by popular vote, they are sometimes controlled by different political parties. For much of this decade, the Senate was controlled by a majority from the Republican Party, while the House has been controlled by a majority from the Democratic Party.

The choice about which party will control the House and the Senate is therefore made by individual men and women at the local level all over America, when they go to the ballot box and decide which candidates will best represent their interests and values.

That's how the people who write American laws are chosen.

The executive power in America is rested in the President, who is elected for a four-year term. Presidential elections, while occurring on the same day as elections to the Congress, are independent of them and involve a more complex process. Rather than amassing a numerical majority of voters nationwide, a Presidential candidate must win a majority in each of as many states as altogether make up a majority of the American population. Nevertheless, because no candidate in the last 101 years has been elected without also receiving the most votes from the American people, the Presidential elections are widely perceived as being just as fair and democratic as those for Congress.

The judicial power in America is also independent. The federal judges charged with interpreting the Constitution and enforcing national laws are appointed by the President, but they must be approved by a majority of the Senate. These judges have life tenure.

As if this weren't enough, there is yet another layer of safeguards to protect the liberty of Americans: the system of federalism. Each of the 50 states has its own popularly elected Governor and legislature and makes its own laws. These state governments, because they are closest to the needs and concerns of their people, have been dynamic innovators in government policy—and much of what is best in our national laws was enacted as a result of its proven success in one or a number of the states.

Constitutional rights and liberties are another essential component of the American political system. That a Congress or a President is elected democratically does not entitle it to infringe on the rights of individuals and minorities. The Constitution's Bill of Rights prohibits the making of any laws that would violate the people's right to freedom of speech, freedom of religion, or any other basic human right.

Central to the economic rights recognized by our Constitution is the provision which holds that "No person shall ... be deprived of life, liberty, or property, without due process of law; nor shall private property be taken for public use, without just compensation."

The Constitution can be amended by common consent of the legislatures of three-fourths of the states to a particular amendment, which can be proposed either by a two-thirds vote of both houses of Congress, or by a convention called by two-thirds of the state legislatures.

By making the amendment process this complex and difficult, the creators of our Constitution ensured that it would not be amended for frivolous and demeaning purposes, or be turned into a tool for the satisfaction of transient passions. And in fact, there have been only 26 amendments in the last 200 years.

It is my belief, based on almost 20 years of experience in American politics, that the American political system works well. The dictum of Prime Minister Churchill of Great Britain, to the effect that democracy is the worst possible form of government except all the other forms that have ever been tried, is true.

To those of us trying to work within the system to promote the interests of the voters of our states, the system is often irritating. It is even sometimes infuriating. But in the last analysis, when it comes to meeting the human needs and protecting the human rights of all the American people, the American system works very well.

Just as the crafters of the Constitution intended, the fragmenting of power has proved a source of great strength for our country. Our constitutional system sometimes fails to prevent bad things from happening, but it usually keeps them from becoming much worse than they already are. In short, the system functions as a self-correcting mechanism—just as its founders had intended.

America's separation of powers makes it much more difficult for any particular party to enact its policies into law. But I think that what America loses by lacking this strong consolidation of power, it more than makes up by giving minority parties and minority interests an opportunity to promote their programs.

The key to a successful representative government is ensuring the rights of the minority while at the same time providing for the enactment of the will of the majority. These structures, then, are important. Democracies do better or worse according to how well their structures provide for the political rights of all their citizens.

But the spirit is the same—the spirit of human rights and democracy. Where this spirit lives, there is a hope of happiness for the people.

And, today, the times are changing here in the Soviet Union. What will become of this union of great nations? Can true democracy be built on a Leninist foundation? Can the slumbering giant of the Russian spirit be reawakened for active service to the world community?

The answers to these questions are written in the hearts of the young people of this country, the first adults of the 21st Century. And I find in those hearts much cause for optimism—because they are the hearts of brothers and sisters, men and women who know the good that is in man if only he is allowed to be free.

So let me ask, along with the great Russian writer Nikolai Gogol: "Whither art thou soaring away to, then, Russia? Give me thy answer! But Russia gives none. With a wondrous ringing does the jingle bell trill; the air, rent to shreds, thunders and turns to wind, all things on earth fly past and, eyeing it askance, all the other peoples and nations stand aside and give it the right of way."

You have it within your power to make this land a wonder of the world, a marvel for all mankind. This is your challenge, and the hope of lovers of freedom all over the world.

Reference: (C.R. 7/11/89, Pg. S-7608)

Poverty
·····••••·

On World Poverty

Excerpts from Speech
in the Congressional Record
by
Hon. Barber Conable, President
The World Bank

As the 1990s unfold, success in reducing poverty should be the measure of global economic progress.

Reducing poverty is possible. Developing countries, bolstered by international support, have made impressive advances against poverty. In the two decades after 1965, developing country annual consumption per capita rose from $590 to $985 in real terms; life expectancy rose from 51 to 65 years; and the net enrollment rate in primary education increased from 73 to 84 percent. These are not mere statistics. They speak of real achievements which have improved the quality of people's lives—achievements to which the World Bank has contributed considerably over many years; achievements of which we can all be proud.

Development on this scale and at this speed is unprecedented. Despite these impressive advances, poverty has proven a stubborn foe. For instance, three of the world's most popular nations—India, China and Indonesia—have made great progress toward reducing poverty. Even so, more than one billion people, half of them in South Asia, still live on less than a dollar a day. Over the next ten years, the population of the developing world is likely to increase by at least 850 million people, many of whom will be born into absolute poverty.

Poverty reduction is an integrating theme for the many facets of the Bank's work, and it is the reason for our operational emphasis. Our World Development Report 1990 sets out a clear strategy for reducing poverty.

The premise of the strategy is that the poor's most abundant asset is their labor. Experience suggests two related ways of improving and utilizing that asset.

First, economic growth which encourages the productive use of labor by removing policy biases will increase income-earning opportunities for the poor, particularly in farming and small and medium enterprise. Second, expanded and better directed educational and health services for the poor augment their income-earning potential.

These two elements form the core of this poverty reduction strategy. In addition, carefully targeted transfers and social safety nets are necessary to assist those most vulnerable—for instance, the children, the aged, the sick and the handicapped—who, through no fault of their own, will not be reached. We can, we must reduce the suffering of these dependent poor.

The precondition for restoring growth to many countries is structural adjustment.

Major economic imbalances must be redressed; the poor suffer most from distortions such as high inflation.

Inadequate restructuring hurts the poor by reducing consumption and availability of social services. We have seen in programs in Ghana and Bolivia, however, that social services can be preserved and even expanded despite budgetary constraints.

In fact, the poor benefit from restructuring. Indonesia's restructuring mainly affected industry, while Tanzania's was directed chiefly at agriculture. Demand for labor is rising in both countries.

Economic growth is driven by the entrepreneurial spirit of individuals. A vibrant private sector, therefore, is vital. Most of the income-earning opportunities for the poor are generated by the private sector, many in the dynamic informal urban sector and in the labor-intensive agricultural sector.

The World Bank is rapidly increasing its lending for the social sectors—primarily education, where we are tripling our lending, basic health care, family planning and nutrition. Our special focus on women in development seeks to expand economic opportunities, while easing their burden in securing food, water and health services for their families. We have intensified our support for efficient food production and for targeting nutrition programs to replace general food subsidies. We are helping countries design better delivery systems for social and public services, and are encouraging the involvement of communities and the private sector.

Poor people and poor countries suffer most from environmental degradation. As the World Bank pursues poverty reduction, our commitment to environmentally sustainable development will continue. We will encourage economically sound patterns of energy use, agricultural development, industrialization and human settlement.

Implementation of the poverty reduction strategy could reduce the number of poor people in developing countries by at least 300 million, roughly one-third, by the year of 2000. Child mortality rates could decline with improved health services, and primary education could become almost universal.

This progress is achievable despite rapidly rising populations, including an expected increase of about 300 million poor people in Sub-Saharan Africa. The World Bank is determined to press Africa's recovery. Special and sustained action is required from the entire international community.

In Africa and elsewhere, governments must be committed to poverty reduction. Scarce resources, financial, natural and human, must be used more effectively. People are seeking better choices and more control over their individual destinies.

Development is most likely to succeed where government is honest, competent, responsive and just; where accountable institutions function according to objective rules, and where red tape is minimized.

Successful implementation of the strategy also depends a great deal on the external economic environment, which is largely determined by industrial countries.

Private direct investment is a powerful engine of growth. Developing countries must improve their investment climates to attract private capital—whether it be foreign, domestic or flight capital.

Despite recent debt-reduction agreements, debt remains an obstacle to growth in many developing countries. We must continue to pursue ways to lighten further the load of both private and official debt.

The Gulf crisis has dampened hopes for a peace dividend. But it should not. Just as an example, if members of NATO cut their military outlays by only 10 percent, they could double their development aid. Moreover, developing countries spend around $200 billion a year on weapons; many spend more on arms than on health and education combined. Financial resources must be redirected to higher priorities.

Development is a slow process, a constantly moving tapestry. Success in reducing poverty will require patience. It will also require determined, collective action. The cooperative spirit in which the international community has responded to the Gulf crisis should inspire our approach to other common causes, especially poverty.

Let me suggest four ways in which we can work together to reduce poverty.

First, developing country governments should establish sustainable growth policies and spending priorities for poverty reduction. The World Bank will work with interested nations to formulate and implement the specific programs which will bring the strategy to life. Others must also help.

Second, we should agree on ways to better measure how a country's policies affect the poor. Good intentions are not enough; objective standards must be built into our efforts to improve the quality of life.

Third, good performance should be increasingly important in allocation of development assistance. Where recipients do not pursue a broad poverty reduction strategy, assistance should be limited and carefully directed towards the neediest groups. Where countries adopt effective strategies, resource flows should be increased to reinforce their implementation.

Fourth, the entire international community should be committed to substantial poverty reduction. We must tap the international reservoir of skills and experience to translate this common concern into action.

Lifting poverty's burden from hundreds of millions of people means new freedom for them—freedom from hunger; freedom from ignorance; freedom from avoidable ill health; freedom to determine their own destinies; freedom to participate in growth and improvement—in short, freedom for a future brighter than the past. Together, we can, and I believe we will, reduce poverty.

Reference: (C.R. 10/1/90, Pg. E-3075)

Chapter 16

Religion

National Prayer Breakfast

Excerpts from Speech
in the Congressional Record
by
Hon. Elizabeth H. Dole
Former Secretary of Transportation

I consider it one of the greatest possible privileges to be invited to share this morning a little of my own spiritual journey with fellow travelers. Like most of us, I'm just one person struggling to relate faith to life, but I am grateful that members of the Congress prayer group have asked me to speak from the heart about the difference that Jesus Christ has made in my life.

But first, I must mention a political crisis, a crisis from which I have learned some very important lessons. Now this is a political crisis involving high stakes, intrigue, behind-the-scene negotiations, influence in high places and even a little romance. The political crisis I'm talking about occurred around 2,450 years ago.

And we learned about it in the Bible, in the Book of Esther.

Esther is the saga of a woman forced to make a decision concerning the total commitment of her life, a decision she was reluctant to make. She had to be vigorously challenged. And it is this part of her story to which I can easily relate in my own spiritual journey. For while the particulars of her challenge may differ greatly from the challenges that you and I face, the forces at work are as real as the moral is relevant. The basic lesson Esther had to learn are lessons I needed to learn. Thus, the story of Esther, over the years, has taken on great significance for me. Indeed, it reflects an individual's discovery of the true meaning of life.

The story takes place in ancient Persia, where there lived a particularly faithful man of God named Mordecai. Now Mordecai, a Jew, had a young cousin named Esther, whom he had adopted after the death of her parents and raised as if she were his own daughter. In fact, Mordecai had raised a young woman literally fit for a king, for Esther grew into a woman of extraordinary grace and beauty.

Then one day, Xerxes, the King of Persia, commanded that a search be made throughout all the provinces for the most beautiful women so that he could choose a new queen. Esther, above all others, found favor in the eyes of the king, and this young girl was crowned Queen of Persia.

Meanwhile, Mordecai, out amongst the people, learned to his horror that one of the top men in government had developed a very careful plan to put to death all of God's people, the Jews, throughout the entire kingdom.

Mordecai immediately thought of Esther, and he sent an urgent message saying, "Esther you must do something, you may be the only person who can persuade the king to call off this terrible plan."

But Esther wants no part of this. Her response to Mordecai: "All the king's officials and the people of the royal provinces know that for any man or woman who approaches the king in the inner court without being summoned, the king has set but one law, that he be put to death. The only exception to this is for the king to extend the golden scepter to him and spare his life. But 30 days have passed since I was called to go to the king."

In other words, Esther is saying, "Mordecai, you don't understand protocol. I have to follow standard operating procedures. Chances are that if I go to the king, I just might lose my head!" Well, Mordecai has no sympathy with Esther's refusal to help. Tens of thousands of her own people stand to lose their heads. So Mordecai sends a second message to Esther.

His second appeal cited three profound challenges which strike at the heart of Esther's reluctance. First, Esther, think not that you'll escape this predicament any more than other Jews. You'll lose everything you have if this plan is carried out. If the thing that stops you from being a servant to thousands of people is your comfort and security, forget it. You are no more secure in there than we are out here.

The second theme is privilege. If you keep silent at a time like this, deliverance and relief will arise from some other place. God has given you the privilege to perform. If you don't use that privilege, He may permit you to be pushed aside and give your role to someone else.

The third theme is providence. Mordecai tells Esther, who knows, that God had placed you where you are for such a time as this.

Finally, Mordecai's appeal struck home. Esther's response: "Go, gather up all the Jews and fast for me. Do not eat or drink for three days, night or day. I and my maids will fast as you do. When this is done, I will go to the king, even though it is against the law. And if I perish, I perish."

That's total commitment. Indeed the story of Esther is for me a very challenging and humbling one. For there came a time in my life when I had to confront what commitment to God is all about.

My spiritual journey began many years ago in a Carolina home, where Sunday was the Lord's day, reserved for acts of mercy and necessity. My grandmother, who lived within two weeks of her 100th birthday, was my role model. She always practiced what she preached and lived her life for others.

And I wanted to be like her. From an early age, I had an active church life. But as we move along, how often in our busy lives something becomes a barrier to total commitment of one's life to the Lord. In some cases, it might be money, power, prestige.

In my case, my career became of paramount importance. I worked very hard to excel, to achieve. My goal was to do my best, which is all fine and well. But I'm inclined to be a perfectionist. And it's very hard to try and control everything, surmount every difficulty, foresee every problem, realize every opportunity. That can be pretty tough on your family, your friends, your fellow workers and on yourself. In my case, it began crowding out what my grandmother had taught me were life's most important priorities.

I was blessed with a beautiful marriage, a challenging career, and yet, only gradually over many years, did I realize what was missing. My life was threatened with spiritual starvation.

I prayed about this, and I believe, no faster than I was ready, God led me to people and circumstances that made a real difference in my life. I found a tremendously sensitive, caring pastor who helped me to see what joy there can be when God is the center of life and all else flows from that center. I learned that Sundays can be set aside for spiritual and personal rejuvenation without disastrous effects on one's work week.

And suddenly, the story of Esther took on new meaning. I finally realized I needed to hear and to heed those challenges Mordecai so clearly stated. Mordecai's first challenge: Predicament. "Don't think your life will be spared from the slaughter, Esther. If you try to save your life, you'll lose it all!"

But I can sympathize with Esther's dilemma. She had all the comforts, a cushy life. And when you get all those things around you, it can build up a resistance to anything that might threaten that comfort and security they seem to provide.

I know all too well how she felt. I enjoy the comfortable life. I had built up my own little self-sufficient world. I had God neatly compartmentalized, crammed into a crowded file drawer of my life, somewhere between "gardening" and "government." That is until it dawned on me that I share the predicament, that the call to commitment Mordecai gave to Esther is like the call that Jesus Christ presents to me.

"If anyone would come after me," Jesus tells us, "he must deny himself and take up his cross and follow Me. For whoever wants to save his life will lose it, but whoever loses his life for Me and for the gospel will save it. What good is it for a man to gain the whole world, yet forfeit his soul?"

Mordecai's second challenge was privilege. "If you don't take this privilege seriously, Esther, God will give it to another." That was a challenge I needed to hear.

What God had to teach me was this. It is not what I do that matters, but what God chooses to do through me. God doesn't want worldly successes. He wants me. He wants my heart in submission to Him. Life is not just a few years to spend in self-indulgence and career advancement. It is a privilege, responsibility, a stewardship, to be lived according to a much higher calling. This alone gives true meaning to life.

The third challenge: providence. "Esther, who knows, but that God in His providence has brought you to such a time as this." What Mordecai's words say to me is that each one of us has a unique assignment in this world given to us by God, to live and serve those within our sphere of influence. But there is one last lesson I had to learn from Esther—the way in which her heart responded.

Esther called on her fellow believers to pray and to fast, and then she cast herself—her very life—upon God in dependence upon Him: "If I perish, I perish."

And how did God work in this situation? Scripture tells us that the king extended the golden scepter, sparing Esther's life, that his heart went out to her cause and that God's people were gloriously rescued.

It has struck me that this is really our purpose in gathering together this morning at this annual National Prayer Breakfast. We have come to humbly acknowledge our dependence on God. We have come to seek the Lord's guidance and strength in our individual lives and in the governing of our nation, with the hope that the power of Christ may deepen our fellowship with one another.

But in this city accustomed to giving directions, it's not easy to seek them instead. Dependence on God is not any easy thing for Washington-type achievers, and it has not been easy for me.

I've had to learn that dependence is a good thing, that when I have used up my own resources, when I can't control things and make them come out my way, when I'm willing to trust God with the outcome, when I'm weak—then I'm strong. Then I'm in the best position to feel the power of Christ rest upon me, encourage me, replenish my energy and deepen my faith. Yes, the story of Esther is actually a story of independence. It's not a story about the triumph of a man or a woman, but the triumph of God.

Total commitment to Christ is a high and difficult calling. And one I will struggle with the rest of my days. But I know that for me, it's the only life worthy of our Lord.

The world is ripe and ready for men and women who will accept this calling, men and women who recognize they are not immune from the predicaments of the day; men and women who are willing to accept the privilege of serving and who are ready to see that the providence of God may have brought them to such a time as this.

(C.R. 3/5/87, Pg. H-1069)

Ministry as a Citizen of the United States
Excerpts from Speech
in the Congressional Record
by
Bishop Leroy Hodapp
United Methodist Church for Central and Southern Illinois

All forms of ministry—as all forms of life itself—exist within a specific context of time and space, and in relationship to other persons and factors.

One of the most fascinating movements in Christian ministry today is happening in China. After many years of underground existence—and ten years of extreme persecution—the Church in China has emerged with new vitality and activity. When

Nanking Theological Seminary announced its reopening in 1981, over 1,000 potential students applied. The seminary has accepted 50 of these (20 of whom are women) as resident students but also is providing resource materials and training for another 30,000 local church workers and lay persons, most of whom work in house churches all across the country.

The church in New China has taken seriously the so-called "three self movement" of 19th Century missionary outreach—that indigenous churches become self-governing, self-supporting and self-propagating. Therefore, Western influence has no place in the current renewal of faith. The form of the church is Chinese—and quite possibly different from any previously experience in the history of our faith.

All forms of ministry exist within a specific context of time and space, and in relationship to other persons and factors.

Scripture makes it clear that the apostle Paul engaged in ministry as a citizen of the Roman Empire. Such citizenship provided him with security and status under very crucial circumstances. Those of you being ordained this evening will carry out your ministry as citizens of the United States. This will be the context of your life. It is a unique setting, defined by a particular time and place. The United States has an understanding of the relationship between church and state, unlike any other nation on the earth.

The basis of our principle of separation of church and state, of course, is the First Amendment to the Constitution. "Congress shall make no law respecting an establishment of religion, or prohibiting the free exercise thereof."

Some implications of this statement may be found in the Virginia Statute of Religious Liberty, written by Thomas Jefferson and considered by him (together with the Declaration of Independence and the founding of the University of Virginia) as one of his three greatest contributions to our common heritage.

In this statute, Jefferson wrote: "To compel a man to furnish contributions of money for the propagation of opinions which he disbelieves is sinful and tyrannical," and "prescribing any citizen as unworthy of public confidence by laying upon him an incapacity of being called to offices of trust and emolument, unless he profess or renounce this or that religious opinion is depriving injuriously of those privileges and advantages to which in common with his fellow citizens he has a natural right." In brief, our heritage does not permit a religious test for public office.

As I hear them, together with other basic documents from our national roots, certain clarification of ministry as a citizen of the United States becomes evident.

First, the United States government should not be in the business of promoting religious faith. We are not a Christian nation; any more than we are a Buddhist nation, or a Jewish nation or a Morman nation or an atheist nation. We are a nation in which persons freely may profess any given religious faith—or no religious faith—and still be qualified and acceptable as United State citizens. That freedom has provided a fertile ground in which the Christian faith has grown to become the dominant faith in the nation.

Second, it is the function of our government to protect the right of any religious faith in the United States to worship, to teach, to evangelize—as long as it does not illegally violate the individual and corporate rights of others in the process. As the dominant faith, it becomes the responsibility of Christians to insist upon the rights of minority faiths. Within our national understanding, the exercise and propagation of faith is a function of the individual, the family and the church—not the state.

Third, inherent in this religious freedom is the right and the responsibility of the church and the individual Christian to interact with the states. The so-called "wall of separation" of church and state does not imply that the two entities ignore one another. The state has a right to demand legal responsibility by the church, and the church has a right to demand moral and ethical responsibility by the state.

Fourth, what the church can and must expect of our government is that its policies and practices live up to the highest moral and ethical ideals expressed in our national tradition and our official national documents. As these traditions and documents were framed, Thomas Jefferson referred to them in his first inaugural address as "the world's best hope." Rarely in national documents does one come upon words like, "We hold these truths to be self-evident, that all men are created equal, that they are endowed by their creator with certain unalienable rights, that among these are life, liberty and the pursuit of happiness."

The traditional and historic ideals of the United States surpass any moral and ethical ideals found anywhere else among the world's nations.

The Declaration of Independence then proceeds to state that, if a government does not maintain and protect these rights, its people have a "right and duty" to alter or abolish it. If it is a foreign government which oppresses them, they have the right to self-determination; if it is their own government, they possess the right to revolution.

Increasingly, oppressed and disinherited people everywhere agree with Jefferson that the U.S. independent documents express "the world's best hope." Therefore, they are determined to alter or replace unjust governments, and cannot understand why we do not support such efforts, given our own historical context. For millions of such people, Emma Lazarus' words on the Statue of Liberty have offered not only hope, but a new beginning—"Give me your poor, your huddled masses yearning to breathe free." But not all victims of oppression can emigrate to the United States. Their plight must be resolved in their own lands.

Since World War II, the image of the United States toward these poor and dispossessed people has undergone a significant transformation. Economic exploitation of already poor nations, immigration quotas established for political purposes, foreign aid programs which enrich United States business interests rather than serve poor and hungry people, regular military and para-military intervention in the affairs of other nations, the threat of military might as the solution to international disagreements, economic and military support for governments which oppress their own people, increasing indifference to the poor in our own nation—all of these types of behavior have challenged positive perceptions of the United States around the world.

However, in a worldwide survey by *U.S.News and World Report*, conducted by its overseas bureaus on attitudes toward the United States, the survey revealed a great reservoir of good will toward the United States especially when compared to the Soviet Union.

From Western Europe came data showing that people preferred the U.S. to Russia as an ally by 56 to 1. One poll in Italy revealed that Italians favored the United States even to their own government.

In Asia there was true appreciation for our refugee and disaster concern, and for our willingness to share technology with developing nations. The Japanese consider us the most trustworthy nation in the world.

African people appreciate the fact that colonialism on their continent did not involve the United States; but they fear current support for the apartheid regime in South Africa, while at the same time we attempt to destabilize some of the newly independent black African states.

In our own western hemisphere, Latin American people are far more apt to blame their own corrupt governments for their poverty and lack of human rights than they are to blame traditional "Yankee imperialism," but they fear our support of unjust ruling elites and our continued threat to intervene militarily when things do not go as we desire.

In summary, any dislike around the world almost invariably is created by our failure to maintain our own ethical ideals. Living up to our traditional ideals of concern for human rights and the needs of the poor not only would reveal the obvious inadequacies of the communist system, but also would be in our own enlightened economic self-interest as the quality of life, including economic purchasing power would rise everywhere in the world market.

As President of the General Board of Church and Society, I receive questions rather regularly about the church being critical of our government and its policies. My answer is that, as one committed to biblical faith, I must criticize ethical and moral failure everywhere, but especially within the systems and structures of which I am a part. If I truly believe in the United States, then I must believe it is good enough to become what its own ideals profess. The Kingdom of God stands in judgment of all human systems. Therefore, I must be constructively critical of my own nation just as I am of my own church and any other institution of which I am a part. I do not strengthen or love my country by blindly praising her faults. I love her best by demanding that she always maintain her commitment to justice, freedom, peace and those human rights so clearly defined in the Declaration of Independence. That, it seems to me, is the essence of ministry as a citizen of the United States. It is "the world's best hope." It may be the world's only hope. It is the key to survival for my children, and my children's children, and the children of the world.

All forms of ministry exist within a specific context of time and space, and in relationship to other persons and factors. Thanks be to God who calls us to ministry today as citizens of the United States.

Reference: (C.R. 7/27/82, Pg. E-3483)

The Second Mile

Excerpts from Speech
in the Congressional Record
by
Lowell Russell Ditzen, D.D., LL.D, L.H.D.

The longer I read the Bible, the more I find myself present when it first came into being.

Let me give you an example. I have visited the land, as have some of you, where Jesus walked and where he spoke to His Day and to eternity. Recently, reading again the Sermon on the Mount, the scene was before me. There came to me a picture of how one individual was affected by what was said on that occasion.

Though the multitude seemed welded into united attention as the Master spoke, one young man seemed to be only partially listening. If you had watched him you would have been aware of a restlessness that came from deep within him.

His eyes roved. His body, naked to the waist, glistened with perspiration. Across his shoulders were raw red bruises, as though he had just been freed from some heavy burden.

Someone, unknowing, might have asked, "Is he a slave?" But any native would have immediately answered, "No, no slave." The tunic tied loosely at his girdle was of too fine a fabric. His face revealed a high-bred youth. If he were a slave, he had not long been subjected to serfdom.

Yet it was obvious, as you looked at him, that there was conflict in that man. His jaw was tense. His eyes smoldered with resentment, and the knuckles of his fists were white, as though anxious to strike a blow of retaliation. And why should it have been so?

A few hours earlier he had been on the road to Magdalena, where it was his monthly custom to spend the day with the wisest man of the area, a great tutor and scholar. Nearing the place he was accosted by a Roman legionnaire, stumbling and groggy with his carousal of the night before. The soldier roughly turned the young man about, tore his tunic down to the waist and taking off the full burden of his impedimenta, lashed it firmly on the other's shoulders. Then he commanded, "You know the law. Carry it now one mile."

The young man burned with anger at every step that he took. The thought of his grandfather's counsel that "as life requires us to do things, we must do them with patience and without resentment," was an old man's folly. Here he was, a man of refined tastes and affections, being required to act like a beast of burden.

Finally, the irksome mile ended. People were gathered on a hillside listening, apparently, to some itinerant preacher. Wearily, he settled among them, trying to find in the scenery about him, in the impersonality of the situation, some release of the inner anger that ate at his heart.

Then the sound of that voice speaking, the quiet authority of the "rabboni," captured his attention. He found himself increasingly alerted—with an electric intensity that began to shock out of his mind any system the dragging anger—as he had heard these words: "You have heard it has been said, 'an eye for an eye and a tooth for a tooth,' but I say unto you, do not resist one who is evil. But if anyone strikes you on the right cheek, turn to him the left also."

He had never heard such daring, such unconventional words!

The books of Exodus, Leviticus, Deuteronomy, all condoned the principle of retaliation—"eye for an eye, a tooth for a tooth."

And then he was surprised and shocked, like some woodland animal that has been pierced by the huntsman's arrow, as he heard the "Teacher" say, "And who so shall compel thee to go one mile, go with him twain."

From years of talking with boys and girls and men and women, I know that there is someone listening in this congregation who feels he's wrongly compelled to go that awful mile—who has a sense of resentment at what life has required him or her to do; burdens that didn't seem to be in the original contract of life; someone for whom duty is a painful thing, who asserts that he's being taken advantage of, who feels he's overburdened, that there are unjust expectations made of him. I know this person is here, because that person is a part of me.

And the words that the Master spoke, need speaking today—the words that say, "There's no real mastery of life—no real mastery of yourself, when you're always struggling against life's minimal requirements."

It could also be put this way, "You really begin to build yourself into a fulfilled person when you let the idea get hold of you to do more than is required! Make of life a quality and a quantity beyond what is expected! Do it and you become a mighty precious person to yourself and to those about you."

The application of this principle is so obvious in our work. Where is the growing edge? Where is the most vital part of any institution, any industry, any profession, any calling? Is it the clock-watching group? The individual lamenting about what he has to do? The dropouts—or the ones who say, "What are the opportunities here?" "What can I do for this company?" "How can I most fully help my customers, my boss, my employees, my clients, my patients, my parishioners, my constituents, my subscribers?"

In this mood, if someone were foolish enough to ask me to nominate a commencement address that was to be emphasized in every graduating class in the country, I would be moved to give the theme in 15 words. There are three points:

(1) Life will always demand that you go one mile!

(2) You go two!

(3) Now get going!

There's power there. There's the rootage of ultimate success wherever we are in whatever we have to do as we get the spirit of not just one mile—but two.

Our country is going through troubled waters. We have grave problems, both nationally and internationally, economically, socially, politically and morally. It's a time of flux and change, with our concerns vastly more complex over what they were when I, as a boy, became conscious of our corporate life. I know few of the answers but I know this: we have portentous opportunities!

One of the fields that intrigues me is that of "Cybernetics." It concerns the various forms of technology and control that will determine the future. For example, with a properly programmed computer we can foresee the end results which will come from any given action. This we could not do with the beginning of the automobile—see the landscape chewed by highways, the parking lots, the air pollution, the mobility of our population, the problems in our urbanization.

But mankind will not be moved forward by these means and instruments ecologically, politically, humanely by people who resent going one mile.

This is Labor Day Weekend. Can I reach someone who will use this occasion to live more unselfishly; who will dedicate himself to our country's welfare more sincerely; who will work for our future with creativity and hope? Friends, our past and our future call out to enroll you as a "second miler."

A helpful book some years back divided life into four categories of work and worship and love and play. Ask yourself when one does what is required—when do the tasks and demands of life turn that corner of drudgery and become play, become fun? When is there delight and love in what one is doing? When does it have a preciousness, almost of sacramental quality? Well, the individuals who are the one-milers will never know, it's only those who go two.

Here's the matter of religion. How do we get the real meaning out of religion? Friends, you and I don't get any treasures of faith until, in this area as in every other one, we get the second mile attitude. There are ethical principles, alive and vital, in every religious tradition. How can these be applied specifically in business, in my industry?

There are Christian ideals of justice in human affairs and good will that have been held up for 2,000 years. People for centuries have talked about prayer, about the healing of the spirit, of the mind and the body. How about going two miles in investigating this avenue of human experience and practicing it in our life?

Where is both progress and joy to be found? One mile? Or two?

I wonder, as I ask myself, if it really is imagination that sees that young man all resentful, centuries ago, by the shore of Galilee, listening to the Master. Is it imagination?" Yes, in a sense.

But perhaps, in an even truer sense, it isn't imagination. For he was there, and is here, too. And the words that were spoken there that day so long ago, and the spirit that prompted them—are they limited to one circumstance, one day in Palestine, centuries ago?

Yes, but also no! For the One who spoke them, speaks them still. And hearts and minds—as then, so now—need to listen to them and apply them, to really get from life these: Who so shall compel thee to go a mile, go with him twain."

Reference: (C.R. 11/12/71, Pg. E-12156)

Republican Party
. . . .

Change, Politics and the Future—
A Challenge to Republicans

Excerpts from Speech
in the Congressional Record
by
Hon. Bob Michel, Minority Leader
U.S. House of Representatives

Nothing better concentrates the mind of someone in Congress than the knowledge that he or she is to face re-election in a few months. So it is our goal to come away from here refreshed, with a better understanding of who we are and how we face the challenges of the fall and the months and years that follow.

I'd like to take a few minutes this evening, as we begin our session, to talk about the future, especially in its special political sense. This brings to mind a more basic question—just what is the future?

Contrary to what Little Orphan Annie sings, tomorrow is "not just a day away." Not, at least, in politics. Those of us in politics just can't see that far.

The only thing those of us in politics can do to prepare for the future is to be aware of and to provide leadership for change. We can't predict the future—but we can deal with change.

The first thing we have to understand is that every change in politics is first preceded by a change in values, technology and basic concepts.

The drug culture eating away at the very heart of our society is proof that a radical change in values can have devastating social and political consequences.

From the Bronze Age to the Iron Age, from the hunting society to the agricultural society, from the Age of Steel to the Age of Information, technological change has always been a harbinger of political change.

Our country—one might say humanity itself—is in the midst of profound transition. The organization of human affairs is being altered, horizons of understanding vastly widened, control of nature extended, perceptions of reality transformed.

Yet both political parties seem helpless to guide this transformation; they cannot even articulate its nature to an anxiety-prone electorate.

Let me give you just a few specific examples of the disorienting, dynamic era of change in which we live.

Johns Hopkins University has developed something called a neural-network computer which, left alone overnight, can teach itself the language skills of a six-year-old.

A symphony orchestra played a concert in Japan, in which a large steel and plastic robot performed as guest organist. The robot, which sight-reads music, played Bach, using its feet on the pedals as well as its ten fingers on the keys.

Experts at Carnegie Mellon University predict that within 20 years, robots will possess the same awareness of their own existence as human beings, have as much intelligence or more, and exercise our kind of common sense—which may or may not be seen as progress!

But as important as these changes are, it is conceptual change that, in my view, is the driving force behind political change.

A recent headline in *The New York Times* about Armenian unrest in the Soviet Union said: " For Gorbachev, a Major Test of Change." The "glasnost" concept has changed expectations, and the recent disturbance resulted.

The American Revolution didn't begin with the "shot heard round the world," but in a gradual change in the perception of the relationship between Great Britain and her colonies.

The Nazi death camps and the Communist Gulag didn't begin when the first strand of barbed wire was laid down—they began with the totalitarian claim to have the right of absolute domination, a basic change in concepts of government.

The Congress of tomorrow is already being shaped by the changing concepts of today. So the first thing we have to do is find out where conceptual change is taking place and then seek to guide it in politically constructive ways.

Take the very basic concept of "family." Twenty years ago it meant a Norman Rockwell painting: Dad at work, Mom at home baking a cake, little Mary Jane with her doll and Junior playing with the family puppy.

These days, Mom is at her job as a truck driver, Dad is in the kitchen learning to work the microwave, little Mary Jane is in college on a basketball scholarship and Junior, a punk-rocker, is undergoing sensitivity training.

And that's only in those traditional families that have a Mom, a Dad and kids in one place.

From child care centers to welfare reform, from creating jobs to building better education, from the problems of the homeless to the need for affordable health care, so much of what we do has to affect the new realities of family life and the increasing importance of family stability to the American future.

We can do better for America. But we face the cold, empty reality that we are in a minority and have been for one-half of my entire life.

Attaining majority status demands that we work harder, be more creative, more aggressive, more daring and more innovative. We must reach for the stars.

To me, a majority is not just to legislate. It is to lead. It is to act, but it is also to think and to learn. To stay in touch with people in Houston and Peoria. To see what they see, and feel what they feel. To experience change and master it. That is not legislating, but it is leadership.

We have to master a level of politics with which we are unfamiliar—the level of the unspoken anxieties, hopes and fears of the people.

Let me give you one congressman's view of what lies at the heart of the deeply rooted hopes and fears of the American people today.

I believe there is a universal and almost desperate longing for a sense of community in America today, a feeling that individuals are not isolated, that we are indeed a nation of communities, not just a mass of rootless individuals, a "lonely crowd." In an era of rapid change, Americans don't want to be left behind, they don't want to be left on the sidelines. They want to direct change with their family and neighbors by values they cherish.

And the only way that can happen is if Americans defend shared values in various communities in the face of enormous pressure from those who want to aggrandize the government's role in our lives.

Don't misunderstand me—I am not saying that government has no role in this nation of communities. To the contrary, we Republicans have to rid ourselves of the cliches and platitudes of yesteryear and realize that most Americans don't believe government is the enemy; most Americans believe bad government is the enemy.

Government can work to enhance, defend and cooperate with communities all across America. Republicans should make this our battle cry.

As I said, this is one congressman's idea. You may have a different one. But I thought I would give you an example of what I mean by "hidden hopes and fears."

We have to remember our party's proud heritage, but at the same time move out to grasp the future, to change it, to shape it, to listen to the hopes and fears hidden in the hearts of the people and to transform what they so deeply feel into public policy.

I came across a sentence the other day that says to me a great deal about what our attitude should be during our meeting. It said: "The future enters into us, long before it happens."

I like the idea, the idea of the future actually coming into our hearts and minds before it happens, waiting for us to make it come alive. That is why we are here—to let the future come into us, to live with it for a few brief hours. And then, fresh and inspired with what we have learned, to move forward to become the majority in the Congress of tomorrow.

Let me conclude by referring to something that everyone by now has seen. I refer to the logo, the photograph of the planet Earth, which is the official symbol of our meeting.

We chose that particular picture for two reasons. The first is a purely aesthetic one. When the first photos of our planet began to appear after the first space flights, we were stunned by the tranquil blue and green and brown and white loveliness of Mother Earth; the sheer beauty of the Earth's serenity. As if seen from God's own vantage point, without a hint of troubles and the sorrow of the human condition—it is always a joy to see it. What better symbol could we have for our purpose here.

But there is another reason we have chosen this view of the Earth. It is to remind us that we are able to enjoy this view because of the courage, ingenuity and persistence of Americans who long ago let the future enter their hearts and transformed it.

It is a wonderful paradox that by going into outer space, we learned not only about space, but about our home, the Earth.

By the same token, by going into inner space for these few days, we will learn not only about ourselves but about our nation and its future.

If we Republicans can let that future into our hearts in Houston, we can, I am certain, become leaders in the Congress of tomorrow!

Reference: (C.R. 3/30/88, Pg. E-904)

Refugees
· · · · · · · · · · · ·
Refugees in the 1990s
Excerpts from Speech
in the Congressional Record
by
Princeton N. Lyman, Director
U.S. Department of State's Bureau of Refugee Programs
to the
Operational Staff Conference of Church World Service

Before addressing the future as concerns refugees, let me take this opportunity to express the appreciation of all of us in government who work on refugee affairs for the extraordinary dedication and conscientiousness which each of you and your organizations devote to refugees coming to the United States. Those of us in government have an important role to play. We must develop proposals, ceilings and budgets which determine just how many and from what countries refugees can come to the United States. But it is you and your affiliates—your volunteers and many families which become involved—which make the program concrete and make it successful. You make each refugee welcome; you give them their start, their first real taste of America. You give the program its heart.

The situation today, and which will define much of our task in the years ahead, is one that is not encouraging. There are some 15 million refugees in the world today, twice the number of a decade ago. Thirteen million of these are under United Nations care. Many of these, it is important to note, are the result of long-standing conflicts; conflicts which today may have even lost some of their original meaning, but which linger nevertheless.

Look at the major sources of refugees today. One-third of the world's refugees are Afghans. The conflict in Afghanistan was triggered by the Soviet invasion in 1979, an invasion from which the Soviet Union has long since withdrawn its troops, but the struggle continues. Or look at the conflict in Mozambique, one which has its origins in a relationship between the Soviet Union that no longer pertains and from a South African policy that is rapidly changing. Mozambique accounts for one million refugees. And there is Cambodia, whose internal wars hark back to the Vietnam War, the Cold War and the rivalry between China and Vietnam—all of which contributed to tearing Cambodian society apart. Bringing just those three conflicts to an end would allow half the world's refugees under United Nations care to return home.

The positive side to this is that, as the origins of these conflicts are mitigated, active efforts to resolve them are under way. In all of the conflicts I have mentioned, intensive negotiation processes are in train, offering the hope that in the 1990s, these three major refugees problems can be finally resolved.

If that does happen, we can rejoice. But the challenge then will be to pay for these settlements. The countries in question have been devastated, mined, people dispossessed while others have taken their land, infrastructure destroyed, education and training virtually brought to a standstill. The bill for each of these settlements—for peacekeeping forces, for repatriation of the refugees and for redevelopment of the countries—thus runs in the billions.

The Gulf War may also exacerbate another old problem, one which has been with us for 40 years: the Palestinian refugees. There are presently some 2 million Palestinian refugees living in Jordan, the occupied territories, Syria and Lebanon. United States assistance to them has been able to focus on education and health, because basic food and shelter did not have to be provided; many refugees were working and sending back remittances, in Israel. But the future of Palestinian workers in the Gulf is uncertain. The invasion and occupation of Kuwait has deprived tens of thousands of their income and life savings. They are returning not as providers but as people needing assistance themselves. Jordan already claims to have received 200,000 Palestinians since the invasion of Kuwait. Thus an old problem may become even worse in the 1990s.

Even as these legacies of past decades carry into the 1990s, new issues are arising. None has grabbed the attention of our friends in Europe—and in a different way in Asia, as the spectra of mass migration.

It is seemingly the changes in Eastern Europe that have brought this issue to the forefront. As societies in Eastern Europe—and we hope in the Soviet Union—become more open, the movement of people takes on a different meaning. When Eastern Europe was under Communist control, we and our European allies treated people fleeing those regimes as refugees. But with Democratic regimes in place, the presence of Poles, Romanians and the Russians takes on new meaning. All over Europe, the issue of migration is being discussed, new mechanisms of both cooperation and control are being fashioned and debated, and old systems are being re-evaluated.

The source of this concern in Europe is easy to see. In the 1970s, the average annual number of asylum requests for all of Europe and North America was 25,000. In 1980, it jumped to 160,000, but then dropped to 70,000 in 1983. However, in 1990, the number went up to an extraordinary 550,000. Many are from Eastern Europe but at least half are from the Third World. So while much of the recent attention has focused on the Soviet Union and Eastern Europe, the roots of the problem are also in the Third World.

The other cause for concern is that it is assumed that most of these applicants today are coming more for economic than political reasons. Europe has less of a clear immigration system than Canada, Australia or the United States, so asylum application becomes in most cases the means of entry. But clearly this will not be adequate or appropriate for the 1990s.

There are many challenges for the 1990s that arise from this concern over migration. One is protecting the principles of asylum for refugees—people fleeing persecution—as nations institute new means of control over their borders. In the backlash against rising numbers of migrants, countries sometimes lean more toward options which threaten that principle. A most disturbing example of that type of action was when Yugoslavia recently forced more than 300 Albanians back across the border.

Because of our concern over this issue, the United States has entered actively into the debate in Europe. One of our objectives is to protect the right to asylum.

A second challenge, however, is to define ways to protect those who are fleeing oppressive regimes for a complex set of reasons that do not fit within our traditional definition of refugee, but which also is not simply a desire for a better job. If the definition of refugee, i.e. someone with a fear of persecution, is broadened too far, we risk losing the sympathy and cooperation of potential first asylum countries in the face of large-scale or even moderate movement of people.

The third challenge arising from this concern over migration is that of international responsibility. How should we share the tasks? How much of European migration should be seen as a European problem, be addressed at least in the first instance by Europe? Or how much an is international problem to be shared out equally? How does one find the right balance that does indeed represent equity?

Let me conclude this discussion of new challenges on the international front with that of new conflicts, conflicts which do not have their roots in the Cold War or other previous international rivalries. The ethnic conflict in Liberia, ethnic and sub-regional conflict affecting Rwanda, and perhaps the same phenomena in Eastern Europe. Will we be able to mobilize the international attention and assistance to these new sources of refugees? Or will they, less directly related to our international positions, be far from our attention and, therefore, our output?

The challenge of the 1990s will also raise new issues with regard to our admissions problem. As in other refugee matters, the refugee admissions program today still addresses in large part legacies of past decades. Some 45 percent of our admissions come from Southeast Asia.

Another one-third of our admissions come from the Soviet Union, with special efforts in regard to religious minorities. The roots of that problem go back not just to the Cold War, but indeed to World War II and the Holocaust. This, too, is a responsibility from which we cannot turn away. If the present trend of migration to Israel and the United States continues, nearly all the Jews in the Soviet Union will have departed by the end of 1995. What will be the people of "special humanitarian concern" after these? How will we define our interests? Or will we reduce our admissions back to those of an earlier period?

Clearly, the 1990s will not be dull, nor lacking in challenges. And we will need to remember the basic purposes of our refugee program: to help those who are victims of persecution. That need, unfortunately, will continue to be with us in the 90s. The sources of persecution, and the nuances of the problems around them will, however, change and challenge us all.

Reference: (C.R. 3/5/91, Pg. S-2598)

Retirement
· · · · · · · · · · · · · ·

Retirement No Longer Makes Sense
Excerpts from Speech
in the Congressional Record
by
Dr. Harlan Cleveland, Director
Hubert H. Humphrey Institute of Public Affairs
University of Minnesota

In January I will be 65 years old, which used to mean I would have to retire. I am beginning to learn what some wag meant by saying of his aging human organs, "If it's working, it hurts. And if it doesn't hurt, it probably isn't working."

As I approach my non-retirement age, it occurs to me to ponder why I wouldn't have been ready to retire if the Courts and Congress and the Board of Regents of the University of Minnesota hadn't recently lengthened the work expectancy of professors. I can present today the fruits of a wholly unscientific inquiry: The truth is that retirement is dysfunctional, which is a fancy way of saying that for most people, it just doesn't make sense any more.

Public policy about retirement is preoccupied with pensions, take home pay for not "working." There is indeed a problem: with a dwindling proportion of working people to retirees, how can the young folks afford to keep supporting the old folks? Some communities are already paying for two fire-fighting teams—the one that responds to fire alarms and the equal number of men who once did and perhaps wish they still could.

If we ask how on earth can the "work" economy afford to support all those people doing nothing, the answer is bound to be some version of "you can't get there from here." But suppose we were to redefine "work" to include both young and old? What if we didn't throw people on the ash heap on a certain date, and organized the work to be done in such a way as to enable them to be "workers"—functional, relevant, engaged, complaining the way real workers do that they never seem to have time to improve that golf score?

Viewed from this perspective, the retirement barrier is a man-made obstruction, a hazard produced by social policy, a cultural obstacle not (for most) a physiological landmark. To be sure, the human body gradually wears out—and, with less frequency, the mind sometimes deteriorates with age. But what about the much larger number of elderly who are coping? Most of them are not visiting clinics or being comforted by their churches or being cared for (and occasionally kicked around) in nursing homes. They are active, they are more or less well, they are at home, and they are available.

Let me digress from my age-group for a moment, because the social disease called retirement is really a subhead of a more pervasive malaise. That larger trouble, just coming into view, can be miniaturized in three words: "After affluence, what?"

Just now, in a society with nearly 10 percent officially unemployed and perhaps three or four times that number unofficially excluded from the labor force, it may seem out of step to be worrying about too much affluence. But bear with me, this argument will shortly lead us back to the case for non-retirement.

Since the beginning of the earliest human civilization, most people in every society were preoccupied with a common goal—to guarantee their own personal security, to achieve an assured and decent standard of life. The bulk of mankind is still too busy making ends meet to worry much about the next goal after that.

But suppose—just suppose—we can in this century achieve a durable prosperity and spread it around in a reasonably egalitarian fashion. What then?

The idea used to be that the purpose of making a living was to stop working when you had it made. According to this philosophy, you would retire as early as possible, pull up stakes and head south to spend the golden years fishing in the sun, snoozing in a hammock, watching the surfers, playing cards in glorious idleness, and happily awaiting the Grim Reaper in bovine indifference to the world about you.

Or, if you were not really old enough to call it retirement, you could work limited hours—as few as your union could negotiate with your boss. You would choose the kind of work that avoided on-the-job excitement and thus avert overtime. Then you could spend long hours and long weekends fishing, snoozing, watching and playing, for all the world as if you were retired. The invention of television, plus the lack of inventiveness in its use of prime time, has made it easier for all of us to do nothing, even when we have something to do, then it ever was before.

There were, of course, more active forms of leisure. When only a few people were rich, they could get away from the others on a yacht, or at least drive into the empty countryside for a spin. They could go to the opera or ballet, hunt elephants, fish for marlin, play tennis, work on their golf stroke, splash in the surf themselves or travel to museums and cathedrals and foreign countries. The object, in any case, was to achieve as much leisure time as possible, then crowd it in with leisure-time activity.

But once a whole production decides to be prosperous, the traditional forms of leisure are somehow not so attractive any more. The lakes and coastlines are crowded, the country lanes become four-lane death traps, the fishing streams get polluted. The need for TV talent runs hopelessly ahead of the talent supply. Even the elephants and marlin have to be rationed. The theaters and courts and golf courses and pools and beaches and restaurants are congested with people who have just as much right to be there as you do. Only the cathedrals are empty. What lies beyond affluence, for most people, is not likely to be the use of the guaranteed income to finance their weekends and vacations. Young people will certainly want to use their economic security as a launching pad for adventure, for "action." And most of them will find their adventure, not primarily in their leisure time, but in their working time—if they can tell the difference.

Luckily, in post-industrial society there should be much more room for work-day adventure. As new machines, new kinds of energy and fast computers take over the drudgery that men and women—and children used to endure, what is left for people to do is the creative, planning, imagining, figuring-out part of each task. Our more complex, agile and intuitive human brains have to feed the fast but stupid computers, which after all they can only count from zero to one and back again. And the handling of relations among people has to be a rapidly growing industry when nearly everyone becomes, through education, a sovereign thinker and communicator—and communications technology makes remoteness and isolation a matter of choice and not of geography or fate.

Now who is likely to be the best qualified for the kind of work that is heavy with personal relations, reflective thinking and integrate action? Who are the most natural members of the "get-it-together profession"? Who are the people among us with the most experience in dealing with other people—the people most likely to have seen more of the world, master or at least dabbled in more specialties, learned to distinguish the candor from the cant in public affairs? The people with the most time for reflection and the most to reflect about. The answer leaps to the eye: they are, on the average, those who have lived the longest.

Our increasingly desperate need for people who can "get-it-together," for integrators and generalists, happens to coincide with technological changes which enable people to work without "going to work." The home computer will put "work," including part-time work, within the reach of anyone willing to retrain his or her brain, and then use his or her imagination.

For those of us in the 60s and beyond, therefore, there will be less and less excuse for advocating a short day in a short week in a short year—and no excuse short of serious illness or death for "retirement." The tasks that machines make possible but cannot do themselves should be creative enough to lure the elderly into work schedules that are lengthened by the sheer excitement of what needs to be done.

In such a society, the people who seek the easy jobs and the earliest retirements will die of man's most readily curable diseases—absence of adventure, suffocation of the spirit and boredom of the brain. The age at which they succumb to these avoidable maladies will hardly matter. "Died at 40; buried at 80" will be their epitaph.

Reference: (C.R. 12/17/82, Pg. E-5273)

Chapter 17

Small Business
· ·

Let Us Compete — Let's Get on With It

Excerpts from Speech
in the Congressional Record
by
Albert W. Gruer Jr., Sales Manager
Waupaca Foundry, Waupaca, Wisconsin

Let me state that the theme for this meeting, "Let Us Compete," was set long before the current bandwagon of the Congress and the President to make our nation more competitive. The Cast Metals Association has been pounding that drum since 1980. This organization represents 500 foundries throughout the country responsible for 90 percent of casting tonnage produced in the United States today.

In 1980 the United States foundry industry operated with 4,000 plants employing 400,000 persons. We began 1987 with 2,900 plants employing 170,000 persons. There have been a few mergers and acquisitions, some joint ventures, but lots of Chapter 11s, Chapter 7s and bankruptcies. Currently the U. S. tonnage production of ferrous castings is about 50 percent of what it was in the early 1980s.

This shrinkage occurred mainly because enormous quantities of foreign castings are coming into this country as rough parts, machined parts, portions of assemblies or simply unclassified castings because of tariff categories. Look around you—and you don't have to look far:

(1) Count the foreign cars—33 percent.

(2) Note the foreign names on electric motors and generators.

(3) See which trucks are delivering merchandise.

(4) Lift the hoods on automobiles and trucks with American names and see who supplied the gasoline or diesel engines—the same with transmissions and powertrains.

(5) Check the innards of your refrigerator and see who made the compressor.

(6) The farm machinery and construction equipment manufacturers—names like John Deere, J. I. Case, International Harvester, Allis Chalmers, Caterpillar—are being devastated and inundated by imported equipment. Some of the names I mentioned have already closed their doors.

(7) Over 60 percent of all machine tools are no longer produced in the U.S.A.

(8) Note the number of new plants being built in America by foreign producers, but ask from where are these cast parts being supplied, their homeland.

(9) I could go on with products like valves, pumps, food machinery, home machinery, garden tractors, lawnmowers, engine parts, construction castings.

The demand for these products, all requiring castings, has gone overseas, along with the jobs. Frankly, we don't need any more government-commission studies to tell us about the impact of imports on the domestic foundry industry—or, as a matter of fact, on our trade deficit for all products.

In 1984, the International Trade Commission conducted an assessment of the U.S. foundry industry in domestic and world markets. The results of that study alarmed us. It provided us with the facts and the statistics. Among the findings: prices on imported castings ranged from 15 to 28 percent lower than our own. Import penetration for certain castings ranged from 10 to 37 percent and was expected to continue upward. The study further showed some distinct disadvantages to United States producers such as:

(1) Their lower cost of labor. (No mention of comparable productivity-man hour or standard of living.)

(2) Their lower cost of capital (many foreign countries favor their industries with the capital costs by special tax concessions, and encourage individuals to save with special tax incentives.)

(3) The assistance in research and development by foreign governments.

(4) Their favorable tariff policies (imports versus exports by foreign governments).

(5) Our U.S. government regulations and mandates impeded U.S. foundries in competing (clean air, clean water, OSHA, EPA, employment policies and benefits).

(6) An unfavorable exchange rate for U.S. producers.

(7) And lastly, the study showed that, "with no substantial changes in world economic or political conditions, it is likely U.S. foundry producers will continue to lose market share."

Our industry followed this study with a 201 case with the ITC (International Trade Commission) and in losing the case we were told that increasing imports were not threatening the domestic industry with serious injury. We were told that "serious injury requires an important crippling, or mortal injury, one having permanent or lasting consequences."

Like it or not, our industry is still alive and breathing. The 201 case found that our foundry employment, productivity, profitability and sales have improved from 1981 to 1983. It showed we were improving our own lot. But there's been some good come out of our present dilemma. We foundrymen have had to search for better means to continue to compete. Some of those means are:

(1) Work as a company team—management and employee—get everyone involved—be receptive to exchange of ideas with an open mind—and be willing to take a chance to improve your costs.

(2) To accept and use advanced technology. Better methods to improve not only productivity, but to improve working conditions—but this needs capital from profit!

(3) To work harder and more efficiently—not all of increased productivity is related to automation—much of it is effort and attitude.

(4) Shut down inefficient parts of a foundry to reduce capacity and overheads and to regain profitability.

(5) Negotiate more realistic wage scales and, in some cases, renegotiate very costly fringe benefits.

(6) Develop new markets for our foundry, and to suggest ideas for reducing costs for your customer.

(7) Fight to maintain market share by performing with superb service and quality.

In summary, get more out of what you have—and do it more efficiently and serve your customers better. The foundry industry is doing just that to be competitive with foreign competition. We can't ask someone else to do the job for us—to accept our responsibility and our challenges.

In the mid 1950s, Eisenhower was pushing a trade and aid program to help the impoverished nations in the world become more industrialized—to improve their standards of living. Obviously, much of this effort was in regard to keeping these impoverished nations from becoming "Soviet" oriented. And may it be said without any fear of contradiction, that since the end of World War II, our nation has helped these former enemies and impoverished nations to revitalize their cultures, their esteem and their economic well-being in the world today.

Without waving a flag—I find that practical, generous and moralistic activity and responsibility on the part of the American people reflects something fantastic that sets our system above all others. In all modern history what other defeated nations have had that opportunity? Let's hope it has not developed into an attitude: "Well, that's what you did for me yesterday—what are you going to do today?"

We don't need more commissions to tell us what's wrong. President Reagan's first Commission on International Competition told us, "For those industries threatened by severe import penetration, U.S. trade law has often granted relief only after their injuries have become irreparable." Amazing, but true.

We need some common sense to make American business competitive—balance the budget and get on with reducing the national debt—fewer government services—toughen our trade and currency policies, a trade deficit that's out of hand—either other countries buy more from us, or they must sell less to us, and stop debating it, do it—stop increasing taxes to American businesses—some have estimated our tax return bill will increase business taxes $120 billion and stop making reckless loans to foreign nations that have no possibility or ability to meet their obligations or pay the interest let alone the principal. Stop mandating useless regulations on our operations that cost money. The United States is in the process of rapid deindustrialization—almost to the point that government has already thrown in the towel. It will be interesting to see what historians write about the current deindustrialization of the U.S.A. in the year 2000.

For several decades following World War II, America had taken for granted that this nation was not only the richest and freest and most powerful in the world, but also was the best educated and most technologically advanced. Unfortunately, many failed to recognize that this status was abnormal and unique due to the way our enemies had been pulverized. Almost all writings of general history of the 1950s, 1960s and early 1970s point to the complacency of these decades. American business was at fault for assuming these attitudes, but so was government. It was the decade of the "giveaways" and flat productivity. Why take a stand—business could raise prices (which it did), government could raise taxes (which it did)—and consumers could pay more (which they did).

So much for history and what it has been. What about today and tomorrow. What about "global competitiveness"? It's a major part of our whole economic dilemma.

(1) Accept that "free" trade is an illusion all over the world—and we're the only nation trying to maintain that position.

(2) Accept that "fair" trade must apply to all nations—without it there can't be free trade.

(3) Accept that American industry often competes with foreign governments—not always with foreign companies.

(4) Accept that there has to be a better solution than retaliation and protectionism—but that applies to all nations—one to another.

(5) Accept that throwing money at a problem doesn't necessarily solve it—it's how the money is managed that's important.

(6) Accept that restoration of a meaningful capital cost recovery system is needed more than ever by capital-intensive companies—so that they can be competitive.

(7) Accept that current trade laws must be enforced; or they must be modified—or be forgotten altogether.

(8) Accept the fact that the trade laws of this country and the trade laws of other nations must be reconciled with the rules of GATT (General Agreement on Tariffs and Trade)—to play the game you need to know the rules.

(9) Accept that real negotiations with other countries are needed—that result in a measurable bottom line. Stop huffing and puffing with threats—negotiate from strength.

(10) Accept that we can neither borrow nor tax our way out of the budget deficit—we must cut spending—we must promote savings for capital formation.

(11) Accept that the trade deficit is not going away overnight—it's going to take time.

(12) Accept that American businessmen and wage earners expect and deserve credibility from the Congress and the Administration in regard to competing worldwide and in keeping their jobs.

Congress could, at no cost, help U.S. manufacturers by subjecting all politically inspired legislation and rule-making initiatives to a test of the proposal's impact on American industry's health and its ability to compete in world markets.

Before passage of any bill, the following five questions should be answered:

(1) Would employment be adversely affected?

(2) Would the U.S. trade deficit be further hurt?

(3) Will capital formation in the U.S. be impeded?

(4) Will it make American industry less competitive?

(5) Will it injure our defense effort and economic stability?

We think a little common sense about sound economics—and less politics—can go a long way toward enabling U.S. industry to begin returning to a more favorable trade balance. It'll take years of industry effort for the good ol' red, white and blue to return to the block. We cannot continue to ignore any more what's happening to us in global competition.

Reference: (C.R. 3/31/87, Pg. E-1210)

Space
U.S. Leadership in Space: Three Reasons Why
Excerpts from Speech
in the Congressional Record
by
Robert Anderson, Chairman and Chief Executive Officer
Rockwell International

For nearly three decades, one of our country's most important sources of new technologies, new companies, new products and services to improve our standard of living—has been the space program.

Today, the promise for future advances from space is greater than ever, but their realization will depend on some very down to earth decisions to be made in Washington, D.C. in the name of the American people.

The basic decision to be made: Will the United States of America invest in its future to assure continued leadership in space?

It was almost 14 months ago that the space program took an unexpected and tragic turn as the shuttle Challenger exploded just 73 seconds into what was to have been the space transportation system's 25th operational flight.

The seven Americans who perished aboard Challenger cannot be replaced. But the spirit with which they faced the dangers of space can be renewed in their names and in the name of the country which they served.

Just four months after the Challenger accident, the President's commission delivered its report. It contained nine recommendations for changes in NASA management and concluded with the following words: "The commission urges that NASA continue to receive the support of the Administration and the nation. The agency constitutes a national resource that plays a critical role in space exploration and development. It also provides a symbol of national pride and technological leadership."

From the events of 1986, I believe the nation has learned some important lessons.

The first lesson is simply that space flight is inherently hazardous and probably always will be. In space, routine is not a synonym for relaxed.

The second lesson brought home by the events of 1986 is that this country needs a mixed fleet of launch vehicles. As a result of the Challenger tragedy and several unrelated accidents with expendable launchers, for about four months last year every one of our large launch systems were grounded. This is affecting virtually every aspect of our usage of space—like the space telescope, the NAVSTAR, many classified projects and a number of civilian communication satellites for United States owners and nations around the world.

Closely tied to our current situation is the third big lesson: the need to push on with the development of new launch vehicles to support our long-range space goals.

The experience curve in space development has trended toward larger and larger satellites and other payloads. This trend will be extended as construction of the space station begins.

Just as with airplanes, ships and trucks, the more you can carry on each trip, or the simpler your operations are, the lower your cost per pound or ton will be.

The final lesson learned from the events of 1986 is the critical need for this nation to get its act together with regard to supporting our space policy and plans.

For me, a person who has spent close to two decades managing businesses on the forefront of technology, the national need to maintain space leadership is obvious.

I see three good reasons why we should strive for leadership in space.

The first is that the American people want to. Opinion polls show that national support for the space program is at an all-time high, even higher than during the years America was putting men on the moon. They also perceive the threat to our leadership.

The second reason for keeping our space leadership is that if we don't stay in front, others will pass us. Many Americans believe it is important to stay ahead of the Soviet Union in space technology. The Soviets are clearly the front-runners among other nations in space activity, but they are not alone. Our international competitors in high technology products recognize the tremendous contribution space programs make to their efforts to maintain global competitiveness.

The third reason for maintaining space leadership: space exploration is a driver of new technologies. NASA can identify tens of thousands of spin-offs from its research that enhance the everyday lives of most Americans.

They include traffic devices, highway safety systems and smoke detectors. Many additional spin-offs are found in medicine. An estimated 12,000 life-saving and health-enhancing devices and processes have sprung from aerospace research, including programmable heart pacemakers, implants that disperse medication or control blood pressure, and surgical tools.

Yet, bear in mind that these advances are only those derived from the process of just getting men and machines into space for relatively short periods of time. Our next step must be to prolong the length of that stay and provide the environment and equipment which will launch truly space-based research.

The space station is the foundation of that next step. And any discussion of the space station should start with the question of manned versus unmanned space exploration. Obviously, unmanned spacecraft offer one major cost and weight advantage—there is no need to protect and nurture that fragile living organism called a human being. Unmanned craft can perform many tasks, gather information, even conduct experiments.

But our experience to date clearly shows the need and effectiveness of men working with machines. Let me give you a few examples.

In April of 1984, U.S. astronauts operating from the space shuttle flew to the non-operational scientific satellite of the so-called Solar Maximum Mission, retrieved it, repaired it and put it back into orbit to continue its mission.

In November, that same year, the shuttle retrieved and returned to earth two satellites, PALAPA-B2 and WESTAR 6, which had been launched earlier but failed to go into their correct orbits.

The final example took place in 1985, but this time it was a Soviet accomplishment. The Salyut 7 space station, while orbiting unmanned, had lost all electrical power and was tumbling through space in a decaying orbit. Two cosmonauts flew a Soyuz spacecraft to the station, manually docked with it as it tumbled, entered and restored power.

Thus the Soviets salvaged through human effort what would otherwise have been a major loss because of machine failure.

Humans, then, have a material role to play in space. Man turns the unexpected into discovery, discovery into knowledge—and knowledge into leadership.

President Reagan has termed the space station our "gateway to the universe" and Dr. James Fletcher, the NASA administrator, has described it as the central focus of all our efforts to expand commerce, industry and science in space through the end of the 21st Century and beyond.

Meanwhile, orbiting factories will be developed and scientists will continue to expand their knowledge of our own planet, the planets near us and the universe itself.

And for the majority of us who will never make that high journey, there will be very direct and tangible benefits.

To keep the space station running smoothly—in the correct orbit and in contact with Earth—using crew members alone would require so much of their time that little would be left for their primary work. So the station itself will be required to do much of this.

The systems developed for these purposes will pave the way for major strides forward at companies which are building products to make industry more productive.

So just within the scope of what we have discussed today, there are two readily identifiable benefits which will most likely result from space station development and construction.

Expanding out into other systems—materials software programs, computer development, the need for food storage and preparation—just to name a few station spin-offs, seems sure to begin soon and continue indefinitely.

For me, obviously, there is no question about the need to maintain United States space leadership. I would hope that few Americans really care so little about their country and their way of life that they could accept the idea of living cooped up under a sky dominated by any foreign nation, but especially the Soviet Union.

How can we fail to fuel one of the two primary drivers of advanced technology, space, especially at a time when there is growing restraint on funding the other one, national defense?

Space has been termed a frontier. Some have called it "The Endless Frontier," and others the "Final Frontier." My own view is that mankind does not yet know enough about the universe to term space either "endless" or "final."

But it is clearly the "Next Frontier." I hope you will agree with me that there are solid, pragmatic reasons to commit both the national will, and a portion of our national treasure, to developing that frontier.

And, ultimately, folding it also into the scientific and economic fabric, not just of this nation, but of all nations.

Reference (C.R. 8/6/87, Pg. S-11466)

Special Days

Columbus Day Address
Excerpts from Speech
in the Congressional Record
by
Rev. William J. O'Halloran, S.J., President
LeMoyne College

In a dark corner of the magnificent Cathedral of Seville in Spain, there remain today some of the most precious historical documents in the world. They are part of the collection which makes up the Bibliotheca Colombina, and contain books which Christopher Columbus annotated in his own hand. Among them is a copy of Seneca's Medea, which belonged to the discoverer's son Ferdinand. It is open to a prophecy written by Seneca 14 centuries earlier.

"An age will come after many years when this ocean will loose the chains of things, and a huge land lie revealed."

"This prophecy," wrote his son in the margin of his book, "was fulfilled by my father in the year 1492."

The ship's log recorded that land appeared two hours after midnight on the 71st day—distant cliffs shining in the glow of a blazing moon. Columbus named the land for the Holy Savior, San Salvador, called the people los Indios. The day was October 12, 1492. The discoverer was 40 years old.

He claimed the lands for Spain, for Ferdinand and Isabella, and for himself. A small ill-fated colony was settled where he had spent his first Christmas in the New World. He called it La Navidad and then sailed off in an easterly direction for his triumphal return to Spain.

The Indies Columbus found were not the Japan he sought—they did not hold the riches and treasures which the King of Spain longed to have from the Orient. Instead, it was the New World, the land of discovery, of beauty, of inestimable resources.

Christopher Columbus was the first of many Italians to discover the New World. The six famous explorers who followed him determined the entire future course of American history. They were Giovanni Caboto, known to us today as John Cabot, in 1497, Verrazzanno in 1524, Marco da Nizza in 1540, Enrico Tonti in 1680, Padre Chino in 1700 and Francesco Vigo in 1779.

With Caboto, the English claimed legal title to their colonies in New England and Virginia. With Verrazzanno, the French laid claim to their holdings in this very part of the America where we are today, New York. They called it Nouvelle France, New France, and with Verrazzanno, there began the parade of famous French explorers of whom Father Simon LeMoyne was one. Marco da Nizza was the discoverer of the Southwest and Padre Chino, whose statue represents Arizona in the Capitol in Washington was its missionary. The lands of our Midwest, from Chicago to New

Orleans, were controlled by Enrico Tonti, a disciple of LaSalle, for over 20 years. Without Francisco Vigo, Michigan, Ohio, Indiana, Illinois, Wisconsin and Minnesota might be part of Canada today.

Ironically and sadly, this great litany of Italians who discovered America—north, south, east and west—did not settle it with those gracious, warm, creative, hard-working and enormously talented people who have given the world its Caesars and its popes.

However, as we honor Columbus today, we also honor those more recent Italians who discovered America and enriched it by building its canals, its industries, its universities, its professions, its churches and its politics. Their discovery is the story of courage, of ambition and of hope. It is the story of the power behind a dream and of the determination and sacrifice which made that dream come true.

The new Italian discovery of America begins in 1880 and continues until this very day. They came from Northern Italy, from Venice, from Lombardy, from Campania and from Sicily. The average Italian arrived in America with a total net worth of $17. They settled in the major cities of the East Coast where they landed. And this for two reasons: First of all, $17 didn't get you very far, and secondly, almost every one of them, at least on arrival, hoped one day to go back home. If they stayed along the coast, the trip back would be easier to make.

The followers of Columbus have peopled this great land of ours with teachers and musicians, doctors and artists, senators and governors, judges, industrialists, builders, mayors, bishops, priests, religious brothers and sisters. They gave us our first American saint, Francisco Cabrini.

How can one summarize or recapitulate that cascade of contributions made to the United States of America by the Italian-American community? It is impossible to do it justice. All the same, while recognizing this impossibility, there does seem to be one characteristic of which we can speak and which more than others captures the true spirit of these wonderful people. It is their love and zest for life. The vitality of Italian people is expressed in countless directions. The affection and devotion which they bestow upon their families and especially upon their children is a thrill to behold. The way in which they reach out, in every community, to all who are burdened with ignorance, poverty, sickness and need make up the daily account of good things going on here. They know how to live and enjoy life and how to share that living and enjoyment with others. They are alive to their country, their church and their communities.

We salute Christopher Columbus on this day of his discovery and we salute the Italian-American people who discover in our own day the new Americas of opportunity and challenge.

Reference: (C.R. 11/21/80, Pg. 11186)

St. Patrick's Day Message

Excerpts from Speech
in the Congressional Record
by
The Friends of Ireland
in the U.S. Congress

Those of us in Congress who follow Irish affairs have in recent years chosen the occasion of St. Patrick's Day to reaffirm our commitments both to help end the violence in Northern Ireland and to contribute by peaceful means to the great goal of Irish unity.

Two years ago, we founded the Friends of Ireland to provide a forum for an informed American role in assisting an overall political settlement. As Friends of Ireland, we shall continue to do all we can in the years ahead to inform the Congress and the American people about the conflict in Ireland, and to further the goal of a just and enduring peace.

It must surely be clear that any lasting political settlement in Northern Ireland can be achieved only by peaceful and constitutional means, through negotiation, compromise and with the consent of all those involved—not by ultimatum, intimidation or violence, which serve only to prolong the anguish of that deeply divided community and frustrate progress toward unity and political reconciliation.

On this St. Patrick's Day, we appeal again to our fellow Americans to reject those who believe in bloodshed, to renounce organizations which are the agents of violence and to deny American dollars to any group that condones or contributes to the killing. Instead, we urge our fellow citizens to be unyielding in their commitment to peaceful political change.

Last year was a year of disappointment and concern for all of us who hope for peace in Northern Ireland. Callous bombings, vicious assassinations and reckless maiming of the innocent carried out by terrorist organizations have contributed to the atmosphere of dependency and aggravated the cycle of vengeance in a community that has already suffered too much for too long. Disturbing allegations about a recent pattern of shooting incidents by the security forces in Northern Ireland and continued reliance by law enforcement authorities on lethal plastic bullets are cause for deep concern.

Chronic unemployment, the continuing British commitment to an unworkable political proposal and the lack of progress toward ending institutionalized discrimination in Northern Ireland have dimmed the hope of early progress in resolving economic and political problems.

At the heart of the Northern Ireland conflict lies a profound crisis of identity and allegiance. Just as the troubles will not be battered or bombed away by terrorists, so they cannot be wished away by measures that serve only to preserve the status quo. The roots of the conflict lie deep in the history of Ireland and in the record of Britain's involvement there. As such, we believe it requires the bold cooperation of both the British and the Irish governments jointly pursuing at the highest levels a new strategy of reconciliation.

In the summit agreements of Irish and British Prime Ministers, there exists the framework for pursuit of such a strategy. We therefore would welcome—and encourage—revival of contacts between the two governments at this time.

We are heartened by the progress within Ireland of the debate on reconciliation. We commend the important recent decision by the Irish government to establish a forum for consultation on the means by which peace and stability can be achieved in a new Ireland through the democratic process. We are especially encouraged by the agreement of all the political parties in the Republic of Ireland and of the Social Democrat and Labor Party in Northern Ireland to participate in this forum. And we welcome their action in seeking the views of all peoples of both traditions in Ireland, North and South, who share the objectives of this constructive new undertaking.

We hope that steps such as these will lead in the very near future to a solemn commitment by all the parties to heal the divisions within Northern Ireland and to reconcile the two major traditions that exist in Ireland.

There should also be an American dimension to this healing process. As Friends of Ireland, we have been heartened by the support we have received for our endeavors from the Irish government and Parliament. We believe that the cause of reconciliation between the Protestant and Catholic traditions in Ireland is one which merits the full support and the responsible involvement of the United States.

To this end, the Friends of Ireland have sought to foster a close working relationship with the Parliament in Ireland, with the government there and with the main political parties of that nation.

On this St. Patrick's Day, we renew our commitment to the great goal of Irish unity, and reiterate our conviction that the only sure road to a just and lasting peace is to end the division of the Irish people. We seek a unity based on democratic principles, achieved by negotiation and persuasion, secured with consent freely given by a majority of the people of Northern Ireland and with full constitutional safeguards for the rights and traditions of all concerned.

Reference: (C.R. 3/17/83, Pg. S-3274)

Flag Day
Excerpts from Speech
in the Congressional Record
by
Hon. Don H. Clausen
U.S. House of Representatives

On June 14, as we celebrate Flag Day, it is appropriate to pause and reflect on what our flag represents.

"Old Glory" or the "Stars and Stripes" had a particular meaning during our bicentennial year. During the past 200 years, the Star-Spangled Banner, like our great nation, has changed while it has remained constant. The alternate red and white stripes represent our steadfast adherence to our concept of one nation under God, with liberty and justice for all, while the ever-increasing number of stars represents the assimilation of peoples, ideas and cultures which developed the United States from a tiny confederation of colonies to our present position as leader of the free world.

The American Bicentennial was a celebration of the American Revolution. But the American Revolution was not simply an event that took place on July 4, 1776. The American Revolution was not even the summation of a series of events, but rather was a venture into the unknown, the culmination of ideals, creativity and common sense that found expression in both the words and deeds of our ancestors.

Nor did the revolution end in 1789 with the ratification of the Constitution of the United States. Its spirit and its principles have remained with us right up through the present.

Two hundred years ago the founding fathers came together to form a more perfect union. They took a risk never before taken in the history of mankind.

This was not the risk of rebellion, for rebellions occur constantly through history. Rather it was a risk of forming a government under which the people would be both sovereign and subject, the rulers and the ruled. It was the risk of uniting persons of diverse races and religions and of unequal education, wealth, intellect and background under a common republican form of government.

Two hundred years later, our vast continent settled, our visions turned to the limits of the universe. We can be proud of the successes in our experiment, and the fact that we Americans are in a position of leadership in the world. But more importantly, we can be proud that we have an enduring system of government which has guided this nation through 200 years of extraordinary growth, challenge and change.

The strength and resilience of our government can be traced directly to the men and women who founded this country. They were truly remarkable, not only for their expression of high ideals but also for their ability to translate those ideals into action.

Our founding fathers were practical people, but their practicability dealt not so much with the specifics of their time as with the implementation of concepts applicable to any time.

Today, as we celebrate another anniversary as a nation, America's genius and common sense are again tested. We again struggle to define who we are and what our real purpose is. Our bicentennial presented us with an unparalleled opportunity to re-examine the origins of our laws, the foundations of our institutions, and the achievements of our forebears. For only if we fully understand our past can we intelligently understand our future.

Two hundred years ago we dreamed of a system of laws that would be equitable for all. We dreamed of ensuring a body of rights to ourselves and our posterity.

One hundred years ago we dreamed of new horizons of invention. We dreamed of achieving affluence, and we dreamed of being a leader among nations.

Almost 50 years ago we dreamed of victory as our troops stormed the Normandy beaches in the largest amphibious invasion across the English Channel since William the Conqueror.

Our goal then was a world made safe for democracy; a world in which we would experience a freedom from want and a freedom from fear.

Many cynics will tell you that the days of dreaming are over.

But they cast their eyes downward, searching for a defect, a flaw, the clay feet of the idol rather than looking up toward distant horizons to discover the unknown, to find new solutions to old problems, and to make a better world for ourselves and our children.

During the past 200 years Americans have consistently dreamed of and worked for a better future, a better way of life, a world with more justice, more peace with freedom, more brotherhood, and more liberty for all.

On this special occasion, let us rededicate ourselves to the attainment of these goals. This is one nation, under God. It is our nation—to defend, to enhance and to protect.

We must be willing to pay a price for freedom, for no price that is ever asked for it is half the cost of doing without it.

Reference: (C.R. 6/14/76, Pg. E-3320)

Sports
Enshrinement, Pro Football Hall of Fame
Excerpts from Speech
in the Congressional Record
by
Alan C. Page

It is a great honor to be here today. Football was very good to me, and my good fortune has continued in my chosen career as a lawyer. But in the world where I now work, professional accomplishment is measured on a very different scale, over a much longer period of time. So I find it a bit strange to again be the object of this much attention for what I accomplished years ago, in a very narrow field of endeavor called football.

As my football career ended, many of my contemporaries were already beginning to make their impact felt in society. And they continued—healing the sick, creating jobs, defending people in trouble and seeking peace among nations. Very few of them will receive a fraction of the tribute lavished on someone like me, who once tackled people for a living.

It's hard to say what today's inductees will mean to future generations, but for now, we are still looked upon as role models. And role models have an obligation, I think, to relate to the needs of the future, and not just relate to the deeds of the past.

It's certainly okay to enjoy the glory and the fruits of bygone efforts. But I think all the men you see here have reached the Hall of Fame because they couldn't be satisfied with their past performances. So as I try to give meaning to this event for myself, I want to focus on what I can do here and now.

On this occasion, I ask myself, "What contribution can I still make that would be truly worthy of the outpouring of respect and good feelings as I have felt here today?" And the answer for me is clear: "To help give other children the chance to reach their dreams."

I don't know when children stop dreaming. But I do know when hopes start leaking away, because I've seen it happen. Over the past ten years, I've spent a lot of time talking with school kids of all ages, and I've seen the cloud of resignation move across their eyes as they travel through school without making any progress. They know they are slipping through the net into the huge underclass that our society seems willing to tolerate.

At first, the kids try to conceal their fear with defiance. Then, for far too many, the defiance turns to disregard for our society and its rules. It's then that we have lost them—maybe forever.

But this loss is not always as apparent as the kid who drops out of school for life on the street. I've seen lost men in the National Football League.

When I played for the Vikings, a new defensive line coach decided the best way for players to learn the playbook was to read it aloud. Maybe it was a good way to learn—

for people who could read. There were nine players in the group—all college products. Three had no trouble reading the book. Two did okay. But for the other four, it was an agonizing struggle. And we all shared their pain.

These same young men were once the heros of their schools, showered with recognition and praise for their athletic achievements—and for their time in the National Football League, at least, these were the fortunate ones. They had beaten the long, 18,000 to 1 odds of even making it that far. But without reading skills, what were their chances of finding a dignified, fulfilling job after football?

We are doing no favors for the poor, young men from Miami and Chicago and Philadelphia and Los Angeles if we let them believe that a game shall set them free. At the very best, athletic achievement might open a door that discrimination had held shut. But the doors slam quickly on the unprepared and the undereducated.

We are at a point in our history where black teenagers constitute the most unemployed and undervalued people in the population. And instead of making a real investment in education that could pay itself back many times, our society has chosen to pay the bill three times.

Once, when we let the kids slip through the educational system;

Twice, when they drop out to a street life of poverty, dependence and maybe crime;

And a third time when we warehouse in prison those who do cross over the line and get caught.

The cost of this neglect is immense—in dollars and in abuse of the human spirit. We must educate our children.

Once we've let it reach this point, the problem is virtually too big and too expensive to solve. But we can make a difference, if we go back into the schools and find the shy ones and the stragglers, the square pegs and the hard cases, before they've given up on the system—and before the system has given up on them.

Then we say to those children: "You're important to our world and to our future. We want you to be successful and have the things you want from life. But being successful and reaching your dreams takes work. It means being responsible for yourself. If you aren't willing to go to class and do your homework and participate in the opportunities to learn, then you have no right to complain about the unfairness of this world. You're not alone in this. But only you can do the work that will make you free.

"If you wait until college—or even until high school—to get serious about an education, you may be too late. It's hard to go back as an adult to learn what you missed in the third grade. It's important to dream, but it's through learning and work that dreams become reality."

We must educate our children. But we can't preach responsibility to our children if we don't accept it ourselves.

We as parents—especially in the black community—must accept that we bear responsibility for our children. We must work with them not just by developing their hook-shots or their throwing arms, but by developing their reading and thinking abilities. If we don't have the skills ourselves to pass on, we can still encourage them, reward them and praise their academic accomplishments. We can educate our children.

We shouldn't put down athletics, because they can teach children the value of teamwork and disciplined effort. But insist that your children take school seriously as well. And if they can't handle the demand of both, school should come first and athletics should go.

Finally, you and I can make a difference as members of our communities. We can't just leave it up to the schools, or the social workers, or the police and the legal system. We ultimately pay the cost of our educational system's failures. But we also have the solutions within our power, if we educate our children.

We can support the schools and the teaching profession instead of complaining about them. We can honor students and teachers who excel with the same rewards and recognition that we give to our athletes and coaches. As it stands, how can we expect kids with poor self-esteem and shaky reading skills to pursue academics when often the only reinforcement they get is in sports?

Now these words may seem too simple to the people on the front lines who have seen too many of the lost and too few of the victorious. The jobless single mother may have too little hope of her own to share some with her children.

To the kid surrounded by drugs and violence and acres of rotting city, a job in a law firm may seem more remote than a shot at the Hall of Fame.

And so we, who have been insulated by our successes from a loss of hope, must not turn our backs on these kids. We must not concede their lives to the forces that have worn so many children down. We must educate our children.

Yes, the things I'm suggesting are simple. But I've learned from school, from football and from the law that even the biggest, scariest problems can be broken down to their fundamentals. And if all of us cannot be superstars, we can remember to repeat the simple fundamentals of taking responsibility for ourselves, and for the children of this country.

We must educate our children. And if we do, I believe it will be enough.

Reference: (C.R. 8/4/88, Pg. S-10898)

Major League Baseball in Seattle
Excerpts from Speech
in the Congressional Record
by
Hon. Slade Gorton
U.S. Senate

"Though some American League owners have expressed disgust at the Seattle situation and openly have opted for transfer of the Seattle transfer, the league as a unit is reluctant to take action."

This line appeared in *The Seattle Times* on January 25, 1970—more than 20 years ago, and only about two months before the Pilots were spirited away to Milwaukee. Milwaukee is a somewhat smaller metropolitan area than Seattle, and one with a far more restricted broadcast media market.

Today, we may be no more than two months away from an attempt to move the Seattle Mariners to Tampa-St. Petersburg, Florida. A metropolitan area considerably less populous than Seattle, with a more restricted market, and with an average annual disposable income of $3,000 a family less.

What does Tampa-St. Petersburg have that Seattle lacks?

First a new domed stadium with an operating subsidy of almost $2 million a year from the city of Tampa.

Second, commitments to a prospective major league baseball team for 23,000 season tickets—four times the number sold for the current Mariners season.

Third, far more potential income from luxury suites and executive boxes—in contrast to Seattle, where more than half of the Kingdome suites lie empty for the Mariners season.

Fourth, a guaranteed local television and cable television agreement with between $8 million and $10 million a year, compared with $1.7 million a year contract here in Seattle.

Fifth, the assurance of 30 years of admission tax rebates from the state and city, together with assurance of "the best lease" in major league baseball.

Sixth, and most important, potential local ownership that is willing to put up $95 million for an expansion franchise and $20-30 million more for the inevitable operating losses of such a franchise during its first several years.

People in Tampa can see—as well as we can here—the impact that the Mariners do have on Seattle and could have on Tampa. Those impacts are both tangible and intangible.

The leading intangible is the fact that having a major league baseball team bestows "major league" status on a city. Seattle is a consummately "livable" town in no small measure because of the Mariners. In a way, major league baseball contributes in a manner similar to the city's art and cultural ambience. And is almost as unlikely to show an annual net profit in monetary terms.

The overall economic impact of major league baseball in Seattle exceeds $100 million a year. It leads to nearly 2,000 direct and indirect jobs—primarily in the service sector—for people who have a relatively limited set of economic opportunities.

Frankly stated, it is in our own economic self-interest to keep the Mariners in Seattle. The business and government communities in Tampa and St. Petersburg are prepared to act on this understanding to bring the team to their community, while those in Seattle have not done so yet to a degree that will assure that the Mariners will remain here.

It is safe to say that, if Seattle loses a major league baseball franchise for the second time, it will not see major league baseball again for many years.

So what is the prescription?

There are three proposals which I do not believe to be likely to hold major league baseball in Seattle.

In 1970, after the departure of the Seattle Pilots, I, as attorney general, began a lawsuit against the American League on behalf of the state, King County and the city. Six years later, as a result of this litigation, the American League agreed to create the Mariners franchise. Although it is remotely possible that the departure of the Mariners might be delayed again by going to court, it is impossible to imagine that baseball can be preserved over the long-term in this community through litigation.

Another solution discussed from time to time is the repeal of organized baseball's exemption from federal antitrust laws. However, legislation to strip baseball of its exemption has been proposed for decades without ever coming close to passage. Furthermore, the Supreme Court of the United States is almost certain not to reverse its own precedents in this respect.

The third alternative that will not solve Seattle's problems in the future is the proposal to require the sharing of local television revenues on an equal basis among all major league baseball teams in a manner similar to that practiced by the National Football League. That is a consummation to be wished for, but difficult to attain.

Seattle, of course, is not the only city that has a baseball team that operates in the red. As Marge Scott, owner of the Cincinnati Reds ,said, "We will not have baseball in small towns like Cincinnati. We can't compete with what New York City gets from cable. It's going to be that baseball is only going to be in the big cities." Fay Vincent (commissioner of baseball) has also recognized the problem. He said, "Baseball is poised for a catastrophe, and it might not be far off."

It is clear that the immediate solution to retaining the Mariners must be found in the business and governmental communities of Seattle, King County, and the state of Washington. Our government entities must be willing to offer incentives comparable to those offered by competing communities. But the primary responsibility for keeping the Mariners in Seattle belongs to the private sector.

One such private sector solution is to dramatically increase the sale of season tickets. But if this effort reached twice its goal, it would in all probability not greatly change the financial disadvantages under which the team operates in Seattle.

A second solution that has generated discussion in Seattle concerns the revenue received by the Mariners for local television and cable television coverage. At $1.7 million per year, the Mariners rank last among all major league baseball franchises. Still, a simple increase in television revenues, standing alone, will not be sufficient to guarantee the retention of major league baseball in this community for the foreseeable future.

Another and more promising proposal that has surfaced recently is the purchase of a minority interest in the Mariners by local business enterprises for a price approximately equal to the loan which has been called by Security Pacific Bank. Nevertheless, even if the Seattle business community could be persuaded to invest upwards of $40 million for a non-controlling interest in a baseball team, it would seem to get very little in the way of directly tangible benefits from such investment.

The best solution to the challenge facing the Mariners is majority local ownership. We have two examples to follow, both of which have been successful. The first is Minneapolis, where a team almost certain to be lost to Tampa-St. Petersburg was restored first by community effort and second by the success of finding a single individual with the willingness and ability to purchase and operate a major league baseball franchise.

Because there are relatively few such individuals in Seattle, the second example, that of Pittsburgh, is perhaps more relevant. There, eight corporations and three individuals combined together to purchase the Pirates and to guarantee sufficient operating capital to keep the team in Pittsburgh.

Majority local ownership has been the key to the success of baseball in other small metropolitan areas. In my opinion, that should be the primary goal in the search for stability for the Seattle Mariners. It is impossible for me to conceive that Boeing, Burlington Northern, Microsoft, Weyerhaeuser, Nintendo, our huge banks and a dozen other corporations will turn out to be so much less concerned with their community than are their precise counterparts in Pittsburgh. What Tampa, Minneapolis and Pittsburgh can do, Seattle can do.

I have discussed the economic impact of baseball in Seattle—the dollars and the jobs. These impacts are substantial and important. But this issue goes beyond dollars. Keeping the Mariners in Seattle is an emotional issue for people everywhere in this state.

Baseball can and should be saved in Seattle, because baseball can work here, and because the benefits to the community far outweigh the costs. But the importance of saving the Mariners goes way beyond just assuring economic opportunities.

People—fans—in Seattle and all across the state care deeply about the team, its stars and their success. The time is short, the money and the skills are available, the occasion is important and the time to start is now.

(C.R. 9/17/91, Pg. S-13078)

Chapter 18

Transportation
· · · · · · · · · · · · · · · · · · · ·

Highways and America's Future
Excerpts from Speech
in the Congressional Record
by
Dr. Ellis L. Armstrong
Former U.S. Commissioner of Public Roads

Many of you may have seen last week's *U.S. News* with the front cover "Honk! Why You'll Be Wasting More Time In Traffic." The question arises: "How did we get into this mess?"

I think the explanation is rather clear. In our comfortable, affluent, self-centered society, we forget that there are two items that make up highway transportation: the vehicle and the road. The cost of the vehicle and its operation and the cost of the highway and its maintenance make up the cost of highway transportation.

Back in the early 1960s, we were spending 88 cents on our vehicles and only 12 cents on our roads; we were spending more on automatic shifts and air-conditioners than on highways. Then we wondered why we were not catching up on our needs. Today, we are spending 93 or 94 cents on our vehicles and only about 6 cents on our highways. How far out of focus and out of balance can we get? We are spending our money but we are not getting the highway transportation we should have.

As highway users, in focusing on our beautiful, comfortable, efficient automobiles, we overlooked the slowly deteriorating pavements and the increasing traffic and changing travel patterns.

We didn't focus on the overall system, nor did we pay attention to our changing society.

We seem to lack the discipline necessary to follow a well-planned, long-range course of action to meet the problems of growth in a changing world. We seem to progress only from crisis to crisis, which is costly and frustrating, and ultimately could destroy us.

I have a nostalgic memory of the dynamic enthusiasm 30 years ago when we launched full speed ahead into the design and construction of America's Interstate Highway System, the world's greatest public works undertaking. Over 15 years of analysis and study, along with growing traffic jam crisis in our urban areas, resulted in all the diverse interests uniting in support of federal legislation establishing the highway user-fee trust fund to finance and build the 42,000-mile Interstate, adequate for 1975 traffic, the year it was to be completed.

That was an exciting, challenging, stimulating time as all across our nation, we shaped the landscape, built the bridges and overpasses, and laid the smooth, riding pavements, tying all America together in one big, social and economic neighborhood, loosening the bonds of an inadequate roadways and creating individual freedom of movement all across the land.

By 1960 we had resolved most problems and every day we were excavating over 20 million cublic yards of earth and rock and compacting it to support the smooth pavements, providing easy access to the vitality and excellence of our great cities, to our farmlands, and to the beauty and magic of scenic America. Along with the Interstate was a stepped-up program on the rest of the federal aid highway system. We were off to a great start.

Then in the late 1960s and the 1970s, we steadily decreased the amount of our highway transportation dollar spent on highways and the programs designed to meet our needs fell further and further behind. The 65 million vehicles on our highways in 1956 have now increased to over 177 million automobiles, trucks and buses. Highway travel since 1956 has increased over 300 percent to a yearly total approaching 3 trillion passenger-miles—at a cost of nearly a trillion dollars. But our highways have been falling further and further behind, even though it is estimated we will spend $60 billion on highways this year—$29 billion in capital construction and $31 billion in operation and maintenance.

The federal aid primary system is now 50 percent inadequate for the traffic it is carrying. Our farm to market roads, our secondary system, has been neglected and in some areas we are heading the farmer back into the mud. One example of problems is the increasingly heavy truck travel resulting from the steady abandonment of railroad branch lines serving mainly the needs of agriculture.

But our most pressing problems are now in our urban areas where over half of automobile travel occurs. Our whole traffic pattern is changing. With decreasing smoke-stack type industry and increasing white collar and service industries, and with our increased standard of living, our centers of origin and destinations of travel are becoming more widely disbursed, so our mass transit facilities are becoming less and less effective.

Multiple breadwinners make two or more cars per family unit necessary because of the required flexibility. For example, the number of married women in the work force is steadily increasing. In the last 15 years, the number of married women in the 15-45 age bracket has increased 58 percent and now totals nearly 70 percent. So most family units have two cars and over 15 percent have three or more cars. This has dramatically affected both direction and timing of highway travel.

The federal aid highway system was never intended, and is not intended, to solve all the automobile transportation problems. It is only part of the overall system, and the rest of the system, provided by state and local governments, has lagged far behind. So we have a crisis situation in many urban areas, not from travel to the city center, but interurban travel and the widely disbursing of employment and retail facilities.

Nationally, we have 575,000 major bridges on our highways and a detailed inventory shows 42 percent are deficient, and the number is increasing. Last year we spent $2 billion replacing and repairing 11,300 bridges but 16,000 more were added to the deficient list, so we are losing ground.

As the era of Interstate construction comes to an end, we must agree on what comes next. And only 6 or 7 cents of the highway transportation dollar will not provide adequate highways to meet our needs. Keep in mind that we highway users pay for good highways whether we have them or not, and if we don't have them, we pay much more in increased costs of vehicle operation, in additional accidents and in lost time. Our highway system, and the freedom and flexibility it provides, is the major underlying support of our whole society—economically, socially, politically and all the rest. We shouldn't forget that the health of our economy depends upon a good, safe, efficient and mobile highway system. If you doubt this, imagine what your life would be like if tomorrow morning all highways disappeared.

Here is what must be done, and you, as the highway users who pay for and use the highways, must be the motivators to see that it is done. First, determine and agree upon what the highway needs will likely be for the next 20 years or so; then determine how the needs can reasonably and practically be met. Careful analysis should be made to determine what construction, reconstruction and rehabilitation is practicable and reasonable to meet those needs, and with what priorities. Then from an examination of the benefits and responsibilities at the national, state and local and private levels, determine how the cost can be most fairly allocated and collected. Legislators and the general public must be involved in this examination process so the full highway system program will be understood and supported. Then required legislation can be enacted.

From studies under way, I'm sure will come a well-conceived, balanced, affordable practical solution to an optimum highway system that will meet the future needs of America.

Here are my ideas of the highlights of such a program:

(1) Generally, we have the basic main framework in place for our highway system, the national federal aid system. However, much of it has reached its design life, and we need to ensure fully adequate maintenance, reconditioning and reconstruction as required.

(2) We must ensure the continuation of the Federal Highway Trust Fund based on the user charge concept of at least the present level, keeping in mind that reconditioning and reconstruction will become increasingly complex and costly.

(3) States, and their local entities, must face up to the need for adequate funding of their responsibilities, based mainly on the highway user pay-as-you-go concept.

(4) Innovative improvements, adjustments, concepts and designs that will im-

prove traffic handling with minimum cost must be continually developed. This requires continual research, training, technology transfers, and direct and effective involvement of the resources we have in our universities.

(5) Research must be better coordinated and greatly increased. And we must ensure that the highway departments fully utilize the information available.

(6) Competent, objective overview of the national, state and local highway programs should be provided consistent with each level of government, to ensure fully adequate administration, and as advisory to the various legislative bodies.

(7) We must especially focus on reducing highway accidents and deaths, which are a disgrace to our society. Deaths on our highways are not deaths by natural causes, but can be prevented. We must also concentrate on keeping drunk drivers off our highways.

(8) We must have a responsible, continuing, truthful, objective and effective program to provide the public with an understanding of our highway problems and how they can be solved.

In summary, an adequate optimum highway system will reduce the number, cost and severity of accidents; highways cost less to build and maintain than neglecting them, they pay for themselves, they accelerate economic development, they improve the way of life for all of us. A well-balanced highway system saves lives, saves time, saves money.

Reference: (C.R. 12/18/87, Pg. E-4879)

Review of the Shipping Act of 1984

Excerpts from Speech
in the Congressional Record
by
Alex J. Mandl, President and Chief Executive Officer
Sea-Land Services, Inc.

Good afternoon. And thank you for the chance to be a part of the South Carolina International Trade Conference's 18th annual meeting.

In my time with you today I would like to take a quick tour of the industry. And in the course of that tour, I'd like to make a couple of points. One—it most definitely is, as the title of this conference says, a new world.

Second, this new world demands some new outlooks, some new strategies and some new thinking if the carrier industry is to effectively meet the needs of you, our shipping customers.

And third, for those new ideas to have any lasting effect in a rough and tumble business, we need some equally new thinking by those who make the rules that govern our segment of this business—at least those of us flying the U.S. flag.

It hardly takes a degree in economics to see that there have been some changes in the world economic order in the past decade or so. Driven by stunning geopolitical and societal events, the balance of economic power has shifted and continues to shift.

Unfortunately, it's been a shift away from those of us in this room. The United States has long ago stopped being the 800-pound gorilla of international trade. We no longer dictate the rules. We no longer dominate the volume of goods moved around the world.

As the United States has stepped back, other ports of the world have stepped forward. Asia, driven by Japan's mighty industrial engine, emerged in the 80s as a world economic power. Japan alone represents a $2.8 trillion market. A similar expansion has taken place in Korea, Hong Kong and Taiwan and now China and Southeast Asia are flexing their economic muscles.

Today, Europe is looming as one of the world's most formidable players as we steam toward 1991. An area covering only 2 million square kilometers will hold almost 325 million people and offer markets that could exceed $4 trillion.

It's no surprise that the world's fastest-growing trade lanes are intra-Europe, intra-Asia, Asia-Europe and Europe-Asia.

And these exploding new markets are there for companies willing to invest now for the long term and increasingly we are seeing companies who are showing that kind of staying power.

Years from now the historians and social scientists will still be arguing what fueled the political, social and economic changes of the past decade. But high on anybody's list is certain to be the information revolution.

If there are any doubts of the pervasiveness of the revolution, consider just a few statistics. Telecommunications—I'm talking here about both voice and data—from the U.S. to international locations was 1.3 billion minutes in 1980. In 1989, it was 6.7 billion. And those minutes will jump by 10 percent a year through the 90s.

Just 10 years ago, faxes were still new, almost a curiosity. Now, there are 4.2 million of them worldwide. In the United Sates alone, there are 11.6 million electronic mailboxes. By the year 2000, there will be 46 million.

Information has ushered in a whole new world where business imagination has combined with an awareness of what technology can do. And the product of that fusion has been new ways of thinking about customers, markets, productivity and service. It's changed the way business views the world. And the way the world views business.

Not too long ago, the top of the pyramid of international commerce was the multinational corporation. Today, that structure is being replaced by a new form—the transnational company. It's lean, on-line and dispersed around the globe.

In a *New York Times* article a senior official of Colgate-Palmolive said simply, "The U.S. does not have an automatic call on our resources." It's a statement backed by facts. Colgate now sells more toothpaste, soaps and other toiletries outside the United States than inside.

Companies like IBM, Ford, NCR and Motorola, and even the Stanley Works, now collect some 30 percent or more of their revenues and large chunks of their profits from products produced outside the country.

America is just one example. Overseas holdings are rising rapidly for just about every other industrial country. Now add to that global equation, alliances and joint ventures. We see them in virtually every industry.

As companies divide, spread out and form new partnerships, efficient transportation becomes paramount. What does it all mean for the transportation industry or, more specifically, for carriers and our ability to meet the needs of you, our shippers?

It means a strong presence in ships, ports and port facilities in the trade lanes of America, Europe and Asia.

In the 60s for example, Sea-Land had eight small ships and a couple thousand 35-foot containers. We had a presence in maybe nine countries, and we employed all of 350 people.

Today, we operate 80 vessels on five trade lanes and call on some 95 ports. And we have more than 9,000 employees. We have around 150,000 containers and more than 200 offices.

But for any transportation company, all of that is merely the price of admission to the big leagues of global service. More important than physical assets is the infrastructure that ties them all together. Ships, trucks, trains, port facilities must come together in a cohesive service offering. And it must go beyond moving goods from one shore to another. It must have the land system that assures timely delivery door to door.

Recently, Sea-Land and Maersk have agreed to an alliance in the Asia-North American trade that will give our customers more sailings, wider port coverage and more direct service among key markets.

We are now proceeding with a number of projects in the Soviet Union. We will share space on Soviet vessels and connect intermodally with Soviet rail and air services and work to improve the country's transportation system. The centerpiece is a land-bridge container service using the trans-Siberian Railway to connect Asia and Europe. It could cut from days to weeks off the Suez Canal routes and the service could be profitable in 1992.

The issue for Sea-Land, like any company today, is to be judged less by what we have and where we are, and more by how quickly and accurately we can gather, process and use information in the name of cost control, productivity, quality and service.

Through information technology, we're working to create a window for our customers on the global transportation pipeline—where information is readily available to everyone who needs it—from the first stages of manufacturing through the final sale.

So in the new world, with its new rules of business, global assets and the infrastructure that ties them together are two criteria for success. But there's also a third. And here our world tour leads back to Washington.

We're an industry that has definitely seen two sides of regulatory change. We've seen what it can accomplish when it happens in a careful, thoughtful and productive way.

And we've seen the price that's paid when it doesn't happen at all.

The best in enlightened policy-making was the Shipping Act of 1984, which, in my view, has been absolutely fundamental in the ability to meet the demands of our customers in world markets.

Prior to the 1984 Shipping Act, it was not a pretty picture. We were struggling along under a patchwork of regulations that were still based on policies set in 1916. I believe the 1984 Shipping Act was a masterpiece of compromise. It protected the viability of the shipping conferences, but allowed independent action and service contracts—both radical ideas at the time.

The master stroke of the '84 Act is that it gives the U.S. a solid platform from which to compete internationally, but it gives us the freedom to build and to innovate.

Let me turn from the '84 Act, a set of policies that has strengthened our industry to the other side of the coin—to a policy that is sapping the strength and vitality of the U.S. Merchant Marine. I am talking about the Operating Differential Subsidy, or ODS, program.

It was established by the Merchant Marine Act of 1936 as a way to equalize the labor cost disparity between U.S.-flag carriers and their foreign competition. In order to qualify for ODS payments, a carrier is supposed to engage in foreign commerce, on certain established trade routes, employ U.S. crews and have its vessels built and flagged in the United States.

All that sounded reasonable enough when the shipping industry just moved goods across the water, and vessels were the core of the business. But today, as failures go, the ODS program is pretty spectacular. By just about any measure, ODS has not strengthened the U.S. Merchant Marine industry. It has weakened it.

Let's start with the subsidized companies. Twenty years ago there were 19 subsidized shipping lines. Now there are just four. For virtually all subsidized companies, the more than $200 millon that is doled out each year, has warped their business focus. It's not how to be a stronger competitor, it's how to keep those subsidies rolling in.

Continued government inaction in phasing out ODS is creating a negative investment climate for those of us who are unsubsidized. Investors are hard-pressed to make a call on where, how and if subsidies will be part of the investment decision.

And one more point. Subsidized firms are benefiting from government-impelled and military preference programs—meaning they are being subsidized twice. This double-dipping is still more money simply wasted.

Reference: (C.R. 6/13/91, Pg. S-7714)

Staggers Rail Act and Competition

Excerpts from Speech
in the Congressional Record
by
Carl Bagge, President
National Coal Association

It's a high privilege to break bread and to share some thoughts with this distinguished group about the Staggers Rail Act and competition.

Let me be clear from the outset. I'm not here to call for a repeal of the Staggers Rail Act. I didn't come to Chicago to lament the coal industry's support of the law.

By way of history, this law never would have been passed unless the coal industry had thrown a lobbying lifeline to the railroads, and we did for two good reasons.

For more than a century, the coal industry and the railroads have shared a strong, mutual economic interest. The rails carry the lion's share of coal to the coal industry's largest customer, the electric utility industry.

For this reason alone, it's in the coal industry's interest to see the railroads financially healthy and able to carry an increasing amount of coal in the coming years. And it's the reason the coal industry was among the first to recognize that the railroads were dying a slow death from regulatory suffocation.

Financial strength, however, wasn't possible unless the railroads were allowed greater rate-making flexibility, and the chance to streamline operations, and to enter into contracts with shippers. Staggers is the mechanism to achieve these ends.

It got the rails out from under the Interstate Commerce Commission's (ICC) oppressive thumb. It ushered in a new era of regulatory freedom, and it made contracts with shippers legal.

Congress fully appreciated the implications of cutting the regulatory ties from the railroads, so the law balanced a measure of deregulation with legal protections for captive shippers. The law says that when captive shippers are present, the shippers have recourse to the ICC when rates are unreasonable and service is poor.

Furthermore, Congress expected the railroads to respond to deregulation by competing vigorously in the marketplace—with other modes of transportation and among themselves.

In this vein, Staggers is a blueprint for the widest possible competition in transportation markets.

It's now time to assess how the law is working and if it's successful. The railroads appear to be making excellent time toward financial health. The contractual sanctions seem to be bearing fruit. To date, 2,000 contacts have been approved by the commission.

But unfortunately, the ICC has lost its way. There is no sense of direction. What's more, the railroads are taking advantage of the ICC's lack of vision in implementing the law—creating a "never-never land" of deregulation without adequate protection for captive shippers.

To be more specific, let me mention three ICC decisions and comment on each one.

One is the ICC decision to ignore the law and set up "guidelines" to determine market dominance. For the ICC to review a rail rate alleged to be unlawfully high, the shipper has to prove market dominance over the involved transportation. When the Act was passed, the commission had precise standards for such a decision. One was a revenue-to-cost ratio of 160 percent. This was changed by Staggers. It now stands at 170 percent.

There were two other tests when Staggers were passed. The most important was a presumption of market dominance if 70 percent or more of a shipper's output from a single source was carried by a single shipper. The other was whether a shipper had made substantial investments in rail transportation facilities.

The Staggers law didn't make any changes in these tests. While the legislative history made it clear they were to be kept in force, in 1981, the commission swept aside these presumptions. In their place, the ICC set up guidelines on the kinds of evidence that shippers and railroads could introduce on the issue, including product competition and geographic competition. With one sweep of the regulatory pen, the ICC turned the table on shippers.

Meanwhile, the coal industry has been jolted by other assaults on Staggers' protections. The railroads have petitioned to put into effect a rate-setting scheme called "Ramsey pricing." Any rail carrier—deemed revenue inadequate—could charge what the market will bear until financial adequacy was reached. Any proposal would exempt from all ICC regulations export coal going by rail to east and gulf ports. The commission not only agreed to consider this proposal, the ICC announced its decision would apply to all export coal in the United States.

Coal exports are an increasingly growing market for the American coal industry. Last year we shipped abroad 110 million tons of coal—a record—and nearly one-third of the total was steam coal overseas. Three years ago the steam coal market didn't exist.

By the end of the century, total coal exports could swell to as much as 200 million tons, making coal America's largest export commodity. The Department of Commerce is on coal's side, because those 110 million tons of coal added nearly $6 billion to America's balance of trade.

In summary, there's a broad consensus that the coal industry must take every possible step to improve the efficiency and effectiveness of the mine to market chain. We've responded with huge investments in new mines, and with management-labor programs to ensure labor peace. Both have resulted in productivity gains.

The point is this: Rising transportation costs are eroding all these gains. They are eating away at coal's marketing advantage by raising the delivered price of coal at home and overseas. The losers are the coal industry, the railroads and consumers. More importantly, the ultimate loser is America's economic strength.

What can we do about it? For years the coal industry has been preaching the gospel of competition in coal transportation markets. We have raised our voices in support of rehabilitating the aging, inland waterway system, which is critical to move more coal in competition with the railroads. What's forgotten, particularly as Congress rushed to tax gasoline to repair roads and bridges, is that the inland waterways are no less important than filling potholes. What's more, the money to start the key projects is setting at the ready Inland Waterway Trust Fund.

Congress can strike a chord for competition and the consumer by granting eminent domain rights for coal pipelines. I know this issue gives the railroads an advanced case of apoplexy and they sit up nights thinking up ways why they don't need competition. Yet, the rails need not fear pipelines.

Instead of pressing their case against coal pipelines, the railroads would be far better off taking advantage of their financial strength and to compete for more coal-hauling traffic. By the mid 1990s, the rails will be carrying as much coal as produced today, creating a windfall of 40,000 new jobs.

A case in point is one which too often is ignored. There always will be locations where inland waterways and pipelines cannot compete with the railroads. To fill this void, the Staggers Rail Act mandated the ICC to promote the fullest possible competition among the railroads themselves.

But why isn't the ICC moving aggressively to create the competition which would permit deregulation and increased rail traffic. Instead the commission is allowing the railroads to erect these marketing fiefdoms, and to build walls of protection around them. It isn't taking steps to foster competition among the railroads—the only path toward achieving full deregulation.

Today, we see the commission embarked on an ideological tangent of mindless deregulations—blindly hacking away at regulations in this philosophical stratosphere, while ignoring the real-life, practical problems of monopolies and captive shippers.

But the elimination of captive shippers must come—not by the stroke of a pen as the ICC has thus far unsuccessfully tried to do—but through a structural market change by injecting competition.

In this vein, the Staggers Rail Act must not become another version of the Natural Gas Policy Act or other legislative monstrosities which require an army of lawyers and bureaucrats to figure out and to administer. We don't need that kind of stifling, oppressive, counterproductive regulatory climate.

If the commission will seize the opportunity to carry out the Act properly, it can be a vehicle to cut regulatory overload, and to promote more intramodal competition in transportation markets.

In this sense, the Act can be a kind of "bill of rights" for shippers, for consumers and industries—a document to achieve the lofty, yet achievable goals of full competition, reasonable rates and excellent service.

In closing, let us recall the words of Abraham Lincoln: "The dogmas of the quiet past are inadequate for the present. The occasion is piled high with difficulty, and we must rise to the occasion. As our case is new, so we must think and act anew."

Reference: (C.R. 12/10/82, Pg. S-14412)

Intermodalism

Excerpts from Speech
in the Congressional Record
by
Nat Welch, Chairman
International Intermodal Expo

I've selected an ambitious subject for my remarks today: "Intermodalism—The Past Decade: The Future Decade." Those of us in the industry live with the word "intermodalism" every day, but it is surprising how few people know what the word means. The Random House unabridged dictionary defined "intermodal" as "transport involving more than one form of carrier such as rail, truck and ship."

In the past 30 years, America has led the world in the container revolution. The container has had as much impact on world freight commerce as the jet aircraft had on passenger business.

The revolution was led by a country boy from North Carolina named Malcolm McLean. He knew the trucking business and had great financial acumen. The advantage of container is pretty obvious. Pilferage in ports was notorious. With strong unions, longshoremen's wages were going through the roof. A sealed container cuts down on pilferage, and can be handled dockside with far less labor than needed to load and unload smaller boxes and bags. Not only did merchandise freight (Hong Kong garments and TV sets) shift rapidly to containers but, in the last few years, American break-bulk commodities such as lumber, cotton, seed grains have shifted to containers. The growth of containers in international trade jumped from a million in 1970 to 12 million in 1990.

Ships are now in service which can handle 2,300 40-foot containers—equivalent to 2,300 trucks with 40-foot trailers traversing the Interstate.

The container revolution was also led by another progressive USA company—American President Lines, which has served the Pacific trade for over 100 years. With the surge in imports from the Pacific Rim, wearing apparel, consumer electronics and toys—APL needed a more efficient system to move its containers from the Pacific Coast to the Midwest and the Northwest. The company was not satisfied with the trailer on flat car (TOFC) and the container on flat car (COFC) service offered by the American western railroads. So APL bought unit trains from the Western railroads to control the quality and timeliness of the service.

Then came the big technological breakthrough of the decade—the introduction of the double-stack flat car. The economic advantage of placing one container on top of another is obvious—two for the price of one. Double-stacks came in the form of five well cars articulated like your backbone. A double-stack train with 100 wells can transport 200 40-foot to 48-foot containers from the West Coast to New York—equivalent to 200 trailer truck rigs covering the same distance.

Having created this enormous eastbound transportation system, American President Lines was confronted with the age-old transportation problem, filling up the back haul. The company created an intermodal sales force to develop domestic back haul service to the West Coast. Because of its aggressive marketing, API is filling up its westbound double-stack trains from Atlanta with textiles, furniture, carpet, aluminum, paper products and motor carrier freight. The success of this program is such that the company's domestic business now exceeds their 100-year-old Pacific trade.

From 1980 to 1989, American railroads' intermodal business increased from 3 million 40-foot units to 6.2 million 40-foot units.

Two significant factors in this growth occurred in 1980. The passage of the Motor Carrier Act and the Staggers Rail Act, both of which essentially deregulated the surface freight industry.

Another American company, CSX Railroad, moved aggressively to become a multimodal transportation company. CSX acquired Malcolm McLean's Sea-Land, which is now the largest worldwide container shipping company serving the USA. It also acquired American Barge Line and formed CSX Trucking. Two years ago, CSX Intermodal, an entirely separate company, was established and is a nationwide intermodal network as well as a principal customer of the Western railroads.

The motor carrier industry is a key player in intermodalism because almost every trailer has to move initially and finally by trucks from plant to rail head or dockside, then after the long haul by rail or ship, by motor carrier to reach its final destination.

Discussing the past is a whole lot easier than predicting the future. I do not see trailers and containers getting larger than 53 feet. The public is rebelling against these larger rigs because of safety and traffic congestion. Also, the longer and heavier the containers, the more difficult it is to lift and load these big heavy boxes. Cost and safety in handling are also negative factors in increasing the size of boxes.

How soon will the piggyback trailer die? The consensus is that piggyback is losing ground but it is not dead yet. The downside is the piggyback trailer gives a "shake, rattle and roll" ride, but the upside is it's flexible and plays a useful role on medium length hauls. The container portion of the U.S. market moved from 38 percent in 1988 to 45 percent in 1990. This percentage growth will continue because of the momentum and the commitment of U.S. railroads.

Some people are enthusiastic about the "iron highway" because of its great versatility in serving smaller markets. The iron highway is a system intended to permit the railroads to participate in the door-to-door truckload market. It consists of a self-powered, self-loading train element that eliminates cranes, locomotives and switching, in combination with a unique loading mechanism. This system has as its goal increasing performance and reliability above the levels attainable with all-highway movement, at lower than highway costs for lanes of under 500 miles. Preliminary tests have gone well.

Promising new markets loom ahead in the 90s. The surface has barely been scratched in transporting refrigerated products, containerized liquids and solid waste. Sharp increases in second, third and fourth class mail have created a growing opportunity for railroads in their bulk mail intermodal business. Conrail and Santa Fe are aggressively pursuing this business.

I predict that more intermodal yards will be located outside the fringes of perimeter highways in our large cities like Chicago, Los Angeles, Dallas and Atlanta. Railroads have frequently built their intermodal terminals on old rail yards in the inner-city. Building new facilities on the edge of the city will reduce urban traffic congestion and be more efficient.

U.S. trucks, railroads and ships did a phenomenal job in moving over 2,000 containers a month recently to the Persian Gulf. Intermodalism needs great teamwork between the modes, strong hands-on management and sophisticated computers. We need the same kind of teamwork demonstrated in the Persian Gulf War to reap the fruits from intermodalism.

The driving force behind the 108 percent in rail intermodal traffic this past decade has been in cannibalizing boxcar freight and the surge of Pacific Rim imports. I predict the driving force behind the continued intermodal growth in the 90s will be the increase in shipments tended by large American shippers such as Proctor & Gamble, General Motors, Ford, Kodak, General Mills, J.C.Penney and others. This will create the momentum for other American shippers to follow.

On the global scene, container volume will increase. Estimates are that from 1990 to 2000, world container traffic will increase from 12 million 40-foot containers to 211.4 million and that the largest container ships will increase from 2,300 to 3,000 of these containers.

It is hard to predict the future 10 to 20 years out. Who would have predicted in the mid-50s that we would put a man on the moon in 1969 or the worldwide impact of the container revolution? I am by nature an optimist—a believer in what can be accomplished by the creativity of human beings in a free society. Let us dream dreams and work daily toward high goals.

Eighteen months ago I toured intermodal facilities in six Pacific Rim countries. While in Taiwan, I visited Evergreen, which has emerged in 25 years from a very small carrier to become one of the very largest container shipping companies in the world. I asked one of Evergreen's middle managers, "What is the secret to Evergreen's success?" His answer, "People—you can always buy the newest ships and computers."

Reference: (C.R. 5/22/91, Pg. E-1839)

Chapter 19

Veterans
• • • • • • • • • • •

American Legion Distinguished Service Medal
Excerpts from Speech
in the Congressional Record
by
Former Senator Howard H. Baker Jr.
On Receiving the American Legion Distinguished Service Medal

Let me say first of all that it's a pleasure to be with my friends in the American Legion once again, and I am most grateful and deeply honored that you have chosen me to receive your Distinguished Service Medal.

And I will say further that when I look at the extraordinary success of modern Germany and Japan, it's sometimes hard to remember who won the war.

But when I look at Poland and Hungary, and the Baltic States, and even the Soviet Union today, I cannot help thinking that not only did we win the war in the 1940s, but we're still winning it in the 1980s.

Indeed the current intellectual fashion in Washington is an essay in which a bright young man at the State Department argues that we may be witnessing "not just the end of the Cold War, or the passing of a particular period of postwar history, but the end of history as such; that is, the end point of mankind's ideological evolution and the universalization of Western liberal democracy as the final form of human government."

I think it goes a bit far to say that we have reached "the end of history," or even that Western-style democracy is about to be universally accepted.

But it is certainly true that the student protest in Beijing, the victory of Solidarity in Poland, the growing reform movement in Hungary, the independence movements in the Baltic states of Estonia, Latvia and Lithuania—and even the creation of a marvelously rambunctious people's parliament in Moscow—are dramatic manifestations of what is truly a universal "yearning to breathe free."

We must deal with the fact that while democracy is the idea whose time has come in Europe today, it is as vulnerable in much of Asia, Latin America and the Middle East as the young man who stood down a column of Chinese tanks.

And we must deal with the fact that even in those countries where the passion for democracy is strongest today, the political leadership is ill-prepared to meet democracy's demands for economic and civil liberty, or with the revolution in expectations which has seized their citizenry.

The response of these leaders has ranged from wariness in Warsaw to tanks in Tiananmen Square. The question we must ask ourselves is, how do we respond?

I believe, first of all, that we should take the advice of our Secretary of Defense, who has quite rightly urged us not to give away our overcoats on the first sunny day in January. We must remain fully prepared to defend ourselves, our interests and our values in a world that remains full of danger.

Second, I think it is important that we understand the nature of the leaders in the countries vying for our attention today. To this end, I am going to Warsaw later this month with a group of present and former American politicians to talk about democracy with the leaders and the people of Poland.

They want to know how a political process as cumbersome and boisterous and self-satisfying as ours produces the kind of economic and social progress the United States has generally enjoyed.

This is really a bigger problem that it may at first seem, because in most of the countries where democracy is pushing its fragile flower through the concrete today, there is little experience with political or social freedom to guide them.

In China, where a political state has existed for 4,000 years, officials still say their citizenry isn't "ready" for democracy, that the peasant class is illiterate, that there isn't the innate respect for law that exists in our country, and that government by the consent of the governed simply won't work in a country of a billion people—even though it has worked relatively well for India's 800 millions.

The Chinese seem to prefer a system in which Ronald Reagan would be considered a promising young man. A system in which being well-born is all but essential to membership in the Communist Party, a system which favors the few at the expense of the many more thoroughly and systematically than the coldest capitalist ever dreamed possible.

And in the Soviet Union, where one-man rule has been a fact of life for over a thousand years, the notion of pluralism may take some time to really catch on.

The man who rules the Soviet Union today, Mikhail Gorbachev, is one of the most impressive men I have ever met. I have seen him "up close and personal" several times and I found him to be the most well-prepared foreign leader I encountered.

He knows when to charm and when to menace. And how to do both well. A leader as experienced and unsentimental as Margaret Thatcher declares appreciatively that she can "do business" with this man, and I will stipulate that if he wanted to, he could be the best businessman in America.

But as Richard Nixon reminds us, you don't get to be general secretary of the Communist Party if your commitment to Communism is in doubt. Gorbachev's isn't. And it's important that we all remember that.

We may say that Communism has failed, that we've won the Cold War, that democracy is the wave of the future. But Gorbachev, who says many extraordinary things isn't saying that, and until he says it—and several of his assistants say it—I say we had better keep our guard up and our defenses strong.

This is surely an exhilarating and hopeful time, especially in Eastern Europe. But it was a hopeful sign in China, too, until June 4, 1989, and the world has brutal ways of mocking our hopes.

Hemingway said, "The world breaks everyone, and afterward many are strong at the broken places." Poland is strong today, and we must help her grow stronger. And so it must be with her neighbors in Europe, in Asia, in Africa, in Latin America, wherever there are people yearning to breathe free.

I am encouraged by much of what I see in the world today. I am worried about much that I cannot see. I hope that we will stay as well-prepared as Gorbachev always is, for I believe this is the only way to keep the peace and the freedom we have won at great price.

I know that you share that hope and that commitment, and I am honored to be in your company.

Reference: (C.R. 9/14/89, Pg. S-11052)

National Veterans' Day
Excerpts from Speech
in the Congressional Record
by
Hon. John O. Marsh Jr.
Former Secretary of the Army

Of all the creatures of the earth, it is only man that has a sense of history. It is this gift which causes us to assemble here today.

In the town where I grew up as a youngster, in the Valley of Virginia, is a beautiful monument to those men of Harrisonburg and Rockingham County who gave their lives in World War I. It is a sculptured figure of liberty mourning her dead.

Carved around the base of the monument are the words: "They tasted death in youth that liberty might grow old."

In the 1930s, I can remember in the classroom on this day the moment of silence as we paid tribute to mark the 11th hour, of the 11th day, of the 11th month when the Armistice was signed to end the war which was to have ended wars—to make the world safe for Democracy.

Now, over 60 years later, we know that the world has not been made safe for Democracy, and wars have not ended. We gather here to pay homage to all of our veterans, far removed from a peaceful and prosperous America.

It was an English poet who captured the solemnity of this moment, when the tempo of a nation slows to honor its dead:

"The tumult and the shouting dies, The Captains and Kings depart; Still stand thine ancient sacrifice, an humble and a contrite heart, Lord God of hosts, be with us yet, Lest we forget—lest we forget!"

The purpose in being here today is twofold: It is commemorative. It is commitment. In our time, the formula for a peaceful world is directly related to United States defense. A defense that defers war—a defense that causes any would-be aggressor to realize the foolhardiness of an attack on any U.S. interest.

As President Reagan recently stated at Yorktown:

"... of equal concern to me is the uncertainty some seem to have about the need for a strong American defense .... Military inferiority does not avoid a conflict, it only invites one, and then ensures defeat. We have been trusted with freedom and must ensure it for our children and for their children. We're rebuilding our defenses so that our sons and daughters never need to be sent to war."

We do not seek empire, nor do we seek to force our will on others. Our record after both world wars is testimony to that.

But, because we are not an aggressive nation, our potential adversaries nevertheless should not forget one of our early flags carried by our successful revolutionary forebears. It was a pine tree displayed on a white background. Around the base of the tree was coiled a rattlesnake and printed across the bottom of that banner were the words "Don't tread on me."

As we set ourselves to the task of strengthening America's defenses, let us remember that we have much to do. That it will not be done in a day. That it will require sacrifice.

Let us speak to this commitment. The world in which we live has three dimensions:

It is a world of crisis.

It is world of change.

It is a world of ideas.

We live in a troubled world. We live in a world of precarious peace, a peace which is maintained only by United States strength. And, to the extent that the United States appears to be weakened, peace is weakened. It is only the United States leadership of the free world and United States power that safeguards an uneasy truce.

A brief global overview points to the difficulties of our times. There are seven major geographic areas of concern today.

(1) Europe—where NATO forces are counterposed to prevent aggression by the Warsaw Pact.

(2) Africa—that continent is the scene of great instability and political cross-currents, but it is vital to the West because of its resources.

(3) The Middle East—which at times appears to be a tinderbox of conflict. This volatile area is the source of enormous energy supplies.

(4) Southwest Asia—where we find 65,000 Soviet combat forces in Afghanistan.

(5) Northeast Asia—where U.S. forces, along with our Korean allies, safeguard the Korean Peninsula.

(6) Southeast Asia—which is still gripped by oppression.

(7) Latin America—where we see growing unrest in our own hemisphere.

To meet these threats of violence, United States forces are organized on the basis of the Total Force Concept whereby the Regulars, the National Guard and Reserves are co-equal partners.

Soviet power today is awesome. The intercontinental strategic arsenal includes 7,000 nuclear warheads. Like their land and sea forces, their air power is a formidable force. A new Soviet blue water Navy is appearing on the world's oceans. The Soviet ground forces have grown to more than 180 divisions.

By any reasonable test, the Soviets have far more than they need to defend their own frontiers. The fact is they have the capability to launch such an attack and project military power beyond their borders.

We live in a world of change impacted by technology, by communications, by transportation, by exploration into outer space. It is a world being changed by exploding population and emerging nations.

However, the world is not changed by armies nor by machines. It is changed by ideas.

The world of ideas and hope is America's world. Its preservation requires dedication, and sacrifice from each of its citizens. It requires your skills, your efforts and it requires your time. You are our greatest resource. You are America's hope for the future.

The last line of the Declaration of Independence is a commitment. "And for the support of this Declaration, with a firm reliance on the Protection of divine Providence, we mutually pledge to each other our lives, our fortunes and our sacred Honor." We must keep this pledge.

President Reagan at Yorktown said: "The freedom we enjoy today has not always existed, and carries no guarantees. In our search for an everlasting peace, let all of us resolve to remain so sure of our strength that the victory for mankind we won here is never threatened."

Perhaps some historian at some future milestone will write: Here passed a small group of Americans, who in their time explored the reaches of outer space and raised the curtain on a new age of discovery.

Through science and medicine, they sought to conquer famine and disease, and helped alleviate human suffering by finding ways to lessen pain. Through quiet strength and reason, they made less shrill the voices of prejudice and hate.

They paid liberty's price of eternal vigilance, yet became neither oppressor nor oppressed.

To a land troubled by drugs and crime—by poverty and loss of destiny—they brought a measure of purpose and order as well as personal dignity.

They helped restore the beauty of the earth and safeguarded the element of our planet vital to all forms of life.

They were people who willingly bore the burdens of defense. Whose forces kept freedom's lonely vigil and were the guardians of their nation's values.

And to a world torn by war, they renewed again the hope of peace.

In closing, let me leave a charge with you today which was the charge that Washington made to the delegates to the constitutional convention at a time when it appeared the convention would fall into disarray and the sacrifices of the American Revolution would have gone for naught because of differences that developed in the convention between regions over political philosophies and economic concerns. Washington, the president of the convention, charged the delegates as to their task with these words:

"Let us raise a standard to which the wise and the honest can repair. The event is in the hands of God."

Let us raise that standard today.

Reference: (C.R. 12/15/81, Pg. S-15398)

Chapter 20

Women
· · · · · · · · · · ·

Women in America Shooting for the Stars
Excerpts from Speech
in the Congressional Record
by
Stella G. Guerra, Director
Equal Employment Opportunity, Department of the Air Force

Let me begin by telling you what an honor it is for me to be participating in the opening session of the Federally Employed Women (FEW) 17th National Training Program. Through my years in federal service I have come to recognize and respect FEW as a leading force in strengthening the careers of women.

As the date of your meeting approached, I began to give serious thought to what I would share with you today. Finally, I decided to talk about women, the progress we've made in the past and the strides we are making today. Most importantly, I want to share some thoughts with you about how each one of us here to day can truly hitch our wagon to a star and chart our own course for tomorrow. A course that will let us share in the fruits of this great nation's success and fuel new generations of achievers for many years to come.

First, let's take a trip back to the past and take a brief glimpse at the road we have traveled. Rocky, and at times filled with a pothole or two, our path has been similar to a newborn baby. We have strived to focus on our personal objectives as well as worked to help America achieve its present-day global status as the most prosperous country in the world.

Dating back to our forebears who first stepped foot on American soil, we have been a part of our nation's progress. We helped America take its first steps toward world prominence. We moved West, we worked in the fields tilling the soil, and in the factories to produce the food and goods that our country needed to prosper and grow.

Moving on in the 1900s, during what some have affectionately referred to "the Rosie the Riveter period," working in shipyards and steel mills, we helped our nation meet labor shortages in a time of national crisis.

Like a child that is anxious to learn about the world and all its opportunities, we began to stretch, to grow and expand our horizons. In the span of less than 50 years, our numbers in the labor force doubled. Our unbridled innocence and energy altered forever the way we lived and worked in this country. In the second half of the 1970s, more of us were enrolled in college and we began to move rapidly into business, industry, the federal sector, the teaching fields, and other professions such as law and medicine.

The early years of America was indeed a time of challenge and a time of change. As women, we were a "spitting image" of that change and challenge. When America dreamed—we dreamed. When our nation stretched to achieve, we stretched. When America laughed, we shared in that laughter.

Today, we are in a time like no other period in our nation's history. With that same belief in achievement and success, we have moved with America from the so-called "smoke-stacked" industries of years past to an economy where three out of four jobs are related to the service industry. In this industry, on average, we've created one million new jobs each year for the past 20 years; of these, two million out of three have gone to women.

In this environment of prosperity we've seen many firsts:

The first female brigadier general.

The first female astronaut.

The first female sky marshall.

The first female ambassador to the United Nations.

The first female justice to the Supreme Court.

The first female director of Civil Service.

The first female to graduate at the very top of the class in a service academy, Navy '84 and Air Force '86.

In business there's been a sharp increase in the number of women who own their own business. The number of self-employed women from 1980-84 jumped 22 percent to 2.6 million people. Three key factors have contributed to this significant upswing.

First, we are gaining experience in positions of leadership in both corporate America and the federal sector. We are moving into middle and upper-level management at a record pace.

The second factor pushing us on and upward has been education. Across the land, numbers increased twofold in the past 21 years for those of us entering the halls of higher education. In the same period, our numbers in law, medicine and architectural schools have gone from 5 to 32 percent. Today, more of us are going to college than ever before. Our search for knowledge and quest for excellence has certainly opened up the doors of opportunity.

As our visions were broadened, women began to move into non-traditional areas—the third major factor for our success. Our movement into presidential Cabinet-level positions, into missile silos as crew commanders, aircraft mechanics and into the officer and enlisted ranks have indeed staggered the imagination.

As attitudes toward working careers change, so, too, will the structure of jobs. The great impact of high technology will shape and mold the jobs of tomorrow. Advances in technology, attitudes about work, and the increase in life spans will demand a change in the way we are educated and trained. More people will have college degrees or have some sort of on-the-job training.

With vision and a sense of direction, we will continue to do what's right for America. We will continue to discuss and help explore ways to resolve concerns such as maternity leave and the use of sick leave to care for our families at times of illness. Like the years of "Rosie the Riveter," we'll continue to do our part to keep America strong, prosperous and upward bound.

As we enter America's early adulthood we find that our hopes and dreams have been uplifted toward achievement. Yes, we are living a time of change but the future holds exciting changes, challenges and opportunities that will tax our abilities, test our skills and require a total commitment from you and I to keep us charging toward the stars.

We are living at a time when commitment, a spirit of achievement and an overriding belief in oneself will help to prepare ourselves for what lies ahead. But sometimes as we travel along the road of life, perhaps we encounter those times when we lose some of that vigor, that drive and carefree spirit that encourages us on. Perhaps on occasion we lose our ability to smile and to turn dreams into reality. Along with the rest of America, now is the time to rekindle that spirit and dream. Now is the time for you and me to look at our commitment and the belief in self.

What is commitment? It has been said that:

Commitment is what transforms a promise into reality.

It is the word that speaks boldly of our intentions and actions which speak louder than words.

Commitment unlocks the doors of imagination. Allows vision and gives us the "right stuff" to turn our dreams into reality.

Now is the time to review and perhaps change our mind set about commitment; it is also time to take a fresh look at ourselves and how we view the world around us. We need to update our strategic road map and recharge our batteries as we continue on the road to success. Changes to come in the years ahead dictate that we get and remain in step with innovative and new ways of doing things. Along with the burning commitment to achieve our individual goals, we'll need an astute ability to look within ourselves and project the positive outward to help our organizations achieve their national objectives.

To meet the challenges ahead and move along the road of progress, we must continue to take charge of our destinies and take responsibility for our own self-development. There are so many factors important to our self-development. However, none is more important that self-esteem. Some scholars have defined self-esteem as the integrated sum of self-confidence, self-respect and self-dignity. I would like to add to that definition—"as we see ourselves so do we act." It is the conviction gained through experience that we are competent to live and be worthy of living.

For all of us self-esteem exists on a continuum: it's not a case of "either you have it or you don't." Self-esteem comes in different doses and different degrees, and its potential is limitless. Scholars also claim "character determines action." I hasten to add self-concept determines destiny. As federal-employed women, if we continue to put faith in ourselves, and strive to develop to our fullest potential, then our boundaries will be truly limitless.

I strongly believe that inner strength and a glowing concept of self carried us through the early developmental years. That positive self-concept has helped us along with America to stretch and grow. It has brought us many firsts and promises much more.

Reflecting on my own youth—I can remember a time when there was little in the way of material things. What I did have was plenty of those simple teachings, later to be appreciated as my "building blocks."

You are a child of God—equal to everyone. No one will do what you must do for yourself.

You must get your education, a never-ending process. It is your right and something no one can ever take away from you.

I leave you with a question:

What better wagon to hitch to a star than: Your dreams. Your vision. Your being.

And if we fail, if we succeed, at least we'll live as we believed no matter what they take from us, they can't take away our dignity.

Reference: (C.R. 5/5/87, Pg. H-3174).

Opportunities for Women
Excerpts from Speech
in the Congressional Record
by
Hon. Elizabeth Hanford Dole
Former Secretary of Transportation

I trust you'll forgive me if I begin by looking over my shoulder—to a day in September 1962, when I entered Harvard Law School, one of 25 women in a class of 550 prospective movers, shakers and Wall Street lions. There were precious few lionesses then. I'll never forget being accosted by a male classmate on my very first day at Harvard, who demanded to know what I was doing there. "Don't you realize," he said in tones of moral outrage, "that there are men who'd give their right arm for your place in law school? Men who would use their legal education?"

That was my first—but by no means my final—exposure to chauvinism in the shadow of Frankfurter and Pound. My colleagues at Harvard seemed to have forgotten that the figure of justice is a woman. They seemed oblivious to the psychological barriers they had erected, ignorant of the fears they inspired or the doubts they nurtured.

Women in 1962 did a lot of wondering. We wondered if there would be jobs when we got out of school. We wondered if we would be accepted by the masculine domain of the legal world, where law books and leather chairs alike tend to be reserved for "old boys" whatever their age.

Today's graduating women have less to wonder about. They have much more to work toward. Those honored today provide heartwarming evidence of just how profound the changes have been. Those honored represent an extraordinary range of skills and achievements, the frontline troops in a quiet revolution taking place all across America.

There is a sense of history in the air. Precedent has few followers in this group. Among its shatterers are Jeane Kilpatrick, the first woman to serve as United Nations ambassador, and Sandra O'Connor, who was offered a legal typist's job in 1952—and who went on to break the type, and interpret the law of the land on the nation's Supreme tribunal.

Yes, we've made progress, but there are still the problems. Even now, too many Americans practice a subtle form of discrimination. Less obvious than the law, more insidious than verbal prejudice, it's called patronization, and it undercuts women just as surely as the old barriers of statute and custom.

Social critic Marya Mannes put it best, I think, when she wrote the following: "Nobody objects to a woman being a good writer or sculptor or geneticist if, at the same time, she manages to be a good wife, a good mother, good-looking, good-tempered, well-dressed, well-groomed and unaggressive."

In other words, in today's society, we are faced with the tyranny of perfection. You, too, can be treated the same as a man—as long as you outperform him. For all our gains, roadblocks still remain on the path to prosperity and job satisfaction. Large segments of our economy continue to regard millions of women as consumers instead of producers. Too many employers regard too many working women as pursuers of pin money—and pay them accordingly, about three-fifths, on average, of a man's salary, despite educational backgrounds that may be identical.

In designating its economic program, the Administration has tried to take into account the sad but true reality that inflation falls hardest on women. In cutting taxes, we've made it a priority to ease the marriage penalty, to all but eliminate estate taxes, permitting for the first time a spouse to inherit a farm or business intact. There are incentives to help working mothers with child care—and additional retirement protection on IRAs for wives who do not work and for women who earn less than $10,000.

The public sector can and should do all in its power to make our own economy color-blind to blue and pink as well as black and white. And ever since my days on the Federal Trade Commission, I've been keeping one hand on the pulse of the private sector, particularly American business, and measuring the slow but steady growth in female recruitment and utilization.

In the years just ahead, America must wake up to the fact that the very interpersonal skills of consensus building, mediating, moderating, and dealing effectively with people in general—skills that studies and surveys have historically identified as predominant in women—are the building blocks of our post industrial society. In the evolving service-oriented economy of the 1980s and 1990s, it's the management of people and not the management of machinery or material that will be crucial.

And with the revolution taking place in this country, the tidal wave of women entering the work force, managers are, I believe, starting to grasp what we have always known: that women share with men the need for personal success, even the taste for power. And no longer are we willing to satisfy those needs through the achievements of surrogates, whether husbands, children or merely role models.

Every person in this room recognizes both the problems and the untapped potential of the 52 percent of America's work force that's female. So do the others who are working outside the limelight to advance justice wherever it is blocked, who understands how far we have come, and who know firsthand how far we have yet to travel.

What all of us—and all of them—have in common is commitment. And with that commitment goes a vision of society as it might, and ought to be.

That vision encompasses a limitless horizon for every woman of courage and conviction. In large measure, it is the product of women whose lives demonstrate an ability to see beyond the common-place, and a reach for greatness that encompasses the distance between their dreams and reality.

One of the country's greatest poets was a women who never left her home in Amherst, Massachusetts. She never worked in an office, never raised a family, never won a headline. The only power she wielded lay in her poetry. But her artistry and her vision inspired millions.

"We dwell in possibility," Emily Dickinson wrote in her clapboard cloister nearly 150 years ago.

But we must adopt the gospel of Emily Dickinson's positive thinking to the world as it exists. We realize that for most women, success is achieved by dwelling in the improbable, by challenging the odds and overcoming the conventional wisdom.

Surely it was a combination of possibility—and a reaching for the improbable— that led Rosa Parks to claim a seat at the front of a Montgomery bus, and thus launch a peaceful revolution a hundred years overdue. Surely it was a brush with the improbable that raised Golda Meir to the Premiership of Israel—or suggested that Mother Teresa's responsibilities to a hungry world involved far more than mere obedience to the rules of her order.

So, even as we join together this afternoon to break bread and break precedent, let us in the pursuit of economic and social equality, continue to strive for the day when the improbable becomes probable. Back in June 1965, I was welcomed somewhat uneasily into a circle known as "the fellowship of educated men." I've seen enormous progress since then. I've seen the circle expand and the opportunities open up.

And I am convinced that today's women stand in the reflected light of a rising, not a setting, sun. Our day has barely dawned. Our dreams are just beginning to be realized. We dwell in possibility—but we challenge the improbable. So as we leave this room, let us not forget why we came.

Reference: (C.R. 6/9/82, Pg. E-2702)

World Order
• • • • • • • • • • • • • • • • •

New World Order
Excerpts from Speech
in the Congressional Record
by
Cyrus Vance
Former Secretary of State

The two and one-half years since 1989 will unquestionably be remembered as a time when unprecedented and unexpected events took place at every turn. And in the wake of those events it will be remembered that literally dozens of people began offering definitions of something called "a new world order." A number of them seem to have in mind only enhanced military security.

For my part, I am convinced that a "new world order" cannot be confined to questions of military security, or based on notions of the United States as world arbiter.

In that spirit and recognizing that the new world situation encourages us to look for solutions that would have been previously impossible, let me offer a few ambitious suggestions.

A new world order, I believe, should be structured along general lines to meet the following imperatives:

International peace and security;

Sustained economic development;

Curbing uncontrolled population growth; and

Strengthening international institutions.

International Peace and Security: The first and primary imperative of a new world order must be the maintenance of peace and security on both a global and regional scale.

Although the Cold War may be over, we need look no further than the nightly television network news to recognize that national, ethnic, religious, economic and other conflicts—both across and inside present national borders—pose potential threats to peace and security.

Beyond maintaining appropriate military capabilities, we should begin our search for peace and greater security by strengthening the mandate and the capabilities of the institution that has the widest and most potentially-effective reach—the United Nations.

The United Nations' potential was at least partially demonstrated during the Gulf crisis. After Iraq's invasion of Kuwait, nations working within the UN framework impressively and effectively applied an unprecedented policy of embargo and containment. And when the war ended, there was no choice but to turn to the United Nations to provide long-term stability and humanitarian aid.

Yet, with new thinking in mind, imagine what might have been possible had the UN possessed the capacity to head off or avert Iraq's aggression.

In this connection, Prime Minister Ingvar Carlsson's Stockholm Initiative recommends the establishment of a global emergency system within the United Nations.

Under this proposal, permanent UN political offices would be established in key places, such as India/Pakistan, South Korea/North Korea, Iraq/Kuwait, and Iran, to provide early-warning of potential aggression. But that, alone, would not be adequate. The UN also needs its own collective security forces—to intervene, forcibly if necessary, when the Security Council so determines.

To make the global emergency system effective, the Secretary-General should be granted greater leeway to deploy the organization's diplomatic monitoring, and dispute-resolution capabilities whenever requested by a member state.

But the UN cannot be everywhere. To keep the peace, we also need to modernize regional security arrangements, particularly in volatile areas like the Middle East and South Asia, where no effective regional institutions now exist.

The Conference on Security and Cooperation in Europe—known as CSCE—has facilitated to a major degree the post-Cold War thaw which has taken place in Eastern and Central Europe. NATO, of course, was the Western shield which kept a fragile situation stable until a thaw could take place. But it was CSCE which helped the West, the Soviets and the Warsaw Pact countries work their way through an essentially peaceful transition to democracy and free-market economies.

In the wake of the Gulf War, this model should be considered for the Middle East. On one level, a regional conference would discuss Arab-Israel relations and the issue of a Palestinian homeland. But on another level, affected nations could tackle a broader range of issues, including regional security arrangements, human rights, environmental degradation, economic cooperation and restraints on all kinds of weapons.

Sustained Economic Development: Peace and development will be served if a prospective new world order includes a recommitment to international economic cooperation and increased development assistance.

Both the United States and other countries have had recent bouts of protectionist flu as economic pressures and changing world trading patterns have endangered the previous worldwide consensus on access to goods and money.

President Kennedy, when he signed the historic Trade Expansion Act of 1962, remarked that "a rising tide lifts all boats." The premise remains true but its support is less widespread than some would hope.

The General Agreement on Tariffs and Trade (GATT) needs to be reinforced, not weakened, as seems to be the drift today. When the International Monetary Fund and the World Bank were created at Bretton Woods, the GATT was seen as the global trade organization which could accommodate the interests of both developed and developing countries while holding back the protectionist and mercantilism forces which were so destructive in the past.

The GATT, World Bank, IMF and UNCTAD (the UN Trade and Development Organization) are all important global institutions. Over the past several years, fresh regional groups have taken on a new life. But it would be tragic for all of us if this were to end up dividing the world into Europe, Asian, and North American economic blocs pitted against each other, while leaving the world's poor nations on the outside looking in.

We must not forget that the history of the past 40 years has been replete with surprising economic success stories. The development process, once begun, takes on a dynamic momentum that carries it forward at a self-sustaining rate.

Investment in human capital, through better education, health, population planning, and training.

Investments in infrastructure and industry which have the long-term prospect of bringing success in international markets.

Development of domestic agricultural production, distribution, and processing.

We must face the dual realities that slow growth in both developed and developing nations illustrates a down-side of interdependence, namely that slow growth in each decreases demands for products of the other. Similarly, we must also recognize that debt service continues to consume a major share of developing country resources. Even resource-rich but heavily indebted potential powerhouses such as Brazil and Mexico will do well in the next decade not to lose ground.

The common threat that links these complex and intersecting factors is evident: No nation can resolve all its problems without the help of other nations. Common action is essential. The worldwide cost of meeting key social-development targets is estimated at $20 billion annually—the cost of sustaining the recent Persian Gulf war for a fortnight. It is all a question of priorities; do we care enough to make a similar investment in the future of humanity?

Confronting Critical Global Issues: There are two commanding issues which both rich and poor must confront if a successful new world order is to emerge. I am talking, of course, about population and environment.

As to population, as nations develop, birth rates invariably recede—another reason why promoting economic development is in our long-term interests. Nonetheless, longstanding religious and social pressures will continue to make it difficult to curb population growth.

Population growth, by definition, tends to reduce standards of living except in nations which enjoy remarkable economic growth. Population growth also adds to environmental pressure—most directly in areas where deserts are created as forests are destroyed to provide land for cultivation. Such growth encourages exploitation of children, migrants and others in the workplace.

It will take political courage, but leaders of both developed and developing nations must commit themselves to population planning programs as an integral part of their plans for economic development.

In contrast to population, the related issue of environment is on everyone's mind. But the question remains: Is the U.S. willing to invest the political and financial capital required?

In the rush to development, humanity has already done irreversible damage to the planet. And both developed and developing nations are to blame.

More than one-half of Africa's arable land is at risk of becoming desert. One-third of Asia's and one-fifth of Latin America's land is in the same state. We know of the environmental catastrophe which exists in the Soviet Union and in most of Eastern and Central Europe.

Issues of global warming and ozone depletion, already high on the international agenda, must not be shunned or postponed simply because they are politically difficult. To come to grips with these challenges, the nations of the northern hemisphere alone will need to reduce emissions of carbon dioxide from the combustion of oil, coal and other fossil fuels by perhaps 50 percent in the next 25 years or so. And we must eliminate the use of CFCs (chlorofluorocarbons) and halons on a far more rapid and comprehensive scale.

Let us hope that next year, at the Landmark UN Conference on Environment and Development, the participants will move from rhetoric to action. And let us hope the United States will take the lead.

Fostering Democracy and Human Rights: There is another issue which is all too often ignored. It is the erroneous belief that the internal affairs of other nations are not a proper subject for state to state discourse, and that internal events in other countries, such as human rights violations, are not our concern. I strongly disagree.

Although our options may at times be limited in dealing with such questions, we should never stop trying to apply diplomatic, economic, and political pressure that will help the human family continue its passage toward a more open, more democratic and freer life.

Lech Walesa and Vaclav Havel, among others, would endorse that view. So would the black citizens of South Africa and other nations where international support and pressure is helping bring about change.

The countries which have attempted to create economic development in a totalitarian framework have found it does not work. The human spirit, liberated, is capable of productivity and achievement undreamed of under the deadening hand of conformist control.

The past two and one half years have been tumultuous. But they have demonstrated that the tide of history is not running in the wrong direction. It is currently flowing toward openness and freedom of the individual—concepts that lie at the heart of much Western thought and certainly of our own American Revolution.

I have suggested several other structural changes which would be steps on the road to greater international peace and security—to shared and sustainable economic development—to curbing uncontrolled population growth and environmental degradation—to fostering democracy and human rights—and to creating a world order in which both law and justice become the norm—rather than the exception.

We have today an unparalleled chance to define the future. Let us seize the time.

Reference: (C.R. 5/21/91, Pg. S-6206)

Chapter 21

Youth
· · · · · · · ·

Boys' Clubs of America
Congressional Breakfast
Excerpts from Speech
in the Congressional Record
by
Arnold I. Burns
Former Deputy Attorney General

We are gathered here this morning to celebrate and honor five "Youth of the Year" finalists. These outstanding young leaders have performed a wide array of valuable services in their clubs and communities. I applaud you for your exceptional dedication to high moral principles.

How I wish that all young people had such strong and healthy attitudes. And how I wish that good physical and mental health were characteristic of all American society. Unfortunately, this is not the case.

No, I cannot in good conscience give a clean bill of health to America. Disease runs rampant in our inner cities. It is a disease of the spirit that cripples and kills.

Our inner cities are plagued by crime, drugs and violence. There is an epidemic of illiteracy, illegitimacy, filth and poverty. And poverty spawns hunger, hopelessness, frustration, anger and despair.

Kids growing up in our cities don't know how to break the cycle of poverty, failure and more poverty. They don't know where to turn for help. They need emergency treatment. But who will cure their ills.

Today I would like to examine the health of America's young people and check their vital signs. As the examination proceeds, I will discuss the symptomology, diagnosis, treatment and prognosis of our inner city boys and girls. So if you will bear with me while I put on my doctor's uniform, we'll begin this important examination.

At 2:03 a.m. a 16-year-old boy was admitted to the hospital by a police officer. The officer found the patient wounded on the street after being caught in cross fire during a drug deal gone sour.

The patient spoke mostly in Spanish, and Dr. Rodrigues, a resident here at the hospital, helped me take a brief history. In taking the history I learned that the patient has no father and that his immediate family consists of four brothers and sisters who are being raised by their mother. The patient ran away from home when he was 14. He has spent most of the last two years on the streets and is a member of a street gang.

I first examined the puncture wound to the right thigh that the patient received during the gunfight. Bone fragments and tearing of tendons were evident, along with resultant weakness beyond the injury to the lower extremity.

As the examination proceeded, I observed needle marks in both ante-cubital fossa and inflammation and excoriation in the nasal passages, indicating heroine and cocaine use. There was also questionable jaundice in the eyes and a fine tremor in the hands.

The patient had old scarring on his back and was missing several teeth. Hospital records obtained when the patient was admitted four years ago indicate that he had been physically abused during childhood. The case had been referred to a social worker at the time, but was never pursued.

The patient weighs 103 pounds and is short of stature, only 5 feet 2 inches tall. He is thin, and loose musculature of the abdomen raises the possibility of malnutrition.

Hematologic studies indicate an increased MCV (meaning corpuscular volume) raising the possibility of alcohol abuse. Chemistries indicate elevated liver enzymes which support this indication and which also strongly suggest hepatitis. I ordered further hematologic studies to rule out the possibility of AIDS.

The patient was then examined by the head of the psychiatric unit, who filed a report indicating severe depression with suicidal tendencies, extreme anxiety, fear and feelings of inferiority. In the doctor's opinion the patient tried to stifle these feelings by using illegal drugs and alcohol. Use of illegal drugs, in turn, explains why the patient was shot in cross fire during a drug deal and, consequently, why the patient has an injury to the right thigh.

What then is the clinical diagnosis of the various symptoms exhibited by the patient? In summary, the diagnosis I believe to be most inclusive and accurate is acute and abject neglect by family and society.

I would like to point out that this diagnosis is not unusual among inner city teenagers. This case is not at all atypical. Today almost two-thirds of all high school seniors have tried illegal drugs. By the 12th grade, 80 percent of all boys and girls are periodic drinkers. Each year, more than 1 million teenagers become pregnant. Remember, more than 14 million youngsters live in poverty.

Acute neglect is a condition that hampers and cripples millions of girls and boys each year. What is my prescription for the ailments afflicting our youngsters? The most successful way to treat them, in my opinion, is membership in a Boys and Girls Club. Clubs provide a secure environment for young people at-risk of drug and alcohol abuse, premature sexual involvement and juvenile crime. By providing a safe place for young people to go, clubs help disadvantaged boys and girls "beat the streets." Clubs give young people a chance to develop self-esteem and the social skills they need to become productive members of society.

Clubs help their members stay out of trouble with the law, and club staff become "second parents" to many boys and girls who often turn to them for advice and guidance. Boys and Girls Clubs serve over 1 million boys and 300,000 girls in over 1,100 club units operated by nearly 600 locally governed organizations. A total of 56,434 board and program volunteers help to make the Boys and Girls Club movement work, and 15,525 full- and part-time staff members enable Clubs to provide youth development services on a daily basis. The care, concern and understanding that young people receive from the club staff foster trust and the development of sound values.

Former club members who felt they had started life with the most obstacles to overcome—blacks, Hispanics, the economically disadvantaged and those from tough neighborhoods—gave their club the most credit for their success as adults.

What, then, is the prognosis for millions of children suffering from abandonment and neglect? This, my friends, will depend largely upon what we as a nation and as a society choose to do about the situation. The prognosis can be very good if we make the concerns of our young people a national priority. Boys and Girls Clubs already look after 1.3 million youngsters. By 1991, at the conclusion of our Outreach '91 program, we will be caring for an additional 700,000 boys and girls, bringing the total number of youth served to 2 million.

A good prognosis also requires that we practice preventive and holistic medicine. It is truly said that an ounce of prevention is worth a pound of cure. Our top priority is to expand drug prevention education. Some people foolishly think that the drug problem is a Columbian problem or a Burmese problem or a Laotian problem. It is not. It is an American problem. As long as our citizens are willing to buy and use drugs, we will have drugs reaching our markets. We have got to change our people's attitudes about drugs—the way we have about alcohol. We've got to take casual users out of the marketplace by arresting and publicly ostracizing them. And we must instill in our children a full understanding of drugs and offer them a viable, exciting, fulfilling substitute or idleness, drugs and then crime.

Making our young people healthy again is going to take a massive collaborative effort on the part of many youth service organizations, private enterprise and government at the city, state and federal levels. These individuals and agencies have joined and financially supported our efforts in public housing. They have helped provide alternatives, as we convince kids to say no to drugs.

We need a determined effort to stem the epidemic of despair that plagues America's young people. Happily, Americans know how to come to the aid of each other, and we know how to fight disease when it attacks the health and well-being of our children. If we band together, we can win the war on drugs, we can win the war on poverty, and we can win the war on crime!

Let me close by reminding you that there is more to medicine than just needles, pills and incisions. Love needs to be a fundamental part of the healing process.

How great it would be if every disadvantaged boy and girl could receive enough love and affection to restore his or her health and vitality. Remember, our children need us. When just one child suffers, the pain is felt by many people. But when millions of children are hurting, our whole nation is at risk.

Let us not be afraid to show our love and concern, and let us resolve here and now to give more of our time, our talents and our treasure to help our children recuperate and get back on the road to good health. Believe me, your kindness will be repaid many times over. In this way, you, too, can experience some of the satisfaction that doctors and nurses feel. For when people help others who are injured and who are in need, they also help themselves and all humanity.

Reference: (C.R. 11/1/89 Pg. H-7913)

Children as Our Priority
Excerpts from Speech
in the Congressional Record
by
Hon. Dan Rostenkowski
U.S. House of Representatives
before the
National Association of Children's Hospitals

This has been a interesting year. Even exciting. It will take years for historians to sort out all the lessons we've learned from our experience in the Persian Gulf, but one thing is clear.

America is hungry for leadership. Americans expect their President to lead. When he does—forcefully and with strong conviction—they will be quick to follow. Americans like to win—and, if the goals are honorable, they are willing to pay the price of victory.

President Bush is riding high—and with good reason. He has an abnormally high public approval rating—and he deserves it. I am happy to be a member of the chorus singing his praises.

But popularity is fickle. The public attention span is short. The President must do more than bask in the applause aimed his way. The logical question is—what can he do for an encore? The obvious answer is—lead us.

The President should set domestic priorities. That's his job. We don't need a thousand points of light. We need a single spotlight that will focus our attention on one important but manageable domestic issue. We don't need to be told we have more will than wallet. We need to know how our limited resources can be invested.

The President should invest some of his popularity and skills to create the same enthusiasm for domestic progress that he did for victory in Kuwait.

If I were the President, I would focus on children. They've been in the dark cellar of policy debates for too long. Their problems are stark. They cannot plead their own case. Their inability to create political pressure means they deserve a strong champion in the White House. And kids are a good investment. If we can help them today, they'll strengthen our economy tomorrow.

I'd like to talk about the long-term impact of neglect, tomorrow's economic cost of today's unaddressed social problems. There's a depressingly logical momentum here—kids who start off on the wrong foot spend a lifetime trying to catch up and often fail.

Kids who don't have enough to eat tend to get sick. Kids who lack adequate medical care tend to miss a lot of school. Kids who aren't in class don't learn how to read. Teenagers who are illiterate tend to drop out of high schools. High school dropouts can't get good jobs at good wages. Often they can't get jobs at all.

They contribute little to the nation's economic growth. Teenage pregnancies cost government more than $20 billion a year. Throughout our nation, one of every five children is born into poverty, and every teenager who begets a child instead of going to college faces an adulthood with very limited horizons.

Consider the parameters of the problem: One child in five is poor. One child in four lives in a single parent family. One child in four is born to a mother who has never been married. Nearly two-thirds of black births are to unwed mothers. Among whites the ratio is one in six.

More than 12 million children don't have any health insurance. Two million cases of child abuse are reported annually. And if you are bothered as I am by the idea of children having babies, I hope you join me in being both offended and appalled by drug-addicted children having addicted babies.

What we have here is simple and cataclysmic—millions of kids are being denied a normal childhood. They're hungry. They're sick. They're not protected and nurtured as they should be by parents and schools that are overwhelmed. They're being cheated by life.

What will happen to American society when these millions of kids become adults? A few will succeed. Many more will be unable to overcome the impediment of their childhood. And some will go out of their way to repay the society for their mistreatment. Not a happy picture.

We know how to respond to their problems. We're not waiting for a major medical breakthrough. There's no magic bullet we can get on the cheap. It requires a long-term commitment to the type of comprehensive programs that we know can work.

If you care, you can do what people traditionally came to Washington to do, lobby. Send a strong message to your elected representatives—including President Bush—that you will follow when they lead. Let them know that you are getting impatient.

You won't be alone. There's a growing realization within the corporate community that our neglect of children is becoming a problem with obvious long-term economic consequences for the country. Earlier this year a delegation of top corporate executives told Congress how adequate funding for the Women, Infants, and Children—or WIC program—is a top priority for them.

But lobbying doesn't yield immediate results. There's a need for growing and constant pressure. The White House must realize that this is more than fad. What you must do is send George Bush a message that you are ready to march. That you elected him to lead. That you might not re-elect him if he fails to lead.

I'd be surprised if you didn't think that larger expenditures on children's health issues should be the first priority. But I urge you to hold your fire on that one. Parochial squabbling has been the death of many a big idea in Washington.

What we need first is a commitment to the general goal. The goal is to create a better life for America's children, especially those who are deprived of the bare necessities, the most basic requirements of a decent life. Unless we can win on that point, there will be no need to discuss whether sex education for teenagers ought to be a higher priority than prenatal care.

Government is often—and properly—criticized for being too friendly to powerful elements in our society. It is true that the squeaky wheel is greased first. And there are those who say that the government tilt toward programs for senior citizens is a direct result of their political participation. Good for them. That's how a responsive political system works—it's called democracy.

But those of us in government, those who have the privilege of exercising power, should also feel a special obligation to the powerless in our society. We can't expect effective lobbying from a 15-year-old pregnant girl who lives in a one-parent home. She's too preoccupied with her own immediate problems to write letters to her congressman—or her President.

Nonetheless, we have an obligation to the powerless—in political, in economic, even in moral terms. They deserve political representation even if they don't have the strength to fight for it. Their humanity entitles them to a decent standard of living.

Kids can't vote in this country. Kuwaitis can't either. But that didn't prevent us from helping them out in their hour of need.

But I think we owe our kids the same kind of commitment we gave the Kuwaiti people. Both cases involve a combination of economic and humanitarian motivations.

One reason we were in the Persian Gulf was because we worried about our oil supply in the future. That's nothing to be ashamed of. Call it enlightened self-interest. This same enlightened self-interest should compel us to invest in kids today because of our same concern about our nation's future.

Let me close by thanking you for all that you and your institutions have done. If I have painted a bleak picture here in trying to promote emphasis on the problem, it is not because I am ignorant of the public service provided by children's hospitals.

Things could be a lot worse. And they probably would be, had your institutions not stretched to help meet this need. But one of the lessons we've learned in the past decade is that community institutions can't solve this problem, regardless of their resolve. It is simply too big. That is why the government must step in.

Don't forget the kids. If you agree with me that they deserve help, let your elected representatives know.

Reference: (C.R. 3/21/91, Pg. E-1052)

Index
....

About the Editor
• •

A native of Pennsylvania, George Berg was raised in the Pittsburgh suburbs where he attended a parochial school, Bellevue High School and the University of Pittsburgh, He is a veteran of World War II and the Korean Conflict.

Upon completing his education, Berg was appointed a special assistant to U.S. Representative Robert J. Corbett (R-Pa.) in 1949. He served as an administrative assistant in the Congress of over 32 years. He was nominated by President Ford to be an Assistant Secretary of Commerce for Congressional Affairs. Berg was a co-founder of the Administrative Assistants' Association in the Congress and has been listed in "Who's Who in Government" and "Who's Who in American Politics."

Upon retiring from government service in 1980, Berg joined the American Farm Bureau Federation as a registered lobbyist, specializing in transportation issues. Widely known and respected by many people in Congress, he frequently testified before the House and Senate on matters involving agriculture, the food industry, agribusiness and transportation matters in general. Berg has traveled extensively throughout the United States speaking at meetings, seminars and conferences on transportation. He is the author of several Farm Bureau publications of interest to the federation's four million member families. Mr. Berg and his wife, Marian, divide their time between Washington, D.C., and Hayden Lake, Idaho.

While devoting most of his adult life to politics and the U.S. Congress, Berg has had ample opportunity to observe that a mark of a leader is his or her knowledge of relevant issues and the ability to discuss them. His compilation of carefully selected speeches excerpted from *The Congressional Record* are outstanding because they express views on a multitude of subjects by distinguished American leaders and dignitaries from around the world.

"The Great American Priorities" will be of interest to every American who is called upon to speak up and speak out and to those who are concerned about the vital issues that will be confronting the American people in the immediate future and as we enter the 21st Century.